C000077063

THEMATIC ANALYSIS

Sara Miller McCune founded SAGE Publishing in 1965 to support the dissemination of usable knowledge and educate a global community. SAGE publishes more than 1000 journals and over 800 new books each year, spanning a wide range of subject areas. Our growing selection of library products includes archives, data, case studies and video. SAGE remains majority owned by our founder and after her lifetime will become owned by a charitable trust that secures the company's continued independence.

Los Angeles | London | New Delhi | Singapore | Washington DC | Melbourne

THEMATIC ANALYSIS

A PRACTICAL GUIDE

VIRGINIA BRAUN AND VICTORIA CLARKE

Los Angeles | London | New Delhi
Singapore | Washington DC | Melbourne

Los Angeles | London | New Delhi
Singapore | Washington DC | Melbourne

SAGE Publications Ltd
1 Oliver's Yard
55 City Road
London EC1Y 1SP

SAGE Publications Inc.
2455 Teller Road
Thousand Oaks, California 91320

SAGE Publications India Pvt Ltd
B 1/I 1 Mohan Cooperative Industrial Area
Mathura Road
New Delhi 110 044

SAGE Publications Asia-Pacific Pte Ltd
3 Church Street
#10-04 Samsung Hub
Singapore 049483

Editor: Amy Maher
Editorial assistant; Esmé Carter
Assistant editor, digital: Sunita Patel
Production editor: Rachel Burrows
Marketing manager: Camille Richmond
Cover design: Wendy Scott
Typeset by: C&M Digitals (P) Ltd, Chennai, India
Printed in the UK

© Virginia Braun and Victoria Clarke 2022

Apart from any fair dealing for the purposes of research,
private study, or criticism or review, as permitted under the
Copyright, Designs and Patents Act, 1988, this publication
may not be reproduced, stored or transmitted in any form,
or by any means, without the prior permission in writing of
the publisher, or in the case of reprographic reproduction,
in accordance with the terms of licences issued by
the Copyright Licensing Agency. Enquiries concerning
reproduction outside those terms should be sent to
the publisher.

Library of Congress Control Number: 2021934969

British Library Cataloguing in Publication data

A catalogue record for this book is available from
the British Library

ISBN 978-1-4739-5323-9
ISBN 978-1-4739-5324-6 (pbk)

At SAGE we take sustainability seriously. Most of our products are printed in the UK using responsibly sourced
papers and boards. When we print overseas we ensure sustainable papers are used as measured by the PREPS
grading system. We undertake an annual audit to monitor our sustainability.

For Marcia, with love and happy memories

CONTENTS

Extended contents   ix

BEFORE THE ADVENTURE...   **xvii**
About the authors and contributors   xix
Acknowledgements   xxiii

Scene setting: What *Thematic analysis: A practical guide* offers you,
    and how to navigate your way through it   xxv

SECTION I   VENTURING FORTH! *DOING* REFLEXIVE THEMATIC ANALYSIS   **1**

1   It's almost time to depart: Getting ready for your thematic analysis adventure   3

   Before analysis: A brief *design* interlude   25

2   Taking an initial lay of the land: Introducing our worked example dataset
   and doing familiarisation   33

3   Exploring this world in detail: Doing coding   51

4   Finding, losing, then finding your way again: Developing your themes   75

5   Arriving home and telling a story about your adventure: Writing your
   thematic analysis report   117

**SECTION II GOING DEEPER FOR TIP-TOP REFLEXIVE THEMATIC
ANALYSIS: THEORY, INTERPRETATION, AND QUALITY MATTERS**   **153**

6   A not-so-scary theory chapter: Conceptually locating reflexive thematic analysis   155

7   So *what?* The importance of interpretation in reflexive thematic analysis   195

8   One big happy family? Understanding similarities and differences
   between reflexive TA and its methodological siblings and cousins   223

9   Getting your own house in order: Understanding what makes good reflexive
   thematic analysis to ensure quality   259

   Fare-well!   281

Glossary   283
References   299
Index   331

EXTENDED CONTENTS

BEFORE THE ADVENTURE...   xvii
About the authors and contributors   xix
Acknowledgements   xxiii

**Scene setting: What *Thematic analysis: A practical guide* offers you,
    and how to navigate your way through it**   xxv
Chapter overview   xxv
Setting the scene for *Thematic analysis: A practical guide*   xxvi
Baking, adventures and maps: Is this a recipe book, a guidebook, or what?   xxvi
Navigating language and imagining the reader   xxvii
This is *our* mapping...   xxviii
Learning through doing: A practice-first approach to learning
    thematic analysis   xxix
Who is the book for?   xxx
A book of two parts   xxx
    Mapped adventure pathways: Navigating your way through the book   xxxi
    Helpful things to support your adventure: The pedagogical features   xxxii
    The companion website: An abundance of teaching and
        learning resources   xxxiii

SECTION I   VENTURING FORTH! *DOING* REFLEXIVE THEMATIC ANALYSIS   **1**

**1   It's almost time to depart: Getting ready for your thematic
    analysis adventure**   **3**
Chapter One overview   3
Let us introduce you to thematic analysis   4
What is *reflexive* TA?   5
Table 1.1: Overview of some key differences between qualitative
    and quantitative research paradigms   6
Can we provide a simple overview of reflexive TA?   6
A qualitative sensibility for reflexive TA   7
Box 1.1: Ten core assumptions of reflexive TA   8
But wait, there's more: Variation within reflexive TA   9
Table 1.2: The variations of reflexive TA   10
Reflexive TA offers guidelines, not rules, but a clear process   10
Mentally preparing yourself to tackle your TA journey: Becoming
    comfortable with uncertainty and discomfort   11

Subjectivity is at the heart of reflexive TA practice   12

Reflexivity: The most important companion for your adventure   13

    Doing reflexivity for reflexive TA   14

Box 1.2: Your values and politics in qualitative research   14

    The time to start reflexivity is ... NOW   15

    Activity pause: A task to get reflexivity started...   16

    Reflective and reflexive journals   19

Box 1.3: What might reflexive journal entries look like?   20

Chapter summary   22

Want to learn more about...?   23

Activities for student readers   23

Before analysis: A brief *design* interlude   **25**

    Getting into design thinking... A guided activity   29

    Some readings to take you further into design thinking   30

2   Taking an initial lay of the land: Introducing our worked example dataset and doing familiarisation   **33**

Chapter Two overview   33

Today's the day!   34

The process of reflexive TA   34

Box 2.1: Introducing six phases of reflexive thematic analysis   35

Introducing and contextualising our worked example dataset   37

Researcher reflection – Box 2.2: Situating myself in relation to these data (Ginny)   38

Researcher reflection – Box 2.3: Situating myself in relation to these data (Victoria)   39

Table 2.1: Anonymised but otherwise unedited comments from *Seven Sharp* Facebook post about "being childfree"   40

    What's my purpose here? Settling on a research question   41

Familiarisation (Phase one)   42

    Activity pause: Familiarisation   45

    Meaning, the dataset and the analytic process: A brief note on language   45

    Note-making for familiarisation   46

Figure 2.1: Familiarisation Doodle for participant 'Franz'   46

Figure 2.2: Familiarisation Doodle for participant 'Frank'   47

Box 2.4: Ginny's overall dataset familiarisation notes   48

Chapter summary   49

Want to learn more about...?   49

Activities for student readers   50

3   Exploring this world in detail: Doing coding   **51**

Chapter Three overview   51

Preparing for coding   52

Box 3.1: Coding, codes and code labels in reflexive TA – a quick guide   53

Coding is a systematic process 53
Coding is organic, evolving and subjective 54
Inductive and deductive orientations to data coding 55
Semantic to latent coding 57
Table 3.1: Dispelling some misconceptions about semantic and latent coding 58
General guidelines for codes and code labels in reflexive TA 58
Doing coding (Phase two) 59
Table 3.2: Some general guidelines for developing code labels 60
    Activity pause: Before coding 60
Box 3.2: A selection of six extracts from childfree dataset 61
Table 3.3: A selection of childfree comments data with Code labels 63
    Actually wrangling data and codes: Technologies of coding 65
Box 3.3: Is using QDAS better than coding in other ways? 66
Researcher reflection – Box 3.4: Thematic analysis and QDAS 67
Researcher reflection – Box 3.5: On Using NVivo 68
    Evolving your coding 69
Box 3.6: Codes as building blocks for analysis 69
    Refining your coding through multiple rounds 70
    Can I stop coding yet? 71
Chapter summary 72
Want to learn more about... 72
Activities for student readers 73

4   **Finding, losing, then finding your way again: Developing your themes** **75**
Chapter Four overview 75
Understanding the *key* concept: What is this thing called a theme? 76
    In reflexive TA, a topic summary is not a theme 77
    In reflexive TA, a theme captures shared meaning, united by a central organising concept 77
Generating initial themes (Phase three) 78
    Developing initial themes[2] from your codes 79
Figure 4.1: Coding and initial theme development with a cup of coffee 80
Table 4.1: A selection of code labels and collated data extracts 82
    Using visual mapping for theme generation, development and review 85
Figure 4.2: An initial mapping of patterns across childfree dataset 86
Box 4.1: Theme levels in reflexive TA 87
    Five key things to keep in mind in the early stages of theme development 88
Figure 4.3a & 4.3b: A dandelion head – fully connected seeds (4.3a) and partially dispersed seeds (4.3b) 90
Box 4.2: How many themes? Some guiding considerations for theme development and review 91
    I quite like it here, should I stay longer? Tackling time management in (initial) theme development 92

I'm struggling a bit, to be honest: Managing anxiety in the TA process 92
Researcher reflection – Box 4.3: Facing the battle of anxiety and OCD when
    undertaking TA for the first time 93
Researcher reflection – Box 4.4: Doing TA when you've got ADHD
    and anxiety: Reflections and strategies 95
Developing and reviewing themes[10] (Phase four) 97
Figure 4.4: "Data says no" 98
    Theme development and revision with coded extracts 98
Figure 4.5: Theme development as wrestling a sea-monster? 100
    Theme development and revision with the full dataset 100
Box 4.5: Can my analysis be based on *part* of the dataset? 101
    What's the point of this part of my adventure? 102
Figure 4.6: Refined thematic map for 'gains and losses' analysis 103
Figure 4.7: Refined (finalised) thematic map for 'choice matters' analysis 104
    Okay, so how would a topic summary be different from a
        shared meaning theme? 104
Box 4.6: Illustrative 'topic summary': Reasons for being childfree 105
    But what about contradiction? 107
Precision matters: Refining, defining and naming themes (Phase five) 108
Box 4.7: The 'contradictory' theme *Good and Bad Parents* [extract] 109
Box 4.8: Definition of the theme 'deficient personhood' 111
    Naming themes 111
Box 4.9: Naming themes related to 'choice' in the childfree dataset 113
Chapter summary 115
Want to learn more about...? 115
Activities for student readers 116

5   **Arriving home and telling a story about your adventure:**
    Writing your thematic analysis report **117**
Chapter Five overview 117
Writing matters for analysis (Phase six) 118
Setting the scene of your story (the introduction or literature review) 119
Describing how you approached your adventure (the method/ology section) 121
    Explaining your choice of TA and what it offers 122
Table 5.1: Is my rationale for TA strong enough? 123
Table 5.2: Examples of rationales for (reflexive) TA from published research 124
    Describing what you actually *did* during analysis 124
Box 5.1: Should I explain why I used TA and not a similar method? 125
Box 5.2: An example of a student analysis process write-up 126
Telling your *analytic* story (the results and discussion section) 128
Box 5.3: How we'd briefly write the analysis part of a methodology section,
    related to the overarching theme around 'choice' 129
    Introducing the analysis 129
Table 5.3: Example of a theme summary table 130

Structuring the analysis section 131

Box 5.4: Writing separate results and discussion sections 132

Selecting data extracts 133

Data extracts and your analytic narrative 135

Box 5.5: Illustrative and analytic treatment of data extracts in reporting a theme 136

Traps to easily avoid when reporting your analysis in reflexive TA 138

Box 5.6: Don't try this at home – paraphrasing your data 139

Is 'thick description' something I should be aiming for? 140

The flow of the story 140

Should I use numbers to report theme 'frequency'? 141

Should I claim generalisability in reporting my TA? 142

Table 5.4: Different types of *qualitative* generalisability 144

Drawing conclusions 146

Reflection and evaluation in your write-up 148

Telling your story *well*: The value of the edit 149

Chapter summary 149

Want to learn more about...? 150

Activities for student readers 151

SECTION II   GOING DEEPER FOR TIP-TOP REFLEXIVE THEMATIC ANALYSIS: THEORY, INTERPRETATION, AND QUALITY MATTERS **153**

6   **A not-so-scary theory chapter: Conceptually locating reflexive thematic analysis** **155**

Chapter Six overview 155

There's no such thing as atheoretical TA! 157

What sorts of theory are we discussing? 157

Key basic starting points for TA and theory 158

The diversity of qualitative research: Revisiting some important conceptual divisions 158

Figure 6.1: It's *all* connected: Qualitative orientation, theory, questions and methods 159

Researcher reflection – Box 6.1: An example of experiential TA: African Caribbean women 'staying strong'? 161

Researcher reflection – Box 6.2: An example of critical TA research: Onward Gay Christian Soldiers? 162

Let's get theoretical! 163

What do we think language does? Three theories of language 163

Box 6.3: Theories of language applied to data 165

Introducing the 'ologies: The big scary theory 166

Theories of reality: Ontologies 167

Realism 168

Critical realism 169

Box 6.4: Some of the complexity of critical realism 170

Researcher reflection – Box 6.5: Coming to critical realism 172
Relativism 173
Do I really have to think about ontology for TA? 175
Theories of knowledge: Epistemologies 175
Table 6.1: Realist and relativist TA: An overview comparison 176
(Post)positivism 177
Contextualism 178
Constructionism 179
Researcher reflection – Box 6.6: Beyond western ontologies and epistemologies:
Using TA in the context of Indigenous knowledge frameworks 181
Box 6.7: Is constructivism just a different name for constructionism? 183
Checking out the view from the houses of epistemology 184
Back to the confusion... Big Theory is contested terrain 186
Theory as it's used: Some TA examples 189
Table 6.2: Some varied use of theory in published TA research 189
Chapter summary 191
Want to learn more about...? 191
Activities for student readers 193

7   So *what*? The importance of interpretation in reflexive
thematic analysis 195
Chapter Seven overview 195
Doing interpretation during theme development 197
What is interpretation? 199
Interpretation needs to be defensible! 201
Different modes of interpretation for reflexive TA 203
From more descriptive to more interpretative modes of analysis 203
Experiential to critical orientations in interpretation of data patterns 204
Box 7.1: Shifting from an experiential to critical orientation to
build analytic depth 206
A deductive orientation: Working with existing theoretical concepts
in doing interpretation 208
Box 7.2: Explanatory theory in reflexive TA 209
Locating data within the wider context 211
Minimising harm in interpretation: Ethics, politics and representation 214
Box 7.3: Interpretation across difference: Power, privilege and positioning 216
Chapter Summary 220
Want to learn more about...? 220
Activities for student readers 221

8   One big happy family? Understanding similarities and differences
between reflexive thematic analysis and its methodological siblings
and cousins 223
Chapter Eight overview 223

A brief and partial history of 'thematic analysis'   224

Table 8.1: Don't believe everything you hear! 10 claims about TA that
    are actually wrong   225

Variation across TA approaches: Core concepts   228

    Coding: Process and/or output?   229

    What is a theme?   229

Table 8.2: Shared-meaning themes vs. topic summaries   231

    Researcher subjectivity (reflexivity)   232

    A process of theme development or identification?   232

Box 8.1: How do I get my themes in TA? Two different conceptualisations
    of the process   233

Figure 8.1: Themes do not emerge!   234

Mapping the main members of the TA family: Our tripartite clustering   234

Table 8.3: Comparing TA: A quick overview of different forms of TA   236

Coding reliability approaches: Small q thematic analysis   237

    What do we think is problematic about coding reliability
        approaches to TA?   238

Codebook approaches to TA (MEDIUM Q)   242

    Template analysis   242

    Do we perceive any problems with template analysis?   244

    Framework analysis   244

    Do we perceive any problems with framework analysis?   246

    Challenges with using codebook approaches in general   246

So is reflexive TA the *best* approach to TA?   247

But wait... there's *even* more? Other approaches to thematic analysis   247

Table 8.4: A quick summary of *advantages* and *challenges*
    for different forms of TA   248

Box 8.2: Thematic coding   248

    The use of TA for qualitative evidence synthesis   250

Box 8.3: Polytextual TA for visual data analysis   251

Researcher reflection – Box 8.4: How I use TA on visual data   252

Figure 8.2: Image of Inverness Castle with white grid lines overlay   252

Figure 8.3: Initial analysis of photograph   253

    'Off-label' TA: Combining thematic analysis with other approaches   254

Researcher reflection – Box 8.5: Combining TA and discourse analysis   255

Chapter summary   256

Want to learn more about...?   256

Activities for student readers   257

**9 Getting your own house in order: Understanding what makes good
reflexive thematic analysis to ensure quality**   **259**

Chapter Nine overview   259

They did *what?* Common problems we encounter in TA work   260

Table 9.1: Strengths and limitations of reflexive TA   261

Figure 9.1: Reflexive TA bingo   262

Table 9.2: Common problems and good practice in (reflexive) TA research   263

    Premature closure of the analysis   266

Strategies for ensuring quality in *your* TA research   268

Table 9.3: Our 15-point checklist for good *reflexive* TA – version 2022   269

    Reflexive journaling   270

Box 9.1: Check yourself! Avoiding 'positivism creep' by developing a   qualitative sensibility   270

    Talking about your data and analysis with others   271

    Allowing time for your analytic insights to fully develop   272

    Working with an experienced supervisor, mentor or co-researcher   273

    Making sure themes are themes, and naming them carefully   274

    Drawing inspiration from excellent examples of published research   274

    Demonstrating quality through an electronic or paper trail   275

Managing quality *during* the publication process   275

Are *generic* qualitative quality criteria and strategies useful in TA research?   277

Chapter summary   279

Want to learn more about…?   279

Activities for student readers   280

Fare-well! Becoming a bold adventurer in the world of reflexive TA   **281**

Glossary   283

References   299

Index   331

BEFORE THE ADVENTURE....

ABOUT THE AUTHORS AND CONTRIBUTORS

The book (and companion website) is mostly written by us, but features contributions from many others – mostly former and current students, and a few colleagues. These contributors offer insights, reflections and sometimes different points of view, along the way. We introduce them and their contributions after our brief bios.

Virginia Braun and **Victoria Clarke's** first co-authored publication was 'Using thematic analysis in psychology' published in *Qualitative research in psychology* in 2006 (this has been translated into Turkish (Şad, Özer, & Atlï, 2019), and adapted into Brazilian Portuguese (de Souza, 2019), with other translations in progress). Since then, they have gone on to write an award-winning and bestselling introductory qualitative textbook – *Successful qualitative research* (2013), translated into both Hindi and Marathi (Braun & Clarke, 2017, 2018) – and numerous chapters, editorials, commentaries and encyclopaedia entries on thematic analysis (TA) (some with other co-authors – most commonly Nikki Hayfield and Gareth Terry). They have taught TA in a wide range of settings internationally (sometimes together, sometimes separately, sometimes with Nikki or Gareth). Ginny's teaching in the Sultanate of Oman even made the national news! More recently, they have begun publishing around two novel qualitative methods – qualitative surveys and story completion (again, often with other co-authors). Their most recent book, prior to *Thematic analysis*, was an edited textbook – with Debra Gray – *Collecting qualitative data* (Braun, Clarke, & Gray, 2017b), which has been translated into (Brazilian) Portuguese (Braun, Clarke, & Gray, 2017a), and includes chapters on qualitative surveys and story completion. They have developed websites on thematic analysis (www.thematicanalysis.net) and story completion (www.storycompletion.net). Ginny and Victoria have worked together on various research and publishing projects (sometimes with others) in the areas of body hair practices, orgasm, infidelity, voluntary childlessness, LGBT concerns in higher education, and *feminist* methods and methodologies.

Virginia Braun is a Professor in the School of Psychology at The University of Auckland, Aotearoa New Zealand. She is a feminist and critical (health) psychologist and teaches around gender and psychology and critical health psychology at undergraduate and graduate levels. When she gets time for it, her research (sometimes in collaboration with Victoria) explores the intersecting areas of gender, bodies, sex/sexuality, health, and (now) food. Her official work page is: www.psych.auckland.ac.nz/people/v-braun. She is on Twitter @ginnybraun, where she sometimes tweets about qualitative research, usually a retweet of an awesome thread by Victoria.[1]

---

[1] Ginny has a variable chronic health condition which impacts her work capacity in unforeseeable ways. She is unable to personally respond to the emails she gets regarding TA, hence has not included her email as a contact here.

Victoria Clarke is an Associate Professor in Qualitative and Critical Psychology in the Department of Social Sciences at the University of the West of England (UWE), Bristol, where she teaches about qualitative methods and supervises student research on a variety of undergraduate and postgraduate programmes. When she's not busy collaborating with Ginny, she has conducted research in the intersecting areas of gender and sexuality, family and relationships, and appearance and embodiment. You can read more about her research on her UWE webpage (https://people.uwe.ac.uk/Person/VictoriaClarke), Google Scholar, ResearchGate, and Academia.edu. She is also active on Twitter – mainly tweeting about thematic analysis and qualitative research @drvicclarke.[2]

Suzy Anderson is a final year trainee counselling psychologist at UWE with a background in third sector support roles, currently writing a thesis on problematic skin picking. She is studying alongside raising a young family and running a small private counselling practice. She has a passion for social justice and an interest in human nature and subjective experience. Suzy's contribution features on the companion website, as reflective commentaries about the analytic process in doing *experiential/inductive* reflexive TA, alongside an abridged version of the paper; you can also find the full version of the paper, co-authored with Victoria, on the website.

Melanie Beres is an Associate Professor in Sociology and Academic Director of Te Whare Tāwharau: Sexual Violence Support and Prevention Centre at the University of Otago, New Zealand. She studies sexual violence prevention and sexual consent with a specific interest in LGBTQA sexualities. Melanie's contribution features on the companion website, as reflective commentaries with Pani Farvid about the analytic process in doing *critical/deductive* reflexive TA, alongside an abridged version of the paper; you can also find the full version of their paper on the website.

Elicia Boulton is a counselling psychologist who undertook her professional doctorate at UWE. Her thesis focused on exploring the lived experiences of sex and sexuality for women with OCD, with data collected using an online qualitative survey. She has worked primarily with children and young adults, and those with learning disabilities and autism. Elicia's contribution – a reflection on doing TA with anxiety and OCD – features in Chapter Four.

Gina Broom is a critical psychology graduate student at The University of Auckland, interested in personal experiences of sexual and relational identities and practices within the contemporary sociocultural context. She has also worked in sexual assault support and is moving into preventative education. You can find her on Twitter @GinaMBroom. Gina's contribution – a reflection on doing TA with anxiety and ADHD – features in Chapter Four.

Lucy Cowie (Ngāti Ranginui) is in the final stages of completing a Doctorate of Clinical Psychology at The University of Auckland. She works with young people and their families in a public mental health service. She is particularly interested in how people navigate and challenge inequity, with a focus on the intersection between psychological distress and power. Her doctoral research explores queer and gender diverse young people's understandings of psychological distress. Lucy's contribution – a commentary on moving from an experiential to a critical position for TA – features in Chapter Six.

---

[2]Victoria has, like Ginny, not included a contact email address. She has a degenerative neurological disease and for this reason is not able to respond to personal requests around TA.

Louise Davey recently completed her Professional Doctorate in Counselling Psychology at UWE with interests in embodiment, dynamics of power and possibilities for change. She works in an inpatient psychology service and in private practice. Louise's contribution – an example of how she wrote her method section to demonstrate the particular TA choices and process of her project – features in Chapter Five.

Panteá Farvid is an Assistant Professor of Applied Psychology at The New School and the founder/director of The SexTech Lab in New York City. She studies evolving ethical issues at the cross-section of gender, sexuality and technology (e.g. mobile dating), broader issues of inequality and marginalisation (e.g. racism, sexism), as well as theoretical and method-ological developments in the psychology of gender and sexuality (e.g. the psychology of heterosexuality). You can contact her at farvidp@newschool.edu. Pani's contribution fea-tures on the companion website, as reflective commentaries with Melanie Beres, about the analytic process in doing critical/deductive reflexive TA, alongside an abridged version of the paper; you can also find the full version of their paper on the website.

Ally Gibson is a researcher in critical health psychology and Lecturer in the School of Health at Victoria University of Wellington Te Herenga Waka. Her work addresses inter-sections of gender, sexuality and health, conducted through a feminist lens. She is also interested in the practice of qualitative methodology – how it's done and the possibilities it offers critical health research. You can find her on Twitter @allyfgibson. Ally's contribution – a reflective commentary on using NVivo for coding in TA – features in Chapter Three.

Rachel Graham is a chartered counselling psychologist, who has an interest in racism, ethnicity and gender, with a particular interest in the lived experiences of UK Black women. She is currently working as a clinician within the NHS and also runs a private practice. Rachel's contributions – a selection of research journal entries, and an example of what 'experiential' TA looks like – feature in Chapters One and Six.

Jade Le Grice is an Indigenous Māori woman from Aotearoa, Te Rarawa and Ngāpuhi iwi (kinship groups). Her research is informed by Indigenous community aspirations for self-determination, decolonisation, sexual and reproductive justice. She is invested in devel-oping Indigenous psychology anchored in Indigenous knowledge, mātauranga Māori. She is a Senior Lecturer in the School of Psychology, The University of Auckland. Jade's contribution – a commentary with Michelle Ong on using reflexive TA within Indigenous psychology frameworks – features in Chapter Six.

Nikki Hayfield is a social psychologist whose research interests are in sexualities. She uses qualitative methods of data collection and analysis and has written with others about thematic analysis (TA). Nikki is currently a Senior Lecturer in Social Psychology and Leader of the Identities, Subjectivities, and Inequalities research theme at UWE. You can read more about her research on her UWE staff page. Nikki's contribution – a practically-orientated commentary on teaching TA to university students – features in the supplementary teaching and supervision chapter on the companion website. A conversation with Gareth Terry, where they reflexively discuss their positionality and their analytic process on a project about the experiences of childfree women, also appears on the companion website.

Michelle G. Ong does research on ageing and migration, children's issues and children's rights, and contributes to Sikolohiyang Pilipino (Indigenous Filipino psychology). She enjoys exploring both qualitative and quantitative methodologies in her work. She teaches at the

University of the Philippines Diliman Department of Psychology. She can be contacted at mgong@up.edu.ph. Michelle's contribution – a commentary with Jade Le Grice on using reflexive TA within Indigenous psychology frameworks – features in Chapter Six.

Matt Sillars teaches psychology, photography and culture studies at the University of the Highlands and Islands, where he specialises in visual research. He focuses on the visual construction of identity in small urban spaces and is co-chair of the Society, Identity, Landscape and Knowledge research cluster. He is a director of the FLOW International Photography Festival. You can contact him at matt.sillars.ic@uhi.ac.uk. Matt's contribution – a discussion and illustration of his process for doing TA with visual data – features in Chapter Eight.

Gareth Terry likes thinking about the various ways bodies intersect with the social – especially why different bodies and practices are privileged over others. His current work explores disability, rehabilitation, and how access is constituted, drawing on critical theory and qualitative research. He is a Senior Lecturer at Auckland University of Technology, working out of the Centre for Person Centred Research. Gareth can be contacted on email gareth.terry@aut.ac.nz and can be found on Twitter @GarethRTerry. Gareth's contributions – a reflection on using QDAS during coding and analysis, and a reflection on combining TA with discourse analysis – feature in Chapters Three and Eight. Two other contributions – a conversation with Nikki Hayfield, where they reflexively discuss their positionality and their analytic process on a project and childfree women, and a box reflecting on and offering advice for teaching TA online – appear on the companion website.

Lisa Trainor is a sport and exercise psychology researcher who uses qualitative methods to explore athlete psychological well-being (eudaimonia), sport injury, and psychological growth. She is currently a PhD student in the School of Kinesiology at The University of British Columbia, Canada. You can find her on Twitter @trainorL. Lisa's contribution – a visual illustration of her coding and initial theme development process – features in Chapter Four.

Matthew Wood is a critical social psychologist who also works as a puppeteer. He often works in Human Computer Interaction and is broadly interested in the qualitative dimensions of social computing. He is a Lecturer in Social Psychology at UWE. You can find him on Twitter @mattywood. Matthew's contributions – illustrations of familiarisation 'doodles' from his analytic process, and an example of what 'critical' TA can look like – feature in Chapters Two and Six.

ACKNOWLEDGEMENTS

Researchers are not isolated and purely self-determining islands, but more akin to individual countries within a collective like the European Union. Nurtured and shaped by others, co-creating shared understandings and meanings, while not always agreeing. We start by thanking all of those people who have contributed to our understanding and thinking around qualitative research, particularly in relation to thematic analysis (TA). As teachers, supervisors, mentors and colleagues, this includes (but is not limited to) Hannah Frith, Nicola Gavey, Kate Gleeson, Celia Kitzinger and Sue Wilkinson.

Those we have taught TA to over the (ahem) decades have also honed our perspectives, not least through the questions and challenges they have presented, and gifted us numerous evocative metaphors and examples that we draw on in our writing. In so doing, they have helped us improve how we teach and provided insights that have informed how we write about TA. Students teach you how to get *better* at teaching; how to explain things in ways that connect and make sense; how to recognise your – maybe forgotten – uncertainties and anxieties, and ways to ameliorate them.

The seeds of this book were sown in 2005 when we decided to write a paper on 'Using thematic analysis in psychology' for the journal *Qualitative Research in Psychology*. Our aim was to provide an accessible and transparent procedure for doing what we felt would be fully qualitative TA. We did not anticipate the popularity of that paper – over 100,000 Google Scholar citations as this book goes to press; the most cited academic paper published in 2006 (according to Google Scholar). Those statistics are rather overwhelming, especially as we'd spent most of our careers engaging with *very* small and mostly like-minded communities of critical sexuality and gender scholars. For giving that paper life, we thank Brendan Gough, one of the editors of *Qualitative Research in Psychology*, and the two enthusiastic and thoughtful reviewers. The anonymous peer review process is robust enough that we don't know who you were (and yes, we have wondered!).

Thank you to everyone – too many to list here – who has subsequently invited us to write about TA, in chapters, encyclopaedia entries, editorials and commentaries. Writing these – alongside insightful and thoughtful editorial feedback and reviews – has provided an opportunity to develop, and sometimes change, our thinking around TA in numerous ways that we capture in this book. Thanks also to our magnificent co-authors.

This book has had a (double ahem) longer-than-expected gestation (aided and abetted by health challenges and the global COVID-19 pandemic). Over the years of development, SAGE have been wonderful to work with. Luke Block initially commissioned this book with great enthusiasm, and insight on how the proposal might develop. He was the publishing editor any writer would hope for, providing critical and engaged support alongside creative freedom. Although we felt the loss when he left SAGE, we have been delighted that he has continued to be an enthusiastic supporter of our work on Twitter – thanks @Luke_Block!

Our current SAGE editor, Amy Maher, has continued the supportive approach Luke enacted. For getting us and our vision, and for support, encouragement and endless patience, we thank Amy, and all the others at SAGE, who have worked hard to make this book possible.

A book is shaped by many people, some visible, some invisible. To everyone who agreed to contribute to the book and companion website – you get a big *thank you*! Not just for your unfortunately-required patience, but for the insights and perspectives you bring, the interruptions to our single authorial voice. We *particularly* thank Nikki Hayfield and Gareth Terry, who have taught many TA courses, both with and without us, and have been our most frequent TA chapter co-authors. Hanan Moller, thank you for being our fabulous cover 'hand model'! The three manuscript reviewers, the first people to read the product of our years of work, provided a perfect mix of enthusiasm and reassurance, questions and critique. Thank you!

Finally, a deep and sincere thank you to everyone who is supportive and sustaining of us, and our writing endeavours, in our workplaces and beyond, anyone who just likes to chat enthusiastically about qualitative research and people who nourish us with chocolate, (minions) memes and general life silliness. Excluding people already mentioned, this includes: Reg Clarke, Toby Clarke, Percy Clarke, Pene Johnstone, Naomi Moller, David Thomas, the UWE psychology team, members of the Auckland Psychology and Social Issues Research Group, the Psychology of Women and Equalities Section of the BPS, and a whole world of academics and students on Twitter, who make our (Twitter) lives interesting and engaging – you'll even encounter some of these tweets *in* the book! Different social research technicians in the School of Psychology at Auckland provided helpful 'mundane task' support at various points... Thank you! Finally, much of the initial editing of this book took place – pre COVID-19 pandemic – in a converted barn in a remote village in the south of France. A huge thanks to Cherie and Oscar for offering your cosy (and *fairly* non-distracting) abode for focused editing and writing time. At that point, we thought we were so close, but it took over another year to finally finish the book. So writing a book about TA, like *doing* TA, always takes longer than you think it will!

As we began the final stages of editing, a deeply loved and valued friend and colleague, a key sharer of gifs and memes, and general bringer of joy, love and laughter to the lives of many – including us – passed away unexpectedly, and far too young. With heavy hearts, but happy memories, we dedicate this book to our feminist psychology colleague, Professor Marcia Worrell.

SCENE SETTING

What *Thematic analysis*: *A practical guide* offers you, and how to navigate your way through it

Chapter overview

- Setting the scene for *Thematic analysis*: *A practical guide*   xxvi
- Baking, adventures and maps: Is this a recipe book, a guidebook, or what?   xxvi
- Navigating language and imagining the reader   xxvii
- This is *our* mapping...   xxviii
- Learning through doing: A practice-first approach to learning thematic analysis   xxix
- Who is the book for?   xxx
- A book of two parts   xxx
  - o Mapped adventure pathways: Navigating your way through the book   xxxi
  - o Helpful things to support your adventure: The pedagogical features   xxxii
  - o The companion website: An abundance of teaching and learning resources   xxxiii

SETTING THE SCENE FOR *THEMATIC ANALYSIS*: A PRACTICAL GUIDE

The scene needs to be set! Captivating first lines grab the reader or listener. Consider some famous opening lines from the canon of White western literature:[1]

> It is a truth universally acknowledged, that a single man in possession of a good fortune, must be in want of a wife. (Jane Austen, *Pride and prejudice*, 1813)

> The first real writer I ever knew was a man who did all of his work under the name of August Van Zorn. (Michael Chabon, *Wonder boys*, 1995)

Such openings entice us, making us want to read or hear more. The words also provide a frame through which we make sense of and interpret what is to follow. A textbook, like literature, also needs an orientation. This scene-setting chapter for *Thematic analysis: A practical guide* aims to give you an enticing taster of what is to come in the book, as well as an orientating guide to *your* engagement with the book. Our scene-setting also reveals some of *our* choices and positionings as storytellers; how we have written this book reflects who we are, as people, and as scholars.

BAKING, ADVENTURES AND MAPS: IS THIS A RECIPE BOOK, A GUIDEBOOK, OR WHAT?

We have sometimes been accused of being methodolatrists who prioritise adherence to procedures as if they are a must-be-precisely-followed recipe, a fail-safe way to produce an analysis. This couldn't be further from how we think about qualitative researching! We imagine qualitative analysis as an adventure, and one that is typically messy and organic, complex and contested – "more messy, more convoluted and more surprising than we thought it would be" (Gherhardi & Turner, 2002, quoted in Nadar, 2014, p. 25). It requires scholarship, reflexivity, creativity, and theoretical engagement. The *joy* of this is often lost on those starting out, uncertain of where to begin, or how to feel confident of doing it well. This book can be considered, in part, a guidebook, like a Rough Guide that bolsters and resources you along the way. It's a *tool* to guide you, to take you through the *process*, and to help you become the thoughtful, reflexive analyst that good qualitative research requires.

Another analogy might be useful: to baking. Baking is often depicted – in recipe books or on TV cooking shows – as a precise process where failure awaits those who dare stray.

---

[1]Googling 'book opening lines' usually produces a list dominated by White male authors! We chose these two examples not just because we love them, but as they have personal resonance for us connected to our qualitative writing. We watched the BBC adaptation of *Pride and prejudice* when writing our original TA paper! *Wonder boys* is about writing and academia; we watched and loved the film version while doctoral students at Loughborough, the place that 'birthed' our passion for methodological thinking and writing (see Braun, Clarke, & Hayfield, 2019; Jankowski, Braun, & Clarke, 2017).

Baking can therefore be scary and intimidating to those who have never baked. But experience can bring a different approach, and there is often more fluidity in baking than might appear to the novice. Victoria's grandfather John worked as a cook (*Downton Abbey* style) and when he baked, not only did he not follow a recipe, he didn't even precisely measure the ingredients (much to small-child-Victoria's fascinated delight). John understood what types of ingredients – and proportions, which he could judge by eye or feel – were needed for a successful bake. He understood how different ingredients worked together, and what needed to happen when, and why, for a successful outcome. Of course, when John first learned to bake, he read and followed recipes. Through following these, and practice, John learned the *general principles* of baking, knowing which rules needed usually to be followed, and which were more flexible. Experienced qualitative researchers tend to approach the process like John approached baking, with a fluid, contextualised application of processes based on an understanding of underlying principles.

We find that metaphors and analogies are useful ways to illustrate or explain concepts and practice in research. Metaphors can "help the researcher understand a familiar process [or, indeed, an unfamiliar one] in a new light" (J. Carpenter, 2008, p. 275). You'll find lots of metaphors and analogies throughout the book (just don't ask us which is which!). The main one we deploy – building on UK-based health and counselling psychologist Carla Willig's (2001, 2013) wonderful *Introducing qualitative research in psychology* – is of research as an adventure, a journey of exploration and discovery, down unfamiliar and perhaps rarely used pathways. We conceptualise our writing as offering *you* a guide, like a map and a compass, to help you traverse the world of qualitative research and the territories of TA, rather than a fully-fledged travel itinerary (Braun, Clarke, & Hayfield, 2019).

NAVIGATING LANGUAGE AND IMAGINING THE READER

One of the things we've grappled with, in writing this book, is how to ensure we describe the process of reflexive TA and deploy language, metaphors and analogies in a way that doesn't reinforce ableist assumptions and norms. Much of the casual or normalised language of qualitative research (like the world!) assumes a non-disabled reader, who navigates the processes and technologies of research in a normative way. Such ableist thinking is hard to avoid, because it's the way the world remains structured, but inclusive language matters to us personally and politically. We haven't gotten it perfect, but we have endeavoured to interrupt these norms as much as possible: to limit our use of terms which assume certain sensory, cognitive, affective or physical capacities; to clarify what we intend with certain language; and to acknowledge the requirements or constraints of processes or technologies when we describe them. And although we love the metaphor of reflexive TA as adventure, as people who both have experience of fatigue-related conditions, we personally know that adventures don't always appeal. We hope the idea of adventuring can be held as something intellectual and conceptual.

In writing a book like this, we also bring *ourselves* into the process. This means that while we're very *serious about* TA, we also don't take all things that seriously in life, and we like to have *fun* in writing. This means you'll find allusions to popular culture in the titles and descriptions we give – though as we're effectively middle aged, in years if not in our psycho-logical maturity, some of these may be obscure, especially if you're not from the contexts we were raised in. You may also notice a few – usually bad – jokes scattered throughout the text; we've tried to make it as obvious as possible where not to take us seriously! We also tend to value complexity and nuance. We add text in brackets, or footnotes, where we feel we have to acknowledge complexity. But we have – honestly! – tried to keep all these aspects to a minimum, as they can work against the accessibility of texts, particularly for some neu-rodivergent readers.

THIS IS *OUR* MAPPING...

The notion of *mapping the terrain* of qualitative research has an authoritative and objective quality, like what we might imagine from a cartographer mapping a landscape: here is a definitive guide to what actually is! But is mapping so straightforward? Consider the worlds depicted in three types of maps:

- Contemporary geographical maps, like the British Mapping Agency's Ordnance Survey maps or Google Maps, which mark out landscape features to scale.
- Maps in art, which provide political commentary on the contemporary social world, like British artist Grayson Perry's embroidered map *Red carpet* (2017).
- Historical maps, which reveal past sense-making of the world. The famous *Mappa mundi*, for instance, shows how 13th-century English scholars understood the world in spiritual and geographic terms (Hereford Cathedral, n.d.).

Mapping is not a simple endeavour, and all maps encode *something* of the worldview of the cartographer and their moment of creation. With medieval maps, where there are profound differences between the cartographers' worldview and contemporary norms, it's much eas-ier to see the act of mapping, and the mapped world, as encoding particular values and assumptions. Our mapping of the terrain of TA is informed by our perspectives on qualitative research, and our positioning as developers of a particular version of TA, and the point in time of writing.[2] We have a stake in this mapping exercise. That doesn't make our mapping wrong, just situated. In reading this book, we encourage you to hold onto an idea of the map as always situated, always partial. If you are new to qualitative research, that might be easier than if the terrain is familiar. Regardless, one of your tasks in learning the terrain, is

---

[2]There is a risk that in writing this book, we might have inadvertently re-shaped others' mappings, others' demarcations of *their* world of qualitative researching, into a form they at best don't find rec-ognisable, and at worst find misrepresentative. For any inadvertent misrepresentation, we apologise in advance. We are of course conscious of the potential hypocrisy of this apology in a book in which we take other authors to task for misrepresenting *our* work, but we hope we are not guilty of the type of misrepresentation we are critical of.

determining which account(s) of qualitative research *you* find most compelling, and what you might do differently, eventually becoming your own cartographer. Or you might reject the mapping metaphor altogether![3]

Despite emphasising an adventurous ethos, we recognise a guidebook can be an essential part of a happy outcome for any adventure, especially for an inexperienced traveller. We hope this book gives you the assurance to boldly adventure with TA! The guidelines for TA we provide in this book operate as tools for learning, for systematic and deep engagement, to be followed openly, loosely, knowingly. Once you understand the principles and purpose, and the context, of qualitative research, once you feel confident about doing TA, such guidelines can be put to one side, maybe to occasionally check back with. They become like the guidebook buried at the bottom of your pack as your adventure hits month three – rarely consulted, but reassuringly there if needed.

LEARNING THROUGH DOING: A PRACTICE-FIRST APPROACH TO LEARNING THEMATIC ANALYSIS

We have organised this book around what we call a practice-first approach. Qualitative research of any kind is a skilled endeavour. As a practice, it combines theoretical and methodological knowledge with *craft* – or doing – skills. The knowledge and practices can seem daunting and overwhelming, especially if you aren't already embedded within the research values and understandings associated with a qualitative paradigm (discussed further in Chapters One and Six). For this reason, we believe there is great value in learning the craft skills and theory *by* and *while* doing. In our experience as teachers and supervisors, we see this approach as a way students can find confidence to start, develop, and finish, their first – and subsequent – qualitative research projects; to gain confidence in their ability as adventurers. As TA offers a fairly accessible method that can be started without *deep* and complex theoretical engagement, it works well with this approach to learning, and as an entry method into qualitative research. We hope that it generates a love of the potential of qualitative research – whether you continue to predominantly use TA or explore other analytic approaches. We also hope it generates a desire to engage *with* theory, to understand theory as *something we do* rather than something separate, abstract and potentially inaccessible. And, finally, to understand that theory is integral to doing TA, and that what we are *not* offering is a way to avoid theory. Theory is always part of what we do as researchers, so it needs to be explicitly considered! Our approach grounds the understanding of the need for theory in practice, in doing.

---

[3]There are many ways of demarcating the terrain of qualitative research. Qualitative research is broad, diverse, complex and contested, and how things connect, or what matters most, varies considerably by discipline. Some authors wouldn't even like our use of a landscape metaphor, rejecting it as too realist, because it implies an extra-textual and essential reality for qualitative research. We get that, but like the imagery nonetheless!

WHO IS THE BOOK FOR?

Writing an accessible and practical guide for those learning about, and doing, reflexive TA was our primary goal. We also wanted to support people teaching about and supervising reflexive TA. So we have written the book for two readerships:

People learning *to do* reflexive TA – our primary readership.

People *teaching* about or *supervising* TA – our secondary readership.

There is overlap between these readerships: those teaching or supervising might not be particularly experienced in TA, or qualitative research *per se*. Our aim is to provide all the resources you need for learning, teaching or supervising reflexive TA. This dual audience made for a slightly challenging task, but it was important to be able to write a book that was both accessible *and* contained depth and context, to support quality practice. The book's companion website offers many additional resources for teachers and supervisors, as well as for student readers.

Do you need *any* qualitative knowledge or experience to read this book? Not a *lot*. We do explain the particular ways in which *we* map and conceptualise the qualitative research terrain throughout, and provide the knowledge and tools you need to do reflexive TA well. But we do assume *some* knowledge of qualitative research, because this is a specialist textbook focused on one analytic approach. Complete newcomers to qualitative research may find our *introductory* textbook *Successful qualitative research: A practical guide for beginners* (Braun & Clarke, 2013) a useful adjunct.

Primarily, this book provides a detailed *how to* guide for doing *reflexive* TA – one particular approach to TA. But it also provides a lot more. You can treat this book a bit like the proverbial onion, starting off at a fairly surface level, and then going deeper into the layers. Your pathway in and through the book will, of course, be whatever you make it, but we have imagined different starting points for different readers – which we'll lay out, as possible adventure routes – after briefly explaining the structure.

A BOOK OF TWO PARTS

The book is divided into two sections:

Section One: Venturing Forth! Doing reflexive thematic analysis is practical and designed for the beginning TA researcher. It's organised around doing TA, orientated to the six-phase approach to reflexive TA we first outlined in 2006, but capturing all subsequent developments in our thinking. The chapters describe the phases of analysis and use a worked example to demonstrate key aspects of the analytic process and outputs. We emphasise the importance of a reflexive, thoughtful and engaged process. The section begins with a basic introduction to key concepts in reflexive TA – everything you need to get started, which you can then learn more about in Section Two.

Section Two: Going deeper for tip-top reflexive thematic analysis: Theory, interpretation and quality matters covers two things that are integral to the whole reflexive TA process – interpretation and theory.

Once you have the foundation in doing TA that Section One provides, this section takes you deeper into the practice of interpretation and the theory that grounds and gives validity to your TA. 'Big Theory' inescapably informs your practice of TA; our theory chapter offers a detailed but accessible guide to various layers of theory that are important to understand. Our chapter on interpretation not only unpacks and explains what interpretation is, and why it matters, but illustrates various interpretative strategies using the worked example from Section One. The third chapter in this section will help you to fully understand the conceptualisation of reflexive TA through considering how it is similar to and different from other approaches to TA. We particularly focus on how core concepts – such as the code and the theme – are understood and how the underlying conceptualisation of the method is reflected in analytic procedures. This chapter provides a gateway to the final chapter focused on quality, by helping you to understand which quality practices from within the wider TA family are appropriate to reflexive TA, and which are not. This final chapter is designed to improve and increase the overall quality of TA analyses – something sadly sorely needed (Braun & Clarke, 2021c). With this chapter, we aim to fully resource you to 'live your best TA life' – to recognise the key problems or challenges in doing and reporting TA, and to avoid these pitfalls. Readers who are teaching or supervising reflexive TA can find a chapter dedicated to tips and techniques for teaching and supervision on the companion website – 'Teaching, supervising, and examining for quality TA'.

The book ends with a few final words of farewell, as you navigate your own TA journey.

Mapped adventure pathways: Navigating your way through the book

Navigating the best path through this book will depending on what your starting point and primary purpose are. Our basic mappings here are far from directive, but we have imagined the following routes of engagement:

- If you're *new to TA* and want to start with the 'what is …' chapter that often starts a textbook, then we recommend heading first to Chapter Eight for an in-depth review of what TA is, and where reflexive TA sits in the field.
- If you're an *undergraduate, taught Master's or honours-level student* using TA for a smaller research project or dissertation, then Section One will provide almost all of what you need. Dip into Section Two as needed for a more in-depth understanding of interpretation, theory and quality.
- If you're a *research postgraduate student*, doing a substantial research project for your research Master's or doctoral thesis: Section One will provide you with a good basic understanding of process, but you'll need to dip into Section Two to better explain and locate your methodological choices and practices.
- If you're an *established researcher new to doing TA*, we encourage taking Chapters Six–Eight in Section Two as your starting point, to reflect on how our mapping of theory in TA coheres with or challenges your mapping of the conceptual foundations of qualitative research and to locate and contextualise your analytic practice. This will provide a richer conceptual foundation for the practical advice offered in Section One, and the quality guidance offered in Chapter Nine.
- If you're *teaching about TA* to an undergraduate or postgraduate class, Chapter Nine and the *online only* chapter on 'Teaching, supervising, and examining for quality TA, available on the companion website, are a good starting point, especially if you're familiar with qualitative research. What you take from Section One and the rest of Section Two will depend on the timescale

and scope of the teaching, as well as the knowledge base you bring to your teaching. The companion website provides a wealth of additional resources for use in teaching.

- If you're **supervising students using TA**, where you start again depends on how much you know about qualitative research, and TA. Chapter Nine and the *online only* chapter on 'Teaching, supervising, and examining for quality TA' on the companion website are again an important starting point. But do dip into Section One and the other chapters in Section Two if your knowledge around TA is limited.

Various *pedagogical features* in the book, and a *companion website*, support both learning and teaching.

Helpful things to support your adventure: The pedagogical features

The book's pedagogical features are designed to *pause the narrative*, to encourage reflexive engagement. They provide a systematic structure for the narrative; they summarise, highlight or develop your understanding of key points; they offer tools to enrich your learning (or teaching) experience. These pedagogical features include:

- Overview boxes outlining the focus and structure of each chapter.
- Three types of 'pop out' features that succinctly note *important* points:
  o Alerts – signalling key things to 'watch out for'.
  o Practice points – highlighting key elements to facilitate better practice.
  o Key concept definitions – succinct definitions of certain key concepts the first time they are used within the main text – these concepts are also defined in the *glossary*.
- A *glossary*, which offers brief definitions of key terms and concepts. The first time a glossary entry term (or close variant) is used in the main text, it will be blue and bold.
- *Boxes* that highlight key information, expand on an important issue briefly acknowledged in the main text, or present an illustration from an actual research example.[4]
- *Researcher reflection boxes* that provide situated and reflexive personal accounts of aspects of research process.
- *Figures* representing elements in the *doing of* reflexive TA.
- *Tables* summarising key information or comparing different approaches.
- *Footnotes* that provide a narrative explanation or counterpoint to a point made in the main text. Typically, these add complexity and nuance and signal – for a more advanced reader – issues they may wish to explore further.
- *Worked-up data examples* from a dedicated dataset, to illustrate the process and outputs of reflexive TA (in Section One).

---

[4]We agonised over whether to use published examples to illustrate what we consider to be poor practice in TA, and although it doesn't feel entirely comfortable to effectively 'name and shame', we decided there is value in using 'real world' instances. Readers can then assess the example in its entirety, themselves, should they wish. Many of the poor practice examples *also* have positive attributes, so their use as examples of poor practice is not a wholesale judgement.

- End of chapter *summaries* highlight the key content and take-home messages.
- Further readings or resources for developing a deeper understanding of particular issues, listed at the end of each chapter as *Want to learn more about...?* These sometimes offer extra insight to a perspective we share; sometimes they offer different 'takes' on an issue.
- *Activities designed for student readers* – practical activities for developing a deeper understanding of core elements of the reflexive TA research process. These are often complemented by materials available on the companion website.
- *Teaching resources* for each chapter are available via the companion website.

The companion website: An abundance of teaching and learning resources

The companion website – which is split between a **student site** and an **instructor site** – provides a vast array of resources to facilitate and enhance your learning, and/or teaching and supervising, of reflexive TA. This content supports and expands considerably what's in the book itself. We provide datasets, expanded illustrations and examples around doing TA, as well as many examples and tools to enhance reflexive practice. We also offer many resources designed specifically to support those supervising TA projects, and teaching TA in the classroom, at both undergraduate and postgraduate level. This includes various PowerPoint- and Word-based activities for instructors to use. Here we summarise the key content:

Datasets

- The full anonymised 'childfree' dataset, that we use as the basis for the worked examples in the book. This includes further contextualisation information. We provide a complete 'as captured' but anonymised version, and a 'corrected' version to aid data readability.
- A small 'men and healthy eating' media dataset, for use with learning and teaching activities. This is intended for use with *postgraduate* students.

Teaching and supervision resources

- An *online only* chapter on 'Teaching, supervising, and examining for quality TA'.
- Extensive Microsoft PowerPoint resources for classroom teaching and learning activities, related to key processes for reflexive TA. This includes the end-of-chapter activities, with a set of resources aimed at undergraduate teaching – based on the childfree dataset – and a set designed for postgraduate teaching, based on the healthy eating dataset.
- A range of activities (in Microsoft PowerPoint and Word), based on the materials we have developed and used in teaching one- or two-day TA workshops over the last decade. Intended for more advanced or specialist TA teaching, these are designed to more deeply engage with processes and phases of reflexive TA. Lecturers may also want to use these to run their own specialist TA workshops.

Reflexive resources to enrich understanding of the reflexive TA process

- A discussion between two experienced TA researchers, Nikki Hayfield and Gareth Terry, about their positionings and process in a project exploring the experiences of childfree women. This highlights the positionality of the researcher in the reflexive TA process.
- Two abridged and annotated reflective reports from published TA work. Designed to unpack and illuminate not only different *forms* of TA, but the active thinking and decision-making processes of researchers, these abridged versions are presented with an interspersed commentary from the lead author(s). The full versions of the original papers are also available:
  - o An example of a more experiential/inductive approach to reflexive TA: Anderson, S., & Clarke, V. (2019). Disgust, shame and the psychological impact of skin picking: Evidence from an online support forum. *Journal of Health Psychology, 24*(13), 1773–1784.
  - o An example of a more constructionist/deductive approach to reflexive TA: Beres, M. A., & Farvid, P. (2010). Sexual ethics and young women's accounts of heterosexual casual sex. *Sexualities, 13*(3), 377–393.

Resources focused on evaluating TA

- A 20-questions list for editors and reviewers to address in evaluating TA.
- The reflexive TA Bingo card.

Find all these resources on the companion website:
https://study.sagepub.com/thematicanalysis

VENTURING FORTH!

Doing reflexive thematic analysis

1

IT'S ALMOST TIME TO DEPART

GETTING READY FOR YOUR THEMATIC ANALYSIS ADVENTURE

Chapter One overview

- Let us introduce you to thematic analysis   4
- What is *reflexive* TA?   5
- Can we provide a simple overview of reflexive TA?   6
- A qualitative sensibility for reflexive TA   7
- But wait, there's more: Variation within reflexive TA   9
- Reflexive TA offers guidelines, not rules, but a clear process   10
- Mentally preparing yourself to tackle your TA journey: Becoming
  comfortable with uncertainty and discomfort   11
- Subjectivity is at the heart of reflexive TA practice   12
- Reflexivity: The most important companion for your adventure   13
  o Doing reflexivity for reflexive TA   14
  o The time to start reflexivity is... NOW   15
  o Activity pause: A task to get reflexivity started   16
  o Reflective and reflexive journals   19

Your adventure into reflexive thematic analysis (TA) is about to begin… *soon*! There is some important orientating information to grasp before you set off. This will get you in the right headspace for doing TA. It might sound like those annoying *terms and conditions* you are supposed to read thoroughly, and agree to, before you can use your new device. Instead, treat this information more like the list of crucial must dos before you are sent off on an adventure, like getting your passport and any visas, immunisations, and learning a bit of the local language or at least downloading the Google Translate app. Don't be a foolhardy traveller in the field of qualitative researching and think that being unprepared makes for a more exciting adventure. Your time reading this chapter will stand you in good stead once your TA adventure begins.

> **ALERT**   Read this chapter before you dive into analysis!

LET US INTRODUCE YOU TO THEMATIC ANALYSIS

TA offers an accessible and robust **method** for those new to qualitative analysis. At a very basic level, TA is a method for developing, analysing and interpreting patterns across a qualitative **dataset**, which involves systematic processes of data **coding** to develop **themes** – themes are your ultimate analytic *purpose*. TA is – more or less – a method for data analysis, rather than a **methodology**. The difference is a bit like getting off a train in a new city, with a range of options you have to choose between, versus arriving in a new city with a pre-prepared itinerary for the day. Methodologies are akin to these complete package itineraries, and things like guiding theory and orientation to language are selected for you, and sometimes data type (Chamberlain, 2011, 2012). Methods, in contrast, leave a wide range of options to be determined by the researcher – such as guiding theory, or data type. This is why **design thinking** is essential for TA, which we touch on in the 'Design interlude' that precedes Chapter Two (for more detail, see Braun & Clarke, 2021b). TA as method offers you a set of tools – concepts, techniques, **practices**, and guidelines – to organise, interrogate and interpret a dataset; but using these well involves thinking, and making choices, about other aspects of your research project and process.

> **KEY CONCEPT**   A method is a process or tool used as part of (qualitative) research – commonly to analyse or collect data.

> **KEY CONCEPT**   Methodology refers to a package of theory, method and other design elements for doing research.

Unfortunately, it's also not *quite* so simple as saying TA is a method. Although TA is often *presented* as a singular and homogenous method, there are dozens of different varieties of, and procedures for doing, TA. What different versions of TA *share* is an interest in patterns of meaning, developed through processes of coding. But these methods are underpinned by a variety of sometimes incommensurate ideas about what constitutes *best practice* for doing TA, based in different qualitative research values. So it's better to imagine TA as method-ish: a method, but with a side of methodology. You don't need to worry too much about such details now! We discuss the similarities and, perhaps most importantly, the differences between approaches to TA in Chapter Eight.

When we first wrote about TA (Braun & Clarke, 2006), we didn't define a specific approach, because the method wasn't established like it is now (Chapter Eight contains a *brief* history). Since then, we've come to recognise that the diversity of orientations, concepts and practices across TA methods makes such differentiation essential. **Reflexive TA** is the

> **ALERT** TA can be understood as a theoretically flexible method, rather than a theoretically-delimited methodology, but different approaches are situated within broad paradigms that shape the method.

term we now use to talk about how *we* approach TA (and the approach as described by some others, e.g. Gleeson, 2011; Hayes, 2000; Langdridge, 2004).[1] Since Section One provides a guide for doing *reflexive TA* specifically, we present the foundational basics here, before you set off on your adventure.

WHAT IS *REFLEXIVE* TA?

We settled on using the adjective reflexive for our approach to TA, because we came to recognise that valuing a subjective, situated, aware and questioning researcher, a *reflexive* researcher, is a fundamental characteristic of TA for us, *and* a differentiating factor across versions of TA (Braun & Clarke, 2019a). **Reflexivity** involves the practice of critical reflection on your role as researcher, and your research practice and process (more later in this chapter). Reflexive TA captures approaches fully embedded within the values of a **qualitative paradigm**, which then inform research practice. We will come back to the much messier question of **paradigms** and TA in detail in

> **KEY CONCEPT** Reflexivity involves a disciplined practice of critically interrogating what we do, how and why we do it, and the impacts and influences of this on our research.

Chapter Six, but for now, it's useful to imagine paradigms as broad value systems encompassing assumptions and principles that guide our ideas about valid, invalid, and ideal research practice (Grant & Giddings, 2002; Guba & Lincoln, 1982). Given that many of us have been trained in a quantitative (and positivist) research paradigm, it's useful to think about how what we will call a qualitative paradigm differs in *broad* characteristics from a quantitative one (we briefly summarise this in Table 1.1, and explore further in Section Two). Also referred to as a **Big Q** framework, this paradigm provides the foundation for reflexive TA; it's what gives the concepts and processes their logic and validity.

---

[1]Encountering different versions of methods or methodologies, based in different conceptual frameworks, is not uncommon in qualitative research. For instance, US sociologist Kathy Charmaz (e.g. 2014) reworked grounded theory into a reflexive, constructionist approach, from earlier iterations with a foot- or toe-hold in positivism (e.g. Glaser 1992; Glaser & Strauss, 1967). We regard our (reflexive) version of TA as similarly unmooring the method from any positivist-empiricist sensibility, crafting it as a fully reflexive Big Q approach.

Table 1.1 Overview of some key differences between qualitative and quantitative research paradigms

Aspect of research	Qualitative paradigm	Quantitative paradigm
Research purpose	Most broadly, focused on *meaning* – from understanding situated meaning to interrogating meaning-making practices. Aims to generate contextualised and situated knowledge.	Recording and understanding truth; often seeking explanatory models or theories. Often reductive, often hypothesis testing.
Big Theory positions related to how reality (*ontology*) and knowledge (*epistemology*) are understood	An only-ever partially knowable world, where meaning and interpretation are always situated practices. Non-positivist; multiple and varied theories (e.g. constructionist, critical realist).	A world knowable through systematic observation and experimentation. Positivist or postpositivist; realist.
Orientation to truth	Situated or life-embedded truth, partial truth, multiple truths.	Singular truth.
Researcher role	*Situated* interpreter of meaning; subjective storyteller. Subjectivity valued.	*Impartial* observer of object of study; unbiased reporter. Objectivity valued, which subjectivity threatens.
Researcher subjectivity	Not just unproblematic, but an asset, especially if reflexively engaged with.	Introduces bias which threatens analytic validity; requires measures to control.
Orientation to influence of subjectivity	Reflexivity as a tool to both interrogate and harness the value of.	Bias control measures to reduce or eliminate influence.
Data purpose and sampling	To gain rich, in-depth understanding; smaller samples valued.	Ideally to gain generalisable understanding; larger, representative samples ideal.
Data analysis	Focused on text and meaning.	Focused on numbers; relationships between variables, cause and effect.
Contributions to knowledge	Part of a rich tapestry of understanding.	Stepping-stone towards complete or perfect understanding.

CAN WE PROVIDE A SIMPLE OVERVIEW OF REFLEXIVE TA?

Yes, and no. The analytic *process* we have described is one of six phases: (1) dataset **familiarisation** (see Chapter Two); (2) data coding (see Chapter Three); (3) initial **theme** generation; (4) theme development and review; (5) theme refining, defining and naming (see Chapter Four for phases 3–5); and (6) writing up (see Chapter Five). But the process is *not* the method. The process *applies* the method to work with and makes sense of data, but is embedded in, and surrounded by, a bigger set of values, assumptions and practices, which, collectively, make up the method. We introduce these values, assumptions and practices in enough depth in this chapter for you to get started on reflexive TA; the rest of the book takes you deeper.

ALERT Don't make the mistake of treating the phases of reflexive TA *as the* method.

A QUALITATIVE SENSIBILITY FOR REFLEXIVE TA

We like the term **qualitative sensibility** as a way to capture the values, assumptions, orientation and skills needed to conduct reflexive TA in a way aligned with a Big Q approach. The term Big Q was used by US feminist psychologists Louise Kidder and Michelle Fine for 'fully qualitative' research. They contrasted this with the use of qualitative data in a limited way, or with values more aligned to quantitative positivist research – which they designated **small q** (Braun & Clarke, 2013; Kidder & Fine, 1987). In *Successful qualitative research*, we identified certain orientations and skills as critical to a qualitative sensibility (Braun & Clarke, 2013):

> **ALERT** Don't conflate qualitative data and techniques with a qualitative paradigm:
>
> - Big Q qualitative uses qualitative tools and techniques within a qualitative paradigm.
> - Small q qualitative uses these techniques within a quantitative paradigm.

- An interest in process and meaning, over cause and effect;
- A critical and questioning approach to life and knowledge;
- The ability to reflect on the dominant assumptions embedded in your cultural context – being a cultural commentator as well as a cultural member;
- The ability to read and listen to data actively and analytically – the development of an analytic orientation to data.

We'd now add a few more to this list:

- A desire for understanding that is about nuance, complexity and even contradiction, rather than finding a nice tidy explanation – you like the *long* answer, not the short answer!;
- The ability to embrace the idea that knowledge comes from a position, and a disinterest in the idea of a singular universal truth to be discovered;
- The ability to tolerate some degree of uncertainty.

At a general level, we'd describe someone as having a qualitative sensibility if they understand the assumptions of reflexive TA and Big Q qualitative research and are able to formulate **research questions** that fit with the assumptions of a qualitative paradigm. For some of us, this is easy. There's an instant attraction to qualitative research; it is the 'one' you didn't know you were looking for, and makes complete sense. Such people – not the majority, in our experience – simply *get it* in some fundamental way. Although there is, of course, always more thinking and learning to be done. For others of us, particularly those well-steeped in quantitative-**positivism**, a qualitative sensibility can take longer to develop, and avoiding **positivism creep** is more challenging. Regardless of your starting point, the more you read, reflect and crucially do qualitative research, the more developed your qualitative sensibility will become. Getting comfortable with **subjectivity** and uncertainty, and getting started on thinking about, and practising, reflexivity – a

> **KEY CONCEPT** Positivism creep refers to the unknowing importation of values of quantitative positivist-empiricist research into qualitative research, such as valuing objectivity, control of 'bias', and the search for ultimate truth. See Box 9.1 in Chapter Nine.

vital tool and process for the qualitative researcher – is central to developing this qualitative sensibility. For that reason, we explain subjectivity and reflexivity in more detail, later in this chapter.

Box 1.1 provides a quick overview of ten core assumptions of reflexive TA, connected to process and concepts. We don't expect this to *all* make sense – yet! As you get into both the book and the TA process, you'll find there's lots to learn. Much like reading the description of norms for social interaction in a foreign country before you get there, Box 1.1 should start you off in the right direction, but might still be confusing. Once you're immersed in the analytic process, it will come alive, start to make more sense, and hopefully eventually become intuitive. Indeed, understanding these ten core assumptions of reflexive TA is a *key learning outcome* for this book. Come back to Box 1.1 as you reach the end of Section

---

Box 1.1

Ten core assumptions of reflexive TA

1. Researcher subjectivity is the primary tool for reflexive TA, as knowledge generation is inherently subjective and situated. Your subjectivity is not a problem to be managed or controlled, to be gotten rid of, but should be understood and treated as a *resource* for doing analysis (Gough & Madill, 2012). This means the notion of **researcher bias**, which implies the possibility of unbiased or objective knowledge generation, and the potential to control such bias, make little sense within reflexive TA.
2. Analysis and interpretation of data cannot be accurate or objective, but they can be weaker (e.g. unconvincing, underdeveloped, shallow, superficial) or stronger (e.g. compelling, insightful, thoughtful, rich, complex, deep, nuanced).
3. Good coding can be achieved alone, or through collaboration – *if* **collaborative coding** is used to enhance understanding, interpretation and reflexivity, rather than to reach a consensus about data coding.
4. Good quality codes and themes result from dual processes of: (a) immersion and depth of engagement; and (b) giving the developing analysis some distance. The latter usually takes time and is often achieved through taking a break from the process.
5. Themes are patterns anchored by a shared idea, meaning or concept. They are *not* summaries of everything about a topic.
6. Themes are analytic *outputs* – they are built from codes (which are also analytic outputs) and cannot be identified ahead of the analytic process.
7. Themes do not passively '**emerge**' from data but are actively produced by the researcher through their systematic engagement with, and all they bring to, the dataset.
8. Data analysis is *always* underpinned by theoretical assumptions, and these assumptions need to be acknowledged and reflected on.
9. Reflexivity is *key* to good quality analysis; researchers must strive to understand and 'own their perspectives' (Elliott, Fischer, & Rennie, 1999).
10. Data analysis is conceptualised as an art not a science; creativity is central to the process, situated within a framework of rigour.

One, to assess your understanding of these core assumptions. Use Section Two to deepen or clarify your understanding where needed.

Don't worry about understanding it all perfectly for now; we explain these concepts more in later chapters (the Glossary contains brief definitions). What is most important to realise at this point is that even reflexive TA is *not just one approach*. Two reflexive TA analyses can *look* quite different, depending on their distinct approach and **research aims**. This flexibility requires the researcher to think through *how* they are doing reflexive TA, and why a particular approach is taken – this is what we mean by being an *active* researcher (Braun & Clarke, 2006). Importantly, although you might have to signal in advance what you *anticipate* your particular approach to reflexive TA might be (for instance, in a research proposal), it does *not* have to be fixed or even fully determined in advance – indeed, our orientations often shift as our analysis progresses.

> **ALERT**   Even *reflexive* TA is not a single method: there are a range of ways you can approach and do reflexive TA.

> **PRACTICE POINT**   You don't have to decide on which version of reflexive TA you will use in advance.

BUT WAIT, THERE'S MORE: VARIATION WITHIN REFLEXIVE TA

Reflexive TA offers a particular orientation to, and form of, TA. That, however, as we have just noted, doesn't mean there is just *one* way to do reflexive TA. The analytic and **interpretative** tools reflexive TA provides can be used to produce analyses from relatively straightforward descriptive accounts to more complex, theoretically-embedded ones (see also Pope, Ziebland, & Mays, 2006). Indeed, one of the *key* advantages of reflexive TA is that it offers researchers a lot of flexibility. You can do reflexive TA using different broad theoretical frameworks, foci for meaning, and orientations to data; these are summarised briefly in Table 1.2. This variability of reflexive TA is one of the reasons the researcher needs to be active, engaged and thoughtful about the approach they take. What TA produces all depends on the particular version you use, and exactly *how you* use it. We'll come back to this point time and again, because the researcher's subjectivity and skill are at the centre of good reflexive TA, and indeed good qualitative analysis more generally.

Both conceptually, and in practice, more **essentialist/experiential**, **semantic** and **inductive** approaches tend to cluster together, likewise **constructionist/critical**, **latent** and **deductive** approaches. But these different approaches are *not* mutually exclusive, and – often – they reflect points on a spectrum, as we have captured in Table 1.2, rather than binary choices.

Table 1.2 The variations of reflexive TA

Orientation to data	More *inductive*: where the analysis is located within, and coding and theme development are driven by, the data content.	←→	More *deductive*: where the analysis is shaped by existing theoretical constructs, which provide the 'lens' through which to read and code the data and develop themes.
Focus of meaning	*Semantic*: where the analysis explores meaning at the more surface, explicit, or manifest level.	←→	*Latent*: where the analysis explores meaning at the more underlying or implicit level.
Qualitative framework	*Experiential*: where the analysis aims to capture and explore people's own perspectives and understandings.	←→	*Critical*: where the analysis focuses on interrogating and unpacking meaning around the topic or issue.
Theoretical frameworks	*Realist, essentialist*: where analysis aims to capture truth and reality, as expressed within the dataset.	←→	*Relativist, constructionist*: where analysis aims to interrogate and unpack the realities that are expressed within the dataset.

REFLEXIVE TA OFFERS GUIDELINES, NOT RULES, BUT A CLEAR PROCESS

We still come across claims like: "little has been written to guide researchers in how to conduct a rigorous thematic analysis" (Nowell, Norris, White, & Moules, 2017, p. 1); that there is an "absence of explicit guidelines on how to undertake it" (Xu & Zammit, 2020, p. 1); and "a detailed description of how researchers identify theme [sic] is under-reported" (Vaismoradi, Jones, Turunen, & Snelgrove, 2016, p. 102). That used to be the case, but it has not been for some time. As well as all our TA writing over the last 15 years, which has centred on helping students and researchers to conduct reflexive, systematic and *rigorous* TA, and to produce meaningful and useful analyses, there is a lot of writing around other approaches to TA. Perhaps these authors sought hard-and-fast rules, failsafe formulae and tools and techniques to apply to a dataset to extract an analysis? *That* is not something we offer, nor would we want to; it's antithetical to a Big Q orientation. What we do provide are clear and detailed guidelines that help you learn the principles and *process* of reflexive TA. But they are not rigid, and they are *not rules*; we don't want people to treat them as if they were. Simply and rigidly following the phases of reflexive TA as a series of 'steps' will not guarantee a good analysis. Likewise, doing things a bit differently will not inherently undermine your analysis. Throughout this book, and based on the values noted in Box 1.1, we will signal those aspects that are conceptually and practically vital for reflexive TA, and those where there is more freedom.

ALERT Reflexive TA offers robust process guidelines, not rigid rules.

Why can't we provide rules? That is because you, the researcher, are a situated, insight-bringing, integral component of the analysis. A computer could not do what you will do, analytically; tech may assist but cannot do the thinking that qualitative analysis involves in the same way as you do it. You are the director of your analytic journey, the author of your analytic **story**.[2] Analysis happens at the intersection of the dataset, the context of the research, and researcher skill and locatedness. The aspiring reflexive TA researcher needs to imagine an adventure, where hidden pathways and surprising revelations, things which cannot be anticipated in advance, are part of the journey. As noted in the introduction, the method that reflexive TA offers is like a compass and a map that guides you through your adventure, to an endpoint (Braun, Clarke, & Hayfield, 2019). What we offer is a set of conceptual tools, heuristics, practice guidelines, and processes to facilitate a deep, rich, and robust engagement with data for knowledge production. But it's up to you to navigate, to make the most of the opportunities along the way, and to avoid potential perils and pitfalls. This is why we like the metaphor of a journey and especially an adventure. Imagine you've travelled before, but it's only been with others who have organised everything – family, or a tour operator, for instance. You've not had to think for yourself or make decisions – big or small – related to your travels. Now you're about to embark on a very different type of travel, where you figure things out and make your own decisions! Exciting – and probably also daunting.

MENTALLY PREPARING YOURSELF TO TACKLE YOUR TA JOURNEY: BECOMING COMFORTABLE WITH UNCERTAINTY AND DISCOMFORT

Some of us revel in uncertainty and a world with many moving parts; others of us find such scenarios stressful and anxiety-provoking, and we want to contain the chaos in nice tidy boxes. Qualitative research and reflexive TA do not flourish when constrained and limited, when placed into nice tidy boxes. If you're new to qualitative research, the idea that you approach data analysis in an *open* way, without a clear structured framework for *what* exactly it is you are looking for, might sound like the approach is therefore random, haphazard, without solid foundation. This is far from the case, because, as noted above, the open, organic approach of reflexive TA is solidly based in qualitative values and a *Big Q* approach (Grant & Giddings, 2002; Kidder & Fine, 1987; Madill & Gough, 2008). Being situated *within* a qualitative paradigm means reflexive TA has a clear foundation and values-base, which guide, support, and delimit the open and organic practice approach. What does this mean for

ALERT The procedures and process of reflexive TA are grounded by qualitative values (Big Q).

PRACTICE POINT Being tolerant of uncertainty is an important skill to practise for good reflexive TA.

---

[2]The idea of qualitative analysis and research as 'storytelling' may sit uncomfortably for some readers, especially if you have been inculcated into 'scientific' values of objectivity, but we find this the most compelling framework for conceptualising what we do as qualitative researchers (see also Nadar, 2014)!

how you approach your analysis? Unfortunately – or fortunately, depending on your inner make up – it means becoming comfortable with, or at least tolerating, some uncertainty and discomfort. The anxiety that this uncertainty might provoke is something we recognise;[3] in Chapter Four, two of our students reflect on their anxiety when doing reflexive TA and share their strategies for managing it.

Try to conceive of openness, uncertainty and discomfort as essential travel companions, the ones who encourage you to take care but nonetheless have an exciting adventure! Reflexive TA is best considered provisional, with the analysis never finalised until it's written up, submitted or published.

Even then, it does *not* aim to produce a simple, fixed and unitary truth, the chaos of a messy dataset brought under absolute control. In fitting with a Big Q orientation, nuance, partiality and messiness remain – constrained within the overarching analytic structure you produce. This means that to do reflexive TA well, you have to live in uncertainty, and to hold on to uncertainty in analysis. If you don't, you risk **analytic foreclosure**, shutting down **interpretation**, and producing a poor and limited analysis.

> **PRACTICE POINT** Reflexive TA is not about *perfect* rule following. At times, we all do 'stupid things' along the way. Good open, interrogative reflexive TA practice involves recognising where we go wrong and changing our practice.

SUBJECTIVITY IS AT THE HEART OF REFLEXIVE TA PRACTICE

If you're a psychologist, like us, you will likely have been trained – at least initially – to view subjectivity as something problematic, something that disrupts the objectivity of psychological science, and needs to be controlled and managed. Such thinking is reflected in the equation of subjectivity with 'bias' – where bias (and therefore subjectivity) is a flaw that threatens the ideal of objectivity. If this view of subjectivity has been ingrained in your thinking, it can be hard to let go. But to do good reflexive TA, it is essential to do so. Viewing subjectivity as something valuable, rather than problematic, is a key aspect of a qualitative sensibility.[4] Your subjectivity is essential to processes of reflexive TA; it is the fuel that drives the engine, and reflexive TA doesn't happen without it. This reconceptualisation of subjectivity as a resource is a key feature of *reflexive* qualitative research (Finlay, 2002a, 2002b; Gough, 2017; Luttrell, 2019). Reflexive research treats knowledge as situated, and as inevitably and inescapably shaped by the processes and practices of knowledge production, including the practices of the researcher. We therefore view researcher subjectivity, and the aligned practice of reflexivity, as the *key* to successful reflexive TA.

---

[3]If the prospect of sitting with uncertainty makes you worried, it might help to know that your feelings around this might change: "I was fearful of the flexibility in [reflexive TA], but now it's starting to become my best friend" (Trainor & Bundon, 2020, p. 13).

[4]Subjectivity is also valued as a key component of much *feminist* scholarship and theorising (Nadar, 2014; Ramazanoğlu & Holland, 2002). A reflexive and subjective approach to TA fits within a wider movement within qualitative research towards situated, partial, reflexive, critically-interrogative and radical scholarship, across a wide range of disciplines and approaches – these ideas are more fully explored in Section Two.

Two titans in qualitative researching, US sociologist Norman Denzin and higher education researcher Yvonna Lincoln (2005, p. 22) described "all research [as] interpretive; it is guided by the researcher's set of beliefs and feelings about the world and how it should be understood and studied. Some beliefs may be taken for granted, invisible, only assumed". Within a qualitative paradigm, researcher subjectivity – who we are, and what we bring to the research, ranging from our personal identities and values, through to our disciplinary perspectives – is an integral part of the analysis. This is captured by the idea that "the researcher becomes the instrument for analysis" (Nowell et al., 2017, p. 2). In this context, striving to '**own our perspectives**' (Elliott et al., 1999) is important for quality, and features among the many robust quality criteria we discuss in Chapter Nine.

> **PRACTICE POINT** Researcher subjectivity is an essential resource for reflexive TA.

> **ALERT** Good reflexive TA depends on the researcher's choices and practices.

Good qualitative research does not just involve embracing subjectivity, it requires us to interrogate it. Reflexivity is the term most widely used to capture both the researchers' generative role in research, and their insight into, and articulation around, this role.

REFLEXIVITY: THE MOST IMPORTANT COMPANION FOR YOUR ADVENTURE

What is reflexivity? We like this definition, by US social work scholar Roni Berger:

> It means turning of the researcher lens back onto oneself to recognize and take responsibility for one's own situatedness within the research and the effect that it may have on the setting and people being studied, questions being asked, data being collected and its interpretation. As such, the idea of reflexivity challenges the view of knowledge production as independent of the researcher producing it and of knowledge as objective. (2015, p. 220)

Reflexivity isn't all navel-gazing and just thinking about yourself; it's also about the knowledge we produce from research and how we produce it (Luttrell, 2019; Wilkinson, 1988). British feminist psychologist Sue Wilkinson (1988) offered a useful distinction between:

- *Personal* reflexivity – how the researcher's values shape their research and the knowledge produced;
- *Functional* reflexivity – how the methods and other aspects of design shape the research and knowledge produced; and
- *Disciplinary* reflexivity – how academic disciplines shape knowledge production.

Feminist and Indigenous iterations of reflexivity in particular emphasise that power is part of knowledge production (Ramazanoğlu & Holland, 2002; Russell-Mundine, 2012; L. T. Smith, 2013). These orientations mandate that our reflexive practice

> **ALERT** Reflexivity also encompasses the researcher reflecting on the methodological choices and disciplinary location, and how these shape knowledge production.

considers the *politics* of our research process, and the knowledge we produce, as well as just interrogating our own positions (see Chapter Seven).

Doing reflexivity for reflexive TA

Reflexivity involves routinely reflecting on your assumptions, expectations, choices and actions throughout your research process (Finlay & Gough, 2003). This process of reflection aims to consider what the researcher's standpoint and choices might enable, exclude and close-off (Wilkinson, 1988). This means locating yourself, which includes having some awareness of the philosophical and theoretical assumptions that inform your research, and working to ensure theory and research practice align. Locating yourself also means developing awareness of your *personal* positionings or standpoints (e.g. your socio-demographic positioning in relation to intersections of race, culture, religion/belief, social class/socioeconomics, sex/gender, sexuality, ability, age, and so on), and your values and assumptions about the world (see Box 1.2). We are all deeply embedded in our values and experiences, even as these may shift, sometimes radically, over time. Who you are and what you bring to the research shapes and informs your research,

ALERT The researcher's positioning inevitably shapes their research and engagement with data.

━━━━━━━━━━ **Box 1.2** ━━━━━━━━━━

Your values and politics in qualitative research

Research cannot be a value-neutral activity, and the ways our personal politics play out, visibly and invisibly, are increasingly under scrutiny for ethical research practice. Beyond a general connection of academia and liberal or progressive politics (Jaschik, 2017), the history of qualitative research is deeply enmeshed with left, liberal or radical politics, and with social justice aims and aspirations (Barnes, 2003). It has been described as "fundamental to the emancipatory research paradigm" (Barnes, 1992, p. 115) and deeply connected to the disability activism slogan – which has since spread more widely – *nothing about us without us* (Charlton, 2000). Such research includes: feminist research seeking to 'bring in', and honour, women's absent or silenced experiences (M. M. Gergen, 2017; Mullings, 2000; Wilkinson, 2001); research seeking to **'give voice'** to patients in healthcare settings (Black & Jenkinson, 2009); participatory modes of research which include as active contributors those marginalised or dispossessed, for social change (Fine & Torre, 2006; P. King, Hodgetts, Rua, & Whetu, 2015); research seeking to deconstruct dominant and taken-for-granted meanings that legitimate existing power relations and oppressive social arrangements (Flowers & Langdridge, 2007; Tischner & Malson, 2012), and provide visibility to the impacts of these on people's lives (Calder-Dawe, Witten, & Carroll, 2020). But what if you have more conservative social or political values? Can you still do reflexive TA? Yes. No matter what your social and political location, reflecting on, interrogating and 'owning' the values that inform your research remains key.

inevitably, through what you do and *don't* notice, and what you take for granted. Locating yourself asks how such aspects have contextualised and shaped the research and analysis, and allows others to appreciate that you do not consider yourself a neutral conduit of information.

The time to start reflexivity is ... NOW

A reflexive researcher is someone who is thoughtful and (self)questioning, identifying and then interrogating their positions, values, choices and practices within the research process, and the influence of these on knowledge generated; someone seeking awareness and new possibilities (R. Berger, 2015; Finlay, 2002b; Luttrell, 2019). Before you get into qualitative researching, it might feel impossible to imagine *how* you might reflect on and articulate the standpoints that inform your research, and how these shape the knowledge produced through your research. In the next two sections, we get you started on reflexivity, and introduce a fundamentally important tool – the reflexive research journal – to set you forth on reflexivity. Journaling is only one of the ways you can engage with reflexivity. Following US sociologist Wendy Luttrell, we encourage you to work on adopting "an eclectic and expansive toolkit" (Luttrell, 2019, p. 15) for being reflexive.

A couple of important caveats and orientating points before we introduce the practical tasks:

1. We don't regard our perspective as something singular *or* fixed. Perspective**s** is better, as it acknowledges that the positions that inform our research are multiple, complex and evolving.
2. Full insight into our positionings is rarely possible: "any reflexive analysis can only ever be a partial, tentative, provisional account" (Finlay, 2002b, pp. 542–543; Gerstl-Pepin & Patrizio, 2009).

This means (your) reflexivity is never final. The positions acknowledged and interrotated, and reported on, should not be framed as complete self-awareness. Reflexivity is – again – a journey, not a destination. The framing of reflexivity as

> **PRACTICE POINT** Reflexivity is never final and complete but an ongoing process of reflection.

"at once subject, method, and product" (Luttrell, 2019, p. 2) captures for us the different threads of reflexivity as a way of thinking about, practising, and writing TA.

Striving to 'own your perspectives' (Elliott et al., 1999) involves being able to begin to articulate things like your philosophical positions, theoretical assumptions, ideological and political commitments, social identities, research training and experience, disciplinary assumptions and frameworks, substantive knowledge about the topic of your research, assumptions and personal positioning in relation to this topic – and to reflect on how these inform and shape your research. When we teach TA, we always start our practical exercises by using an activity that invites everyone to reflect on *who* they are as a researcher; likewise, we encourage all readers to do this. We include this exercise here, rather than at the more traditional placement at end of the chapter, because we think it is *essential* for good reflexive TA practice, rather than an optional extra.

Activity pause

A task to get reflexivity started...

Consider, and write[5] about where you belong in relation to the following dimensions. Exactly *how* you write this is not important; writing is the tool to push you deeper in your thinking around these.

Getting into personal reflexivity

First up, consider what might relate to more personal aspects of yourself – which Wilkinson (1988) referred to as *personal* reflexivity. This relates to your intersecting *social positionings* – for example, your sex/gender, sexuality, social class/socioeconomics, race and ethnicity, ability, age, belief, immigration status. In particular:

- Consider where you occupy positions of social *privilege*. In high consumption westernised countries this is typically male, non-trans/cisgender, straight/heterosexual, middle class, rich, White, culturally Christian, non-disabled, younger, non-migrant.
- Also consider where you occupy positions of social *marginality*. In the same contexts, this would typically be female, transgender/nonbinary, asexual/pansexual/queer/gay/lesbian/ bisexual, working class, poor, Indigenous, Black or person of colour, disabled/neurodivergent, elderly, culturally or religiously Jewish, Muslim or Atheist, migrant.

How do these social positions shape how you experience the world, and how you view others, and how they might view you? Do these social positions relate to any political, ideological or theoretical commitments you have (e.g. Black feminism, queer theory, disability studies, decolonising academia and Indigenous knowledge frameworks[6])?

Also consider your *personal background and life experiences*, as these shape how we engage in research and with data. In particular:

- Think about how these shape your *worldview*. To use us as examples – we are shaped by: growing up poor but Pākehā (White) and middle class in a geographically and socially isolated hippie commune in the culturally-mixed and economically-deprived Far North of Aotearoa New Zealand versus growing up in a predominantly working class and racially diverse suburb in outer London; being in a relationship versus being single; choosing to be childfree versus being circumstantially childless; being chronically ill but fully mobile versus being disabled with limited mobility...).

---

[5]We use 'write' here and elsewhere in this book, but it's intended as a shorthand for a more inclusive range of ways of recording thoughts – which includes making voice memos or using voice recognition software, handwriting, or typing, or some combination of these.

[6]For more discussion of how political, ideological or other theory can inform reflexive TA, see Box 6.6 in Chapter Six, and the sections 'Working with existing theoretical concepts in doing interpretation and locating data within the wider context' in Chapter Seven.

Our *political and ideological commitments* (both overt and implicit) are another important aspect of personal reflexivity:

- If you are struggling with this one, think about how you have voted or would vote in elections, and what news sources you'd follow or trust. Are you religious, or an atheist/humanist? What is your position on subjects often deemed controversial or matters of conscience such as animal welfare, abortion, the right to die (euthanasia), and the sex industry? What organisations are you a member of? What charities do or would you support? Are you engaged in *activism* of any kind? Reflecting on such questions will help you to map your political and ideological commitments. This is important for all forms of qualitative research, but particularly important for research deemed 'critical', as it is strongly tied to 'leftish' political orientations such as socialism, feminism, humanism, and queer theory (see Crotty, 1998), and often has an overt political agenda (see Box 1.2). Such research is often criticised because of this, or because its politics are *overt*. But ideology and politics are inseparable from research, embedded in all areas of research, whether we reflexively acknowledge this, or not. Consider, for instance, criticism of the way dominant social values, including gender biases and racism, are inbuilt into AI development (Buolamwini, 2019) or the area of so-called 'race science' which sounds neutral, but is imbued with ideas of racial superiority and White supremacy (Evans, 2018; Saini, 2019).

Getting into functional and disciplinary reflexivity

We then encourage you to think about yourself specifically in relation to knowledge, scholarship, and research practice – these cover 'functional' and 'disciplinary' reflexivity (Wilkinson, 1988):

- Your research training and experiences. What practical experiences of research do you have? What have you learned makes 'good quality' research? What methods are associated with that? What research values can you identify? How are the questions you are interested in subtly and not so subtly shaped by your disciplinary context and training – it can be tricky to recognise the ways you 'view the research world' as, for instance, a psychologist, or a geographer, or a sociologist (friends and collaborators from other disciplines, and attending other- and cross-disciplinary events can help with this).
- If you're not a student, your affiliation, status and context as a scholar. What type of institution do you work for? Are you a new or an established scholar? What internal and external pressures do you face – such as to publish, to publish in particular 'high ranking' journals, to seek external research funding, to seek promotion?
- The methods or approaches you are drawn to, and how the methods you use might shape the research process and the knowledge produced. For example, the data for our worked example are online comments about people choosing to be childfree (see section 'Introducing and contextualising our worked example dataset' in Chapter Two), but we could have run a focus group and asked people to discuss the topic. How might these different data collection methods shape the resulting data?
- Any philosophical and theoretical assumptions or commitments related to research. Do you think qualitative research captures the truth of people's lives and experiences? Do you prioritise Indigenous knowledge and research practices? Do you want to interrogate meaning-practices? How do these shape the research questions that interest you?
- Your fears, anxieties, hopes and expectations about your research. Both about your research in general, and then connected to the specifics of the topic for a particular project.

(Continued)

Depending where you are on a research trajectory, some of these might be quite challenging – so don't expect to have answers for them all. In practising disciplinary and functional reflexivity, you want to consider how these might shape your design choices, and your use of TA?

Reflexivity around your specific topic

Once you have a specific *topic* for research, it is vital to come back to reflexivity related to your identities, and life experiences, and consider these in relation to your topic, and to your participants (if your research design includes data from participants):

- How are your positionings and/or life experiences related to your topic?
- What assumptions do you hold about your topic?
- How might your participants perceive you?
- Where and how do you occupy positions of privilege and marginality *in relation to* your topic and your participants?
- And are you an **insider researcher** (a member of the group you are studying) or outsider (not a member)? Or are you both? How might this shape your research, and your relationship with your participants? What advantages and risks can you imagine to being an insider and/or **outsider researcher**? Aspects to reflect on include: access and recruitment; developing trust and 'rapport' with participants; devising and asking questions, including what we latch on to as important in participant's accounts, and what we might miss in participant responses; participants withholding information; and representing participants' accounts (R. Berger, 2015; Hellawell, 2006).

KEY CONCEPT An insider researcher is in some or many ways a member of the group they are studying (e.g. sharing a racial or ethnic heritage or particular life experience with the participant group); an outsider researcher is not a member of the group. We can be both insiders and outsiders in multiple ways.

What participants might *not* tell us, because of how they perceive us, and then how we represent participants, connect to longstanding challenges, from Indigenous and marginalised/exploited communities, to the idea that *anyone* is entitled to research any topic they wish, and with any community (L. T. Smith, 2013). Such challenges have, in some contexts, become more mainstream and accepted, with rich discussions for how privileged or outsider researchers *might* engage in research in ethical and politically sensitive ways (e.g. Cram, McCreanor, Smith, Nairn, & Johnstone, 2006).

ALERT Our assumptions always influence our research – it's not a question of *whether* they influence but *how* they influence.

Acknowledging your assumptions is essential for taking a step back from them and reflecting on how they shape and inform your research. It's important to remember the question is not *whether* these assumptions influence the research (trust us, they do!), but *how* they influence, and how that might matter. Influence is not contamination to be worried about; it is an inevitable part of the knowledge production process (Finlay, 2002b). This is why good quality qualitative research – and reflexive TA – requires a reflexive researcher. That means this type of reflection is not a one-off activity at the start of your research, but an ongoing process, something you consciously need to keep returning to in all phases of the research (R. Berger, 2015; Luttrell, 2019; Trainor & Bundon, 2020).

Reflective and reflexive journals

Keeping a reflective or **reflexive journal** is one of the most important practices you'll undertake on your research journey. US education researchers Cynthia Gerstl-Peplin and Kami Patrizio (2009) argued the *pensieve* is a useful metaphor for a reflexive journal. If you're a Harry Potter fan,[7] you'll immediately know what they're referring to: a magical instrument for storing and viewing three-dimensional visual memories. In the Harry Potter books and films, the *pensieve* allows Dumbledore – a powerful wizard, and headmaster of Hogwarts, the school the young wizard Harry Potter attends – to revisit and reflect on his memories, and share them with others, including Harry. A reflective or reflexive journal is similarly a repository for documenting and storing thoughts for subsequent reflection, interrogation, and meaning-making. And *potentially* for sharing with others, such as a collaborator or supervisor (Gerstl-Pepin & Patrizio, 2009). The reflexivity task we've just outlined could be the first few entries for such a journal (there's a lot to reflect on!); we would expect you to revisit such questions at many points across a research project.

There is no rule for how to keep a reflexive journal – how often, or how much to record, or indeed *what* to include – but you should use it to reflect, and to ask questions that unpack the initial responses you come up with. This latter process helps *you* push yourself deeper into reflexivity, so note your responses to things, but also interrogate those. Ask, for instance, why *might* I be having this particular type of response, and how *might* this matter for my research? This is kind of like a de-socialisation process, where things you take for granted are put in the spotlight and questioned. If you're looking for parallel examples of this sort of activity, it's akin to the work asked of White people by anti-racism or decolonisation activists and scholars, as White people start to recognise they are embedded in systems and structures that privilege them and oppress others (e.g. Eddo-Lodge, 2018; McIntosh, 1992; Saad, 2020). It's what's evoked in the idea of becoming and being a White person who 'shows up' against racism. Like White people reflecting on their racial privilege, good reflexivity isn't a surface reflection, it isn't a comforting feeling or something designed to make you feel like a better person; it can and should be discomforting, unsettling, and change-bringing.

Sometimes our reflexive journal entries are mundane, pragmatic, and not very engaging. But sometimes they provide a nuanced account of the process and struggles of reflexive TA. In Box 1.3, we provide a rich and moving example of a series of reflexive journal entries, generously shared by our former student, Rachel Graham. As a therapist and doctoral student, Rachel was experienced in reflexive practice, and asking questions of herself. Therefore, the slightly edited entries – selected for different points in the research process – capture vividly the complexities of research and the value of keeping a journal for unpacking

---

[7]We acknowledge the position of 'Harry Potter fan' was troubled for many following JK Rowling's 2020 tweets around trans issues.

and interrogating your research process. The journal entries include a poem – not something we'd typically include in *our* research journals. But it evocatively and powerfully illustrates that the reflexive journal is a *tool* for you to make sense of your research and research journey, in whatever ways facilitate insight and critical engagement.

Box 1.3

What might reflexive journal entries look like? A selection of entries from Rachel Graham

For my counselling psychology professional doctorate thesis, I researched UK Black women's perceptions and experiences of emotional distress. I was particularly interested in how the 'strong Black woman' construct – the notion, with origins in slavery, that African heritage women are psychologically strong, independent and have an innate capacity to withstand adversity – shapes these women's experiences of emotional distress. I collected data in five focus groups with a total of 18 Black African Caribbean women living in the UK, recruited via my personal Facebook page, the University of the West of England psychology participant pool, and snowball sampling through my personal and professional networks. Like my participants, I am a Black woman of Caribbean heritage, living in the UK, and my positioning was communicated to participants in my recruitment process.

25/06/2016 Reflecting on my first focus group

I had my first focus group today, after the group I did try to write some reflections, but I was feeling so full and heavy with emotion, I needed some time to process what I was feeling.

Having had some time to do this, I now know I was simply overwhelmed with the emotional content in the focus group. Throughout the focus group, I was shocked at how often the participants' experiences mirrored my own, how their feelings were so similar to mine.

I also felt grateful and humbled by their openness – I am not sure if I would have been so honest, willing and comfortable to talk about my own vulnerabilities in a group to that extent (unless it was a friendship group). I admire their honesty and courage.

I think that, however, I was reluctant to probe deeper with some members of the group because of my own uncomfortable feelings about sharing my own emotions with others. I feel that this limited the types of questions that I asked. In hindsight, I could have asked for clarification on several comments, which would have provided more insight.

It is important for me – in the next focus group to not be afraid to probe deeper.

02/08/2016 Reflecting on personal subjectivity and research practice after discussing my first and second focus groups with my supervisor

Racism appears to be a common theme so far. I have never looked at my own experiences of racism, I have never really acknowledged it unless it was explicit, such as being called a racist name, etc. I think my inability to acknowledge my own experiences of racism has limited my ability to hear the participants' accounts.

I have often viewed my racist experiences as normal (i.e. that's what happens when you live in a White society) and thus I have always just brushed them off, trying to not absorb them, trying to not let them affect me in anyway. And I feel that this coping strategy affected the way I heard the participants' stories, when they spoke about being subjected to racism, I did not ask them about their experiences because instead I viewed them as normal, which led me to brush over them.

For the next focus group, I plan to ask more questions about racism (if it comes up) in relation to strength and emotional distress. Additionally, in the meantime, I feel that it is important for me to continually reflect upon my own experiences of racism on my own, but also through talking to others (friends and family) about their experiences.

15/01/2017 Reflecting on coding

I think I now have the hang of coding, it was very tricky at the beginning as I was not sure what I was doing, and my codes seemed more like sentences than codes. I was also finding the coding unbelievably slow, since I was constantly evaluating and revaluating every **code** to make sure that I was capturing what the participants are saying rather than imposing my own assumptions into the codes. Although, it is currently going slightly faster, since I am more familiar with the coding process.

One topic that is jumping out at me is the participants' perceptions of Black men. I find it interesting how they were speaking about them in such a negative way – almost burdensome. They implied how Black men lacked emotional strength and thus felt that being strong was not a choice but a necessity – since it compensated for the Black man's inability to be emotionally strong.

02/03/2017 Reflecting on coding

I have so much data. It feels overwhelming. I have had to take a day off work to try and figure out what I am going to do with it. It all seems so important. I think I am going to find it hard to narrow it all down into themes. Since this is new to me, I am constantly worried that I am doing it wrong – I am worried that when I hand it in to be reviewed, I will be told to re-do it all. I might email Victoria for some advice.

15/04/2017 A poem I wrote about the women in the focus groups

Black women's pain

My pain is silent

Do not despair, I will not shout nor scream, run around chaotically

My pain is silent

It resides within me

(Continued)

I will remain strong, stand up tall, carry the load

My pain is good like that, it will not let itself show

I will not ask for help

Don't worry, I will not lean on you

Instead you lean on me and I will carry us both through

Yes, I will be hurting and sometimes I will want to scream

but the sounds of my pain are just for me

For my pain is loyal it knows how to hide,

just under the radar, sitting awkwardly underneath my pride

12/05/2017 Reflecting on writing

Writing the research is difficult. I keep thinking about wanting to do the women (participants) proud. I keep thinking about wanting to not misinterpret them. I want to make sure that I am capturing their voices. However, I know this is an impossible task, because this subject is so close to me, and thus will be coloured by my own experiences.

In order to stay as close-as-possible to the participants' experiences, I need to make sure that I am not rushing the write-up, that I take regular breaks and take my time.

CHAPTER SUMMARY

In this chapter, we wanted to give you a quick introduction to the method we call *reflexive* TA, and an orientation to significant things to grasp about the approach. Having read the chapter, you should understand that reflexive TA is characterised by (Big Q) qualitative research values, and a subjective, situated researcher who reflexively strives to own their position and can tolerate or accept some degree of uncertainty. You should understand that reflexive TA is not a neutral activity, but a values-based, situated practice. You should recognise that there are different ways to approach reflexive TA, but that you don't have to know exactly which approach you'll use when you start. You should understand that quality reflexive TA requires you to be a thoughtful, knowing practitioner, understanding yourself as an active researcher who makes choices related to method and to theory. We introduced you to the idea of a qualitative sensibility or headspace, for orientating you as you start reflexive TA, and explained the importance of reflexivity for TA. That such practice is vital is emphasised by our decision to explicitly call *our* approach to TA *reflexive* TA. We provided practical guidance for getting started with reflexivity. You should now have a good sense of what reflexivity involves and have started your own reflexive practice. With this foundation, you are *perfectly placed* to start your reflexive TA journey.

WANT TO LEARN MORE ABOUT...?

Our original paper is a good place to **start reading about reflexive TA**: Braun, V., & Clarke, V. (2006). Using thematic analysis in psychology. *Qualitative Research in Psychology*, *3*(2), 77–101.

For an updated account of how **our thinking has evolved**, see: Braun, V., & Clarke, V. (2019a). Reflecting on reflexive thematic analysis. *Qualitative Research in Sport, Exercise and Health*, *11*(4), 589–597.

For resources related to reflexive TA, we recommend starting with our **TA website**, hosted by The University of Auckland. The site includes a long list of further reading, FAQs, links to lectures, and much more: www.thematicanalysis.net.

For a general overview and introduction to the field of **qualitative research**, our qualitative textbook provides an accessible introduction to concepts and practice: Braun, V., & Clarke, V. (2013). *Successful qualitative research: A practical guide for beginners*. London: SAGE.

For more about **subjectivity** as a resource for quality inquiry, see: Gough, B., & Madill, A. (2012). Subjectivity in psychological research: From problem to prospect. *Psychological Methods*, *17*(3), 374–384.

There's no *one* paper we'd recommend on **reflexivity**. Sue Wilkinson's classic paper is an accessible place to start: Wilkinson, S. (1988). The role of reflexivity in feminist psychology. *Women's Studies International Forum*, *11*(5), 493–502.

For a book length discussion and a range of perspectives on **reflexivity**, we recommend: Finlay, L., & Gough, B. (Eds.). (2003). *Reflexivity: A practical guide for researchers in health and social sciences*. Oxford: Blackwell Science.

For a useful discussion of the value and practice of **keeping a research journal**, see: Nadin, S., & Cassell, C. (2006). The use of a research diary as a tool for reflexive practice: Some reflections from management research. *Qualitative Research in Accounting Management*, *3*(3), 208–217.

For a practical and layered example of **reflexive practice for reflexive TA**, see: Trainor, L. R., & Bundon, A. (2020). Developing the craft: Reflexive accounts of doing reflexive thematic analysis. *Qualitative Research in Sport, Exercise and Health*, 1–22. Advance online publication https://doi.org/10.1080/2159676X.2020.1840423

ACTIVITIES FOR STUDENT READERS

Get journaling. One of the first bits of advice we give our new research students is to start a research journal, in whatever format works for you. Your first task is therefore to formally start your research journal, considering what you've read in this chapter. The earlier reflexivity task could be your first few entries – or you might want to treat that separately and start your research journal with this activity.

Level 1: Starting off. Writing *for yourself*, use these questions as a prompt for reflection:

- How much does the mode of research depicted in this chapter – *reflexive* qualitative research – sit comfortably with you? How much does it feel uncomfortable and challenge you?
- How do you feel about starting your reflexive TA journey? If you feel uncomfortable or anxious about this, what might you be able to do to manage this?
- Which values or principles about research might influence your response to the material in this chapter?
- If you imagine a continuum from the unbiased objective researcher to the subjective situated researcher, where feels most comfortable to you? Why might that be? How might that affect your qualitative research practice?

Use such questions as a tool for starting to *locate yourself* in relation to research as a values-based activity. If you want to then go a bit deeper, you can tackle Level 2.

Level 2: Going deeper. One of the challenges of journaling is not just to record our immediate or more obvious or surface-level responses, but to explore deeper assumptions, and indeed question them for the ways they bring value to or constrain our practice. For this activity, we recommend revisiting your previous entry a few days after writing it. Read your reflections, and use the following questions as a tool to start to explore and reflect more deeply on the assumptions and values they might be based on:

- Why might I have had this response?
- What ideas or values does it rely on?
- How might I have responded differently?

If you're teaching content related to this chapter…
Don't forget to check the companion website for a range of teaching resources:
https://study.sagepub.com/thematicanalysis

BEFORE ANALYSIS
A BRIEF *DESIGN* INTERLUDE

Sometimes, we're adventurers in a land not of our choosing: we do TA with an already-collected dataset as part of an already-existing project. Other times, we consider and map out the scope of our own adventure: we use reflexive TA as part of a project that we *design*, a project where we make decisions about things such as project scope, research question, participant group or dataset of interest, selection criteria for, and number of, participants or data items, data collection mode and ethics. In the latter scenario, the options open to us are broad: reflexive TA comes shackled by few constraints around elements like suitable research questions, viable datasets and numbers of participants, and even appropriate theory (within limits). That doesn't mean we shouldn't consider such issues. We should! All the elements that make up a research project fall under the umbrella of **research design**. A full design discussion is not within the scope of this book, however, as we focus on *doing* TA, rather than the broader project design within which we do TA. There are several works that specifically address qualitative design, all of which conceptualise qualitative research rather differently (see suggested readings below), and many that discuss particular design elements, such as ethics.

> **KEY CONCEPT**   Research design refers to the overall plan for, and approaches to, the research you will do.

The concept of qualitative research design *overall* is, however, not universally embedded in the existing qualitative methodological literature. Given that, we take this interlude to signal ten key elements to take into account around design.

1. *There are many routes in to design for reflexive TA.* One or more elements in research design might take precedence in the decision-making process. How you conceptualise a project might be shaped or determined by theoretical assumptions, or political commitments (see Chapter Six). Research questions constitute another common starting point for designing a project. Design is also often guided by quite pragmatic considerations – such as available time or researcher experience. Pragmatic starting points don't necessarily lead to poor design, as long as design is considered thoughtfully, and the overall design is coherent.

2. *Design should be considered and coherent.* The concept of overall **conceptual coherence** or **'fit'** (Braun & Clarke, 2013; Willig, 2013) or **methodological integrity** (Levitt, Motulsky, Wertz, Morrow, & Ponterotto, 2017) is a useful guiding tool for design: do your research aims and purpose, philosophical, theoretical and methodological assumptions, and methods cohere together (Chamberlain, Cain, Sheridan, & Dupuis, 2011)? Questions that can guide you in thinking through coherence include ones like: "Can my data provide an 'answer'[1] to my research question?"; "Does my research question make sense with my theoretical framework?" (see Braun & Clarke, 2021b).

> **ALERT**   Good qualitative research design evidences 'fit' or methodological integrity – where all the different elements are conceptually coherent.

---

[1] In qualitative research, your analysis is *often* not about providing a singular direct Q&A-style answer to a research question, so much as offering insight and understanding around the topic of interest. Although we sometimes use the word 'answer' in our writing, we intend this broadly.

3. *Your research question always matters for design.* The thing you're trying to understand through research, through collecting and analysing data, is encapsulated in your **research question**. Sometimes it might be learning about and understanding people's experiences. Or the ways they make sense of phenomena. Or their views or perspectives. Or the ways they behave. Or the factors and social processes that influence, or the norms and rules that govern, particular phenomena. Sometimes it might be about interrogating or unpacking **representation** or meaning-making around a topic. Reflexive TA can address a wide variety of research questions (Braun & Clarke, 2013, 2021b). Importantly, the specifics of your research question do *not* have to be locked in right at the start of a project. For reflexive TA, research questions can evolve, narrow, expand or sharpen as your analysis takes form – as long as your final questions are part of a conceptually coherent design. No matter what route you take into your research design, it will always be guided by your research question and purpose: your design has to be able to address what you – broadly – want to understand.

4. *TA has few inherent restraints around data.* Depending on other design elements, your dataset potential for reflexive TA may be more or less limited or constrained by design. But in the absence of any particular design restriction (such as a research question orientated to understanding people's experience) reflexive TA offers much freedom of choice for researchers related to data and dataset.

5. *You have a lot of flexibility around dataset composition.* TA can be done with datasets generated from participants specifically for your project (e.g. through chat-based interviews), sampled from material that exists out there in the world (e.g. magazine articles), or with previously gathered materials (e.g. open-source qualitative survey responses collected in a different project). A very wide variety of data collection methods – such as focus groups, or story completions – and data types – such as interview transcripts, diary entries, or social media postings – are amenable for analysis with reflexive TA (Braun & Clarke, 2013, 2021b). We encourage people to make the most of the flexibility this analytic method offers, and explore the wide range of data collection methods and data types available to qualitative researchers,[2] within a framework of design coherence (see suggested readings below).

6. *You need to be systematic in your approach to data.* Research as an empirical activity is based on the idea that we don't reach assessments or draw conclusions based on a random or haphazard engagement with the world (data), but through a deliberate and thought-through strategy. This means data need to be collected, compiled, or prepared for analysis systematically. Audio data will need to be transcribed – turned into a text version – ahead of analysis. Such data transformation itself again requires a system so that we can assure our readers of the robustness of our process. To facilitate systematic transcription, our companion website contains a detailed Microsoft PowerPoint guide for transcription for reflexive TA.

7. *You have lots of flexibility around dataset size and composition.* Reflexive TA accommodates datasets from the comparatively heterogenous to comparatively homogenous, made up of individual data items that are 'thicker' or 'thinner', and that are overall smaller or larger in size and scope. Thicker individual data items (such as an in-depth interview) will often contain rich, complex, nuanced and detailed data – the ideal for many qualitative researchers. You can balance depth and breadth of data. In our experience, a dataset made up of a larger number of thinner or shorter

---

[2]Here we set aside much more complex discussions around 'qualitative data' taking place in certain domains, where data are seen as "an increasingly contested term and concept in qualitative research" (Torrance, 2018, p. 743; see also Denzin, 2013; Flick, 2019; Sandelowski, 2011).

individual items can also provide a rich dataset for reflexive TA – such as short qualitative survey responses (Braun, Clarke, Boulton, Davey, & McEvoy, 2020) or social media comments.

8. *Data quality matters.* Thinking about the quality of the data you will use, as well as the volume, matters in design. Not all text- or image-based information makes *quality* data – data that can give you access to a rich range of meanings, perspectives or experiences related to your topic, and from which you can explore, develop, and interpret patterned meaning. We recommend reflexively assessing the quality of the dataset you're starting to generate or gather early in the process. Reflect on whether the data items themselves, and (growing) dataset, provide data that are rich and diverse in meaning. Such evaluation might also involve piloting (fixed) tools like qualitative surveys or story completion to assess whether the responses deliver data of sufficient quality (e.g. Clarke, Hayfield, Moller, Tischner, & The Story Completion Research Group, 2017; Terry & Braun, 2017). Or reviewing your interviews after the first few, to assess whether you're getting only superficial and shallow answers to your interview questions. Although interviews are often idealised in qualitative research (Silverman, 2017), they are not a guarantor of quality data *per se*. Interviews lacking sufficient depth to provide meaningful and useful analyses has been highlighted a problem for TA research (Connelly & Peltzer, 2016).

9. *There's no easy answer to the question of dataset size.* There is no simple way to take all data related elements – such as data depth, richness, complexity – and determine the *right* size of dataset for a particular project. Numerous statistical models and formulae that have been proffered for determining TA 'sample size'[3] are problematic in various ways (Braun & Clarke, 2021b). The concept of data **saturation** – widely touted as a 'gold standard' for determining 'sample size' – is also deeply problematic (Braun & Clarke, 2019b). We recommend avoiding claims of 'saturation'; instead, we find concepts such as **information power** useful (Malterud, Siersma, & Guassora, 2016). Rather than precise calculations, it invites the researcher to reflect on the information *richness* of their dataset and how that meshes with the aims and requirements of the study. Chapter Five also contains a brief discussion of how to *describe* your dataset and selection strategy.

10. *Ethical thinking is a really important element of design.* Ethical thinking includes consideration of where, and how, and from whom we collect data. We frame this as ethical *thinking* not just ethics, to emphasise that it should be integral to all elements of research practice, before, during, and after analysis (see Tolich & Tumilty, 2020). Indeed, as the British Psychological Society's 2009 human research ethics code highlighted, ethical "thinking is *not* optional" (2009, p. 5, our emphasis). Alongside the important ethical considerations around dataset *generation*, there are also considerations during analysis. While *doing* analysis using reflexive TA, your ethical thinking should be primarily around your responsibilities to participants and the power dynamics inherent in representing the voices and stories of participants, particularly those from socially marginalised groups. We discuss this further in Chapter Seven (e.g. see section 'Minimising harm in interpretation: ethics, politics, and representation'). We encourage TA researchers to pursue a complex and sophisticated *reflexive* approach to research ethics. To exemplify *best practice* with regard to relating to and representing participants, especially around questions of difference. And, to conduct research that is genuinely inclusive, culturally sensitive and politically astute.

---

[3]The notion of 'sample size' is a key consideration in positivist-empiricist research that aims to capture a selection of data items/participants that ideally provide a representative subset from a larger population. Due to an inconsistency between those assumptions and the values associated with reflexive TA, we now try to avoid using the language of 'sample' and 'sample size' – though you will find it in our earlier writings – and so put it in scare quotes here.

Getting into design thinking... A guided activity

This design interlude has intended to pique your curiosity and signal the **domains** of thinking and planning for a well-designed, conceptually coherent, ethical TA project. If much of this is new to you, we end with an activity intended to get you into a design-thinking space (the readings below provide additional resources for this, if needed). Imagine you're designing a small student project to explore *how young people – or a particular group of young people, such as trans and non-binary or disabled youth – make sense of the role of social media in their lives.* You plan on using reflexive TA to analyse the data. You have a research proposal and ethics application to write, so need to make some fairly concrete decisions about design. To write your proposal, you need to answer the following questions, and provide a rationale for your choices. In working this through, keep the principle of *design coherence* in mind:

Will your design reflect an interest in gaining an 'empathetic' insight into people's own perspectives, understandings and views about an issue? Or are you more interested in unpacking and questioning the ideas or concepts related to a particular issue. These interests reflect different orientations in qualitative research, respectively referred to as 'experiential' and 'critical' (discussed more in Chapters Four and Six)? Do you think one of these approaches might be better-suited to this research project, or are both equally appropriate? Why? What might distinguish *your* approach to researching this issue as experiential *or* critical?

Having decided your broad orientation, what 'version' of reflexive TA (see Table 1.2, in Chapter One) might you select for this project, and why? If you already have some understanding of research values or ontology and epistemology (which we discuss in Chapter Six), what ontological and epistemological framework would you select for this project? Why?

Consider whether the research question (in italics above) fits to the orientation (and ontology and epistemology, if you are familiar with these) you have selected – if not, how would you reframe it to fit better?

What are potential suitable data collection methods or sources? Which will you choose? How would you justify your choice (or choices) in the proposal? (See the suggested readings below if you are new to qualitative data collection.)

What dataset selection strategy might you use? What type of dataset will you seek (e.g. homogenous or heterogenous), what are your inclusion and exclusion criteria, and what size of dataset do you think would be appropriate for a dissertation project? How would you justify your dataset selection strategy?

How will you source your dataset? If using human participants, how will you recruit them?

Within reflexive TA, which particular 'version' might – at least initially – seem most suitable (e.g. more inductive, more deductive, etc.; see Table 1.2 in Chapter One)?

What specific ethical issues might there be with this project, research question and dataset/participant group?

Imagine you have seven months to complete this project, and you will be spending about a third of your time on this. Plan out a timetable for conducting your research, considering

(Continued)

that you need to allocate *at least* a third of your time to analysis (see 'Allowing time for your analytic insights to fully develop', in Chapter Nine). What will you do when? How long will you allocate for each element of the project?

Finally, reflect on your experience of and expectations of the topic, your role as researcher for this topic, and, in research with participants, your relationship to the participant group (as discussed in the 'Activity pause' in Chapter One). If your proposal had to include a statement of researcher reflexivity, what would you say?

These are some of the questions you typically need to consider when writing any qualitative research proposal. Reflecting on these aspects, how confident do you feel that you have designed a TA study that is conceptually coherent and demonstrates good fit? What *questions* do you still have, that you'd need to think further about, to feel confident about this? (Note that at this stage, if you're new to qualitative research, we'd expect you to have quite a lot!)

SOME READINGS TO TAKE YOU FURTHER INTO DESIGN THINKING

Understanding and putting design thinking into practice for reflexive TA requires more than just reading our 10-point list here – as we hope the guided activity demonstrates. Here we list some readings we like and find relatively accessible and useful. These readings are akin to a pile of books we might give you if we heard you were about to plan an adventure. They're intended, like most of our TA advice, to provide a starting point for you to take *yourself* deeper in your thinking and understanding. We don't expect you to read them all – which ones are most useful will depend on your particular situation.

For an engaging and eminently practical **guide to planning and conducting research**, which discusses many elements often not covered in other texts, we recommend: Boynton, P. (2016). *The research companion* (2nd ed.). London: Routledge.

For an accessible **introduction to qualitative research theory, design, and a range of methods**, including face-to-face and virtual interviews and focus groups, and textual methods such as surveys and story completion for readers new to qualitative research, we recommend our textbook: Braun, V., & Clarke, V. (2013). *Successful qualitative research: A practice guide for beginners*. London: SAGE.

For a range of useful general **guides to design in qualitative research**, see:

Creswell, J. W., & Poth, C. N. (2016). *Qualitative inquiry and research design: Choosing among five approaches*. London: SAGE.

Levitt, H. M., Motulsky, S. L., Wertz, F. J., Morrow, S. L., & Ponterotto, J. G. (2017). Recommendations for designing and reviewing qualitative research in psychology: Promoting methodological integrity. *Qualitative Psychology, 4*(1), 2–22.

Marshall, C., & Rossman, G. B. (2015). *Designing qualitative research.* Los Angeles, CA: SAGE.

Maxwell, J. A. (2012a). *Qualitative research design* (3rd ed.). Thousand Oaks, CA: SAGE.

Patton, M. Q. (2015). *Qualitative research and evaluating methods: Integrating theory and practice* (4th ed.). Los Angeles, CA: SAGE.

Willig, C. (2013). *Introducing qualitative research in psychology* (3rd ed.). Buckingham, UK: Open University Press.

For our advice on **conceptual and design thinking for (reflexive) TA** specifically, see: Braun, V., & Clarke, V. (2021). Conceptual and design thinking for thematic analysis. *Qualitative Psychology.*

To read more about our **critique of saturation** as a concept for sampling within TA, see: Braun, V., & Clarke, V. (2019b). To saturate or not to saturate? Questioning data saturation as a useful concept for thematic analysis and sample-size rationales. *Qualitative Research in Sport, Exercise and Health, 13*(2), 1–16.

To read more about our **critique of statistical models for determining 'sample size' in TA**, see: Braun, V., & Clarke, V. (2016). (Mis)conceptualising themes, thematic analysis, and other problems with Fugard and Potts' (2015) sample-size tool for thematic analysis. *International Journal of Social Research Methodology, 19*(6), 739–743.

There are lots and lots of books about **qualitative interviewing**, but our favourites include: Magnusson, E., & Marecek, J. (2015). *Doing interview-based qualitative research: A learner's guide.* Cambridge: Cambridge University Press. And Rubin, H. J., & Rubin, I. S. (2012). *Qualitative interviewing: The art of hearing data* (3rd ed.). Thousand Oaks, CA: SAGE.

For a useful guide to **focus group research**, see: Stewart, D. W., & Shamdasani, P. N. (2015). *Focus groups: Theory and practice* (3rd ed.). London: SAGE.

For an accessible and practical guide to implementing a range of **textual, media and virtual methods and data source**s, including blogs, online forums, qualitative surveys, story completion, vignettes, diaries, broadcast and print media, instant messaging (IM), email and video-calling interviews, see: Braun, V., Clarke, V., & Gray, D. (Eds.). (2017b). *Collecting qualitative data: A practical guide to textual, media and virtual techniques.* Cambridge: Cambridge University Press.

For useful guides to the wide range of **creative and visual methods** used across qualitative research, see: Kara, H. (2015). *Creative research methods in the social sciences: A practical guide.* Bristol: Policy Press. And Mannay, D. (2016). *Visual, narrative and creative research methods: Application, reflection and ethics.* London: Routledge.

For a good starting discussion of **ethics and** *(but not limited to)* **qualitative research in psychology**, see: Brinkmann, S., & Kvale, S. (2017). Ethics in qualitative psychological research. In C. Willig & W. Stainton Rogers (Eds.), *The SAGE handbook of qualitative research in psychology* (2nd ed., pp. 259–273). London: SAGE.

For in-depth discussion of **qualitative research and ethics**, see: Miller, T., Birch, M., Mauthner, M., & Jessop, J. (Eds.). (2012). *Ethics in qualitative research* (2nd ed.). London: SAGE.

2

TAKING AN INITIAL LAY OF THE LAND

INTRODUCING OUR WORKED EXAMPLE DATASET AND DOING FAMILIARISATION

Chapter Two overview

- **Today's the day!**   34
- **The process of reflexive TA**   34
- **Introducing and contextualising our worked example dataset**   37
  - What's my purpose here? Settling on a research question   41
- **Familiarisation (Phase one)**   42
  - Activity pause: Familiarisation   45
  - Meaning, the dataset and the analytic process: A brief note on language   45
  - Note-making for familiarisation   46

TODAY'S THE DAY!

You're about to start your TA! You might have woken early, fingers tingling with excitement at the prospect of exploring the things you can do with, and say about, your data. You might, instead, be gnawing the tips of your fingers with anxiety – uncertain in your ability to notice anything interesting in relation to the data, and to tell an analytic story. You might feel a mix of excitement and anxiety, or indeed neither of these sometimes-intense emotions. However you feel, feeling *is* a part of qualitative analysis. Qualitative analysis is riddled with emotional highs and lows, delights and frustrations, and acknowledging that up front is important. Especially if, like us, you've trained in a discipline (in our case, psychology) that promotes the neutral model of the analyst, where emotion is *not* supposed to be part of the process. But it is. You can't avoid it, and key is learning both to accept it, and to not let it derail your analytic process. Forewarned is forearmed, as they say – and so in these next chapters, alongside demonstrating how to *do* reflexive TA, we discuss the emotional and real-life aspects of analysis.

> **PRACTICE POINT** The process of qualitative analysis can have emotional highs and lows – as the researcher is integral to this process. Awareness and taking a break are important for self-care.

This chapter first introduces you to our 'six phase approach' to *doing* reflexive TA, and then we guide you through the *first* phase – *dataset familiarisation* – a process common to many qualitative analytic approaches (Braun & Clarke, 2013). We outline what familiarisation involves, and demonstrate *how to do it*, with key analytic processes illustrated. For the practical worked examples of the method (here, and in Chapters Three to Five and Seven), we use a single dataset, which we introduce and contextualise before setting you off on your adventure, with familiarisation.

THE PROCESS OF REFLEXIVE TA

Our reflexive approach to TA involves a six-phase process – starting with dataset *familiarisation*, moving into a rigorous and systematic *coding* process, before starting to explore, develop, review and refine *themes*, and finally producing the written analytic report (Braun & Clarke, 2006). Box 2.1 overviews these phases, so you have a general idea of what's ahead in your adventure. Don't worry if it doesn't all make sense: the core aspects of each will be introduced at the appropriate point across the chapters in Section One.

In your excitement to set off, remember, as we emphasised in Chapter One, that *reflexive TA offers guidelines rather than rules for the process of analysis*. We use the term *phase* rather than step quite deliberately, because language matters, and it conjures up an image of what the process is like. 'Steps' evoke a passage up or down, clearly segmented,[1] or the act of walking. But the different phases of reflexive TA are not always sharply delineated. Moreover, the term *steps* evokes a fairly linear and *unidirectional* model.

---

[1]Steps and stairs are also one of the ways our physical environments are made inaccessible for many – an additional reason not to use the term!

━━━━━━━━━━ **Box 2.1** ━━━━━━━━━━━━━━━━━━━━━━━━━━━━━

Introducing six phases of reflexive thematic analysis

Phase 1: Familiarising yourself with the dataset. Here, you become deeply and intimately familiar with the content of your dataset, through a process of immersion. Practically, this involves reading and re-reading your data (and, if working with transcripts of audio data, listening to the recordings at least once), and making (brief) notes about any analytic ideas or insights you may have, both related to each **data item** and the dataset as a whole.

Phase 2: Coding. Here, you work systematically through your dataset in a fine-grained way. You identify segments of data that appear potentially interesting, relevant or meaningful for your research question, and apply pithy, analytically-meaningful descriptions (**code labels**) to them. Your focus is specific, and detailed, with coding aimed at capturing single mean-ings or concepts. In reflexive TA, you can code at a range of *levels* – from the very explicit or surface meaning (we and many others term this **semantic**), through to the more conceptual or implicit meaning (we and others term this **latent**). Coding isn't *just* about summarising and reducing content, it's also about capturing your 'analytic take' on the data. You code the entire dataset, systematically and thoroughly. When done, you collate your code labels and then compile the relevant segments of data for each code.

Phase 3: Generating initial themes. Here, you aim to start identifying shared patterned mean-ing *across* the dataset. You compile clusters of codes that seem to share a core idea or con-cept, and which *might* provide a meaningful 'answer' to your research question. Although we originally identified this phase as *searching for themes*, that language can be misleading: the process is not like an excavation, where meaning is lying there, waiting to be uncovered and discovered through the right search technique. Rather, theme development is an active process; themes are constructed by the researcher, based around the data, the research questions, and the researcher's knowledge and insights. Where codes typically capture a specific or a particular meaning, themes describe broader, shared meanings. Once you've identified potential or *candidate* themes that you feel capture the data and address your research question, you collate all coded data relevant to each **candidate theme**.

Phase 4: Developing and reviewing themes. Here, your task is to assess the initial fit of your provisional candidate themes to the data, and the viability of your overall analysis, by going back to the full dataset. Development and review involves checking that themes make sense in relation to both the coded extracts, and then the full dataset. Does each theme tell a con-vincing and compelling story about an important pattern of shared meaning related to the dataset? Collectively, do the themes highlight the most important patterns across the dataset in relation to your research question? Radical revision is possible; indeed, it's quite common. Certain candidate themes may be collapsed together; one or more may be split into new themes; candidate themes may be retained; some or all may be discarded. *You have to be prepared to let things go!* In review, you need to think about the character of each individual theme – its core focus or idea (the **central organising concept**) – and its scope. You also need to starting considering the relationship *between* the themes, and existing knowledge, and/or practice in your research field, and the wider context of your research.

(Continued)

Phase 5: Refining, defining and naming themes. Here you fine-tune your analysis – ensuring that each theme is clearly demarcated, and is built around a strong core concept or essence. Ask yourself 'what story does this theme tell?' and 'how does this theme fit into my overall story about the data?' Key activities in this phase involve writing a brief synopsis of each theme. You also decide on a concise, punchy and informative name for each theme. In this phase, you still need to be prepared to *let the analysis go*, if your refining process indicates more development is needed.

Phase 6: Writing up. Writing is an integral phase of the analytic process for TA, as it is for many qualitative analytic approaches, so you start writing early on. In reflexive TA, formal analytic writing often starts from Phase 3; the more informal (just for you) writing you do from the start of the process – familiarisation notes and reflexive journaling – can feed into the more formal writing. In *writing up*, you finesse and finish the writing process. Ultimately, you're aiming to weave together your analytic narrative and compelling, vivid data extracts, to tell your reader a coherent and persuasive story about the dataset that addresses your research question. Final writing up also involves producing the introduction, method and conclusion sections of a research report. And a lot of editing. Never underestimate the importance and value of editing.

PRACTICE POINT Do not expect a linear progression when doing reflexive TA.

This means that if you need to take a step backwards, it can seem like you're getting it wrong, or regressing. *The process of reflexive TA is not strictly linear*, and so you are *not* regressing if you go 'backwards'. It's better to understand TA as a progressive but recursive process. You're moving along a trajectory from dataset to developed analysis, but that *often* involves going sideways, backwards, and sometimes even around in circles, as you move from the start to the end of the process. Knowing that is important, because it's not only part of the process, it's part of doing TA *well*.

The phases and process we outline in Section One of this book are not only guidelines for *doing* reflexive TA, they are guides to *learning to do* TA. They offer a process for discipline in familiarising, coding and theme development, and this disciplined activity is designed to help you engage more deeply with the data, to understand what the data offer in ways that might be quite different from what you notice during data collection (or familiarisation, or even early coding). If you're an inexperienced qualitative analyst, and/or working on data on an unfamiliar topic, you will likely spend more time at certain earlier phases than if you're more experienced. Qualitative analysis is a skill that involves *treating data as data* (discussed further in the 'Familiarisation' section), both noticing and exploring beyond the obvious meaning and content. With experience, or with intense familiarity with a field, you may have deeper insight into the analytic potential of your dataset in the familiarisation process (see our familiarisation notes in Box 2.4 and on the companion website), and you may code more quickly and easily, and identify less immediately-obvious meaning early on. We say may, as this can vary hugely across projects! Similarly, the processes of theme generation, development and review (the focus of Chapter Four) may be more integrated as a fluid process, particularly if you're working with a smaller dataset. Experience can help develop a more intuitive sense of what a theme might look like, something we find researchers new to

TA are sometimes concerned about. This is not
the same as saying that with experience, you
will develop a fully-worked-up analysis right
away, or that your analysis won't evolve, but
that there are certain analytic skills, and ways of
engaging and working with data, that develop
with experience. Just like with a new hobby –

> **ALERT** The six-phase process provides
> guidance both for doing reflexive TA
> and learning to do reflexive TA. As you
> become more experienced, how you
> engage with the process may change.

we're rarely brilliant at it right away, and things can feel awkward and hard to grasp, but with
a bit of time and practice, we often develop more fluid almost 'intuitive' skills.

INTRODUCING AND CONTEXTUALISING OUR WORKED EXAMPLE DATASET

The dataset we use to demonstrate TA procedures and practices in this section is one that
you will come to 'cold' – in the sense that it's not a topic you've chosen to research, and so
not one you probably know a lot about in terms of scholarship – though you may have lots
of life experiences or thoughts on the topic. The topic relates to adults who have chosen to
be childfree.[2]

This dataset consists of Facebook comments[3] related to a clip posted on the official
Facebook page of a New Zealand current affairs show, *Seven Sharp*. At the time of the post,
Seven Sharp positioned itself as having "a goal to keep you informed, discuss what you're discussing but never take ourselves too seriously". They broadcast weekly in a prime-time 7pm
slot on mainstream television. This particular *Seven Sharp* story raised the issue of *choosing* to
not have children. In the few minutes of the pre-recorded short film, it briefly introduced the

---

[2]We aimed to select a worked example topic that would resonate for lots of readers, be engaging and
thought-provoking, and would require readers to reflect on their personal positioning and assumptions
in relation to the topic. We were also mindful of feedback that we received relating to our use of an example from Ginny's PhD research on the social construction of the vagina in our 2006 paper. A lecturer contacted us to ask if we'd written anything else on doing TA, because some of his conservative male students
were refusing to read a paper that included the word 'vagina'. The only other piece we had available at
that time featured a worked example of gay students' experiences of university life – which turned out to
be just as problematic. So, when planning this book, we gave a lot of thought to potential topics related
to our own research interests that would be less sensitive. The topic of being childfree has research and
personal resonance for both of us, and compared to some of our other research interests, we assumed
it wouldn't be a particularly sensitive topic. We have used this dataset a lot in TA workshops over some
years, and for most people, the topic appears to function as we intended – it's engaging, resonant, and
thought-provoking. But a purely intellectual or dispassionate response isn't universal, and we acknowledge that for some people the topic of 'childfree' or not having children can be a sensitive one, and even
a dataset like this – social media comments, rather than personal stories – can be deeply affecting.

[3]Comments on social media posts can provide a rich source of data for qualitative researchers, giving
access to wider societal understandings and meaning-making around a topic (Giles, 2017). Facebook
comments provide a textual form of data, and 'naturalistic' data in the sense that the researcher doesn't
influence the data production – although of course they have *some* influence if selection is involved
during sampling.

perspectives and experiences of one single woman, and one straight couple, who had made deliberate choices *not* to have children. Ginny is one member of the couple (she situates herself in relation to the dataset in Box 2.2; Victoria does the same in Box 2.3). The reporter (a woman) contextualised how difficult this choice can be, especially for women, by presenting evidence of the abuse women who are childfree have received. After the film played, the two studio hosts discussed it. The Facebook clip included the (male) main *Seven Sharp* host, Mike Hosking,[4] dismissing the perspectives expressed, and stating that the people interviewed were 'clueless'/deluded. He evidenced his position by stating how great being a father (to many children) is, but that he used to think the same way as the people in the story.

Researcher Reflection – Box 2.2

Situating myself in relation to these data (Ginny)

I have a complex relationship to these data. As well as having a keen analytic interest in the topic (Clarke, Moller, Hayfield, & Braun, 2021), it's one I'm *personally* invested in (something that is not that unusual for qualitative research). I am a woman who knew early in life she didn't want to have children, and who made that decision permanent. I am very critical of most arguments that get associated with women who don't have children by choice, and the ways such women are typically represented in the media and wider Anglo-western cultures. That's my basic starting point, but with these data it goes deeper, as I was a key interviewee for the story the dataset relates to. This means there's potentially a real trickiness in trying to separate out what are just personal (emotive, reactive) responses, and what are analytically-useful and relevant responses. These things aren't necessarily in opposition to each other(!). Key in tackling this analysis will be being reflexively aware and questioning throughout data engagement, and examining both my scholarly and more emotional responses to things, as they come up. I will also need to ask myself to what extent my analytic insights are being limited by, or can be expanded by, my emotional or other responses. It's important to treat my reactions as a *starting* point, rather than endpoint – for instance, if I feel angry about something someone says, that doesn't mean anger is the only, or even the appropriate, response. To be a good qualitative researcher, to be in a position where I can work well with the data, my responses to the data have to be *up for grabs* – or interrogatable. After years of working analytically around sensitive topics, and doing lots of reflexive scholarship, I think I'm quite good at disengaging from my responses, meaning I feel comfortable pushing them into the analytic foreground, and interrogating them. But we're always only partially capable of this, and we have questions we never think to ask ourselves. Working with Victoria provides a nice check-in for the limits of my reflexivity, and also for what I think are important insights. She can interrogate and question things that I might not be noticing, or ways I am noticing things, that are based on my own locations and positions. In this instance, it's *really* useful having a co-researcher.

---

[4]Mike Hosking is one of the highest profile and highly popular radio and television hosts in New Zealand. He is right wing/conservative, and much-criticised for presenting uninformed and/or biased perspectives (https://en.wikipedia.org/wiki/Mike_Hosking).

━━━━━━━━━━━━ **Researcher Reflection – Box 2.3** ━━━━━━━━━━━━

Situating myself in relation to these data (Victoria)

My starting point for reflecting on these data is quite different from Ginny's, as I have previously conducted *research* with childfree women (Clarke, Hayfield, Ellis, & Terry, 2018; Hayfield, Terry, Clarke, & Ellis, 2019) and supervised doctoral research on childfree men. Furthermore, one of the strands of my own research has centred on family and relationships, and particularly how people *do* family when they are located outside of dominant and normative notions of family (e.g. family equals a straight couple with their genetic 1.9 children). This ranges from my PhD research on lesbian and gay parenting to my current collaborative research on embryo donation for family building.[5] My research with childfree women has focused on how these women make sense of their experiences, which is rather different from analysing Facebook comments around the choice to be childfree in response to a television current affairs story. However, my research on lesbian and gay parenting had a very similar focus – examining and interrogating public debates and **discourses**. This means both the topic and the data feel like familiar territory to me. Therefore, I bring to the data a sense of how the legitimacy of particular choices or relational/family practices are debated and some of the recurrent tropes in discussions of the choice to be childfree (e.g. women who choose to be childfree are selfish…, parents have children for selfish reasons – to look after them in later life…, there's no guarantee your children will look after you, they will more than likely dump you in a home…). I also have lots of experience of holding such tropes at a distance from my own personal experience and focusing on them as social *ideas* and getting excited by interrogating the logic and assumptions underlying such ideas. This is relevant here because, like Ginny, I don't have children and I conform to the image of the stereotypical childless woman – a White, middle-class professional. But unlike Ginny, this is not something I think of as a choice (some people who are *unable* to have biological children subsequently do chose to identify as childfree, so this might change). As a result, although our lives without children of our own and our experiences of adulthood are similar in many ways, our pathways to that were quite different. This means we bring different personal *and* academic experiences to this topic, but potentially productively so.

The story aired in late March 2014,[6] and the Facebook comments were compiled two days after the clip was posted on the *Seven Sharp* Facebook site. The dataset comprises *all* postings over the 48-hour period after the video link to the story was posted – to capture the full scope of commentary and debate.[7] A total of 187 posts were made over this timeframe, made up of 151 comments, 35 replies (a comment in response to someone else's comment), and one posted link. The negative features that can be part of online comments, such

---

[5]Embryo donation is when embryos often created for IVF are then donated to, or adopted by, couples or women who typically don't have any genetic relationship to the embryo.

[6]Neither the original story nor the Facebook commentary is still available online – inadvertently highlighting the importance of ensuring online data collection methods and record keeping are thorough and rigorous.

[7]No selection criteria were required as the dataset was not unworkably large for our purposes.

Table 2.1 Anonymised but otherwise unedited comments from *Seven Sharp* Facebook post about "being childfree"

META: People should just respect other's choices, we all choose our own paths.

CAHO: Having had 3 kids and 2 stepkids I say get a dog

DEMO: im the same I now have 2dogs , 9 grandchildren .

FIMA: Why do people think it's selfish not having children? It's no one else's business!!

CHCA: Why do people assume that choosing to be childfree automatically means that you won't have children in your life? My partner and I have decided not to have kids for a range of personal, environmental and social reasons. But I am a Godmother, an aunt, an older cousin, and a friend to many children. Contrary to common misconception those who choose not to have kids are rarely lonely, just more self-aware. In many cases those who choose not to have kids have usually thought a lot more about that decision than those who reproduce.

DARE: Very, very well said. Clearly you have never had baby brain.

MACL: And conversely, in many cases those who choose to have children have thought a lot more about that decision than those who choose not to have children. We're an ageing society .... And I think parents are pretty self aware as our children's behaviour is reflected right back at us. For better or for worse.

GRKO: lets not forget those who would die to have kids of their own, but for one reason or another cant. . .

DARE: Agreed. The pity is there's no shortage of people who shouldn't have kids. Should almost have to take a pill TO have a kid.

SHHA: I think you have to want to amd be prepared for the challenge ahead. Those who dont have kids might have other goals they want to achieve good for them im not hating and I wouldnt change my life for anything my daughter did it for me amd I am grateful :)

MAMC: not many ppl plan to have kids hehe an dwhen they plan it dusually doesnt happen :)

NAMI: It's selfish to spread your legs and expect everyone else to pay for your kids through welfare!!! Why should I pay for someone else's kids when I choose not to have any of my own. I'm tired of being taxed and seeing it go to someone who doesn't deserve it ... But I also see families that do need help and do deserve it.

TIJA: Hear hear! Agree totally!

BRMA: better not to have kids than have trophy kids and dump them in childcare from 7am to 6pm every day and then say I'm too busy to come to special events. Poor sprogs, selfish parents

---

HATU: Yep seen plenty of those kids , infact seen a lot of very bad parenting along the way too, gosh it frightens me at these kids are going to be the next generation, bunch of spoilt brats!! Btw I have 3 well rounded kids and love being a mum!!

SARO: Some people are child orientated, others aren't. Its as simple as that

---

SARO: Its also a lifestyle choice people make, more money and luxury, or the ups and downs a family brings along with different social skills needed

---

RITA: My wife and I are not having kids,we do what we want,when we want how we want......and we always have money.....always

---

CLPR: Grandkids are your reward for not strangling your kids.

JOWI: My husband and I chose not to have children and have never regretted this decision. The majority of our friends have no children and we all have brilliant fulfilled lives. It is a personal choice, respect it!

SAWH: No kids for us and we are fine with that it's our choice!!! I laugh when people say there won't be anyone to look after us when were old, because let's face it people how many of you are really going to look after your ageing parents and by that I mean not putting them in a rest home!!!

ANLI: I will look after mine. They are amazing parents and it's the least I can do. Tis the natural order.

DARE: Its a sad old argument isn't it? That I should breed humans to take care of me in my old age? Absolute pish.

SAWH: Don't get me wrong my parents have been amazing but me having to care for them when they can't I'm sorry but I'm honest it's not for me!

HEWI: Don't have kids & do not regret our decision not too!...But love our nieces & nephews to bits !

JAOB: Children AREN'T for everyone... never have been. It's purely a personal choice and some people who choose to become parents should have thought far more about WHY they had their children. I love my children, but they have always been loved and cared for, fed, clothed and taught well. This is not always the case

as trolling (Mkono, 2018) were occasionally apparent, but most posts were *on topic*. Posts ranged in length from a few words to multiple paragraphs. Table 2.1 provides a selection of posts (the sequence is as they were displayed by Facebook's algorithms). Each post is presented after an anonymised code, made up of four capitalised letters, which replaces the commenter's Facebook username. The full anonymised dataset, including information about each post (e.g. comment/reply, time of posting, likes) is on the companion website. We include a 'corrected' version to aid readability, and a discussion of the ethics of using online comments as research data.

We cannot know much about the commenters and what preceded their posting. Some may have watched this broadcast and come to the site *to* comment; others may have watched it via the *Seven Sharp* Facebook site; some may not have watched it at all (Tait, 2016). *Who* the commenters are is unknown, and again we can only speculate – although it does not seem unreasonable to assume that most of them are people who follow the *Seven Sharp* Facebook page. Beyond that presumption – which itself would need empirical verification – we have no way of knowing anything demographically about them. Any identity information we have depends on claims or indicators of identity in their posts (e.g. gendered names, discussion of having children). But as we know displayed online identity doesn't always match offline identity, we cannot treat those as *truth*. For the purpose of our analysis, this doesn't *really* matter, because we're not tagging meaning to *who said what* or the identity categories they might belong to.

What's my purpose here? Settling on a research question

There's one more aspect to consider before you depart on your journey: clarifying what you want the *point* of that journey to be. In TA terms, this becomes: what research question am I exploring? From the beginning of analysis (or before – see 'Design interlude'), TA needs a research question to address.[8] It's fine for that question to be quite loose and broad, at your starting point, but you do need a sense of *what* it is you're trying to gain insight into. A good research question meshes together considerations of the wider context, existing empirical scholarship, and the scope and potential of the dataset. We know childlessness, including *chosen* childlessness, is increasingly common in culturally/economically high consumption westernised countries like Aotearoa New Zealand and the UK: around one in five of

---

[8]We avoid the term 'answer' here (which is the typical pairing with question in the English language), preferring instead 'address'. The concept of answer risks evoking a singular truth model, and the idea that there is a *correct* answer to find. Although reflexive TA does provide *an* answer, we emphasise it's not the only one possible. Furthermore, the word 'address' evokes the way reflexive TA – in a Big Q qualitative orientation (see 'A qualitative sensibility for reflexive TA' in Chapter One) – provides nuanced and complex, and sometimes contradictory, *insights* into the topic, rather than a straightforward answer to a research question. Analysis can be conceptualised as a *reading* of the data, not the *only* way of making sense of it.

women born in the early 1970s (like us) will remain childless (Office for National Statistics, 2016). The last decade or so has also seen a resurgence of a childfree movement and the development of *childfree* as a social identity, particularly in the context of online social networks (Moore, 2014; Morison, Macleod, Lynch, Mijas, & Shivakumar, 2016). However, in an ongoing context of pronatalism – the assumption that having children is a natural human instinct, something deeply fulfilling, *essential* for human happiness and a meaningful life, and a marker of a successful adulthood (Morison et al., 2016) – this is not always viewed as a positive choice. Those who are childless/childfree are often stigmatised (Morison et al., 2016) with women, particularly, perceived as emotionally unstable, unfeminine, unnatural, unhappy, immature and selfish, among other characteristics (e.g. Rich, Taket, Graham, & Shelley, 2011). Mainstream media coverage is often unsympathetic to those who choose not to have children (Giles, Shaw, & Morgan, 2009; Graham & Rich, 2014; H. Peterson, 2014). Online communities often deploy more positive meaning frameworks (Moore, 2014; Morison et al., 2016).

> **PRACTICE POINT** Having a clear but still broad research question is beneficial for keeping the scope of your TA open in the early phases.

In this context, we took a very broad focus in working with the data through the early analytic stages: *what is the nature of contemporary meaning-making around voluntarily not having children?* The phrase 'voluntarily not having children' is a bit clunky, but it builds in no assumptions about how people might frame the issue. All the language and ways of talking about people who do not have children of their own volition are problematic, often ideologically or politically slanted. Take child*free* or child*less*, the terms most commonly used to refer to such people (usually women, given entrenched gendered associations of motherhood as essential to women's identity in a way that is different from fatherhood). We don't *really* like either term, because both orientate to a child/children as the key organising principle for a person's life. In line with our critical analysis around contemporary parenting (Clarke et al., 2021; Hayfield et al., 2019), we want to avoid implicitly reinforcing this through language. We will regularly come back to the point: that the detail, specificity and nuance of language *matters*, both in life, in this book, and in doing reflexive TA! That said, for simplicity's sake we do refer to the 'childfree dataset', as childfree reflects the experience of the original story participants; it is also, we think, the least problematic term – and least disliked (Hayfield et al., 2019).

Now – with a sense of what the process of reflexive TA involves, the dataset we'll be working with, and the research question we'll orientate around, let's jump into *familiarisation*.

FAMILIARISATION (PHASE ONE)

Familiarisation involves two *seemingly contradictory* practices, and a third, *complementary*, one. The first is about developing deep and intimate knowledge of your dataset. This is often referred to as immersion. The second is starting to critically engage with the information *as data*, rather than simply as information. This orientation to data is about being active as a reader or listener. This means developing a way of reading the data that involves both close-ness and familiarity (immersion) and distance (critical engagement). Both of these processes take time – qualitative research always takes

> **PRACTICE POINT** Qualitative research always takes more time than you anticipate it will.

much more time than you anticipate it will – so try to give yourself dedicated time and space for this. Consider disconnecting from potential distractions for a bit (put your device on flight mode; mute notifications), and focus on really absorbing and thinking about the con-tent of your data. The third process – note-making of thoughts related to the dataset – can be interspersed throughout, and facilitate the other two practices; it also needs to happen in a more focused way at the end of this phase.

The first practice of familiarisation is immersion in the data. Think of it as the analytic equivalent of settling in to the cinema to avidly enjoy the latest, much awaited release in your favourite movie series. Practically, familiarisation involves reading and re-reading through text-based data items, repeatedly viewing visual data items, and if working with transcripts of audio data, also listening to the audio recordings. You want to get to the point where, if suddenly your data got stolen (this horrific scenario can happen! See Meth, 2017), you'd be able to describe the broad content fairly well, even if precise detail was gone. This practice is important for *everyone* doing TA, but it's *most* important if you as ana-lyst *didn't* collect your data yourself, and the data were not generated through interaction with participants (e.g. qualitative surveys). Perhaps you've been given pre-collected data for a student project? Perhaps a research assistant conducted your interviews? Perhaps you collected social media data based on some criterion – as we did for our worked-example project. In these instances, you tend to start out less familiar with the data content than

if you've moderated some focus groups or con-ducted online interviews. This means deep engagement to identify the rich diversity of meaning, particularly interesting or intriguing elements, as well as *possible* patternings across the dataset, is important. That's what we mean by immersion.

> **PRACTICE POINT** Immersion in familiarisation is about gaining deep familiarity with the content of your dataset

At the same time as you are becoming deeply immersed, you want to *critically* engage with the data. As a reader of the data, you want to be active, critical and analytic. Back to our imagined movie. If you participate in fan culture, that's kind of like what we're talking about (McDermott, 2018): instead of simply summarising the plot and detail of the film, you're effectively engaged in dialogue *with it*. You are actively making sense, contesting and challenging, critiquing and imaging how things could be different (L. Green & Guinery, 2004). During familiarisation, you stop just *taking in* the information, and start asking your-self deeper questions about the data. In reflexive TA, you're trying to make meaning of the

world that has been presented to you in your data, to develop potential patterns of meaning. Imagining a textual dataset collected from peo-ple, useful things to ask about the dataset to facilitate this critical engagement include:

> **PRACTICE POINT** Familiarisation also involves critical engagement and asking questions about the content of your dataset

- *How* does the person make sense of whatever it is they are discussing?
- Why might they be making sense of things in this way (and not in another way)?
- In what different ways do they make sense of the topic?
- How 'common-sense' or socially normative is this depiction or story?
- How would I feel if I was in that situation? (Is this different from or similar to how the person feels, and why might that be?)
- What assumptions do they make in describing the world?
- What kind of world is 'revealed' through their account?

These questions aren't all compatible with all data types (e.g. textual versus visual, researcher generated or not), but provide a sense of the types of questions we ask ourselves during familiarisation. Importantly, they are not rigid questions to be *answered*, but things to *think about*. The purpose of questioning is to facilitate depth *and* distance in engagement.

It's important to recognise that such questions are the *starting* point, not the limit, for the things we might want to ask as we start to engage with our data. There are many other questions you can ask to facilitate critical engagement, depending on the topic. These include questions you ask of *yourself*, such as:

- Why might I be reacting to the data in this way?
- What ideas does my interpretation rely on?
- What different ways could I make sense of the data?

Interrogating yourself in this way as you start – and continue – doing reflexive TA is important. We often begin having analytic thoughts before analysis, both *during* data collection and even *before*, as we conceptualise a project. This cannot be avoided, and it isn't necessarily a problem, if we recognise and interrogate it. It highlights the importance of being reflexive *throughout* the analysis. Reflexivity reduces the likelihood of developing a poor-quality analysis through either fitting data to pre-existing ideas or shallow interpretation – by forcing you to interrogate how you're making sense of the data.

The familiarisation processes of immersion and critical engagement can be sequential, with critical engagement flowing out of immersion, or more concurrent. In our experience, it's much easier to critically engage if you're really familiar with the topic, an experienced qualitative researcher, and/or have a well-developed **analytic sensibility** (see Braun & Clarke, 2013). An analytic sensibility refers to the skill of reading and *interpreting* data to produce insights into your dataset that go beyond the obvious or surface-level content, and to noticing connections between the dataset and existing research, theory and the wider context. Essentially, it relates to taking an inquiring and interpretative position on data. If you don't find critical engagement easy at this point, don't despair! This is a skill that can be developed. Often, you only really start to engage critically as you move to coding, because that process orientates you towards unpacking meaning within the dataset more systematically.

> **KEY CONCEPT** The idea of an analytic sensibility relates to taking an inquiring and interpretative position on data.

Activity pause

Familiarisation

We encourage you now to pause in the reading of this chapter, and engage in a familiarisation activity for the childfree dataset. Either read the excerpts provided in this chapter, or the full dataset on the companion website, and try to engage in the dual processes of immersion and critical questioning.

As well as the generic familiarisation questions we've just discussed, you might ask things like:

- What sort of assumptions about adults without children are being made here? And about those with children?
- How are children characterised?
- What purposes are children imagined to serve (e.g. for parents, society, etc.)?
- What ideas about parenthood and family are being drawn on?
- What purposes of parenthood are articulated?
- Why might a commenter understand something as positive? Or as negative?
- What makes a particular claimed-experience be possible?
- What moral frameworks do commenters rely on?
- What sorts of assumptions are made about how the world is – or should be – organised?[9]

Take a few notes of the things you're noticing, so that you have a record of your thinking about the data at this point in time.

Meaning, the dataset and the analytic process: A brief note on language

In describing the process of analytic engagement for TA, it's very hard to avoid using language describing meaning as *in* or *within* the dataset, as we just did. There will be places where we use such language. Although meaning is clearly connected *to* the content of the dataset, we want to make it clear that *our* use of such language is not intended to suggest the meaning is simply there, waiting to be discovered, to be 'excavated'. As we noted in Box 1.1, this model does not align well with either reflexive TA, or the Big Q qualitative framework it is embedded in (Kidder & Fine, 1987). Instead, analysis is a process of meaning-making, at the intersection of the researcher, the dataset, and analytic and data contexts.

---

[9]If you're a bit stumped by this one, it could be about noting whether commenters assume a heterosexual nuclear family, or that children are raised by two parents, and 'leave home' in the late teens/early 20s.

Note-making for familiarisation

Your critical engagement *can* be facilitated by the third aspect of this phase – where you note ideas around the data that you have developed through familiarisation. Depending on the format you're engaging with your data, this might involve hand-scribbling notes on hard copy printed data items, using voice recognition software to comment on electronic data items, making fuller written notes or voice memos for yourself, in a separate file, or some other option that works for you. *For yourself* is key here – if you're working alone, you're the only one who will engage with these, and so they can be as messy and as casual as works for you. Familiarisation notes don't have to just be textual. *Visual* notes might also facilitate getting a grasp on the data. For instance, Matthew Wood, one of our former students, found that drawing text-and-image 'doodles' helped him make sense of the ideas he was noticing in his interview data (see Figures 2.1 and 2.2). Emphasising the point about these being *for yourself*, these doodles don't make sense to us, and they won't for you, either. But they don't need to. They were tools *for Matt* (Box 6.2 in Chapter Six has a summary of Matt's final analysis). Familiarisation notes (or doodles) are analytic tools for your *own* use, not least so you don't forget ideas that you've started to engage with. Rachel Graham's poem in Box 1.3 in Chapter One is another creative example of a familiarisation practice.

Figure 2.1 Familiarisation Doodle for participant 'Franz' (Matthew Wood)

Figure 2.2   Familiarisation Doodle for participant 'Frank' (Matthew Wood)

There is a second note-making process in familiarisation, which is important preparation before coding. This involves making brief but systematic *overall* familiarisation notes related to the *whole dataset*, capturing your ideas about potential patterning of meaning, and questions you may have. The point of overall dataset familiarisation note-making is to take the time to reflect on your responses and the dataset as a whole, rather than just individual data items, so you can head into coding with an already-engaged, critically questioning mindset. Box 2.4 presents Ginny's overall familiarisation notes for the childfree dataset, as an example. They are quite analytically developed, but they are also reflexive, focused on reactions and responses as well as data content. That's appropriate in familiarisation notes – as they are tools for *ourselves*. We have also included Victoria's familiarisation notes, which provide a looser set of overall impressions, on the companion website. We encourage you to look at Victoria's as well – not only do they show a different style of overall familiarisation notes from Ginny's, but by reading both, you can appreciate similarities and differences in our initial noticings around the dataset. The companion website also contains an exercise related to our two sets of familiarisation notes.

After discussion, following individual familiarisation, we decide to code in such a way as to keep the possibility for a research question somewhat open, depending on what develops as our insight deepens through close and systematic engagement. This means we will continue to work with the very broad research question: *what is the nature of contemporary meaning-making around voluntarily not having children?*

Box 2.4

Ginny's overall dataset familiarisation notes

Meta-comment: As a woman who has chosen to be childfree, I know quite a bit about this topic, and, as a person interviewed in the story the dataset relates to, the detail of Facebook comments affected me. When I started to engage analytically, however, and read the comments *as data*, quite a few things struck me. Initially after familiarisation, I noticed that:

- There's far less (explicit) criticism of being childfree, or specifically being a childfree woman, than I had expected. By and large, the criticisms aren't that brutal, and there seems *on the surface* to be lots of support...
- There's a really strong 'liberal tolerance' thread – it's your choice (it's my choice), each to their own sort of thing... So a quite striking individualism – very little in the way of a structural or situated analysis.

Combined, and on the very surface, this suggests that things *aren't so bad* for women (or men) who might want to remain childfree... Great!

But... I still feel marginalised by the data overall, and annoyed by it, and this suggests that there's probably more going on. Getting a bit more engaged, I started to notice a few other things, not least of which is that there actually is quite a bit of criticism, but it's less obvious (most of the time). There seem to be lots of norms and assumptions – as well as contestation of these (I can't help noticing some of these in very critical psychology/discourse terms – because that's how I've been trained):

- Not having children seems often to be construed in terms of missing something – the idea of 'fur-babies', for example.
- Parents as *really* the selfish ones – so contesting that common trope of not having kids as about selfishness.
- Contestations over things like: the purpose of life; what counts as contributing; being a good person; right/wrong ways to be a parent; right/wrong motivations and intentions; responsibility/irresponsibility.
- True love – something you only ever can experience through parenting. Well I've failed there then ☹!
- Freedoms and joys of not having kids (money).
- 'Compensatory' kids – not having children doesn't mean having a childfree life, but claims to having kids in your life seems to be a key way people avoid judgement.
- There seems to be a lot of 'identity work' going on here... people presenting themselves as liberal, 'good people' in subtle ways – probably not relevant for our TA analysis, but it might connect to the themes we develop.
- Use of "don't have a clue" as a way of dismissing other people's views or experiences.

I finish the overall familiarisation excited by the richness of our small dataset, but realising I have too many potential research questions I could address with the analysis – including lots that are more appropriate for **discourse analysis** (Wiggins, 2017) than TA, so I – or we! – have to think about what questions are useful and appropriate *for* TA specifically.

When is it time to move on from familiarisation to coding? There's no right answer. In general, it's once you're familiar with, but also potentially starting to be critically engaged with, your data; once you start to have a sense of some possible patterns and interesting features. You can spend too long in familiarisation, for all sorts of reasons, such as anxiety about coding, or feeling like you need to understand *everything* before you can move on to coding. But to come back to the idea of an adventure, this phase is you getting a lay of the land, not a full understanding of every possible nuance. Coding shifts you into a *systematic* mode, and so it's important to have a good sense of the sorts

> **PRACTICE POINT** If you're reluctant to stop familiarisation and start coding, try to assess whether uncertainty and anxiety around starting coding might be keeping you in this phase.

of things you'll be noticing and coding for. But remember, those understandings and meanings will also be developed *through* the discipline of coding. Don't wait until you feel you understand *everything* that's going on in your dataset, before moving to coding.

CHAPTER SUMMARY

This chapter set you off on your analytic journey. We aimed to do three main things. First, we wanted to give you a quick introduction to method and process for analysing data using reflexive TA. This set you up for a basic understanding of the *plot* of this and the next three chapters. Second, we introduced you to the dataset we use for our worked example through all the phases of reflexive TA. Our description of the dataset demonstrated the practice of contextually locating the data; our reflexive boxes illustrated the practice of situating yourself in relation to the data (reiterating the importance of reflexivity discussed in Chapter One). We emphasised the importance of having a *purpose* – a research question – to guide your analytic focus through the phases of reflexive TA, and discussed the broad research question we will orientate to in demonstrating how to do reflexive TA. Third, we explained the principles and practices of *familiarisation* for reflexive TA (Phase one), noting three key aspects: immersion in the dataset; critical distancing and questioning (aka an analytic orientation); and note-making, the latter illustrated with visual and written examples. Having engaged with familiarisation in a thorough and reflexive way, it's time to move on to *coding*.

WANT TO LEARN MORE ABOUT...?

For a chapter that illustrates the **process of reflexive TA** with a worked example, including familiarisation, see: Terry, G. (2021). Doing thematic analysis. In E. Lyons & A. Coyle (Eds.), *Analysing qualitative data in psychology* (3rd ed., pp. 148–161). London: SAGE.

For a more detailed discussion of **research questions in reflexive TA,** see: Braun, V., & Clarke, V. (2021). Conceptual and design thinking for thematic analysis. *Qualitative Psychology*. Advance online publication https://doi.org/10.1037/qup0000196

If you want to better understand **meaning and experience around being 'childfree'**, our critical feminist review chapter highlights many of the key contestations: Clarke, V., Moller, N., Hayfield, N., & Braun, V. (2021). A critical review of the interdisciplinary literature on voluntary childlessness. In H. A. Cummins, J. A. Rodgers, & J. D. Wouk (Eds.), *The truth about (m)otherhood: choosing to be childfree* (pp. 29–54). Bradford, Ontario: Demeter Press.

ACTIVITIES FOR STUDENT READERS

Topic-based reflexivity exercise: Our worked example dataset is on the topic of people who choose to be childfree. Spend about 15 minutes reflecting on the *topic* and where you would place *yourself* in relation to it, both personally (e.g. have children, want children, don't want children, uncertain) and more general views. Write as you reflect. Writing – be it using pen or pencil on paper, typing on a keyboard, dictating to some voice capture device, or some other mode – is an important tool *for* developing reflexive depth. Start with your own experiences/understandings/views, but then also try to interrogate those. Ask yourself questions like: what assumptions am I basing my thinking on? What broader experiences and values might inform my thinking on this? How might these be connected to myself as a person, my various identities, my personal experience in relation to the topic, and the communities I am part of?

Familiarisation activity – reading data as data: For this activity, we will use the topic of *healthy eating* and a specific research question of 'how is healthy eating for men represented online?'

- First up, note any initial reactions to the topic (think of this as a quick reflexive check-in on yourself).
- On the companion website, you'll find a PDF of a *healthy eating dataset*, made up of four articles that comprised top relevant hits from a Google search for 'men healthy eating'. Access this dataset in whatever format works for you (there is a simplified-text version for text readers).
- Read the first article in the dataset through once. Note any reactions or observations about the data item that relate broadly to the research question.
- Read it again with a more critical orientation, thinking about the key areas that might make up *your* research interest. For example, we both have a longstanding interest in gender research. So if we were examining men and healthy eating, we would be interested in gendered or masculine ideas or tropes or assumptions, as well as ideas about what might count as healthy eating or healthy food. We'd also be interested in the ways race or class or ability seem to be relevant.
- Make some familiarisation notes related to the data item, noting your initial observations and any questions that you have.
- Continue this process for the remaining articles in the dataset.
- Compile some overall (reflexive) familiarisation notes for the whole dataset.

If you're teaching content related to this chapter…
Don't forget to check the companion website for a range of teaching resources:
https://study.sagepub.com/thematicanalysis

3

EXPLORING THIS WORLD IN DETAIL
DOING CODING

Chapter Three overview

- Preparing for coding   52
- Coding is a systematic process   53
- Coding is organic, evolving and subjective   54
- Inductive and deductive orientations to data coding   55
- Semantic to latent coding   57
- General guidelines for codes and code labels in reflexive TA   58
- Doing coding (Phase two)   59

  o   Activity pause: Before coding   60
  o   Actually wrangling data and codes: Technologies of coding   65
  o   Evolving your coding   69
  o   Refining your coding through multiple rounds   70
  o   Can I stop coding yet?   71

You've taken the lay of the (new) land you've found yourself in; you've had some initial observations about what things are like; you've spent some time reflecting on your impressions, both overall, and specific aspects you've encountered. Now is the time for a more detailed and systematic exploration. In reflexive TA terms, you're about to start *coding*. Coding is a process and practice across many forms of qualitative analysis, but one where there is quite a bit of variation, even across TA (in Chapter Eight, we discuss different conceptualisations of coding in TA). In the first half of the chapter, we explain how coding is understood within reflexive TA, and clarify some key concepts. In the second half, we discuss and demonstrate how you *do* coding in reflexive TA.

PREPARING FOR CODING

Before you get into coding, you need to understand some key things *about* codes and coding. In reflexive TA, a code is the smallest unit of your analysis. Your codes form the building blocks of your analysis; from these you will go on to develop your themes.

KEY CONCEPT Codes are the building blocks of analysis in reflexive TA, capturing meaning relevant to the research question.

Your codes capture specific and particular meanings within the dataset, of relevance to your research question. They have succinct *labels* that evoke the data content. In writing about reflexive TA, we've often conflated the concept of a **code *label*** and a code, through simply using the term code for both, but it's useful to be clear that a richer analytic idea often sits 'behind' the short code label, and this is what the code captures. Although codes in reflexive TA focus on singular ideas, these don't necessarily lack depth. This is because coding is more than just a way to *reduce down* the detail of the data. Codes often also provide a pithy take on what is of analytic interest **in the data** – they offer some interpretation. This means codes can range from the more

KEY CONCEPT A code label succinctly summarises the analytic ideas and data meanings captured by a code.

ALERT Codes both reduce the data content and provide an analytic take on what is of interest.

summative or descriptive to the more interpretative or **conceptual**. Coding can capture a range of meaning abstraction, from the semantic or **manifest** content of the data, to latent or underlying meaning. The coding process can also be driven by a more inductive or a more deductive orientation to data. We will describe all these elements in a bit more detail, below; before we do, we briefly synopsise the three core concepts of coding for reflexive TA (see Box 3.1).

========= **Box 3.1** =========

Coding, codes and code labels in reflexive TA – a quick guide

Coding   The *process* of exploring the diversity and patterning of meaning from the dataset, developing codes, and applying code labels to specific segments of each data item.

Code   An *output* of the coding process; an analytically interesting idea, concept or meaning associated with particular segments of data; often refined during the coding process.

Code label   An *output* of the coding process; a succinct phrase attached to a segment of data, as a shorthand tag for a code; often refined during the coding process.

CODING IS A SYSTEMATIC PROCESS

In reflexive TA, coding is a *process* – it's how you work with data in this phase – and codes and code labels are *outputs* of this process.[1] When you engage in this process in a thorough and rigorous way, your codes should set you up well for the next phase of initial theme development.

> **ALERT**   Coding in reflexive TA is a *process* – an activity you are engaged in – with codes as the *outcome* of that process.

Where familiarisation is engaged-but-not-yet-systematic, coding is engaged-*and*-systematic. The coding *process* involves reading each data item closely, and tagging all segments of the text where you notice any meaning that is potentially relevant to your research question with an appropriate code label. This means some segments of data will not be tagged with any codes, because there isn't anything of relevance to the research question.[2] In contrast, as the coding example in Table 3.3 later in this chapter shows, some segments might be tagged with many *different* codes – because a number of *different* meanings are evident in a particular segment of data. You use a different code label for each different meaning because coding is a process for parsing out diversity of meaning. Individual codes shouldn't capture multiple meanings. Sometimes, your code applies to just

> **PRACTICE POINT**   Make sure each different meaning you identify has its own code, so you're using coding to parse out the diversity of meanings from the data; codes should not capture multiple meanings.

---

[1]Not all forms of TA conceptualise coding and codes as, respectively, process and outputs. We conceptualise themes in a similar way to codes, as meanings developed *through* our analytic engagement with our data. See 'Variation across TA approaches: core concepts' in Chapter Eight for more discussion of these different conceptualisations.

[2]For reflexive TA, we do *not* advocate line-by-line coding in the traditional, grounded theory-developed sense of coding each single line of text (see Glaser, 1978). Instead, you only need to code data relevant to the research question – broadly framed.

a few words in a data item; other times, you might affix a code to a whole paragraph, or an even longer segment of text. Often the meaning you identify will be very narrow or 'tight'; other times it might be broader or 'loose'. There's no *right* or specific level here, as exactly how you code is ultimately guided by your research question and purpose. But what doesn't vary is that, with coding, you're aiming to generate lots of different codes that differentiate between meanings. It's also crucial to remember that *codes are not themes*, and so you're trying to capture a singular or particular idea through coding, not a multi-faceted one.

Coding often helps us to shift to fully engaging with the data *as data* – as materials we are grappling with to make analytic sense of, to address a specific question – rather than straightforward sources of information. A systematic coding process is important for two reasons – insight and rigour:

Insight, because your analysis typically becomes deeper, more interesting, and less obvious through a repeated process of close engagement. Insight takes time, and this disciplined practice forces us to not 'leap ahead' into developing themes. We regard thinking about themes as very important to resist during coding, not only because themes are typically an *outcome* of later phases of the analytic process in reflexive TA, but because this risks foreclosing analysis (Braun & Clarke, 2021c). Your analytic insights will evolve throughout the phases of reflexive TA.

Rigour, because coding ensures a systematic engagement with meaning and patterning *across* the entire dataset, so theme development is based on a robust and detailed analytic interrogation. Systematic engagement also helps avoid the accusation of *cherry-picking*. This is the idea that qualitative analysts select 'patterns' in their data to fit their own predetermined ideas about what meanings are evident, through poor analytic practice and/or partial data engagement (Morse, 2010) (see also Box 4.5 in Chapter Four).

> **ALERT** A 'quick and dirty' analysis can result in *analytic foreclosure* – stopping analysis after an only superficial engagement with the data and producing a set of themes that don't realise the full potential of the data.

CODING IS ORGANIC, EVOLVING AND SUBJECTIVE

Coding is an *organic* and *evolving* process, an open process, in reflexive TA. Coding begins without any list or set idea of what codes will be used.[3] Codes can *evolve* through the coding process – shifting as your understanding of meaning in relation to the dataset develops through coding. Codes can be sharpened or expanded, so that the meaning they capture is associated with more than just one segment of data. The evolution of codes and code labels

> **ALERT** Codes should usually connect to more than one segment of data; coding is about starting to capture repetition of meaning.

---

[3]There is *no* codebook or framework that guides the process of coding in reflexive TA (as there is in some other forms of TA – we outline the different approaches in Chapter Eight).

might sound like a flaw in the process, but it reflects *good practice* in reflexive TA, for two reasons. First, as noted already, insight develops through analytic engagement. Earlier codes *may* lack nuance, subtlety or depth; evolving rather than fixing your codes early in – or even before – analysis ensures more nuanced coding, and that richer analytic insights are systematically captured. Second, as TA is about identifying *patterns* of meaning, your task in coding is not only to demarcate differences, but to start to notice shared or similar meaning. An evolving coding process supports this practice, through allowing you to shift and change the code labels to capture closely-related ideas or meanings within single codes, where appropriate. You're looking for some repetition in coding

> **ALERT** Codes and coding labels can shift and change throughout the coding process, to better evoke and differentiate between the range of meanings in the data.

for most, but not necessarily all, codes. A code can still be useful and relevant to addressing your research question even if it occurs only once, since themes are typically developed from *multiple* codes that identify different facets of the meaning focus of a theme.

We also view coding as a *subjective* process shaped by what we bring to it. Coding is a process of *interpretation* – or meaning-making[4] – and researcher subjectivity fuels that process. As discussed in Chapter One, in keeping with an overall Big Q qualitative orientation, we view analysis as a process of meaning-making rather than truth-seeking or discovery (Braun & Clarke, 2021c). This means subjectivity is a strength, rather than a weakness or a source of 'bias' (Nadar, 2014). The coding achieved through this open, organic process can be stronger or weaker, depending on the depth and rigour of engagement. But it cannot be understood simply as right or wrong. This is because of the subjective and situated nature of the analytic process in reflexive TA, which means that different coders will notice and make sense of data in different ways.[5] Having only one person coding – usually the researcher – is normal practice, and indeed good practice, for reflexive TA. Where multiple coders *can* be useful is in developing *richer* and more complex insights into the data. But it is *not essential*, or even more desirable than having a single coder. If multiple coders *are* part of your reflexive TA process, the purpose is to collaboratively gain richer or more nuanced insights, *not* to reach agreement about every code (we discuss this further in Chapter Eight).

> **PRACTICE POINT** A single coder is normal – and good – practice in reflexive TA.

INDUCTIVE AND DEDUCTIVE ORIENTATIONS TO DATA CODING

In Chapter One, we signalled different variations in reflexive TA, including different orientations to data (see Table 1.2). It is during coding that these variations *start* to take shape.

---

[4]Meaning-making and interpretation are core in the reflexive TA analytic process, so important that we dedicate the whole of Chapter Seven to interpretation.

[5]This means we *do not* recommend using multiple coders as a way to guarantee a 'true' or 'accurate' analysis. Some other versions of TA do recommend this, which we discuss in Chapter Eight.

ALERT Coding doesn't have to be either inductive or deductive, although it can be; your analysis can have elements of both orientations. What's most important is that your coding orientation fits your purpose.

One really important dimension in coding and theme development is the way you tackle the question of where and how meaning is noticed: this ranges from inductive (data-driven) to deductive (researcher- or theory-driven) orientations.[6] As we noted in Chapter One, it's more a spectrum than a dichotomy, and coding of a dataset can encompass both types. What is important is to recognise how you're approaching the meaning-making (coding) process, and how that shapes the things that you notice about the data.

An *inductive* orientation takes the dataset as the starting point for engaging with meaning. At some 'pure' level, it would only capture that meaning – it's evoked by the idea that qualitative research can 'give voice' to participants and tell their stories in a straightforward way. In Big Q qualitative analysis, the subjective and embedded process makes pure induction impossible: we bring with us all sorts of perspectives, theoretical and otherwise, to our meaning-making, so our engagement with data is never purely inductive. We cannot simply give voice, because who we are always shapes what we notice about our data and the stories we tell about them (Fine, 1992). This is why reflexivity matters (as discussed in Chapter One). Consider your disciplinary training so far: even if you don't realise it, you will be starting to think like, and view the world as, psychologists, or sociologists, or economists, or whatever it is you might be, or be training to be – and unless you spend lots of time in an inter-disciplinary environment, it can be hard to notice how much that constrains and limits your sense-making.

ALERT In Big Q qualitative, an inductive orientation is never 'pure' because of what we bring to the data analytic process, as theoretically embedded and socially positioned researchers.

This is not to say an inductive orientation is not possible! In reflexive TA, your analytic process *can* emphasise the data meanings, and aim to be grounded in and depart from these meanings *as your starting point*. If you want to figure out whether an inductive orientation fits your project, a useful basic question is: am I interested in things like the experiences, perspectives, and meanings of the participants? If the answer is an emphatic *yes*, then you'll probably be working more inductively. Often this connects to your research question: for the childfree dataset, for instance, you might want to understand people's *experiences of* being childfree. Within the dataset, people's articulated experiences would then form the starting point for your coding and theme development.

---

[6]The meanings of the terms induction and deduction in a qualitative analytic context are different from the more traditional – quantitative – use of these terms, as representing research that is either theory generating (inductive) or theory testing (deductive; determining a hypothesis, making observations, and confirming or revising the theory). Another – less commonly used – analytic orientation you might encounter is *abduction*, where situated scholars use theory to make sense of curiosities in the data, and/or use data to extend, modify or dispute existing theory (e.g. see Blaikie, 2010; Collins, 2019; Kennedy, 2018).

What about a *deductive* orientation? In reflexive TA, a deductive orientation refers to a more researcher- or theory-driven approach, where the dataset provides the foundation for coding and theme development, but the research questions asked – and thus the codes developed –

ALERT In reflexive TA, a deductive orientation means theory provides an interpretative lens through which to code and make meaning of the data.

reflect theoretical or conceptual ideas the researcher seeks to understand through the dataset.[7] In some cases, existing theory and concepts might provide a lens through which a researcher interprets and makes sense of the data. As an example, Icelandic education researchers Kjaran and Jóhannesson (2013) drew on the concept of heterosexism to make sense of varied experiences of lesbian, gay, bisexual and transgender (LGBT) school pupils. Heterosexism captures the normative assumption that everyone is heterosexual, and the societal privileging of heterosexuality as normal and natural (Pharr, 2000). The researchers used this concept to make sense of students' experiences, including feeling different and less valued, and an implicit pressure to talk openly about a heterosexual sex life. Prior theory might also inform your coding, and subsequent theme development and interpretation, in a more precise way – perhaps to enrich the empirically based understanding of a theoretical concept (e.g. Beres & Farvid, 2010). Finally, TA can be more deductive when the researcher notices strong connections to theoretical ideas, early on in the process, and starts to code around such concepts.

No matter whether your analysis is more inductive or deductive, or indeed a blend of both, *theory* is still important – it's what gives reflexive TA, and indeed all forms of qualitative

ALERT Reflexive TA, like all forms of qualitative analysis, gets its analytic power from theory.

analysis, both its foundation, and its analytic power (Chapter Six provides a deeper discussion of theory and TA).

SEMANTIC TO LATENT CODING

A second consideration is the level at which you will code meaning. Reflexive TA can capture meaning from semantic (participant-driven, descriptive) to latent (researcher-driven, conceptual) levels. *Semantic* coding involves exploring meaning at the surface of the data. **Semantic codes** capture explicitly-expressed meaning; they often stay close to the language of participants or the overt meanings of data. **Latent codes** focus on a deeper, more *implicit*

ALERT The 'best' coding is the coding that best fits *your* purpose in analysing your data.

ALERT Coding in reflexive TA ranges from semantic to latent. These are again best thought of as two ends of a spectrum, and approaches that can be combined in any one analysis, rather than either/or choices.

---

[7]Some describe quasi-deductive rather than purely deductive orientation to coding (Jaspal & Cinnirella, 2012).

or conceptual level of meaning, sometimes quite abstracted from the obvious content of the data. Because it can be easier to code meaning at the semantic level, initial coding is often semantic. As you become more experienced, or your analysis develops, you may find it becomes easier to generate latent-level codes. What this does *not* mean is that latent coding is better – that idea is one of several misconceptions about semantic and latent codes we clear up in Table 3.1. Whether latent or semantic meaning is the most *relevant* depends on the aims of the project. Furthermore, in practice, the boundaries between semantic and latent codes are not always distinct. Semantic and latent codes are not a dichotomy, but instead represent ends of a continuum of ways of looking at data.

Table 3.1   Dispelling some misconceptions about semantic and latent coding

Misconception	Response
Coding is *either* semantic *or* latent	Semantic and latent are end points on a continuum, and your coding can sit at one or many points along this continuum.
Latent coding is *more sophisticated* and *better* than semantic	Latent coding can be harder to do than semantic coding, because the meaning might be less immediately obvious to you. This doesn't make it necessarily more sophisticated, or indeed better.
Semantic coding is *more respectful* than latent	This idea is based on two assumptions: (1) that if the analyst engages semantically, they are not shaping or reading into the data, but simply capturing *what is there*; (2) that to engage latently, and look at meaning beyond what is obviously stated, *is* disrespectful. But we always shape the analysis, no matter how we approach coding, and neither approach is more inherently respectful (to participants) or disrespectful. Respectful interpretation is *not* tied to coding level (for more on the politics of representation, see Chapter Seven).
Latent codes capture *unconscious* meaning	We hear this especially among the counselling and psychotherapy students we teach – reflecting the use in psychoanalytic theory of latent to refer to unconscious meaning and experience. In reflexive TA, latent is used in a broader sense to refer to non-obvious, *hidden* or *concealed* (that is, non-explicit) meaning. But *if* your theoretical lens allowed, latent codes could capture 'unconscious' meaning.
Semantic codes *have to* use participant words	Semantic codes are not about summarising the words participants say (or the words written in a text); they are about capturing explicitly-stated ideas, relevant to answering your research question.
Codes are latent if they use words that weren't in the data	Not using the words participants say (or the words written in a text) is *not* what makes a code latent. A code is latent if it captures ideas and concepts that are implicit – that is, sit behind or underneath, the obvious, surface-level meanings in the data.
Semantic codes *should not go beyond* the data content	As codes can offer a *take* on the data, codes – even semantic ones – can go beyond the data; they can have some aspect of interpretation in them, connected to why you think the meaning is relevant to your research question.

GENERAL GUIDELINES FOR CODES AND CODE LABELS IN REFLEXIVE TA

Our organic and open approach applies to the codes themselves – and the associated labels you tag segments of data text with. Codes are *your tools* for developing the analytic depth you need, to do justice to the dataset in addressing your research question. Codes aren't (ontologically) real, in the sense concrete is real or a wheelchair is real. Codes are **heuristic devices** we use, to foster our engagement, to enrich understanding, and push ourselves into interrogating the dataset and our meaning-making with it. That sounds vague, but really the key point is not to worry about getting codes right or wrong. The aim of understanding different *ways* to approach coding is not about doing things perfectly, so much as understanding what you're doing, and why. The point of coding is to develop codes that help you understand meaning in relation to your dataset in a different way than you did before, and to gain insights that address your research question. Given the flexible and organic process for reflexive TA, you might shift your analytic interests as your analysis develops. That's absolutely fine – as long as your research question shifts too. Similarly, your coding might become more latent – or indeed more semantic. Keep in mind that codes should be specific and precise, as your aim is to demarcate and capture (with the code labels) a rich diversity of meaning within the dataset. This is to allow you the widest scope for theme development in subsequent phases: you might cluster code labels into patterns of meaning that aren't even apparent to you in the coding phase.

> **PRACTICE POINT** Don't worry about whether you're getting semantic or latent coding right – use this distinction to reflect on how you're coding the data, and at what level you're working with meaning. If you're only or mainly working at one level, might the other have anything to offer your analysis?

As noted, the label you use for each code offers a shorthand for the broader idea you're working with. Good code labels are pithy and brief – they offer a quick *in* to what the code is about. Generally they are *your* words (but occasionally a particularly evocative pithy data quote might be used). There is no easy formula for what a code label could or should be, but we offer a few useful general guidelines in Table 3.2, with examples of code labels related to 'choice' to illustrate these.

Qualitative analysis is an interpretative, rather than mechanical, process, so absolute rules are impossible. We call these *general* guidelines because they do not have to apply for *every single code*. Understanding the logic behind the overall process and techniques provides the grounding for making *in situ* decisions around analysis.

> **PRACTICE POINT** Reflexive TA offers much flexibility. Understanding purpose and principles behind the tools and techniques allows you to apply them as needed, during your own analysis.

DOING CODING (PHASE TWO)

With all that information to set you going, you are now ready to start coding! We'll explain the process *and* illustrate it with data extracts and codes from the childfree dataset. We start with the initial coding process, then talk about the different technologies you might use for doing coding, and then discuss the process around *developing* your coding to the point you're ready to move into theme generation.

Table 3.2 Some general guidelines for developing code labels

General guideline	Principle	Example
Don't just copy the data	A code label should reduce the mess of the data, and summarise the meaning you're identifying in the data extract.	A code label like 'choice is important' summarises an idea that is often more loosely or fluidly expressed in data (and from semantic to latent levels).
Identify the particular angle of the meaning	A good code label should not be too broad, and should contain some indicator of the specific meaning in the data.	A code label like 'choice' potentially captures very contradictory meanings related to choice, and is too broad to be effective. Better code labels would indicate what specifically was stated or evoked around choice in a particular segment of data – such as 'choice is important' or 'it's not always a choice'.
Indicate your analytic take somehow	A code label often contains some indication of your interpretative take – what you think is particularly important or interesting about this particular meaning.	Rather than being based in the meaning-frameworks expressed by the commentators, a code label 'having choice is what is *ultimately* important' captured *our* analytic take. Although the commenters rarely expressed it in quite these terms, *having* choice was regularly expressed in a way that framed it as the most important principle of all.

 Activity pause

Before coding

Before we show you what coding looks like, read the excerpts in Box 3.2. Hopefully it's apparent that there are lots of assertions and contestations around the meaning of choosing not to have children and being a parent. There are lots of explicitly stated (or semantic) ideas, as well as different assumptions and concepts that underpin what the commenters write – the logic-frameworks behind what is claimed, that allow it to make sense (latent ideas). Think about what and how you might code it.

The process of coding involves systematically working through each data item and your entire dataset. So where do you start? Take your first data item. Start reading,[8] and stop when you think you have spotted something relevant to addressing your research question, even if

---

[8]We assume here an analytic process centred on textual data, but TA is starting to be applied to visual data – Boxes 8.3 and 8.4 in Chapter Eight offer some guidance.

======= Box 3.2 =======

A selection of six extracts from childfree dataset

CHCA: Why do people assume that choosing to be childfree automatically means that you won't have children in your life? My partner and I have decided not to have kids for a range of personal, environmental and social reasons. But I am a Godmother, an aunt, an older cousin, and a friend to many children. Contrary to common misconception those who choose not to have kids are rarely lonely, just more self-aware. In many cases those who choose not to have kids have usually thought a lot more about that decision than those who reproduce

DARE: Very, very well said. Clearly you have never had baby brain.

MACL: And conversely, in many cases those who choose to have children have thought a lot more about that decision than those who choose not to have children. We're an ageing society... And I think parents are pretty self-aware as our children's behaviour is reflected right back at us. For better or for worse.

GRKO: lets not forget those who would die to have kids of their own, but for one reason or another cant. . .

DARE: Agreed. The pity is there's no shortage of people who shouldn't have kids. Should almost have to take a pill TO have a kid.

SHHA: I think you have to want to amd be prepared for the challenge ahead. Those who dont have kids might have other goals they want to achieve good for them im not hating and I wouldnt change my life for anything my daughter did it for me amd I am grateful :)

---

it's only *potentially* relevant. Each time you spot *something* interesting or potentially relevant, tag it with a code label. Each time you encounter some text you want to code, consider whether an existing code applies, or you need to develop a new code.

> **PRACTICE POINT** Each time you notice something potentially relevant in your data, code it with an existing code, tweaked if necessary, or create a new code.

What might you *want to code*? We love sport psychologist Lisa Trainor's description of her approach to coding for her Master's research, which captured the idea of 'data of analytic interest' for us:

I approached coding as a 'consciously curious' researcher, attended to the athletes' stories, open to hearing (and reporting) different experiences than mine, and looking to connect the data and place it in the box of 'currently know' but also make sense of the 'unknown' data outside the box. (Trainor & Bundon, 2020, p. 9)

We coded each of the data items[9] in Box 3.2 in multiple ways, using a mix of semantic and latent codes (see Table 3.3). When you look at these, you'll probably note that sometimes our code labels here contain information in brackets and/or contain a forward slash with different ideas included in the code label – the label *superiority/hierarchy (childfree on top)* illustrates both points. We do this to signal codes that aren't yet fully clarified or where the exact scope of a code is not settled on; we do this when we're still evolving and refining our codes, which we typically do for much of the coding phase. Remember, code labels are *working tools* for us to parse the meaning we notice. We find this strategy useful for not feeling like we have to fix all our ideas or have analytic clarity on everything too early on. We also often retain some of these features in our final coding, as even final coding is still provisional, in the sense that there is no absolute end point to coding; there is always potential for new understandings.

Let's look at some semantic-level codes first. In CHCA's post, the codes *childfree can be for personal reasons, childfree can be for environmental reasons* and *childfree can be for social reasons* all relate to what is explicitly expressed by CHCA. They state they decided not to have children for a mix of reasons. Note, however, that the code label does not simply summarise this with a *mixed reasons for not having children* code, but instead parses each one out into a separate code. Furthermore, the label phrasing 'childfree can be for...' isn't what CHCA stated. This code labelling was deliberately chosen – even though it wasn't how we initially named the code. We evolved this code label throughout the coding process, and eventually settled on this precise language, because it allowed us to code a wider range of places where a reason for being childfree was discussed. For instance, CHCA talked about their *own* decisions; other posters wrote about *other people's* decisions. In the environmentally orientated code, for instance, any environmental explanation around (not) having children could be included, even oblique references to overpopulation (e.g. PAMA: "the world is so over populated already"). This demonstrates the value of open and organic coding and a thorough code revision process, to settle on useful codes that balance precision and inclusivity.

The example of PAMA's reference to "overpopulation" demonstrates the ways codes *can* capture both quite semantic and quite latent expressions of an idea – while CHCA explicitly links not having children to the environment, PAMA only obliquely references the idea that environmental considerations (connected by some to planetary population) might motivate or justify not having children. Some codes may solely capture a semantically or latently expressed meaning, but qualitative analysis works with *messy* data and, as noted earlier in the chapter, many codes are unlikely to be purely semantic or (to a lesser extent) purely latent.

What might a more purely latent code look like? Consider the code label *good/bad parents* related to DARE's second extract in Table 3.3. This offers a good example of the way code labels operate as analytic shorthand, capturing concisely an idea, without spelling out all the analytic thoughts contained by the code. It might appear that this captures semantic content – there is talk of 'good' parenting and 'bad' parenting in the dataset. But the code label actually signals something deeper – related to hierarchy and legitimacy around parenting. When coding the dataset, we noticed that people often made claims about good and bad

---

[9]We're treating each comment as a data item.

Table 3.3   A selection of childfree comments data with code labels

Data	Codes
CHCA: Why do people assume that choosing to be childfree automatically means that you won't have children in your life? My partner and I have decided not to have kids for a range of personal, environmental and social reasons. But I am a Godmother, an aunt, an older cousin, and a friend to many children. Contrary to common misconception those who choose not to have kids are rarely lonely, just more self-aware. In many cases those who choose not to have kids have usually thought a lot more about that decision than those who reproduce	Offspring are not the only children in people's lives Childfree by choice Childfree can be for personal reasons Childfree can be for environmental reasons Childfree can be for social reasons Compensatory kids Relationships with other kids The childfree more enlightened than parents (hierarchies) Parents (often) don't make deliberate choices/aren't thoughtful Childfree as a thought-out choice (kids as non-thoughtful action) Superiority/hierarchy (childfree on top) Logic/rationality trumps emotion
DARE: Very, very well said. Clearly you have never had baby brain.	Children destroy (women's) rationality Logic/rationality trumps emotion
MACL: And conversely, in many cases those who choose to have children have thought a lot more about that decision than those who choose not to have children. We're an ageing society... And I think parents are pretty self-aware as our children's behaviour is reflected right back at us. For better or for worse.	Parents (often) *do* make deliberate choices/are thoughtful Childfree as not thoughtful Parents as self-aware Superiority/hierarchy Society needs children (ageing society) Having children as investment for future Parents produce society of tomorrow
GRKO: lets not forget those who would die to have kids of their own, but for one reason or another cant. . .	Childfree isn't always a choice The 'real' victims are those who can't have kids Some people are desperate for kids Childfree are selfish? (because the real victims are those who want but can't have kids) Genetic relatedness and offspring are important
DARE: Agreed. The pity is there's no shortage of people who shouldn't have kids. Should almost have to take a pill TO have a kid.	Good/bad parents Social engineering/forced sterilisation/eugenics Many/some people shouldn't have kids (the ones who often do)
SHHA: I think you have to want to amd be prepared for the challenge ahead. Those who dont have kids might have other goals they want to achieve good for them im not hating and I wouldnt change my life for anything my daughter did it for me amd I am grateful :)	Each to their own but... Good/bad parents – being prepared/deliberate Kids are a challenge Gratitude for having kids/wouldn't change anything Childfree have other goals Kids are life-fulfilling

parents, creating a hierarchy that seemed to denaturalise the idea that we should all be parents, because only some people are 'fit' for the role. In the early analytic phases (familiarisation, coding), we were not quite sure what was going on with this, and whether it would be relevant. So we developed this code to capture our analytic *questioning* around a common pattern that seemed to underpin statements that contained quite *different* obvious semantic content. This operates as a *latent* code, because it is getting at some pattern or idea *beyond* the explicit or obvious meaning.

Another example of a latent code is the code labelled *compensatory kids* associated with CHCA's extract in Table 3.3. Many of the commenters described relationships with children in their lives who were not their biological children. The code labelled *relationships with other kids* captures this explicit or semantic expression. In contrast, the code *compensatory kids* captures our initial speculation that the commenters might somehow need to demonstrate that they are not emotionally cold-hearted child-haters, one of the negative stereotypes of childfree women, in particular (Hayfield et al., 2019; Rich et al., 2011). However, our analytic ideas developed even further with this code, captured by the word *compensatory* – as we worked through the dataset, it seemed as if not having children in your life suggested you might be in some way deficient as a human being. This analytic idea was, again, something we wanted to *explore*, but the ideas were still bubbling around, not yet very clearly formed; the label again succinctly summarised a bigger idea we were working with.

Both of these codes also help to illustrate the other code continuum discussed earlier in the chapter: from data-driven or *inductive* codes to researcher-driven or *deductive* codes. Although the code *good/bad parents* initially derived from the data, it reflected *our knowledge* of the parenting literature, the ways good and bad parents get constructed within society, and the work of legitimating and de-legitimation this does around parenting (Clarke, 2001; DiLapi, 1989). So the code captured an analytic idea that reflected *our* knowledge and skills, rather than more directly capturing meaning or interpretation as expressed by the commenters.

Similarly, the code *compensatory kids* captured an analytic idea that went beyond the data. While many non-parent commenters described relationships they had with other children, the code captured our analytic take around this as compensation – based in our knowledge that non-parents and non-normative family structures (e.g. single or lesbian parents) are often characterised as somehow deficient (Clarke et al., 2018; Lampman & Dowling-Guyer, 1995). The codes indicate that we want to do more with these data excerpts than just explore the semantic meaning – they hint at something deeper that can potentially offer important insight into how being childfree is made sense of (by those who are, as well as those who are not, childfree). As noted, at this stage, these analytic ideas are just that – *ideas* we're trying to capture through coding, to get a sense of potential prevalence and scope within the dataset, to assess whether they are worth exploring and developing further.

> **PRACTICE POINT** Coding is quite exploratory, especially earlier in the process. Keep all potentially relevant ideas 'in play' at this point, as you don't know what themes you will develop later.

At the other end of the inductive–deductive spectrum, codes related to choice, such as *childfree by choice* (CHCA) or *childfree isn't always a choice* (GRKO) (see Table 3.3) offer examples of more data-driven codes. The dataset was permeated with *explicit* references to choice, in all sorts of different ways. These quite semantic codes reflect a prominent pattern, immediately obvious to us on a first read. Even though there is scope to engage with choice in a more theoretical way (see for instance Figure 4.7 and Box 4.9 in Chapter Four), these codes capture the dominant *explicit* meanings around choice within the dataset.

These two continua – semantic to latent; data- to theory-driven – are aligned but not perfectly: more theoretical codes are often more latent; more inductive codes are more often semantic (see Table 1.2 in Chapter One). Remember, though, that these are continua.

Most importantly, remember that types of codes are not *real things*, but rather tools and devices that we use to develop our analytic insights. Understanding the process and purpose of coding, and recognising *how* you've engaged with your data – for instance, in a primarily deductive or latent way – through coding and theme development, are what's important for later writing up and producing a cohesive, high quality, reflexive TA (we focus specifically on quality and TA in Chapter Nine).

Actually wrangling data and codes: Technologies of coding

But what about actually *doing* coding? You can use all sorts of technologies – in the broadest sense – to code your data. Ranging from totally manual to entirely electronic, the way you can label data segments includes:

- Handwriting code labels *on* the printed data – it's helpful to print with wide margins to facilitate this. You need to indicate what bit of data the code relates to. You can do that with circles, underlining, highlighting, etc. – whatever works for you.
- Writing code labels on sticky notes and attaching those to printed data. Again, you need a way to clarify which bit of the data the code relates to.
- Writing each new code label on a hard-copy file card and clearly noting where to find each associated extract of data (and where each extract starts/ends).
- Typing the code label beside the data in an electronic version of the dataset formatted into a two-column table – as in Table 3.3.
- Using the *comment* box in Microsoft Word to select a section of text and tag it with a code label (Box 3.4 contains a handy hack, if coding in this way).
- Attaching electronic sticky notes to a PDF version of the dataset.
- Using one of the many software programmes specifically designed to assist coding and analysis of qualitative data, originally collectively referred to as **CAQDAS** (computer assisted qualitative data analysis software), and now often just **QDAS** (see Box 3.3).
- Finally, if you've collected data using an online data *collection* programme, such as SurveyMonkey, you may be able to electronically tag data with code labels within the programme itself.

The way you code intersects with all sorts of things, including circumstances and ability. If you're new to coding, and you have options, play around to find what works best for you. Don't automatically assume that (various) electronic ways are better than hardcopy modes, or vice versa. Each presents opportunities and challenges or constraints, intersected by your circumstances. For most of our careers, we used a manual, handwriting approach. This approach *worked* for each of us – no doubt *partly* because of our age and our training, but also because we have found we think and engage with data differently when we read it as hard copy compared to electronically. We also liked to leave the screen behind, and to code in all sorts of different spaces – which

PRACTICE POINT There is no best or ideal way to manage the practicalities of coding. Do whatever works best for you, but be mindful of the opportunities and constraints different coding technologies offer.

can bring subtly different things to the process. You might notice we're writing this in the past tense. That's because this has changed for Victoria recently, as she no longer has full use of her right hand (she is right-handed), necessitating a shift to coding electronically using voice recognition software. This has caused us to reflect more on these processes. We now consider our previous advocacy for manually coding – or at least learning to code manually before using software, if using software at all – as reflecting an ableist worldview that assumes all people have the same opportunities for, and processes of, engagement.

PRACTICE POINT You don't need to stick to one coding technology – you can shift between different tech. Again, we emphasise doing what works best for you.

How you start to do coding does not lock you into an unbreakable contract! It's possible to start with one approach and move to another (e.g. see Box 6.5 in Chapter Six and Box 7.1 in Chapter Seven). For instance, you might start with some hard-copy coding first, then develop your coding further using QDAS. You might start with QDAS and switch to comment functions in Microsoft Word. With a larger dataset, you might start some initial coding based on semantic content using QDAS and develop a fuller and more latent coding, with the full dataset or a subset of the dataset, using a different technology. What's best might change with our circumstances, with each project, or indeed *within* a project. Despite that, we find ourselves increasingly encountering the view that QDAS makes for better or at least more thorough or rigorous coding and analysis (see Box 3.3). To give some *different* perspectives, we also asked two colleagues who have used and teach QDAS in TA to reflect on this – see Boxes 3.4 and 3.5.

Box 3.3

Is using QDAS better than coding in other ways?

QDAS programmes have evolved over more than three decades to provide often-sophisticated tools to assist coding, code development, and even pattern-development. These programmes offer varied resources for (TA) coding and analysis – and some even allow for some (online) data collection (Silver & Bulloch, 2017). Does this mean they are the best way to code? We want to emphasise there is no decontextualised best way! We share some of the concerns raised by others, about the ways programmes have the potential to embed or implicitly validate certain assumptions around the purpose of qualitative research, which can shape your research practice or outputs (e.g. Zhao, Li, Ross, & Dennis, 2016). Some programmes reflect the early dominance of **grounded theory** (GT); reflexive TA and GT do not share processes or (necessarily) assumptions (Braun & Clarke, 2021a). The language in the promotional material can tell us much about how qualitative research is imagined, reflecting implicit research values. The NVivo website, for instance, states: "Unlock insights from your research: What is your data really trying to show you?" This quotation offers a realist, extractive model of research, where the data reveal their (singular) truth, a truth that exists in there, waiting for you to find it – if you have the right tools. NVivo's claims for speed and efficiency in analysis ("Connecting the dots in your data is faster, easier and more efficient with NVivo") position these as ideal in qualitative researching.

But this is at odds with deep and questioning engagement, and allowing plenty of *time* for reflection and insight to develop (Braun & Clarke, 2013, 2016, 2021d).

Advocates of QDAS have argued that while there are important questions we should be engaging with, related to critiques of distancing, standardisation, dehumanisation, quantification, and decontextualisation (e.g. Jackson, Paulus, & Woolf, 2018), these critiques are themselves often decontextualised. Furthermore, changes in what QDAS offers and facilitates have shifted their possibilities and limits. Without a thorough and conceptual sense of what the purpose and process of reflexive TA is, and without an understanding of the foundations, principles and process of the software we use, we do, however, fear there is a risk that analytic development and depth within reflexive TA can be foreclosed. This might be through an over-emphasis on highly stratified and detailed coding, through over-focus on very semantic, and obvious expression of meaning, or developing themes too early (Braun & Clarke, 2021c). Relatedly, we have concerns about the way the user-engagement with QDAS and the tools the programmes offer *can* risk framing qualitative analysis instrumentally, treating both analysis and the technology as a neutral tool or technique you *apply to* data – rather than an interpretative subjective and reflexive process and practice developed through *engagement with* data (Zhao et al., 2016). The shift in the acronym to QDAS – the disappearance of "computer assisted" – risks implicitly promoting a view of the technology as something that *does* the analysis for you, or allows you to do it, something we find problematic. QDAS provides tools, but analysis is a *process* of mind, and it is important to remember this (Evers, 2018). Useful questions for anyone using QDAS include: how do we challenge our ideas once we're getting comfortable with analysis, and how might we move away from the screen/programme and create space for different ways of data engagement (Jackson et al., 2018), and (therefore) different analytic possibilities? This is not just a question of QDAS versus manual modes, but could be about switching between different digital modalities of engagement – such as using voice recorders to make voice memo notes.

Of course, such questions are important for any developing analysis, regardless of QDAS use – as we'll continue to show.

Researcher Reflection – Box 3.4

Thematic analysis and QDAS, by Gareth Terry

My training as a qualitative researcher tended toward the old school, and I still prefer manual approaches when I do (reflexive) TA, and I have the capacity to code in this way. I have dabbled in the use of QDAS, and like many doctoral students, attended an NVivo workshop when it came to analysis time. I hoped that the software would enhance my analytic processes and reduce the time burden – instead I found the opposite. I enjoyed aspects of the software as a data management tool but found that my preference toward flexible coding was strongly curtailed by features of the programme. The node structure nudged me toward clustering much earlier than I would normally want, which had the effect of creating notable superficiality in my analysis. In other words, my use of the software, the way I interacted with it, worked *against* both the style of analysis that I had been trained in and my existing analytical craft skills. This may have been a

(Continued)

consequence of not fully understanding NVivo, or a constraint I imagined rather than something more tangible, but at the time I found it counterproductive.

My current orientation, and one I use with my students, is to focus on the craft skills of qualitative analysis, using QDAS products only insofar as they *support* existing ways of working and capabilities. I have found a happy medium, where I code using the comment function under the review tab in Microsoft Word. This means my preference for coding multiple facets of various data extracts is not constrained. A colleague (Duncan Babbage at the Auckland University of Technology) has helped develop a bespoke macro for Microsoft Word that can then turn these comment codes into a Microsoft Excel spreadsheet, where each code is listed alongside the data.[10] This mechanism, while 'computer aided', allows me levels of engagement with data that I am invested in, reducing the writing (and reading) burden, while also providing opportunities to present lists of codes and data for other members of a research team to easily access. I am definitely not opposed to QDAS in principle, as long as it facilitates good research practices (e.g. immersion in data and flexible and ongoing coding, without premature clustering).

Researcher Reflection – Box 3.5

On using NVivo, by Alexandra Gibson

I can chart my use, and subsequent views, of NVivo in much the same way as other aspects of my research journey – with elements of curiosity, exploration, and always a healthy dose of critical scepticism. Coming from a strong background in critical qualitative research (see Chapter Six), I had developed firm opinions about various analytical approaches. This was paired with undergoing my research training in a context where QDAS was virtually unheard of and an anathema. So during my PhD, I baulked when I heard about peers having to use NVivo in their work as research assistants – virtually a job requirement for those working in multi-disciplinary teams in health research. I felt wary about the ramifications for the role of the researcher-as-analyst, the loss of interpretation, and possibly even a standardising effect of boxing data into pre-defined units. I had also heard of tools, such as counting instances of words; it concerned me that quantification might take precedence over meaning and context.

It was only post-PhD when I was faced with analysing much larger qualitative datasets, involving upwards of 50–200 participants and projects spanning multiple sites, that I started to think that there might be some benefit in having a programme that could help to store and organise what could be an unwieldy amount of data. In that particular context, using NVivo can be very helpful, in that you can organise data files according to participant groups, method of collection, or study site, making the data feel more manageable at the start of analysis. Having all of your coding in one place and being able to more easily re-code extracts are advantages

---

[10]The macro is *not* currently publicly available. If it does become available, we'll provide a link to it from the companion website.

I have found with NVivo compared to coding by hand or in a Microsoft Excel spreadsheet. More recently, I was in a role where I had to facilitate NVivo training. My co-facilitator and I always spent considerable time emphasising the importance of some initial hand-coding (if you can, or using the comments function in Microsoft Word), reflexivity, interpretation, and theory. Yet, even while having taught students how to use this programme, I remain sceptical of certain functions and promises that NVivo offers and make it clear to others that analytic rigour comes from knowing the foundations of qualitative research, not from the touch of a few buttons in a programme.

Evolving your coding

Because of the organic nature of coding in reflexive TA, your codes will likely evolve as your analytic insight develops. You may decide your first code was a bit too precise or narrow, and want to make it a bit broader, to capture more related data extracts. If you're finding each code is *unique*, and there's little repetition or patterning starting to happen as you work your way through your dataset, your developing coding is likely too **fine-grained**, particular, and ultimately fragmented. You will need to look for ways to broaden your codes. For instance, we noted the *childfree can be for environmental reasons* code label earlier (see Table 3.3), which expanded from a narrower scope into a broader one – encompassing own and others' reasons, and not just focusing on a *particular* environmental reason (e.g. overpopulation).

Conversely, your codes may be *too* broad or general, and you may hone them to identify a range of meanings related to the same general concept. Take codes around 'choice' that we've already noted. Even in the few extracts shown in Table 3.3, there are different codes related to ideas about choice: *childfree by choice; parents (often) don't make deliberate choices/ aren't thoughtful; childfree as a thought-out choice (kids as non-thoughtful action)* (all from CHCA); *parents (often) do make deliberate choices/are thoughtful; childfree as not thoughtful* (both MACL); and *childfree isn't always a choice* (GRKO). The whole dataset contained yet further ideas and codes related to 'choice' (as we will go onto discuss in later chapters).

--- **Box 3.6** ---

Codes as building blocks for analysis

At the start of this chapter, we identified codes as the building blocks of your themes; we've often used an analogy of building a dwelling – say a stone house – to illustrate the relationship between codes, themes, and a final analysis. Codes are like the stones you would combine with other stones to build bigger things – walls, for instance (where walls are akin to themes). In coding, you're trying to identify all the different forms of stones you might need, from your big

(Continued)

pile, for the structure you're building. For the sake of our analogy, imagine you have a whole lot of stones, with quite different features. Initially, you identify the basic size differentials as important, and you start to separate them into piles by size – small, medium and large. But as you start to work with the stone, you notice all sorts of other variations. You realise other features, like shape, colour and texture will *also* be relevant to the walls you're about to build. And so your sorting process becomes more refined as you prepare for the build. You end up with *many* different piles, based around relevant differentiations in the stones. These many, many piles will set you up to build good strong walls in a systematic and coherent way. Coding is somewhat akin to this – it is about demarcating the variation in the dataset, in order to develop themes robustly based on clusters of pertinent similar meaning.

The issue of coding precision and capturing diversity of meaning also highlights the value of good familiarisation. We started our coding of the dataset knowing there were lots of different expressions around choice that we wanted to capture; we knew a single code around choice would not be enough. Sometimes familiarisation sets you up well for this task. Sometimes, the close work of coding leads to the refined noticing of meaning in the dataset,[11] and the refinement of codes. Other times, later analytic phases reveal a need for even further refinement around coding. The importance of acuity for difference and shared meaning developed through coding is illustrated by the analogy in Box 3.6.

Refining your coding through multiple rounds

You systematically work your way through the dataset, more than once, when coding, to ensure rigour. Sometimes, you might refine codes across multiple data items 'as you go': "as I continued coding the interviews, I moved back and forth between interviews, making notes on previous interviews as well as the interview I was currently coding" (Trainor & Bundon, 2020, p. 9). But don't be haphazard! Be systematic and thorough. Because possible analytically-interesting meanings evolve *through* the coding process, we recommend going through your dataset *at least* twice, to ensure this process is thorough and rigorous – and there may be further value in additional coding 'runs'. It depends on how close and deep you get initially. We recommend that with each different coding run, you go through the dataset in a different order. If you have 20 data items, for instance, your first coding run might start with item 1 and work sequentially through each data item, finishing with item 20. For your second run, maybe start in the middle of the dataset (e.g. data item 10) and work

PRACTICE POINT Do at least two rounds of coding – to capture evolutions in your codes and coding labels – and vary the order in which you code the data items – to give you a fresh perspective on your dataset.

___

[11]As we noted in Chapter Two, the phrasing 'noticing of meaning in the dataset' does *not* imply the meaning is just there waiting to be found.

'backwards' – initially towards item 1, and then from item 20 down, finishing on item 11. We recommend mixing up the coding order for two reasons: (1) disrupting what can become a familiar 'flow' for the dataset; and (2) as your coding will continue to be refined, changing the order means certain (later) data items don't get a doubling up of extra depth of insight, while earlier ones miss out – risking an unevenly coded dataset.

Coding is never completed, because meaning is never final; you could (in theory) always notice something more or different in the dataset. In reflexive TA, you aim to reach a point at which you decide it's time to adventure forth to the next phase of your journey. At this point, in

> **PRACTICE POINT**   There isn't an absolute endpoint for coding – you make a subjective judgement about when to stop.

preparation for the next phase, you collate together all your codes (and relevant coded data). If you want an example of this, flick forward to Table 4.1 in Chapter Four. The data extracts for each of the codes illustrate how a code label tags similar but not identical content, similar but diverse articulations of the code (including some that are semantic and some latent).

Can I stop coding yet?

How do you know if you're at the point when it is time to stop coding? Coding can be alluring – it can draw you in, and make you want to stay. It can tempt you to feel you *need* to go on coding, *ad infinitum*. Although it's important to be thorough, remember coding is only an *early stage* in the analytic process. You are not trying to get at everything that you will say about the dataset at this stage, or even develop the analysis. You're still effectively in the preparation stages. You're trying to parse out a whole range of possible meanings and ideas, which you'll then look at combining and evolving, and sometimes rejecting, as you develop your TA.

So when do you know your codes and code labels have done a *good enough* job of capturing and differentiating diverse meaning? Once you've gone through the dataset thoroughly a couple of times, and refined and finalised your code labels and checked coding for consistency and thoroughness, you're probably in a good position to stop – especially as you know you can come back to coding, if you need to.

> **PRACTICE POINT**   If you've reached the point when you're just tweaking your codes and coding labels, perhaps even over-tweaking, you've probably reached the point when it's time to stop and move on to theme development.

There's no absolute test for whether your reflexive TA coding is *good enough*, but we have found an exercise we call 'take away the data' useful for our students, to test both their developing coding and whether the code labels do a good job of capturing meaning (Terry, Hayfield, Clarke, & Braun, 2017). Imagine you had compiled all your code labels, but lost your dataset (Meth, 2017) – gaahh! Look at your list of code labels and ask whether they provide you with a summary of the *diversity* of meanings contained in the dataset? Do they also provide some indication of your analytic take on things? This activity should illustrate clearly why a code label 'choice', mentioned above, would be a weak code and doesn't do what it needs to do. It doesn't parse out the diversity of meaning *in* the dataset, and it doesn't provide any indication of why or how you might have been interested in choice. If your code labels similarly don't deliver, you need to do more coding refinement before moving on. But if they do, you've probably done a good job of coding. Another way to look at this activity is to ask: can I make sense of the meaning richness, diversity and any contradiction in the dataset through the codes *alone*? This is important, because that is exactly how you start building your themes – initially working with the codes, not the full dataset.

CHAPTER SUMMARY

We have done two primary things in this chapter: (1) discussed key principles and concepts of coding for reflexive TA; and (2) discussed and illustrated the *process* of coding. We highlighted the way coding in reflexive TA is a process, with codes and code labels an outcome, a product, of the coding process. Moreover, coding is an organic and evolving process, capturing an interweaving of the knowledge, subjectivity and analytic skill of the researcher, engaging closely and systematically with the dataset. We discussed and illustrated the ways codes and coding can be more or less inductive ↔ deductive and semantic ↔ latent. We explored different technologies for coding and emphasised that no matter what technology you use, your thinking, your subjectivity and your analytic insights are the driving force of coding. Even though this is still effectively 'preparatory' work, by the end of coding you should feel that you're getting yourself ready for the theme development part of your adventure.

WANT TO LEARN MORE ABOUT...?

For a detailed worked discussion of **coding in reflexive TA**, see: Terry, G. (2021). Doing thematic analysis. In E. Lyons & A. Coyle (Eds.), *Analysing qualitative data in psychology* (3rd ed., pp. 148–161). London: SAGE.

For all things **QDAS**, see the University of Surrey's Computer Assisted Qualitative Data Analysis (CAQDAS) networking project: www.surrey.ac.uk/computer-assisted-qualitative-data-analysis.

For a **critical and reflective evaluation** of such software, see: Zhao, P., Li, P., Ross, K., & Dennis, B. (2016). Methodological tool or methodology? Beyond instrumentality and efficiency with qualitative data analysis software. *Forum Qualitative Sozialforschung/Forum: Qualitative Social Research, 17*(2). www.qualitative-research.net/index.php/fqs/article/view/2597.

ACTIVITIES FOR STUDENT READERS

Coding your own dataset: This activity works with the same *men and healthy eating* dataset you worked with in Chapter Two, downloadable from the companion website. Once you've completed familiarisation, you're ready to start this coding activity. Remember your research question is 'How is healthy eating for men represented online?'

- Systematically work through all four data items, following the coding processes outlined.
- Compile a list of all the code labels you have identified. For each, list the data items associated with each.
- Examine the list to determine that codes in general are evident across more than one data item, and to identify similarities, overlaps, or inconsistencies, that might benefit from refinement.
- Go back and recode the dataset, in reverse data item order, making any adjustments necessary.
- Compile a list of final code labels. For each, list the data items associated with each.

If you're teaching content related to this chapter…
Don't forget to check the companion website for a range of teaching resources:
https://study.sagepub.com/thematicanalysis

4

FINDING, LOSING, THEN FINDING YOUR WAY AGAIN

DEVELOPING YOUR THEMES

Chapter Four overview

- **Understanding the *key* concept: What is this thing called a theme?**   **76**

  o In reflexive TA, a topic summary is not a theme   77
  o In reflexive TA, a theme captures shared meaning, united
    by a central organising concept   77

- **Generating initial themes (Phase three)**   **78**

  o Developing initial themes from your codes   79
  o Using visual mapping for theme generation, development and review   85
  o Five key things to keep in mind in the early stages of theme development   88
  o I quite like it here, should I stay longer? Tackling time
    management in (initial) theme development   92

- **I'm struggling a bit to be honest: Managing anxiety in the TA process**   **92**
- **Developing and reviewing themes (Phase four)**   **97**

  o Theme development and revision with coded extracts   98
  o Theme development and revision with the full dataset   100
  o What's the point of this part of my adventure?   102
  o Okay so how would a topic summary be different from a
    shared meaning theme?   104
  o But what about contradiction?   107

- **Precision matters: Refining, defining and naming themes (Phase five)**   **108**

  o Naming themes   111

Aha, you might think, we're finally about to get to the good stuff – the *real* analysis! This is, indeed, the point at which you shift the scale of your focus, back out from the micro detailed scope of the coding process, towards exploring, at a more macro scale, for connections and alliances that might develop into broader patterns of meaning. Ultimately, your whole dataset will be your focus. We find it useful to conceptualise TA as a process in which your closeness to the dataset needs to shift and change, moving very close in, focusing on the micro, and moving further out, shifting to a wider lens. This isn't a unidirectional movement, but shifts in and out across the analytic phases.

To come back to our adventure analogy. Imagine you'd planned something big, bold and somewhat daunting as a highlight of your travels – what that might be will vary depending on your own circumstances. Starting theme development is like being at the point it's about to begin: what comes ahead is unknown, super exciting, and maybe slightly terrifying. The quality and comprehensiveness of your preparation thus far will be important for how well these next phases go. The analytic work you've already done – the data preparation, the familiarisation, the coding, the reflexive journaling – is akin to adventure preparation, such as ensuring you've got strong hiking boots that are fully worn in (if your adventure involves hiking), or robust new tyres on your all-terrain mobility scooter (if your plan involves an off-road scooter expedition). Unfortunately, there is no simple cause and effect, however – excellent coding doesn't automatically lead to an easy process of theme development; unexpected twists and turns are part of the process. You might hit really bad weather that turns your chosen route into a bog that your scooter cannot navigate. You might sprain an ankle and need to pause progress on your hike for some days to let it heal. Disaster? Not necessarily, if you're prepared for things to not go completely smoothly. The unexpected is part of adventuring, as it is part of reflexive TA. Using a hiking analogy, that means taking enough supplies that a sprained ankle doesn't mean you run out of food.

What is one of the most helpful tools for making your TA adventure as good as it can be? Allowing yourself enough time! The adventure *will* take longer than you anticipate. It'll probably take at least *twice* as long as you expect. Given all that you and others (e.g. any participants) have invested to get here, you need to make sure you have time to do the experience justice. Such advice isn't to put you off – but to allow you to do justice to the potential offered by the method, and by your data.

> **PRACTICE POINT** Aim to give yourself twice as much time for theme development as you expect you might need.

For reflexive TA, you need to be psychologically ready for a rich, unexpected, sometimes frustrating, but ultimately achievable adventure. So, let the adventure continue!

UNDERSTANDING THE *KEY* CONCEPT: WHAT IS THIS THING CALLED A THEME?

Your analytic focus now shifts from codes to themes. But what *is* a theme? Simple, we thought, when first writing about TA: a theme captures the *patterning* of meaning across the dataset (Braun & Clarke, 2006). Except it's not quite so simple. Even if you just look across those who write about and use TA, there are some quite *different* conceptualisations of themes in TA (see Chapter Eight). For reflexive TA, a theme has to capture a wide range of data that are united by, and evidence, a *shared* idea, sometimes quite obviously, and sometimes far less obviously, and sometimes in quite different ways. We have variously called these 'shared meaning', 'conceptual pattern' or 'fully developed' themes; often we have simply called them *themes*, which we will do in this book. Before you get into theme generation and development, the distinction between themes and another conceptualisation of 'themes' – which we call topic summaries – is *fundamental* to understand.

In reflexive TA, a topic summary is not a theme

A **topic summary** is a summary of everything the participants said about a particular **topic**, presented as a theme. One of the main problems with topic summaries for us, and for reflexive TA, is that they unite around a *topic*, rather than a shared meaning or idea. Topic summary 'themes' from the childfree dataset would be something like *reasons for being childfree* or *perceptions of people who choose not to have children*. The topic summary conceptualisation of a theme is prevalent in practice – especially in some other forms of TA. But they are also presented as themes by people who say they're doing *reflexive* TA (Braun & Clarke, 2021c). For this reason, we have given an example of what a topic summary *might* look like, to highlight *what not to do* in reflexive TA (see Box 4.6). As topic summaries capture the *range* of responses around a particular issue, they potentially contain quite different and even contradictory data. A topic summary around *reasons for being childfree* might include environmental, psychological, emotional, financial, and many other different reasons (see Box 4.6). What can you conclude from such a 'theme'? Simply that there

> **ALERT** A topic summary – whereby you report all the different responses or meanings around a topic in the dataset – would not count as a theme for reflexive TA.

are varied reasons people have for choosing not to have children, and what some of these are. That might be useful to know, but it's not the analysis that reflexive TA *should* result in!

In reflexive TA, a theme captures shared meaning, united by a central organising concept

In reflexive TA, with themes defined by meaning-unity and conceptual coherence, each theme has its own distinct **central organising concept** (Braun, Clarke, & Rance, 2014). Your analytic

> **ALERT** A theme in reflexive TA is a pattern of shared meaning organised around a central concept.

task is to explore the expression of shared or similar ideas or meanings, across different contexts. Sometimes this united-pattern might be evidenced at a quite semantic or concrete

---

[1] The theme *compensatory kids* is an example of a code label being reworked as a theme name. In this case, that code label captured the core idea – central organising concept – of the developed theme, which included more codes than just *compensatory kids*.

KEY CONCEPT   A central organising concept is the idea or meaning that unites a theme.

level. Sometimes it might be more conceptual or latent. Conceptual pattern themes from the childfree dataset include *it's making a choice that's important* or *compensatory kids*.[1] These themes are conceptual because they dig down below surface meaning, and are united around an idea that isn't necessarily obviously evident in the data. We explain both of these themes further in this chapter, and in Chapters Five and Seven.

As the level at which you're exploring shared meaning can vary dramatically, some themes might contain data extracts that *on the surface* appear quite dissimilar. And indeed,

PRACTICE POINT   A contradiction in, or dichotomisation of, meaning can form the basis for a theme.

a contradiction or dichotomisation *might* form the basis for a theme itself, if the theme focuses *on* that dichotomisation; if that contradiction *is* the pattern (see 'But what about contradiction' and Box 4.7 later in this chapter).

Understanding that basic definition and distinction, it's time to move on to the theme development phases. In these phases, you start to build alliances and networks between codes, to explore shared-meaning patterns. In doing so, keep in mind your research question. As a reminder, for our worked example, our research question is – broadly – *what is the nature of contemporary meaning-making around voluntarily not having children?* (as discussed in the section 'What's my purpose here? Settling on a research question' in Chapter Two).

GENERATING INITIAL THEMES[2] (PHASE THREE)

We've often suggested the idea of a sculptor is a useful analogy for the process of TA – where the sculptor uses their creative thinking and craft skills, and engages with the potential of the 'raw' materials (data), making choices and working to shape a final product. A creative-process analogy usefully evokes the various constraints and possibilities in the analytic process:

- The skills the person has, in working with their material(s);
- The personal positioning, knowledge, and traditions they bring to the process;
- The limits the initial materials place on the possibility for the final product – not *everything* is possible;
- That a *range* of outcomes are, however, possible. There is no single correct end-point, no destination. You might end up somewhere quite different from where you started; and
- That the quality of the end-product can vary, quite considerably.

---

[2]In our original TA paper (Braun & Clarke, 2006), we called Phase three *searching for themes*. It's become clear that the word 'searching' – which we imagined as an active engaged process – risks evoking theme development as akin to fishing, where you catch something that's there already (and, in the case of fishing, unlucky enough not to escape), or to archaeology, where you 'uncover' some hidden and pre-existing treasure. Where 'searching' risks suggesting that theme development is a fairly passive, extractive process (Braun & Clarke, 2019a), generating does not.

In terms of thinking about exploring, developing, reviewing and refining themes (this phase, and the next two), we like the sense of 'finding, losing, and finding your way again' that an *adventure* evokes. To come back to our earlier example of an off-road scooting adventure: imagine you're trying to reach a mountain pass, the way is unmarked, and there are differ-ent potential routes through, or ways to tackle, the task. No matter where you start, getting to the top involves a whole series of choices, some of which will get you there, but many of which will lead you in impassable directions, or on long side-tracks. There's no one *right* route to the end; getting there inevitably has some hiccups, and backtracking, as well as some fairly straightforward passages. This scenario evokes not just the messiness, the uncer-tainty and tentativeness of analysis, but also the freedom, creativity, playfulness (and indeed *excitement*) of analysis. Analysis is a constrained-but-open process in reflexive TA. So when starting theme development, try to hold onto the *possibility* contained in the question *where will this journey take me?* rather than the more pragmatic and destination-orientated *how do I get to my endpoint?*

> **PRACTICE POINT** In theme generation and development, focus on the process, the journey, not the destination.

We call this phase *generating initial themes* to emphasise that it's generative and part of the theme development *process*, but also that you're still early on. In this phase, your analysis *starts* to take a form, as you shift analytic attention from smaller meaning units – codes – to larger meaning patterns – themes. As the form of your analysis will likely change quite a lot as you progress further, it pays not to get too attached to these early themes.

> **PRACTICE POINT** Don't get too attached to early-developed themes.

Developing initial themes from your codes

What does this phase involve, practically? It involves a range of processes of engaging with the data codes to explore areas where there is some similarity of meaning. Then cluster-ing together the potentially connected codes (into candidate themes), and exploring these initial meaning patterns. This exploration considers each cluster: on its own terms; in relation to the research question; and as part of the wider analysis. Key to remember at this stage is that you are exploring clustered patterning *across* your dataset – not just within a *single* data item. So even if you have one data item or participant who expresses an idea repeatedly, if it's not evident in *any other* data item, it probably isn't the basis for a *theme* in TA.[3] That's not to say it's not interesting, but the point here is to discuss patterned meaning.

> **KEY CONCEPT** A candidate theme is an initial clustering of codes and a potential theme – one that requires further exploration before it can be considered a more settled theme.

---

[3]Reflexive TA calls for *in situ* assessments about the 'themeyness' of a potential pattern, and sometimes there *might* be patterned meaning within only one or two data items that, in the context of the dataset, the research question, and the wider context of the research, warrants focus and possibly becomes a theme.

The initial way to explore patterned meaning is to consider all the codes (collated at the end of Phase two, see Table 4.1), and explore whether there are any broad ideas that a number of different codes could be clustered around. For an example of this early clustering, see Figure 4.1. Lisa Trainor, a doctoral student in sport and exercise psychology at the University of British Columbia, posted this on Twitter. We loved it so much as an illustration of her process, we asked if we could share it in the book.[4] In starting to develop candidate themes, remember that themes capture multiple facets of an idea or concept – whereas codes capture a single facet or idea. These multiple facets all need to contribute to the same core idea or central organising concept. This means you're trying to cluster codes into broader patterns that are coherent, and meaningfully tell you something important and relevant in relation to your research question.

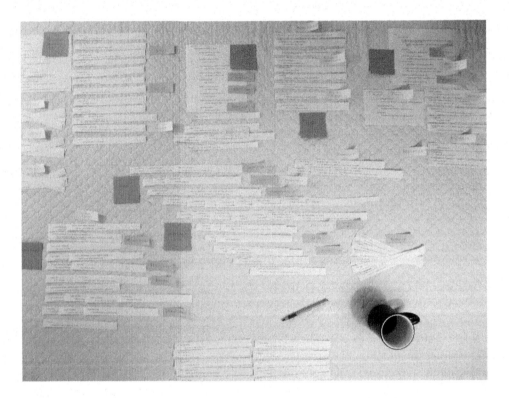

Figure 4.1 Coding and initial theme development with a cup of coffee (photo courtesy Lisa Trainor)

Depending how narrowly or broadly you have coded, the number of codes you combine into potential themes will likely vary. If your coding is more fine-grained, you'll usually be working with more already-identified variation as you develop your themes. But don't conflate overly-**fine-grained coding** with more conceptual depth; such coding can

---

[4]This image of coding has since been published in a reflexive methodology paper, with many more useful images of Lisa's reflexive TA process (Trainor & Bundon, 2020).

remain superficial. Sometimes, you may have coded something complex at a quite broad level, and this often happens if an idea is complex, and you're still working out what you want to do with it. It is often the case that trying to *refine* your coding at that point is futile, because the meaning you're interested in becomes *more* apparent as the analytic phases progress. In our experience, codes that we get a bit stuck on often relate to a conceptual idea or something more latent – such as the *good/bad parents* code in the childfree dataset (see Table 4.1; an extended version of this table is on the companion website).

In theme generation and development, you may occasionally decide that one of these broader and nuanced codes seems like it might *actually* be a theme. There is a core idea, but also variation. In such instances, it's perfectly reasonable to 'promote' a rich or complex code to a candidate theme.[5] This reinforces the point we made in our 'Scene setting' opening chapter: that with reflexive TA, we aim to provide practical guidelines for robustly doing what really is a conceptual *process*. Understanding what the process is about provides the foundation for a conceptually coherent practice, rather than rigid rule-following. Repeat after us: these phases are not rules!

> **ALERT** Once you have a sound understanding of the conceptual foundations of the process of reflexive TA, you will have more confidence to bend or break what might feel like 'rules' for good practice.

As we worked with the codes from our childfree dataset, we started to explore a number of different clusters. We tried to generate ones that might be relevant to our analysis of *the nature of contemporary meaning-making around voluntarily not having children*. We'll illustrate this with four – quite different – code clusters/candidate themes:

1. A cluster around choice was an obvious one – so many codes and extracts either explicitly referenced choice or evoked the concept of choice in some way. In the codes and coded data in Table 4.1, choice is expressed in the code *each to their own*. Similarly, data related to the *absence* of choice seems relevant to understanding choice around parenting and non-parenting, so the code *the 'real' victims are those who can't have kids* was also included in this clustering, alongside other codes connected to choice.

2. We started to feel that there were some interesting meanings clustering around the notion that people are missing out in some way, if they aren't a parent. For this, we started to cluster together a wide range of codes that spoke to quite different elements of missing out. This included the *fur babies* code, as well as *other kids in my life* (see Table 4.1) – such codes seem to evoke a sense of compensations for an absence created by not being a parent. Another code that appeared to relate here was the articulation of *kids as the ultimate* (also in Table 4.1). Such data seemed, to us, to speak to an idea that *nothing* can truly compensate for what people miss, if they don't have children.

3. We were interested in a number of ideas that related to some kind of differentiation between good and bad parents. The code *bad parents* (Table 4.1) was included here, as was the code *good parents*. And, naturally, the code discussed in Chapter Three, *good/bad parents* (see Table 3.3).

4. We felt that there seemed to be a potential pattern around social responsibility – or possibly social *and* environmental responsibility – and having children, or not having children. We clustered a number of different codes together (e.g. *environmental benefit/overpopulation* in Table 4.1) to explore a theme around this aspect of the dataset.

---

[5]The promotion of codes to a theme happens in other analytic processes too, such as grounded theory and IPA (Charmaz, 2014; J. A. Smith, Flowers, & Larkin, 2009).

Table 4.1 A selection of code labels and collated data extracts

Code	Example data extracts
Each to their own	*META*: People should just respect other's choices, we all choose our own paths.
	FIMA: Why do people think it's selfish not having children? It's no one else's business!!
	SARO: Some people are child orientated, others aren't. Its as simple as that
	JOWI: My husband and I chose not to have children and have never regretted this decision. The majority of our friends have no children and we all have brilliant fulfilled lives. It is a personal choice, respect it!
	GLSH: Isn't it funny how most of the judgemental comments seem to be coming from people with kids. I cannot understand why we cannot all respect each others decisions, each to their own I say.
	ALBR: Good on ya if you have kids and good on ya if you don't!
	ANMA: Not my uterus, not my business!
The 'real' victims are those who can't have kids	*MIBE*: I feel for those men and women who really want children but can't have them.
	JOBR: Um [SUST] some of us would love to have the choice
	BRDU: There are folks who would love to have children but nature is against them. Having science to intervene can be ok if u can afford it but for others just take things in their stride and enjoy the company of nieces and nephews which means a lot. I am ok with this and we just have each other me and my guy.
	GRKO: lets not forget those who would die to have kids of their own, but for one reason or another cant. . .
	WAFL: Some couples can't have kids; no choice involved, it's just fate...
	REMA: Each to there own really, and sometimes you don't have a choice.
Fur babies	*DEBA*: My partner and I have been together 32 years - no children and we both love it! We are not shrivelled up selfish misfits! we have fur babies who we love to bits but who don't limit our enjoyment of the things we love doing.
	RADE: ...I have a kitten called Fanta and she is my furbaby and she adores my partner to pieces also. When he comes over to see me she will run to him and purr.
	MAWA: Didnt like them when i was one. Most people.. i know with them wish they didnt. Fur babies better... will never tell you they hate you then expect you to hand over money.
	MSND: They Probably are dog or cat owners thinking they are parents to them both because that's their children Lols

Code	Example data extracts
Other kids in my life	*CHCA*: Why do people assume that choosing to be childfree automatically means that you won't have children in your life? My partner and I have decided not to have kids for a range of personal, environmental and social reasons. But I am a Godmother, an aunt, an older cousin, and a friend to many children.
	ANWH: My partner and I decided long ago we didnt want kids. I have nieces I love to bits but I still dont want my own kids. Ive seen people have kids and regret it and others who have them and dont regret it so I say each to their own.
	RADE: ... I love children and I volunteer at the YMCA two mornings a week. I also have two wonderful nephews and a niece as well and adoption is out of the question ...
	BEJO: At 42 we don't have kids and wouldn't change it. Love my nephews but love I can give them back.
	KAHA: My husband and i dont have kids and dont want kids. We're happy being the aunty and uncle who buys the cool gifts.
Kids as the ultimate	*CALO*: By choosing not to have children, you're depriving yourself of the greatest love of all.
	TRBA: I think its absolutely a personal choice . If you choose to have kids that's great. Its the hardest and most wonderful thing I've ever done .
	JAFO: I didn't want kids. Didn't like babies. No interest at all. Ended up with 3 gorgeous sons. 2 not exactly planned... All within 4 1/2 years. Am incredibly grateful. Feel for people that don't get to experience that sort of love.
	JOAS: I never wanted kids... Then my first was born.. He was so perfect , such a miracle that I made a human wow! I thought I knew love but he showed me what it really felt to love someone with all the love I had. Now I have three and as stressful as it can be it's amazing. I am never lonely , I'm loved everyday, I have a purpose in life. Sure it would be great to be rich but love is worth more than any material object on earth. I didn't want kids but I'm glad I accidentally got pregnant. It's one if those things you don't know what you were missing until you have it :-)
	RAIS: As a lot of people said , it's everyone's choice . We have one 4 year old and that's the best gift we ever had. She comes before anyone. We put our life on hold to take care of her needs and absolutely love it. That's what's our parents did for us and theirs for them. We believe in unconditional love and sacrifices and that creates very strong family bond. As for some said kids are waste of money, that saddens me. To my wife and I, the love we get from our daughter is priceless. All the money we make we spend a whole lot of it on our daughter, our parents and family members who have hard lives. Maybe that's why God gives us more and blesses us with happiness.

(Continued)

Table 4.1 (Continued)

Code	Example data extracts
Bad parents	*SHHO*: Itz a choice, y ave kidz if u cnt aford them. Too many hungry children goin to skool without food.
	MIBE: There are so many amazing parents out there. Sadly there are also some appalling parents out there. My only judgement on the world is that I wish more men and women would give themselves a warrant of fitness before becoming a parent. It's such a huge responsibility, and it's for a very long time.
	JAOB: I love my children, but they have always been loved and cared for, fed, clothed and taught well. This is not always the case
	BRMA: better not to have kids than have trophy kids and dump them in childcare from 7am to 6pm every day and then say I'm too busy to come to special events. Poor sprogs, selfish parents
	NAMI: It's selfish to spread your legs and expect everyone else to pay for your kids through welfare!!! Why should I pay for someone else's kids when I choose not to have any of my own. I'm tired of being taxed and seeing it go to someone who doesn't deserve it ...
Environmental benefit/ overpopulation	*ELBR*: I think that there is beauty in children, their innocence, the love of life, and the knowledge that the children are the future of the world. But we also are in a world where we face overpopulation in many countries. It takes a balance of people having children, and people choosing not to have kids to ensure the survival of our planet.
	RITA: 5.3billon humans on this planet putting it under so much pressure.....so really...who's being selfish
	SIMA: The world has far too many people! Good on those who don't want kids they should be applauded.
	TESI: This planet is far to over populated ADOPT if you feel the need

We really want to emphasise the provisionality here. You're effectively *trying things out*, to ascertain how they feel – kind of like an initial scouting of different routes up to that mountain pass. Our four clusterings could have been made in different ways, even with the same research question. For instance, with our fourth clustering, a narrower cluster might have focused *just* around the environment.

This is still early in the initial theme development process, but it is important to consider the value of your developing analysis at this point in Phase three. Your aim here is to generate a number of working, provisional themes, and consider the story they allow you to tell about your dataset, to address your research question. Good themes are distinctive and, to some extent, stand-alone. This means that, in theme generation, each theme needs to be assessed on its own merit. We discuss this in more depth in the next phase of theme development and review, but note here some useful theme-evaluation questions:

- Does this provisional theme capture something meaningful?
- Is it coherent, with a central idea that meshes the data and codes together?
- Does it have clear boundaries?

As, ultimately, your themes need to work together as a whole to tell a coherent story, you also need to begin to assess themes in relation to the *overall* story the analysis tells.

Using visual mapping for theme generation, development and review

We find using a visual mapping technique – drawing **thematic maps**, either by hand or electronically – very useful, both as a general analytic practice and in three specific ways: (1) for starting to think about provisional themes in their own right; (2) for exploring how provisional themes might relate to each other; and (3) for starting to consider the overall story of your analysis.

KEY CONCEPT Thematic maps capture visual or figurative representation of potential themes, and relationships between themes.

The map in Figure 4.2 presents a way of charting patterned meanings to help identify potential themes and **subthemes**, with interconnections between different recurrent features of the data. You'll note it's slightly

KEY CONCEPT Subthemes share a key concept with the theme of which they are a part.

evolved from the initial four clusterings we just described. In our initial making sense of the data, we kept coming back to a range of quite different aspects. We wanted to explore how all these would work together, or not, in telling a story about the data. In this thematic map, we have three 'core' ideas or provisional themes, captured within central circles: (1) choice rulz ok; (2) you're missing out without kids; and (3) kids and socially responsible actions. Alongside these, two closely connected potential themes were: (1) kids bring personal gains and (2) gains in/for society.[6] You'll notice there's a lot going on – we reproduced Ginny's hand-drawn version to emphasise that messiness is okay![7] That's pretty much what this phase is about, starting to make sense of a range of different ways of clustering the data.

You should notice in Figure 4.2, that there are what appear to be smaller or more specific patterns of meaning, generally contained within straight-sided shapes (mostly rectangles). These are possible subthemes. In navigating this messiness, mapping provides a tool to start exploring possible *layers* within your analysis. In TA, the primary focus is the theme, and your main task is identifying patterning at the theme level, and telling a rich, interpretative, contextualised story

---

[6]Just as provisional are the names we've used in Figure 4.2 for these early candidate themes. Theme names are refined in Phase five.

[7]For a *tidier* hand-drawn example of a thematic map, see Trainor and Bundon (2020).

ALERT Don't slice your analysis too finely: more layers of theme level do not usually make a better analysis; indeed, they often mean a thinner, poorer and underdeveloped one.

ALERT Subthemes should be used judiciously rather than as a matter of course in TA.

about these patterns. Your aim is not to develop a highly particularised, multi-layered model demarcating meaning, sub-meaning, sub-sub-meaning, and so forth. That said, some judicious use of subthemes might sometimes help to frame and tell your story in the most meaningful way. They might, for instance, help highlight salient elements of a theme – salience being determined in relation to the topic and wider analytic context, rather than simple frequency. For reflexive

TA, we recommend never more than three layers in total, organised *around* the themes; these are described in Box 4.1.

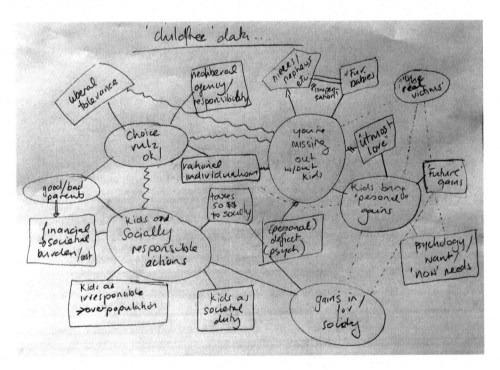

Figure 4.2 An initial mapping of patterns across childfree dataset

Thematic maps are working documents to help *you* figure out patterns of meaning, and possible connections, interconnections, and disconnections. The different lines in Figure 4.2 – wavy, dotted, straight single or occasionally double, straight with arrows, even straight with a two-intersecting-lines mark, akin to a does *not* equal sign – are intended to convey this alive and in-process aspect. The different types of lines are our way of signalling, *to ourselves*, that we feel there are different types of relationships between candidate themes and subthemes.

At this stage, it's all tentative, and we don't have a full sense of what's going on, and whether it matters (or, even, whether much of this will make it into our final analysis). But it's useful to have a visual reminder for ourselves to *think about* relationships, and the different forms of relationship we've started to conceptualise. In the early stages of mapping, you might use few if any lines. There are no rules here. Remember, mapping is a tool for *you* to use to develop your analytic understanding, and so you should do it in the ways that best suit you.

The mapping in Figure 4.2 might give you the impression that we had lots of ideas about potential themes (and subthemes) and indeed what a possible (final) analysis *might* look like. If you're thinking we had started to anticipate and shape the overall final analysis at this point in the process, stop right there! Everything was still *up for grabs* at that point. That said, one aspect we have noted in relation to mapping potential themes (and subthemes) when working with data, is that with more conceptually or theoretically orientated versions of reflexive TA, patternings *might* seem clearer or stronger or just more visible, earlier in the process. With more inductive, descriptive or semantic versions, the shape of the analysis *may* be harder to pin down. With more conceptually-driven analysis, our *story* of the dataset (which we report in our write up; discussed in Chapter Five) can start to take form earlier – as the theoretical 'take' shapes and delimits the analytic possibilities more so than an inductive reading of the data.

■■■■■■■■■■■■■■■■ **Box 4.1** ■■■

Theme levels in reflexive TA

Themes are the core analytic concept and focus in reflexive TA, but there are times when some additional structuring can add interpretative depth or clarity. Reflexive TA reports patterned meaning at three different levels, which we call **overarching themes**, themes and subthemes.

An *overarching theme* is like an umbrella concept or idea that embraces a number of themes. The point of an overarching theme is to demonstrate some broader conceptual idea that you identify as anchoring a number of themes together – in a way that goes *beyond* the central organising concept of each (see Braun & Clarke, 2021e). For instance, as we developed our analysis, we held choice as a potential overarching theme (see Box 4.9), since there seemed to be some different – but potentially related – choice themes. It's not typical for reflexive TA to report overarching themes, and they're not something to *aspire* to, as you develop your TA. We think it's useful to think of them as some extra additional contextual information, where relevant: a footnote, rather than the main text. If you use an overarching theme, you don't necessarily discuss or evidence this in great detail in your analytic narrative; it's more of a structuring or organisational device.

The *theme*, capturing the multi-faceted manifestations of a single, central concept from the dataset, is the key analytic unit in reflexive TA. The central organising concept of each theme demarcates it from other themes in the analysis. There is nothing *wrong* with simply reporting at the level of themes: analysis that only reports themes without other layers is doing precisely what reflexive TA is designed to do.

(Continued)

A subtheme sits 'under' a theme. It focuses on *one* particular aspect of that theme; it brings analytic attention and emphasis *to that aspect*. A subtheme needs to share the central organising concept of the theme it is part of.

Within an analysis, the relationship *between* themes is horizontal. The relationship between overarching themes, themes, and subthemes is vertical: subthemes are *subordinate* to a theme (and *only* contained within that individual theme); an overarching theme is *superordinate* to more than one theme. An analytic structure with all three levels of theme might look like this:

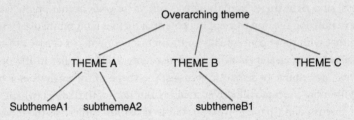

Our best advice around the use of overarching themes and subthemes? Watch out for adding structural complexity at the cost of analytic *depth*. If you do use subthemes or an overarching theme, do so sparingly.[8] Too many subthemes, and the analysis will likely start to feel fragmented and thin, and lacking in analytic depth (Trainor & Bundon, 2020). Remember, your task is mapping the rich nuance and complexity of the data, not demarcating a model of the different elements within them.[9] If you do use subthemes, there is no need to have subthemes across every theme, or indeed the same number of subthemes within any theme that has them. This emphasises the point that subthemes should be used *when they serve the purpose* of telling the strongest story about the data. (We focus much more on how you tell your analytic story in Chapter Five.)

Five key things to keep in mind in the early stages of theme development

First, your initial (and indeed final) themes do not have to capture *everything* in the dataset, or indeed all the codes that you have developed. For instance, we developed lots of codes that didn't make it into the patterns tentatively sketched in Figure 4.2. Your job in analysing the data, and reporting them, is to tell a *particular* story about the data that addresses your research question. It isn't to

> **PRACTICE POINT** Your analytic task is to tell a particular story about the data that addresses your research question, not to represent everything in the dataset.

---

[8]You might, however, be encouraged by others to use lots of layers in your thematic structure; we have heard this come back from reviewers. Resist! A more layered reflexive TA is not a better reflexive TA (Braun & Clarke, 2021c)!

[9]If developing a model is your aim, grounded theory may suit your analytic task better (see Braun & Clarke, 2021a).

represent *everything* that was said in the data – that would be a *different* analytic process. There is, however, value in keeping codes 'in play', even if they don't fit into any initial themes or ideas. Because the analysis will develop, sometimes changing quite radically, they *may* become relevant. You could keep them in play by keeping a record of 'unallocated' or 'miscellaneous' codes you revisit as the analysis develops. Some or all of these codes can be 'resuscitated' into the analysis if relevant further along your theme development.

Second, each theme should have a central organising concept. The idea of a central organising concept is a really useful one to work with, as it clarifies your purpose. It can help you determine the 'essence' of what a theme is about, and, through that, whether or *not* any particular code fits within it. This is not about discovering the *truth* of each theme, but about gaining clarity around what sense you're making of the codes and the data. What *is* it that holds this theme together? One useful visual metaphor is of a galaxy or solar system – something at the core unites many connected but disparate and variable elements. We also find the image of a dandelion seed head evocative of this concept (see Figures 4.3a and 4.3b): The fluffy seed head is made up of many *individual* seeds, each with a fluffy 'umbrella'. All seeds are connected by, and attached to, a central anchoring point – the calyx (visible in the partially dispersed seed head in Figure 4.3b). The partially dispersed seed head also illustrates an important point about themes: a theme does *not* need to be evidenced in every single data item. You can have themes developed from some, many, or all data items.

Third, as we keep emphasising, don't get too attached! The themes you're exploring at this stage are provisional, tentative; they are *candidate* themes – vying for a position, but not settled. Your analysis will almost certainly change, and that's good; change shows you're really engaging with the data and questioning and developing your analytic 'take' on the data. Trying to finalise your themes early on is likely to produce a superficial reading of the data. You need to be prepared to let things go throughout the whole theme development and refinement process. Indeed, *even* as you write your report, you may identify elements of the analysis you ultimately decide don't work as part of the full reported final analysis.

Fourth, it's okay to have a larger number of possible themes that you play around with and explore the potential of, than you will end up with. This raises the very thorny question of *how many themes should I have?* There is no right or wrong answer to this, or indeed a formula that can magic up an answer from the matrix of your dataset, the particulars of your theoretical and analytic approach, and the scope of your output (e.g. a dissertation or journal article) – *sorry!* But from our experience, we generally recommend somewhere between two and six themes (including subthemes) for an 8,000-word report. A longer output – such as a 10,000-word dissertation or an 80,000-word thesis, offers *greater* scope to explore more themes in depth (see some further suggestions in Box 4.2).

Fifth and finally, try to avoid a 'question and answer' orientation in the way you engage with codes and data. If you generate clusters related to 'answering' quite specific or concrete

> **ALERT** There is no right answer to the question of 'how many themes?' However, in practice it is difficult to do justice to more than six themes (including subthemes) in a roughly 8,000-word report.

Figure 4.3a & 4.3b   A dandelion head – fully connected seeds (4.3a) and partially dispersed seeds (4.3b) (photos by Virginia Braun)

questions, such as *how is being childfree negative?* or *how is being childfree positive?* or even *why are people childfree?* you can be pulled towards quite surface readings of the data, as well as topic summary-type themes. This type of 'asking questions and seeking answers' can stymie theme development by inadvertently: (a) constraining your ability to notice patterned meaning *across* the dataset; (b) preventing you from exploring patterns or clusters that aren't immediately obvious, but might ultimately offer the most useful and important analytic insights. Although we advise keeping your research question in mind when developing themes, we imagine this quite loosely. It does not mean looking *for a direct answer to* that research question, or developing a series of very specific questions related to the research question. It means instead *generally* keeping in mind what your interest in the topic (dataset) is, and exploring patternings that might illuminate our understanding of the issue.

A crucial thing to realise here is that your task is both to generate themes/interpret patterned meaning *and* to tell the reader *how* it addresses your research question – and what the implications of it are. The themes you develop provide the reader with 'evidence' for *your* 'answer' to the research question; themes themselves do not directly have to address the research question. We illustrate this from Ginny's analysis exploring how New Zealanders made sense of poor sexual health statistics (Braun, 2008). Her overall analysis claimed that people draw on ideas of a 'national identity' or 'how we are as Kiwis' to

Box 4.2

How many themes? Some guiding considerations for theme development and review

The question of the number of themes is not an abstract one, but relates to broader issues in theme development and quality. The following are important considerations in the theme development phases of reflexive TA:

- Each theme needs the space to be developed fully, its various facets explored, and the richness and complexity of the data captured in the account you write up.
- If you're wanting to present an overall summary or overview of key patterns in your dataset, you may need more themes; if you're exploring one or two facets of the dataset in depth, fewer themes are likely more appropriate.
- The richer and more complex the themes, the fewer you'll be able to do full justice to.
- A large number of themes can produce an incoherent analysis – kind of like a quick once-over that effectively says *hey look at these interesting things I noticed* instead of exploring the richness of each and telling a nuanced story about them.
- A large number of themes can result in a thin and underdeveloped analysis (e.g. Fornells-Ambrojo et al. [2017] reported 18 themes, organised under seven 'superordinate' themes).
- If you have a large number of 'themes' and 'subthemes', it's worth reflecting on whether you have codes rather than themes. Are the themes thin? Do they report only one dimension or facet? If so, they're probably codes.
- It's fine to produce an analysis (e.g. in a journal article) that focuses on just one or two themes, even though there were more to discuss – if there's a good rationale for this, and the analysis is contextualised and not presented as if it were the *full* TA of the dataset. For instance, you might report a few themes within an overarching theme in a single article with a particular focus (e.g. Li & Braun, 2017), or you might report a whole dataset analysis over several articles (e.g. Terry & Braun, 2013a, 2016; Terry, Braun, Jayamaha, & Madden, 2018).

---

explain these statistics. The four themes collectively provided evidence for this answer to her research question, but each on its own did not. Each theme instead evidenced a *particular* way sexual health statistics were framed; together the themes evidenced the salience of national identity.

It's important also to emphasise here that data do not speak for themselves. Not only do data not speak for themselves; themes do not speak for themselves either. *Your role*, as researcher, is to speak for your themes (and your data), to tell the story *you* have made from and of the dataset.

> **PRACTICE POINT** Your role as analyst is to tell the reader what the data and your themes mean and why they matter. A key mantra for analysis is 'data do not speak for themselves' – alongside 'themes don't emerge' of course!

I quite like it here, should I stay longer? Tackling time management in (initial) theme development

As with coding, don't be tempted to rush through clustering codes and initial theme development, racing towards an imagined finish line. But at the same time, you could cluster codes *ad infinitum*, and a concern that you haven't gotten *everything* can stop you progressing deeper into the analysis.

ALERT Don't get stuck in initial theme development, as you are not *finalising* your analysis at this stage. You need to ensure you have plenty of time for the next phase(s).

There is, unfortunately, no easy guidance on how long generating initial themes should take, but don't spend *ages* here – you want to make sure you have quite a bit of time for the next phase. Once you've really engaged with the *codes*, and clustered and re-clustered them into tentative themes, and explored the scope of the developing analysis through some kind of mapping exercise, you're likely ready to move on to the next phase of theme development and review, where deeper theme development takes place through re-engagement with the data themselves.

Two things can help with any anxiety around knowing whether you're moving into Phase four too early (or too late):

1. Recognising the *recursive* nature of TA. You will be moving back and forth in the process, as doing TA is not like a one-stop train journey that once you have started, you cannot get off or change direction!
2. Remembering that no (reflexive) TA analysis is ever *final* or *complete*, because it's a subjective situated engagement with data. There is a point at which we decide to stop our adventuring, but it's not by crossing some actual finish line (Trainor & Bundon, 2020)! It's useful to understand there isn't a *perfect* analysis of your data, waiting in the Cloud, that someone will use to judge *your* analysis against. There are quality criteria (Braun & Clarke, 2021c; see Chapter Nine), and these are useful to guide *good practice* in TA, as is the advice we provide *throughout* the book. But the very nature of the task means that there is no perfect final product to identify. What you have to do is follow a robust and rigorous engaged analytic process to produce a compelling story about your data. But think of your goal as an analysis that's *good enough*, rather than 'perfect'. Phew!

I'M STRUGGLING A BIT, TO BE HONEST: MANAGING ANXIETY IN THE TA PROCESS

Before we move into the next phase, we want to pause to acknowledge that many people find themselves worried, stressed or anxious about the reflexive TA process. They can find it daunting, overwhelming, can feel stuck through worry or indecision. That's very normal.

And the absence of simple easy-to-apply *rules* for reflexive TA can add to feelings of uncertainty, doubt and worry. If anxiety is something you experience in your everyday life outside analysis, reflexive TA can provide fertile ground for anxiety to take hold. Anxiety can easily *get in the way* of your adventure, adding extra hurdles to navigate, including ones that feel impossible, and reducing the pleasure that might otherwise be involved. But anxiety doesn't make reflexive TA an impossible task. Two of our former students have generously provided reflections on their experiences of doing reflexive TA while experiencing anxiety related to ADHD and OCD (see Boxes 4.3 and 4.4). As well as describing the challenges they faced during the analytic process, they share things that helped them in managing the process and successfully completing their research projects. Anxiety is far more widely experienced than just related to specific diagnosed conditions. Elicia and Gina's experiences and suggestions will hopefully be useful for any and all researchers facing some level of anxiety throughout the research process.

=== **Researcher Reflection – Box 4.3** ===

Facing the battle of anxiety and OCD when undertaking TA for the first time, by Elicia Boulton

My research for my professional doctorate in counselling psychology used a qualitative survey to explore how obsessive-compulsive disorder (OCD) shaped women's experiences of sex and sexuality (e.g. Braun et al., 2020). I took a critical realist approach to TA, to capture participants' **lived experiences**, but understand them as contextually located (e.g. social, political, historical). As well as tackling a topic where knowledge is lacking, my research was motivated by my own experiences of living with OCD.

OCD involves trying to reduce harm to self and others, manifesting differently for each person through intrusive thoughts and compulsions, which can cause high anxiety levels. Intrusive thoughts are anxiety provoking due to their frequency and intensity, and are upsetting because of being in stark contrast to the person's values and/or beliefs. In short, they are like your worst nightmare on loop in visual form or through your own internal voice. My experiences of OCD impacted on various aspects of the TA process and here I reflect on some of these challenges and my strategies for managing these.

The most difficult aspect of data analysis was anxiety-related intrusive thoughts (e.g. you don't know what you're doing; what you're doing is rubbish; you're not intelligent enough to do this; you can't remember anything...) that affected my ability to engage and focus. At times when I was trying to analyse the data, it felt like I was in a room full of people all talking at the same time. Hardly the 'ideal' conditions for analysis, so trying to focus could be a battle. Obsessing about doing TA 'perfectly' (although I know logically

(Continued)

there is no such thing as 'perfect' TA) involved intrusive thoughts about 'missing something' important in the data. This led to my supervisor noting that I seemed to want to comment on every single tiny nuance and detail in the data and was getting pulled away from overall patterning. The intrusive thoughts also resulted in anxiety around my analysis not having depth and not being 'good enough' – part of the anxiety being driven by perfectionist thoughts. This led to self-doubt: it can be challenging to develop your own researcher identity and make assertive choices about your research when OCD and anxiety lead you to continually question your academic ability. I was also very anxious that how I wrote my analysis might inadvertently harm participants, through misrepresenting their experience, coming across as judgemental/critical and, to a more extreme level, that a participant may commit suicide because of what I wrote (this links to feeling responsible for keeping everyone safe).

I developed some useful strategies that helped manage these challenges. Perhaps the most important was accepting the value of 'time out' and not assuming it meant I was just avoiding analysis and writing. Taking time out meant learning to recognise that analysing data and writing about data while consumed by intrusive thoughts and anxiety is unlikely to be healthy. Time out was also good for the writing process, because when I returned to writing I found I had more space cognitively to think – the critical OCD thoughts had diminished somewhat, and it felt less like trying to write in a room full of people. In hindsight, I needed to find a way to have regular time out – time management when also dealing with anxiety is difficult, and something I am still working on. I found doing exercise extremely important not just as a break from studying but for reducing overall anxiety levels. Finally, conversations in supervision helped pull me out of being lost in worry of what participants may think about my analysis; they enabled me to develop my analysis as grounded in the data, rather than anxiety-related intrusive thoughts.

Self-care included therapy, where I could remind myself of coping strategies and have somebody point out if I had become lost in self-defeating anxious thoughts. Engaging with an OCD support group was also invaluable to recognise 'the battle with critical internal thoughts' as anxiety/OCD and to then notice and accept the negative thoughts without engaging in them – allowing better focus for developing my analysis.

Overall, although anxiety can feel like an all-consuming force battling against you during the TA process, I believe it is worth bearing with it. Despite my 'battle with intrusive thought' and doubts and anxieties, I made myself do various presentations along the way (and got positive feedback). I also prepared for and passed my doctoral oral exam (viva) with just minor corrections; now I'm working on publications. Hopefully, as I have found, the questions and doubts from anxiety are not just challenges, but bring positives. They can be used to help develop a deeper level of reflection during data analysis, and empathy for participants.

━━━ Researcher Reflection – Box 4.4 ━━━

Doing TA when you've got ADHD and anxiety: reflections and strategies, by Gina Broom

My Master's research explored the topic of attractions or feelings toward someone other than your partner(s). I was interested in exploring this because it's something that isn't often talked about, and there was very little research on this topic. I was sure I must not be the only person who had found the experience confronting, particularly in a culture where monogamous exclusivity is idealised.

I have ADHD, and I'm not a stranger to anxiety – especially when it comes to producing structured work (like a Master's thesis) in a timely fashion. I had never *done* TA (or even critical/qualitative research) before, which was also challenging, because I was learning this method *and* my subject area simultaneously. I experience various ADHD-related challenges, but also strengths, which can help with the challenges. Likewise, anxiety brings challenges, but these also can bring value (which I've briefly summarised in a table):

Challenges	Strengths
ADHD	
Attention regulation – sometimes lacking focus, sometimes 'hyperfocus' (can get lost on tangents)	Creative thinking – more readily making unique connections between otherwise seemingly abstract concepts
Time management	
Becoming overwhelmed	Hyperfocus can be useful (when directed well)
Anxiety	
'Analysis paralysis'	You care about your project
Avoidance – of both work and communication about work	When managed, can be a great motivator

Time-management and 'analysis paralysis' – how to avoid leaving things till the last minute

One of the worst things for me was when my plan for the day was simply 'work on X' (e.g. work on coding today). I would carry the *whole* task in my head, and it would be overwhelming; I would procrastinate and feel lost before I had begun. My main strategy for managing this was *chunking*. I would break tasks down into smaller and smaller chunks till they all fit evenly within my timeframe with a buffer at the end. This was particularly useful with structured/methodical tasks like transcription or coding, but a good strategy throughout the process overall. If the first chunk – and the first chunk *alone* – felt overwhelming, I realised I needed to break it down further, until it felt manageable. On a particularly anxious day for me, this may have been something like an hour set aside to just look at the data and think. This would allow me to focus on just one small thing at a time (instead of holding it all in my mind) *and* know that it would all get done – I could almost physically feel the psychological weight lift! So to apply this strategy more broadly, if say you had three weeks to code 10 interviews, coding one interview per day (in a 5-day week) will have it done in two weeks, with a one-week buffer in case some take longer than you expect (which they almost always do!). The buffer also allows you to move on from

(Continued)

parts that you are tempted to spend too long on, because you can return to add detail at the end *if there's time*. Breaking each day into four time slots gives you a quarter of an interview per slot – I found this is a good way to check my progress throughout the day.

Communication

Developing a relationship with my supervisor where I felt I could talk openly was very important to me, as well as actively remembering that she was there to help me. They *want you to succeed*. It's easy to feel intimidated (it certainly was for me, due to a prior harsh work environment), but a lack of communication can really hold you back. Sometimes I would feel afraid to talk to my supervisor if I felt like I was falling behind, or I didn't feel like I knew what I was doing. In hindsight, my anxiety would build, I'd have no new information to help me, and I would find myself in a deeper and deeper paralysis. After talking to my supervisor, I *always* had a clearer idea of how to proceed, and I *always* felt better. Throughout the course of my thesis, I found it easier and easier to be upfront and get the help that I needed sooner rather than later.

Regular meetings and deadlines also don't allow for anxiety-driven perfectionism – you *have* to get something in. Sometimes feedback would take me in a different direction, and I'd be glad I hadn't wasted too much time going in one direction. I had to embrace the feeling that I may get something wrong, because I was uncertain through most of the process – but that was okay. Whenever I dropped the ball, I would try not to be hard on myself. I would just make a new plan and try again (however much that is easier said than done!).

Extra tips on things that helped me

- Don't think in circles – talk it out or jot down thoughts if you get stuck. Talk to an inanimate object if you have to! (I had a stuffed bear who learned a lot about epistemology and ontology.)
- Get out of the house – go into your office space (if you have one) or find a quiet space on campus (or even in a café) to work in. Working at home may allow for pyjamas, but it also makes it hard to avoid procrastination and to get into a working headspace.
- If there is software that can help you, try it out – or plan in some time to let yourself experiment with your options:

  o I know some prefer to handwrite codes on hard copy, but I preferred to use the comment function in Word because typing was faster than writing for me, and I was lucky in that someone I knew could write a macro in Microsoft Excel for me to organise my coded excerpts into themes and subthemes (see also Box 3.4 in Chapter Three).

  o I also discovered and really liked using MindMup (www.mindmup.com) to visually map my themes and subthemes, because I could move things around and edit more easily than on paper.

- Give yourself time to figure out what works for you.
- If your university has support services for mental health or study support, *try them out*. I found these services helped me with planning, managing anxiety, and they supported my need for an extension, which allowed me to finish the project when I otherwise wouldn't have been able to.

DEVELOPING AND REVIEWING THEMES[10] (PHASE FOUR)

For the initial theme generation and development (Phase three), you've worked mostly with codes to explore possible clusters of meaning and generate tentative themes. Getting a good **thematic mapping** by the end of that phase relies on the quality of your coding, because it's usually not possible to hold your entire dataset, and all the nuance within it, in your head as you work with the codes to explore patterning – even with a small dataset, like the childfree dataset. Phase four extends, and offers a vital check on, the initial theme development in Phase three, through a process of re-engagement with: (1) all the coded data extracts; and (2) the entire dataset. The purpose here is to review the viability of the initial clusterings, and explore whether there is any scope for *better* pattern development. This phase is *partly* about providing a validity check on the quality and scope of your candidate themes. But it's importantly *also* about developing the richness of your themes; you're aiming to develop a rich, nuanced analysis that addresses your research question. For us, a good TA is evidenced by themes that: are built around a *singular* central idea or argument, and do not try to be *all things to all people* (i.e. they are *not* topic summaries); illustrate richness and diversity in the manifestation of that idea within the dataset; are not too fragmented or multi-layered; are distinctive – each theme has its own focus, its own boundaries, and themes do not merge into each other and weave together to tell an *overall* story that addresses the research question.

We have emphasised TA as a recursive process – like following a hose that loops randomly across a long grass lawn, back and forth and round and round in every direction, rather than an escalator or a train sending you inevitably in one direction. This phase is *particularly* recursive. You move backwards and forwards between the data and developing analysis, to check that you haven't taken your developing analysis in a direction that either: (a) doesn't tell a compelling story to address your research question; or (b) takes you too far away from the data. This latter can happen if you get too attached to the story *you* have been developing through code labels, one step removed from the data. The *Mr Lovenstein* cartoon in Figure 4.4, posted by student Nicole Watson on Twitter (Watson, 2018), captures this last point nicely.

---

[10]We've renamed Phase four from our original *reviewing themes*, because, like Phase three, we felt it risked evoking something other than what we mean here. The original name risked *suggesting* that by this time, you're not still actively *developing* themes, but are rather just checking to make sure they fit. That isn't the case, and imagining it is, makes it harder to fully engage in the spirit of what you're trying to do with this phase.

Figure 4.4   "Data says no"[11]

Theme development and revision with coded extracts

The initial part of this phase involves reviewing your tentatively developed themes against all the data that have been tagged with any of the codes clustered for each theme. Does *each* candidate theme *work* when it is read in relation to all the data that are supposed to evidence it? Keeping your (broad, potentially shifting) research question in mind: does each theme capture a (different) core point, and some rich diversity and nuance (multiple facets), about the dataset, that *you* want to convey in addressing your question?

The most useful basic question to guide this development and review process (both now, and in relation to the full dataset) is:

- Is this pattern a viable *theme* – a pattern that has an identifiable central organising concept, as well as different manifestations of that idea?

---

[11]However, within reflexive analysis, interpretation happens at the intersection of the data, the subjectivity of the researcher, and the scholarly and societal context of the research, so the data are not the final or only arbiter of the 'truth' of the analysis.

If your candidate themes meet that basic criterion, then useful review and development questions for each theme include:

- *Can I identify boundaries of this theme?* Am I clear about what it includes and excludes? Understanding each theme's central organising concept is vital for determining this. The dandelion seed head images (Figures 4.3a and 4.3b) are useful to revisit here: there is a clear boundary for what is, and what is not, part of the dandelion. If a bug had landed on the exposed calyx in Figure 4.3b, you would be clear that it was *not* part of a 'dandelion seed theme'.
- *Are there enough (meaningful) data to evidence this theme?* Are there multiple articulations around the core idea, and are they nuanced, complex, and diverse? Does the theme feel *rich*? A useful heuristic here is to ask yourself, do I have quite a bit I could say about this theme? If not, perhaps it is too *thin*? It may just be a code, an important and interesting, yet ultimately single-faceted, meaning.
- *Are the data contained within each theme too diverse and wide-ranging?* Does the theme lack coherence? If you go back to your imagined dandelion, are you trying to scrape together all the blown-away seeds (those missing from Figure 4.3b)? Instead of a connected, coherent and delineated seed head (Figure 4.3a), you now not only have a range of dandelion seeds (which may actually come from some different plants), but also a few bugs and other flowers and plants and seeds that you've accidentally gathered as you've tried to capture the seeds as they floated and landed in different directions. That is what a theme without coherence is like.
- *Does this theme convey something important?* It can be useful to reflect on whether each theme conveys information and interpretation that you judge to be *important* in relation to the dataset, your research question, and the wider context (which we discuss more in Chapters Five and Seven). This can be where you grapple with the question of importance versus prevalence. Some meanings might be common, but nonetheless pretty *meh* in terms of the insight or interest they offer. Your analysis does *not* have to report *the most common* meanings in the dataset but rather clearly tell a compelling story to address your research question.

Sometimes, initial themes work well, but that's rare. Often, they don't work that well, and they need considerable (re)development. It may be that the themes don't work against the coded data – consider whether you need to rework the code-clusters, or even go back to Phase two and recode. Or the themes might not work because they aren't coherent, distinct and/or comprehensive enough. Or they might not work because you realise you've inadvertently over-emphasised particular aspects of the dataset you found personally interesting or intriguing but that aren't hugely relevant for your research question. Or they might not work for some reason you can't quite pin down or articulate. If you're a student, you may feel like you've done a good (enough) job at this point, but your supervisor may have a different take on it.[12] If that happens, it's not because what you've done is necessarily wrong, but that more development work is needed around theme conceptualisation, focus and scope.

So, you should expect some revision to the candidate themes at this stage. This could be at the level of tweaking – refining boundaries, clarifying central organising concepts, or slightly expanding or narrowing a theme. Often, it will be more substantive. You might combine two potential candidate themes into one broader theme. You might realise part of

---

[12]We imagine our students heaving a collective sigh of empathy right now!

one theme doesn't fit, so you pull it out and redraw the theme boundary. You might split a theme into two, or even three themes. And, sometimes, you might just reject one or more of your initial themes completely.

At this stage, you really need to prepare yourself psychologically to discard the initial themes you generated in Phase three and start over. That may send shudders down your spine, but good reflexive TA involves being provisional about your developing analysis, and being prepared to ask yourself tricky questions like: *am I trying to massage the data into a pattern that isn't really there?* and *what am I missing or not noticing here?* You shouldn't try to *force* your analysis into coherence, if it isn't working. We loved the idea, expressed on Twitter by UK-based occupational health psychologist Elaine Wainwright (2020), that the process of theme development felt like wrestling a sea-monster (see Figure 4.5). The vivid imagery evoked reflexive TA so well for us: a process of meaning-making that shifts and changes form, and sometimes feels slippery, tricky to grasp hold of. Such moments are ones where taking a break, and just letting the analytic ideas ferment in your head, can be really helpful in shifting how you're making sense of the data.

Figure 4.5 Theme development as wrestling a sea-monster?

Given the recursive nature of reflexive TA, this part of Phase four can blur into Phase three – for experienced qualitative researchers, especially if working with a smaller dataset. We really want to emphasise this combination of robust processes and flexibility. It is *your* process with TA, *your* reflexivity and thoughtful engagement, that offer the most important tools in developing your analysis, not 'following the (perceived) rules'.

ALERT Don't treat phases as rigid entities that have to be followed precisely to give you the right analysis. Remember this is a 'recipe for your adventure' – where reflexive engagement leads to the most compelling outcomes.

Theme development and revision with the full dataset

Once you feel you have a set of themes that work in relation to the coded data extracts, that tell a good story, with each theme offering something distinctive, you then expand the focus of revision and development by going back to the entire dataset. All the processes and caveats just outlined apply here, including still being prepared to let things go.

Why do we regard this stage as so important? As noted, coding moves you *away from* your dataset, and in initial theme generation you effectively work at two steps removed from the dataset: one step from the full dataset to the coded dataset; another from the coded dataset to your list of code labels. With theme generation, you're initially just looking at the code labels themselves. When you move to development and revision with the coded data, you get closer to the dataset again, but you're still a step removed, as you're only working with pre-selected segments of the dataset – the data you have tagged with code labels. Each step of removal allows greater scope for misremembering, decontextualisation, or just plain forgetting the full scope of the dataset, and thus an analysis that potentially misrepresents the data content.[13] Furthermore, as we go deeper and deeper into analysis, there's a good likelihood that we'll *notice* different (relevant) things in the data. This is especially the case if our analysis is more latent, conceptual or theoretical. So full, thorough, and open engagement with the whole dataset at this stage is important. This is a quite a different point from developing an analysis from *part of* the dataset – see Box 4.5.

============ **Box 4.5** ============

Can my analysis be based on *part* of the dataset?

If you're working with a very large dataset, you may develop analyses based solely on part of the dataset. It's entirely acceptable within qualitative frameworks to reanalyse the same dataset with different foci or to address different research questions, and sometimes with different methods (e.g. Spiers & Riley, 2019). That is *not* the same as the 'cherry-picking' critique noted in Chapter Three, where a researcher either selectively presents only the data that support their argument, or misrepresents their dataset (Morse, 2010). In some cases, you might do this across a subset of the dataset (for instance, participants with a particular experience); in other cases, you will home in on a particular data domain. Victoria, for instance, with her colleagues Carol Burgoyne and Maree Burns, collected interview data from same-sex couples for a project initially on money management, that evolved to encompass views on civil partnership and same-sex marriage as the government introduced legislation to recognise civil partnership for same-sex couples as the project started. Victoria led on several thematic analyses relating to discussions of civil partnership and marriage in the interviews – including on naming practices (Clarke, Burns, & Burgoyne, 2008) and weddings (Clarke, Burgoyne, & Burns, 2013). She first extracted *all* data relevant to the topic, and the extracted dataset became her new working dataset. Such partial dataset analysis is fine to do in reflexive TA – but it needs a clear rationale for dataset selection.[14]

---

[13]The likelihood of misrepresenting your dataset is diminished greatly by a thorough coding process (as discussed in Chapter Three).

[14]A dataset is not a thing that we can develop (or extract) only one analysis from. Indeed, we like the argument that US nursing researcher and qualitative methodologist Margarete Sandelowski (2011) made, that each time we consider our dataset in relation to a different question, the data become a somewhat *different* dataset, through responding to different research questions and reading through different interpretative lenses.

What's the point of this part of my adventure?

Where are you aiming to get to by the end of this revision and development phase? Having produced a set of well-worked-up (but still provisional) themes – along with any sub- or overarching themes – that capture the most important and relevant elements of the data, *in relation to your research question*. It's your job as analyst to determine the most relevant and important patterned meaning that 'speaks' both about the data, and into the existing field of scholarship and the wider context. As noted earlier, sometimes the most common patterns are not particularly relevant or salient. Whether the *pervasiveness* of meaning is a key important factor in deciding on themes, depends on your research question. If your research question seeks to understand something experience-based or concrete, like Black experiences of driving–policing in the US (see Bell, Hopson, Craig, & Robinson, 2014) – check out #DrivingWhileBlack – then commonality may be a key aspect to consider, especially if you want to be able to make claims around frequency of experiences. But often the types of questions we have with qualitative research mean frequency is not the most important element – if it were, we would probably use quantitative measures (see Terry &

> **ALERT** Theme importance is NOT determined by (numerical) frequency so much as salience and importance to addressing the research question.

Braun, 2013a). Sometimes, a minor theme (in terms of frequency) may offer a *vitally* important meaning to capture and report. It all depends on the research question, data and context.

Thematic mapping is again your friend in this part of the process, providing a tool to visualise the overall story the analysis tells, identifying boundaries around themes and connections across themes, as well as the overall structure of the analysis. Mapping can be a useful technique for identifying if there's something interesting, but that doesn't fit with the overall story. Or if the overall story appears disconnected, like a series of unrelated anecdotes vying for attention, instead of having a logical, connected narrative. Our initial clustering (seen in Figure 4.2) presented a mass of patterned and intersecting ideas, but didn't map an *overall* story. We soon shifted our analytic focus in two separate directions, exploring two quite different topics or ideas from the dataset; each seemed like it would provide rich, nuanced and important understanding in relation to our research question – *contemporary meaning-making around voluntarily not having children*. We show revised thematic maps for these developing analyses in Figure 4.6 (related to: *the gains and losses of (non)parenthood*) and Figure 4.7 (related to: *choice*). At this point, each topic effectively seemed to be working as an overarching theme (see Box 4.1) for a number of candidate themes. But note: even after this revision and development phase, each map is still reflecting somewhat provisional themes.

The first mapping, in Figure 4.6, captures three themes we were *starting* to develop and review related to an idea of *gains and losses* – an overarching theme which evolved around the idea of parenthood as beneficial and non-parenthood as lacking. It's still not finalised, but has more clarity than the earlier stages of mapping (Figure 4.2), and a sense of the likely scope of themes within the umbrella of the overarching theme.

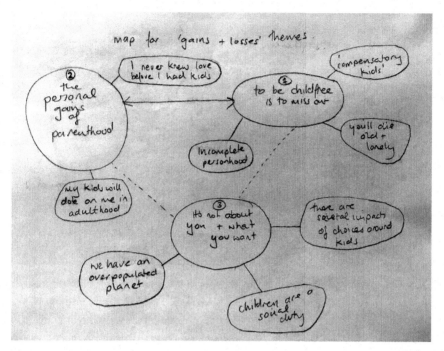

Figure 4.6 Refined thematic map for 'gains and losses' analysis

The second thematic map (Figure 4.7) starts to map out what we anticipate will be a *final* analysis within an overarching theme of *choice* – three distinctive patterns, clustered around choice. This map shows a *considerable* shift from the initial mapping in Figure 4.2. Notable in Figure 4.7 is a potential 'satellite' idea (floating in the periphery, like a satellite around earth) – here called *the 'real' victims* (connected to the code in Table 4.1 *the 'real' victims are those who can't have kids*). This was articulated in the data as people who want to have children but who cannot, and who deserve empathy; this **category** of people was often used as a contrast with people who *choose* not to have children. Although it didn't seem *directly* connected to how our main 'choice' themes were developing, it still *seemed* like it might be an important meaning to consider in our understanding of how choice operates in this dataset – and hence we retained it in mapping our developing analysis. Further refinement around this choice analysis can be seen in Box 4.7.

After the two layers of review and theme development, you need to decide if you feel your analysis fulfils the criteria we described at the start of this section. If so, great! Move on to the next phase. If not, you may need to proceed 'backwards' for a while. You may need to revisit your coding, re-coding some or all of the dataset; you may even discard some coding if the scope of analysis has shifted. A common reason for going backwards to go forwards is realising you have inadvertently developed topic summaries, rather than themes. We now consider the distinction between topic summaries and themes in a bit

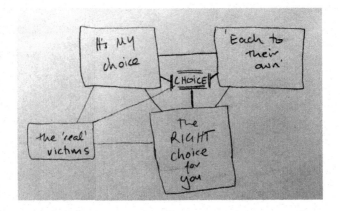

Figure 4.7   Refined (finalised) thematic map for 'choice matters' analysis

more detail, to guide you in assessing the 'themeyness' of your developing themes. Before that, we want to re-emphasise that a step or two 'backwards' in TA should *not* be framed as failure, but instead as having the courage to reverse on your adventure, recognising that the path you've gone down has proved too dull, or too complex, or is just a plain dead end, and reassess the path forwards. The best adventures are rarely linear.

> **PRACTICE POINT**   Going 'backwards' to develop TA is an important part of the process. Instead of representing 'failure' it represents the researcher's commitment to producing a quality analysis.

Okay, so how would a topic summary be different from a shared meaning theme?

In teaching around TA, as we wrote this book, we have sometimes used part of the 'childfree' dataset for practical exercises – some readers may even recognise it from those contexts! In those classes, we found people sometimes struggled to differentiate between *shared meaning* themes and topic summaries, in the context of the dataset. For this reason, we thought it would be really useful to include an example *of* a topic summary, something that would *not* count as a theme in *reflexive* TA (but might in other versions, see 'What is a theme?' in Chapter Eight). We use the topic *reasons for being childfree* to demonstrate what a topic summary might look like (see Box 4.6; Table 8.2 in Chapter Eight provides another comparison from published research). There were lots of places in the dataset where people described or hinted at their own reasons for being childfree, and/or others' potential or actual reasons for not having children. A topic summary is what would result if we were to cluster all these reasons in one place – kind of like an overview of what's in the data on the topic. It's the sort of 'theme' you get when you base it around answers to a particular question. You can tell that there is no central organising concept, no dandelion calyx, no sun at the centre of the solar system.

=== **Box 4.6** ===

Illustrative 'topic summary': Reasons for being childfree

Why are people childfree? Within the dataset, and in the context of a wider framing of childfree as a choice that people make – "Children AREN'T for everyone... never have been. It's purely a personal choice" (JAOB) – lots of explanations were given for childfree status. People were commonly characterised as having a *reason* for being childfree:

> Before you judge anyone on not wanting children maybe just listen to their story of why they don't want children or just can't have them (RADE)

> Those who dont have kids might have other goals they want to achieve good for them (SHHA)

Commonly, participants who spoke of their own context simply framed their reason in terms of individual psychology – of 'not wanting' children:

> My husband and i dont have kids and dont want kids (KAHA)

> I have no children and that was by choice. Never wanted any, never will. (JATH)

The most common *reasons* could be described as reflecting personal (including psychology), lifestyle, environmental or societal elements. When the reasons given for being childfree were identified as *personal*, this was sometimes simply described in generic terms:

> Some people are child orientated, others aren't. Its as simple as that (SARO)

Others referred more specifically to particular traits that made them unsuitable for parenting or not desiring of parenting. For some this was psychological; for others, physiological:

> I personally like the idea of being a parent but recognised very early on that I had too much of a temper, and that my moods were too up and down. I seriously looked at myself like giving myself a warrant of fitness for parenting, and declined the warrant (MIBE)

> I wish I could have children but I can't because I have a rare syndrome [...] I can pass on my syndrome to my children and I have seen first hand what my syndrome can do and I don't want that for my children (RADE)

More lifestyle-type reasons were evident where participants simply described the reason around the type of life they wanted to live:

> I'm so sick of people saying, "You'll change your mind" when I say I don't want kids. I want to travel, have a career and have nice things so no kids for me (CLGR)

Such descriptions evoked the *cost* of children, either indirectly through reference to things one could otherwise afford – like travel – or directly:

(Continued)

I cant afford them (LIPO)

No i wouldnt because children cost too much money to cloth feed, educate. Why have babies when we have a rich kid hating goverment. (MEMI)

In these reasons, costs are a barrier, whether it is in recognising the inherent cost of raising a child (Hamilton-Chadwick, 2017), as in "I can't afford them" or through restricting the person's ability to spend their (always limited) money – or indeed time – on other things. In some instances, these personal reasons were characterised in familiar selfishness terms around "lifestyle":

Its also a lifestyle choice people make, more money and luxury, or the ups and downs a family brings along with different social skills needed (SARO)

Comments related to reasons tended to be quite brief – and hint at or provide a summary of a more complex reason – SARO's quotation here, for instance, evokes a range of reasons. These brief reasons seemed often to operate as a shorthand of something wider the readers should understand. For example:

the worlds overpopulated as it is lol (ALRO)

Reasons appeared sometimes blended together, suggesting there is not necessarily a *single* motivation – though whether that is the case cannot be determined precisely:

My partner and I have decided not to have kids for a range of personal, environmental and social reasons (CHCA)

As the data excerpts have illustrated, discussion of reasons around being childfree sometimes appeared when people described their own personal reasons for choosing not to have children, or reasons within the context of a relationship. Other times, people described the real or imagined reasons of *other* people. In the latter, the rationale or logic was not always framed in terms of what might motivate the choice, but as a framework for understanding the choice. As noted above, and as many of the excerpts hinted at, the reasons supplied often worked, in a context where being childfree is often framed as selfish (Morison et al., 2016), to explain the decision as a *reasonable* choice, and not a selfish one. These appeared perhaps most explicitly when having children or not having children was framed in terms of *environmental* impact:

The world is so over populated already, so if people choose not to have kids, they are not being selfish at all (PAMA)

5.3billon humans on this planet putting it under so much pressure.....so really...who's being selfish (RITA)

People's reasons for being childfree, or understanding why others might be childfree, covered a wide range of different motivations that were, in the dataset, rarely fully articulated. Given the nature of the dataset – Facebook comments – this is not surprising.

The topic summary in Box 4.6 evidences a wide range of reasons for choosing to be childfree, and so the analysis does tell the reader something potentially useful. But it has no *core* meaning that these reasons cohere around. We think it's worth pointing out that the topic summary contains many micro patterns, such as *personal reasons* or *environmental reasons*, but they are thin and unidimensional – they are more like codes. Within the dataset, there is simply not enough rich and diverse data to form a number of *different* meaning-based themes related to the topic of reasons for being childfree. Looking beyond the semantic responses in the data, we do notice some patternings, across the reasons given – such as something related to *selfishness*. But this patterning is *not* related to the type of *reason* people give to explain being childfree. For a reflexive TA, we might explore whether topic-connected patterns like *selfishness* might be developed into a theme (or themes) that addresses our research question. However, were we to do that, we wouldn't limit our data instances where reasons for being childfree are discussed explicitly; we'd look across the entire dataset for anywhere ideas related to selfishness appeared.

But what about contradiction?

Often your dataset will contain contradictory meanings or tensions; sometimes, individual data items will themselves contain contradictions or tensions; sometimes, the contradiction will be between different data items. How should we make sense of contradictory meaning within a reflexive TA? There are three main points to make around this:

First, each individual theme should not contain meanings or interpretations that are contradictory to the central organising concept of the theme. Let's go back to the topic summary versus shared-meaning theme distinction: a topic summary, which overviews the diversity of responses in relation to a topic, potentially *contains* contradiction. For instance, if you developed a topic summary on *views of childfree women*, it would likely contain points like *childfree women are viewed as selfish*, and *childfree women are viewed as generous and loving towards others' children*. These views are in tension. In reflexive TA, if there were enough complex data related to selfishness, you might develop a shared meaning theme around *the selfishness of childfree women*. That theme could capture data that didn't just express overt views of childfree women (e.g. *childfree women put themselves first*), but articulated the idea in less obvious ways (e.g. *I like to travel* – which subtly evokes a curtailment of personal options when having children). Likewise, if there were enough complex data related to generosity, you might develop a separate theme called something like *childfree women make the best aunties*, which, again, would develop a distinctively different – and in this case somewhat contradictory – meaning evident across the dataset.

These examples evoke our **second** key point – that your *overall* TA *can* contain themes developed around contradictory meanings. Different themes can *be* contradictory to *each other*, just not *internally* contradictory. Such contradictory-to-each-other themes *might* be contained within one overarching theme. For instance, the idea that *childfree people are missing out* and that *children ruin your life* – contradictory meanings sometimes articulated by the same participant or within the same data item, as noted – might co-exist within an overarching theme around children as core to organising life. Life and meaning-making are often messy. Your task with reflexive TA is not to tell a uniform, singular story (see Nadar, 2014), but to convey the key patterned meaning evident from your engagement with the data, related to your research question.

Finally, there is one other way that contradiction *can* appear in reflexive TA, and that is when the tension or contradiction is what the theme is *about* – where the central organising concept itself focuses on that tension. What do we mean? Let's go back to the childfree dataset, and the potential theme we discussed called *good/bad parents* (see Box 2.4 in Chapter Two; Table 4.1; Figure 4.2 above). Often, as noted in Chapters Two and Three, commenters evoked a hierarchy – or, more usually a dichotomy – between right and wrong ways of being parents. What constituted *good* or *bad* parenting was less of interest to us, analytically, than the way that parenting was effectively described in one *or* the other terms: you're either a good parent *or* a bad parent. What constituted good or bad differed greatly across the accounts; what did *not* was the sense of *splitting* parents into two distinct and dichotomised *types*. Where childfree people sat in this good/bad parent dichotomy varied – so this dichotomy was used to make sense of being childfree, but in lots of *different* ways. Hence, the central organising concept of our theme became *the dichotomisation* – this separation of parents into *either* good *or* bad. The theme did not focus on *what* constituted good parents or bad parents, but rather how this dichotomy was made, and what the implications of it were. See Box 4.7 for an extract from the write-up of this theme.

PRECISION MATTERS: REFINING, DEFINING AND NAMING THEMES (PHASE FIVE)

This phase involves further development around your themes, as well as more precise analytic work refining your analysis. As analytic refinement involves writing, it necessarily blends into the final phase of TA – *writing up* – so we will discuss refining your analytic argument *primarily* in Chapter Five. In Phase five, you also do the refining work of figuring out the structure and flow of your analysis; you effectively *map* the way you will report on your adventure, once you're home.

> **KEY CONCEPT** A theme definition can be thought of as an abstract for your theme – outlining the scope, boundaries and core concept of the theme.

The disciplined task of writing a **theme definition** – effectively an abstract for your theme – is a good test of the quality of your themes. A definition, in a few sentences, clarifies and illustrates what each theme is about – the central organising concept or key take-away point of the theme, as well as the particular manifestations (and *sometimes* implications in relation to the research question) of the theme, and any subthemes. In addition to checking for internal theme clarity, theme definitions can be useful for thinking about the organisation and flow, the overall story your analysis builds towards. The theme definition for *deficient personhood* from the childfree dataset exemplifies this (see Box 4.8). The theme *deficient personhood*, from within the overarching theme of *gains and losses*, was first identified as '(1) to be childfree is to miss out' (see Figure 4.6). Through development and review, we concluded the scope of this theme was wider than just missing out through not having children, but encapsulated an impossibility of experiencing full humanity, and so ultimately called this theme *deficient personhood*.

> **PRACTICE POINT** Writing theme definitions is a good way to test the 'themeyness' of a theme. If you can't sum up the gist of a theme, and its core concept, in a few sentences, further review and refinement may be necessary.

====== **Box 4.7** ======

The 'contradictory' theme *Good and Bad Parents* [extract]

A pattern evident within the dataset related to a dichotomisation that commenters regularly made, both explicitly and implicitly. This evoked two separate groups: good parents and bad parents. *Good* parents are people who do parenting appropriately – and is embodied in concepts like 'respectable motherhood' (Mannay, 2015). *Bad* parents are people who do parenting inappropriately – for instance in ways that regularly leads them to be characterised as 'unfit' parents, a label which has been applied to everyone from lesbian and gay parents, to single women, to those with mental health challenges and physical disabilities (e.g. Clarke, 2001; Clarke, Kitzinger, & Potter, 2004; Van Brunt, Zedginidze, & Light, 2016):

> The pity is there's no shortage of people who shouldn't have kids. Should almost have to take a pill TO have a kid. (DARE)

> Itz a choice, y ave kidz if u cnt aford them. Too many hungry children goin to skool without food. (SHHO)

> I love my children, but they have always been loved and cared for, fed, clothed and taught well. This is not always the case (JAOB)

Sometimes this characterisation was explicit, such as through reference to "bad parenting" or "people who shouldn't have had kids". Other times it was more subtle, such as in evocations of a beneficiary parent who either cannot support their children without state assistance, or the resilient trope of the beneficiary mother, who has children to access more state money, so she selfishly does not have to work (Matthews, 2014): "Plenty of people out there having kids who have never payed a cent towards society but feel free to bleed it dry" (RALA). Or through often-implicit contrasts with one's own parenting, such as: "I have 3 well rounded kids" (HATU), implying that children in the world who aren't "well rounded" are simply a consequence of poor parenting. There was considerable variation in *what* people claimed *as* good or bad parenting – related to domains like financial or emotional support, or child-centred or 'present' (at home) parenting. Sometimes these connected to some inherent quality of the person, sometimes to (potentially) more changeable behaviours or circumstances.

We do not focus on the content of these characterisations, so much as on the pattern *of* dichotomisation, and consider what impacts it has. Effectively, two different groups of people were constructed: good parents or would-be parents, and bad parents (and sometimes would-be parents). These categorisations tended to be fixed and absolute – by which we mean someone was either a good or a bad parent, rather than being a mix of good and bad, which might vary with circumstance. In this, parenting was simultaneously naturalised and denaturalised – if people have the potential to be bad parents (or good parents), then parenting cannot simply be a 'natural' instinct. This dichotomisation potentially achieves two different things in relation to people who choose to be childfree. First, it could be seen as serving a *positive* social justice purpose in debates, shifting parenting from the domain of the natural, by deconstructing the idea that parenting is natural and (should be) an automatic part of the life trajectory for everyone. In this way, parenting becomes something one should reflect on, and evaluate the self in relation to:

> some people who choose to become parents should have thought far more about WHY they had their children. (JAOB)

(Continued)

I personally like the idea of being a parent but recognised very early on that I had too much of a temper, and that my moods were too up and down. I seriously looked at myself like giving myself a warrant of fitness for parenting, and declined the warrant. [...] I make an awesome part time, respite care mum, but I know my limits. There are so many amazing parents out there. Sadly there are also some appalling parents out there. My only judgement on the world is that I wish more men and women would give themselves a warrant of fitness before becoming a parent. It's such a huge responsibility, and it's for a very long time. (MIBE)

In MIBE's quotation, the decision to parent or not is characterised around a "warrant of fitness" to parent, akin to a test for road-worthiness that most nations require of motorised vehicles – *Warrant of Fitness* is the term for this certification in New Zealand. Unfitness is a familiar trope in 'bad parenting' discourse (e.g. Clarke, 2001), and people who made the wrong choice were described in fairly judgemental terms:

You're clear evidence that the ability to breed doesn't mean it should happen (DARE)

better not to have kids than have trophy kids and dump them in childcare from 7am to 6pm every day and then say I'm too busy to come to special events. Poor sprogs, selfish parents (BRMA)

However, although a dichotomisation into good and bad parents potentially disrupts an (often gendered) naturalisation of parenthood – through suggesting not everyone is naturally fit to parent – it also echoes a long history of discourse, policy and practice that has policed the fitness of parents, and especially mothers. This policing has occurred through legislation that prohibited same-sex adoption (Clarke, 2001), societal condemnation of the (particularly non-White, working class, teenage) single mother (Duncan, Edwards, & Song, 2002), and the removal of children from homes where their welfare is deemed under threat (Choate & Engstrom, 2014). Ironically, it also echoes recurrent concerns and debates about the risk to children of mothers *who work* (McGinn, Ruiz Castro, & Lingo, 2019).

At the same time, it does not necessarily disrupt a latent pronatalism, and alongside it the idea that those deemed fit *should* be parents. Or that those who choose not to parent should have a (valid) reason, of which 'I would not be a good parent' is key. Although it appears to situate childfree as a choice, it risks echoing a kind of voluntary eugenics, where one determines one's *un*fitness to parent and takes oneself out of the gene pool through being childfree, as MIBE effectively positions herself as having done. In this way, being childfree is not constructed as a positive and equally-valid-to-having-children life-choice that people might select, but more a service to society (and in some cases a personal sacrifice in so doing). Given a wider association of having children as a social good, this construction allows those who are childfree to position themselves as not reneging on their social contract. Yet it retains a stain of pathology and stigma, and potentially shores up the existing moral order, in which to be a childfree person (and particularly woman) is an invalid or negatively judged life choice (Morison et al., 2016).

By utilising existing (moral) discourse in relation to good and bad parents, this pattern of meaning-making around being childfree, then, effectively, works against equality for those who are childfree.

Box 4.8

Definition of the theme 'deficient personhood'

The theme *deficient personhood* explores a core idea expressed in various ways throughout the dataset – that those without children are missing out through not having children, and specifically in ways that construct them as somehow less fully human. One aspect of this idea was relational, that without our own children, we have some kind of relational deficit. We notice this articulated within the dataset when people describe relationships they have with pets ("fur babies") and also with other people's children – which we broadly characterise as a *subtheme* of this theme, which we called *compensatory kids*. The other main expression of a deficient or incomplete personhood was captured by the repeated idea that you cannot really know love until you have a child – often expressed in the form of an unexpected revelation once someone had had children. This situates the emotional landscape of anyone without children as, therefore, somehow lacking. Alongside the idea of a *gap* filled by compensatory kids or pets, the childfree person is never able to achieve the full emotional and relational personhood of the parent. Moreover, because such insight was often positioned as only coming from *being* a parent (sometimes willingly, sometimes not), the person without children is positioned as eternally unable to *really* know themselves, their desires, or indeed *really* make informed choices; they are positioned ironically as somehow childlike, not *fully* adult.

In writing a definition for each theme, it's useful to ask yourself whether you can clearly state:

- What the theme is about (central organising concept).
- What the boundary of the theme is.
- What is unique and specific to each theme.
- What each theme contributes to the *overall* analysis.

If you cannot clearly answer these, your analysis will probably need some reworking. Here we come back to our 'broken record' point about *still* being prepared to let things go.

A final aspect of this refinement is, if you're working with data that have been transcribed, that you go back to the recordings to do a check on the data segments you quote. Although the validity of a theme should *not* hang on any one individual extract, taking care that you have not inadvertently misrepresented what or how something was said through the data translation process is important. For example, that obvious sarcasm was not captured in the transcript, and a response was analysed as genuine.

Naming themes

Another important aspect of this phase is to think about the name you will give each theme. A good theme name will be informative, concise, and catchy. If you're like us, you'll find

PRACTICE POINT   A good theme name is a short phrase, or perhaps a heading and subheading, that captures the essence of the theme and engages the reader.

this to be a *fun* part of the process! It's not just that we *like* creative or fun names for themes (though we do!); theme names are really important, for two main reasons. **First**, because they provide the reader's initial encounter with your analysis – an article abstract, for instance, rarely offers space for more than just theme names to be reported. You're trying to 'sell' your analysis in advance; you want to entice, but not mislead! Theme names operate a bit like an advertising tag-line – try for something as memorable as some of those.

Second, sometimes a poorly named theme not only misrepresents the analysis, it suggests that you've actually developed topic summaries instead of themes. *Quelle horreur!* If a theme name doesn't signal its *meaning* and *analytic direction*, but rather just names a *topic*, there's no way to tell what exactly the analysis will say *about* that topic. Consider the difference between *stigma* and *the subtle stigma of being childfree*. The former names a topic; the latter captures *your analysis* in relation to that topic *within the dataset*. Single word theme names typically don't work well for reflexive TA.

ALERT   In general, avoid one-word theme names in reflexive TA – one word can capture a topic but rarely the patterning of meaning evident in a theme.

Using brief data quotations in theme names can provide an immediate and vivid sense of what a theme is about, while staying close to the data language and concepts. Such quotations usually require an explanatory subheading. If using a quotation for a theme name, make sure it captures the *essence* and *scope* of the theme, and don't use quotations as names just for the sake of it (as tempting as it can be). A risk here is that a catchy quote doesn't *really* capture the central organising concept for the theme, or the scope, and has been used because it's catchy. If you do use quotations, its good to be aware that not everyone likes this, but it's your analysis, not theirs!

ALERT   If publishing your TA, you may encounter the notorious 'Reviewer 2' – a particularly negative reviewer, often sandwiched in between more positive reviews (hence Reviewer 2). One such reviewer recently derided theme names based on data quotations in one of our co-authored papers as "cutesy" and unscholarly.

Naming themes might feel stressful – a need to get it *right* somehow. Or that there is a perfect name if only you can find it. Not only is that *not* the case, but naming things can be fun. The discussion in Box 4.9 highlights *our* process around choosing theme names, and also the interconnection between theme definitions and names. Our discussion relates to our analysis around *choice* in the childfree dataset, which we had mapped out around a possible overarching theme of *choice matters* in Figure 4.7. We reference popular culture often in how we name themes (see Braun & Clarke, 2013). Popular culture can be a great source of inspiration for theme naming, which can quickly and richly evoke the theme concept. But in referencing popular culture texts or tropes, do be wary

PRACTICE POINT   You can use pop cultural references to name things, but be wary of using anything too obscure.

and make sure it's not so particular, subcultural, or narrowly time-based that the theme focus is obscured rather than revealed by the use of the reference.

================= **Box 4.9** =================

Naming themes related to 'choice' in the childfree dataset

Choice was evident to us as a broad pattern of meaning, and likely overarching theme, early on in the analytic process (as discussed throughout Chapters Two and Three). *Choice* would be a poor name for a theme, or even an overarching theme, because it simply captures the topic or concept, without telling us *anything* analytically useful about it – what exactly *about* choice?

Looking across the instances of *choice* – both latent and semantic – within the dataset, what appeared key was that having or making a choice was important. The right to have and/or enact a personal choice seemed to be pervasive. As children of the 1970s and 1980s, we were tempted to call this provisional theme *choice rulz ok* – in reference to a popular slogan from our youth! But that name would only make sense to those who got the reference, so it was probably too obscure. We kept it as a working title as the theme developed, to amuse ourselves.

This candidate theme was quite a theoretical and latent one, where the idea of choice was expressed in quite subtle ways. We drew on our theoretical knowledge of the wider sociocultural logics of choice, and how choice operates (something we have written about, e.g. Braun, 2009), to interrogate the data. Our development of the theme helped us clarify two things: (1) that choice *per se* wasn't *really* a theme, but functioned more as an *overarching* theme (see Box 4.1); and (2) that there were three *distinct* ways the idea of choice appeared across the dataset – three themes in their own right, each with their own central organising concept. Each theme was developed around a different kind of logic or rationality around choice within the dataset. Each theme contained a somewhat different idea of choice, the choosing person, and the act and responsibility of choice – and although distinct, they interconnected with each other. Our three themes became:

Each to their own. This pervasive notion of choice appeared widely across the dataset. It is based within the notion of liberal tolerance, and the idea that we must not judge the free choices of others, as long as no harm is done. It carries echoes of Christian morality and biblical dictates such as 'judge not lest ye be judged'. This articulation of choice focuses on not *who* the choosing subject is, or *what* their choice is, but on ourselves, our relationships with others. It offers a morality for living with others. The theme name captures that this articulation of choice is located in sociality, and not judging other people for their choices.

It's my choice. Another pervasive articulation of choice appeared based in neoliberal ideas of individual agency, where the individual is expected to make choices about their life and how they live it (Gill, 2008; Gill & Orgad, 2018). Within neoliberal logic, choosing is the right thing to do, and being a choosing subject is a strong and powerful responsibility – hence this theme name identified 'my choice' as the key element. This theme focuses on choice in relation to the person who is *doing* the choosing. We situate choice within ideas about how to live a proper life and be a proper person within the contemporary Aotearoa New Zealand context.

(Continued)

Making the right choice. This third theme closely connects to *It's my choice* but focuses particularly on the *process* of choice. This theme is conceptually connected to rational individualism and evokes a strong articulation of the right way of choosing. Although there were some instances where choice was framed as *right* or *wrong* in terms of outcome, the primary focus of this theme was on the foundation and process of choosing. To us, it evoked echoes of Descartes' declaration 'I think therefore I am', or Rodin's sculpture, *The thinker*, in valorising a rational, thinking, choosing subject. Choice needs to be thought out, rational, and reasonable, rather than emotional or spontaneous, and thus there are right and wrong *ways* to make choices. We fluctuated between calling this theme *making the right choice* and *the right way to choose* – and decided on *making the right choice*, as this name emphasised process, but still allowed us to discuss the outcome of those choices.

These three themes and names very closely resemble what we mapped in Figure 4.7. The theme names here are somewhat ambiguous however, and in fully writing up and developing an analysis (which we discuss next, in Chapter Five) we refined them further with subheadings, to become: (a) *Each to their own: liberal tolerance*; (b) *It's my choice: neoliberal agency*; and (c) *Making the right choice: rational individualism*.

In addition, we developed a fourth theme – related to the 'satellite' candidate theme in Figure 4.7. Although this theme wasn't about who and how we *choose*, it focused on those who *cannot choose*, and the articulations demonstrated the value placed on ability *to* choose. In this, it illuminated the power and value given to choice. We called this theme *the 'real' victims*, because commenters often expressed a deep sense of empathy or sympathy for those for whom biological parenting is desired but not (easily) possible, often without any comment around those who are childfree by choice. Here, having one's choice *removed* effectively victimises, and so this fits within the logic of what we realised was an overarching theme around the importance of choice.

Developing these theme definitions and names helped us to clarify the distinctive patterning around choice within the dataset and reinforced our earlier perception that it could *not* be captured by a single theme of *choice rulz ok*. There were too many distinct facets. But an overarching theme worked perfectly to encompass these distinctive themes, as each theme was related to and connected by an overall conceptual pattern. A trope of choice was *central* in making sense of the actions of the individual or couple who do not have children, and indeed, often those who do. Choice did, indeed, 'rule ok' in the logic of the dataset. For this reason, we wanted to retain the idea of the importance of choice, and we settled on the name *choice matters* for the overarching theme. *Choice matters* can be interpreted in two ways, which works well for an overarching theme:

1. It signals the scope of the analysis is about choice, as the matter at hand is choice. But it doesn't signal a particular focus. This is fitting for an *overarching* theme, but would not work so well for a theme, where you want to indicate the direction of the analysis. Compare *choice matters* with our individual theme names.
2. It can also be read as a statement of importance: choice is something that *matters*. This second reading resonated well with the emphasis on the importance of choice within the dataset.

So *choice matters* is a clever overarching theme name (if not quite as fun as *choice rulz ok*), but also one which works well to indicate the scope and focus of what is contained within it. The theme names within this overarching theme signal far more clearly the dimension and direction of particular ways choice played out.

CHAPTER SUMMARY

With this chapter, you have gotten to the heart of your adventure. You have gone deep into the analysis phases of TA, from the early moments in theme generation, where you start to cluster codes, through development, revision and refinement, to precise questions of language in theme names. To guide you through the process, we: discussed the structure and different theme levels of a reflexive TA; emphasised the importance of clear theme boundaries and a core idea, captured by a central organising concept for each theme; and discussed and illustrated some of the challenges and missteps that can take place. We provided an example of what a topic summary 'theme' might look like and discussed why such themes don't fit with reflexive TA – don't try this at home! We explored the complex challenge of contradiction in relation to themes, and illustrated how contradictory meaning *might* be incorporated into reflexive TA. We discussed various tools and techniques you can use to facilitate your TA: the value of visual mapping; the usefulness of theme definitions. We finished by emphasising the importance of well-crafted and thoughtful theme names.

WANT TO LEARN MORE ABOUT...?

For a worked example of **coding and theme development** related to sport and exercise, that also illustrates the analysis of focus group data and an orientation that is both **semantic and latent**, see: Braun, V., Clarke, V., & Weate, P. (2016). Using thematic analysis in sport and exercise research. In B. Smith & A. C. Sparkes (Eds.), *Routledge handbook of qualitative research in sport and exercise* (pp. 191–205). London: Routledge.

For a worked example related to health and clinical areas, that also illustrates the analysis of interview data and a more **latent orientation**, see: Braun, V., Clarke, V., & Terry, G. (2014). Thematic analysis. In P. Rohleder & A. Lyons (Eds.), *Qualitative research in clinical and health psychology* (pp. 95–113). Basingstoke: Palgrave Macmillan.

For a worked example related to counselling and psychotherapy, that also illustrates the analysis of interview data and a more **experiential approach**, see: Braun, V., Clarke, V., & Rance, N. (2014). How to use thematic analysis with interview data. In A. Vossler & N. Moller (Eds.), *The counselling & psychotherapy research handbook* (pp. 183–197). London: SAGE.

For a worked example related to social research, that also illustrates the analysis of interview data and a more **experiential approach** (but one firmly embedded in the wider social context), see: Clarke, V., Braun, V., & Hayfield, N. (2015). Thematic analysis. In J. Smith (Ed.), *Qualitative psychology: A practical guide to research methods* (3rd ed., pp. 222–248). London: SAGE.

For an example of a paper that **reports just two themes** – each richly developed and presenting contradictory meanings – related to the topic of the worked example study, see: Hayfield, N., Terry, G., Clarke, V., & Ellis, S. (2019). "Never say never?" Heterosexual, bisexual, and lesbian women's accounts of being childfree. *Psychology of Women Quarterly, 43*(4), 526–538.

ACTIVITIES FOR STUDENT READERS

Initial theme development and revision: Using the men and healthy eating dataset you've already worked with in Chapters Two and Three (on the companion website), start to explore potential broader patterns of meaning – you may have already started to think about these through coding, but try not to be too limited by that. Cluster codes together in *different* ways to explore what potential patterns you can make. Draw rough maps of possible meaning clusters to help develop your thinking for ways you can combine and divide the dataset.

Working with the same research question 'how is healthy eating for men represented online?', reflect on questions like:

- Does this pattern tell us something important and interesting in relation to my research question?
- What assumptions might I be making in clustering meaning in the ways I am?
- Is there a clear central organising concept for this potential theme?

Once you're fairly certain you have some distinct candidate themes, go back and review your candidate themes against the previously coded data. Then re-read the entire dataset. Ask yourself:

- How well do these patterns capture key meaning?
- How internally coherent and yet distinct from each other are they?
- What, if anything, am I missing?
- Is more refined coding needed?

Revisit your theme development and/or coding as necessary.

Write a theme definition: Select one of your candidate themes and write a definition for that theme (recognising that if you were actually doing this with your own dataset, this would involve skipping a few parts of the process). Try to describe the central organising concept of the theme, and the different manifestations or dimensions of the theme – its scope and boundaries. Discuss how it addresses the research question.

Reflect on this exercise. If you found this tricky, think about why, and what analytic work might be needed to develop the theme further.

If you're teaching content related to this chapter...
Don't forget to check the companion website for a range of teaching resources:
https://study.sagepub.com/thematicanalysis

5

ARRIVING HOME AND TELLING A STORY ABOUT YOUR ADVENTURE

WRITING YOUR THEMATIC ANALYSIS REPORT

Chapter Five overview

- **Writing matters for analysis (Phase six)** — 118
- **Setting the scene of your story (the introduction or literature review)** — 119
- **Describing how you approached your adventure (the method/ology section)** — 121

  o Explaining your choice of TA and what it offers — 122
  o Describing what you actually *did* during analysis — 124

- **Telling your *analytic* story (the results and discussion section)** — 128

  o Introducing the analysis — 129
  o Structuring the analysis section — 131
  o Selecting data extracts — 133
  o Data extracts and your analytic narrative — 135
  o Traps to easily avoid when reporting your analysis in reflexive TA — 138
  o Is 'thick description' something I should be aiming for? — 140
  o The flow of the story — 140
  o Should I use numbers to report theme 'frequency'? — 141
  o Should I claim generalisability in reporting my TA? — 142

- **Drawing conclusions** — 146
- **Reflection and evaluation in your write-up** — 148
- **Telling your story *well*: The value of the edit** — 149

Stories enact a form of mutual hospitality. What is story if not an enticement to stay? You are invited in, but right away you must reciprocate and host the story back, through concentration: whether you read or hear a narrative – from a book or a person – you need to listen to really understand. Granting complete attention is like giving a silent ovation. Story and listener open, unfold into and harbour each other. (Basil, 2019)

This evocation of the place of storytelling does not reference analytic writing, but it captures how in qualitative research reporting, we *are* telling a story (Nadar, 2014). We want to write in a way that invites our readers to stay, and ultimately rewards them for staying. A recognition of the gift of their time and attention. This chapter is about analytic writing, which is how you *complete* the analytic work you're doing in reflexive TA. Your analytic writing needs to be grounded in a solid theoretical foundation, and a rich, robust interpretative process. For this reason, we encourage readers, especially those completing a Master's or doctoral thesis, or writing for publication, to take a deep dive into Chapter Six (on theory and reflexive TA) and Chapter Seven (on interpretation), alongside reading this chapter.

WRITING MATTERS FOR ANALYSIS (PHASE SIX)

PRACTICE POINT Writing is integral to the process of reflexive TA because your analysis takes shape in the writing you do around your data. Writing your report provides a final opportunity for refinement, and you may find that you make big changes even at this late stage.

ALERT Think of writing your analysis as telling a story – your story should engage the reader and convince them of the validity of your analytic claims and argument.

This phase isn't an add on to analysis. Writing *is* a key component of the analytic process for reflexive TA, because the analysis is *in* the writing around your data. Because writing is embedded in the analytic process, you will have been writing in all sorts of ways, before you get to a point where you finalise your analytic report – such as a dissertation, a thesis chapter, an academic journal article, or a public report. With TA, you will still be *producing* your analysis *as* you write it, not simply describing the analysis you finished before writing started: "themes shifted until the final manuscript was published" (Trainor & Bundon, 2020, p. 14). This contrasts with much statistical or quantitative research, where reporting often happens *after* the analysis has been completed. This final phase of doing reflexive TA, then, is about deep *refining* analytic work to shape the detail and flow of the analysis. But it is also the work that has to be done to tell your *whole* analytic story, to bring it all together and convince the reader of the validity and quality of your analysis (for further discussion of quality, see Chapter Nine). It's about understanding what makes a good TA story and then working to produce that.

This phase shifts your writing into the fully formal realm of academic writing. Up until this point, all the writing you've done for your project has been more or less disciplined, more or less developed, but mostly for you (and sometimes for supervisors or collaborators). It has not been finessed and finalised for an audience. Here you're writing for that audience, within the conventions and expectations appropriate to your context and the type of report you are writing. The writing you've done up until this point is like stories you might tell friends and family about your adventure: sometimes it might be casual, sometimes introspective, sometimes fully-developed – like a planned presentation at a big family party celebrating your return. In these instances, the audience is known and private. With formal writing, you're moving into a more 'public' domain – to be read by people like examiners or reviewers, readers who haven't been involved in the project. Imagine that as part of your adventure, you participated in a volunteering scheme organised by a charity. The task of formally writing up is like you giving a public lecture hosted by the charity, where anyone interested in the volunteering scheme can come to hear about your experience. Such a presentation is more formalised, with a clear(ish) audience in mind, and clear expectations for what you should do, and *not* do. In this chapter, we focus on these more formalised aspects of writing for TA.

SETTING THE SCENE OF YOUR STORY (THE INTRODUCTION OR LITERATURE REVIEW)

Every good story needs a set-up, and an academic paper is no different. There are two broad approaches to this within the scholarly traditions, which we refer to – clearly with *no judgement whatsoever* – as the-dull-and-boring-facts versus the-curiosity-fuelled-questioning approaches. Our clear preference is for the latter, but we recognise that sometimes the former is needed – for instance, it might be expected by a journal editor, or a supervisor, or a funder. We hope to encourage more people to embrace the latter model for reflexive TA, where they can.

So what are these? Imagine you're planning your trip to a part of the world you don't know and haven't been to. Even worse (or better!), no-one you know has been there either. How do you tackle the question of preparation? Here are two possibilities:

1. You read the Wikipedia entry for the country and follow up with some of the key references. You attend a lecture at a local university, describing the current socio-geo-political landscape of the country. You read up on flora, fauna, and local culture, to prepare yourself with all the relevant facts. TripAdvisor reviews provide the final pieces of evidence to prepare you for what lies ahead. Prepared like this, you are ready to go. In discussing what you know before the trip with friends and family, you provide a rich summary of existing knowledge, clearly and logically organised, ending with the things you're still curious or want to know more about.
2. After reading the Lonely Planet guide, and Wikipedia entry, you sign up to a few Twitter and Instagram users specific to the country. You find a vlog from some young people living in the country, as well as a few online talks from local researchers. You join a couple of traveller-forums with people talking about their experiences, challenges and adventures, and pose your own questions on social media. You feel like you have some sense of what to expect, but the picture is more subjective, and you're unsure quite what you will experience, or how you might make sense of it. Your curiosity is piqued, and you're excited to engage more. In discussing what you know at a 'bon voyage' party with friends and family, you're less descriptive, less linear, and instead present a rich, partial, situated and questioning account of different insights into the country you've been able to glean. You end with the questions you think you'll find answers to, on your trip.

These two trip preparation modes capture – in a way – the different approaches researchers take to a literature review/introduction section of a report. Elsewhere, we've described these as either building up an evidence case for a *gap* in what we know, or making an *argument* that locates and rationalises the question we're going to explore (Braun & Clarke, 2013). Both the making an argument and the filling a gap approach involve making *a case* for your research. But they differ in how you go about it.

> **KEY CONCEPT** The establishing the gap model of a literature review provides a rationale for your research question by summarising what is known about a topic, and any limitations or gaps in existing knowledge.

A more traditional literature review validates a project's focus, based on what we do not know – let's call it the *establishing the gap model*. As an example, following their review of relevant literature on Irish men and healthy eating, British psychologists Aiden Kelly and Karen Ciclitira (2011, p. 226) stated: "what emerges clearly from the existing research is that the issue of maintaining a healthy lifestyle through healthy eating for Irish men has not been adequately addressed by researchers or policy-makers, and needs to be further explored." In its purest rendering, we find the idea of a gap problematic. It effectively reproduces a positivist-empiricist idea of research as truth-questing, where there are gaps in knowledge – produced either through a lack of *any* research or through existing knowledge being inadequate or flawed – and these gaps *need* to be filled. The notion that this is *the* right way to locate research produces much (unnecessary) anxiety. Especially as it doesn't necessarily fit well with qualitative paradigms and localised, contextualised knowledge. But to some extent, which of these models for writing an introduction is expected depends on *what* you're doing and *where* you're doing it – the audience for your TA matters! For instance, if you're working in applied fields, you're likely to encounter the establishing the gap model – often for good reason. Editors and reviewers of journals, or supervisors and examiners, may expect or demand this approach: check the expectations and needs of your context.

> **KEY CONCEPT** The making an argument model provides a rationale for your research question by situating and contextualising it within existing knowledge, theory and/or context.

Why do *we* advocate for a different approach – one we call the *making an argument model?* Because reflexive TA and Big Q qualitative research are more *adventures* than recipe-following-procedures (Willig, 2001). In qualitative research, you're providing a rich, contextualised examination of a topic that contributes some or many facets to our existing understanding(s) of the issue, and maybe even changes it. You are *not* seeking to show that you have found an empty cell in the spreadsheet of ultimate truth about the topic, which your study will fill. We think it's useful to get beyond the filling the gap idea(l), and conceptualise our qualitative analyses as contributing something to a rich tapestry of understanding that we and others are collectively working on, in different places, spaces and times. Within the making an argument approach, you're aiming to set the scene and provide a theoretically-informed and located rationale *for your research*. You're aiming to give the reader a contextualised understanding of what is currently understood, that situates what you've done, and convinces them that it is interesting and important. You do of course cite literature in telling this story about your topic, but you are *not* seeking to provide a *comprehensive* review of the existing evidence to date.

So what does this making an argument type introduction look like in practice? One of our analyses of a story completion dataset related to counter-normative[1] body hair practices offers an example of a 'scene setting' introduction (Jennings, Braun, & Clarke, 2019). In that paper, existing scholarship was used to argue that "body hair non-removal among women [is] more strictly policed than body hair removal among men" (p. 77), which provided a rationale for exploring gendered variation around body hair norms, and resistance to those norms. Another analysis of men and body hair removal stories offers an introduction that blends elements of both 'styles' of introduction (see Clarke & Braun, 2019b). As this latter article shows, such demarcations are *not* a dichotomy (just to continue a theme that characterises *much* in reflexive TA).

The mythical scientific method would suggest this part of the research project should be done *before* you do your analysis (or even collect your data), but given the open and evolving process of reflexive TA, we advocate writing (the final version of) this section later.[2] Some knowledge of the research domain and literature is necessary from the start of a research project, and indeed *increasingly* helpful during the analytic phases. However, you don't know in advance exactly how the analysis will turn out in reflexive TA, and, therefore, what literatures you will need to engage with, to build your convincing rationale. For this reason, we advocate for engaging with existing scholarship by reading *throughout* your research process, but actually writing the final version of this section towards the end of your analysis. Again, this is akin to the scene-setting you would do, on telling the story of your adventure when you were safely back home; the things you have encountered along the route would necessarily shape how you wanted to set your story up.

> **PRACTICE POINT** You may be required to write a version of your literature review/introduction early on in the research process, but we recommend only writing the final version after you have completed your analysis. You can't fully set the scene until you know what that scene is!

DESCRIBING HOW YOU APPROACHED YOUR ADVENTURE (THE METHOD/OLOGY SECTION)

The next component of writing your TA is to describe your analytic process, alongside key design choices and other procedural practices and processes for the study (see 'Design interlude'). In this method or methodology section, your task is a combination of *description* – what you did – and *explanation* – for the choices you made.[3] As well as discussion of aspects

---

[1]By counter-normative body hair practices we mean body hair practices that aren't the typical gendered norm in our westernised contexts – so for women, this is body hair retention; for men, body hair removal.

[2]An early version of a literature review/introduction may be required for things like ethics applications, research proposals, doctoral progression and funding bids.

[3]For various reasons, we generally prefer the name *methodology* for this section of a report, compared to method. The name method risks, in certain disciplines (e.g. our own discipline of psychology), a practically oriented *descriptive summary*, rather than a more theoretically-orientated and reflexive *discussion* of what, why and how one did the research. However, just using the term methodology without including such discussion does not suffice – a methodology section needs to deliver what the name promises (for a wider discussion, see Chamberlain, 2011, 2012). In some circumstances, there isn't a choice, and method it must be.

like recruitment/participants and ethics (see Braun & Clarke, 2013), this is the section where you explain your analytic choices and processes.

Explaining your choice of TA and what it offers

PRACTICE POINT Your justification for why you used reflexive TA needs to discuss which particular version you used, and why.

It is important to provide an explanation for *why* TA – and specifically *reflexive* TA – is an appropriate method to use to address your research question. In justifying why reflexive TA, you also need to explain and justify the particular choices you made around reflexive TA (e.g. more inductive or deductive, experiential or critical; see Chapter One), and locate this within theoretical frameworks (see Chapter Six). Justification typically connects to the purpose of your research, and to your specific research question, as well as to theoretical underpinnings and research design. For instance, why the theoretical positions you have taken around your TA, and your analytic orientation, are relevant to your research question.

Locating your TA theoretically, by acknowledging the philosophical (ontological and epistemological) assumptions underpinning the research, *can* be done well and relatively briefly (if circumstances require). For instance, a research team exploring family counsellors' perceptions of their primary care work located their analysis as follows:

> The epistemological stance taken in this study was a form of tempered realism. While assuming a broadly uncomplicated relationship between language and reality, the authors were aware that researchers and participants would impact on one another, and that the authors' values and assumptions would contribute to both the questions asked and the reading of the data. It was therefore important throughout the research to reflect on the authors' subjectivity and how it impacted on the collection and perception of the data [...] The analysis was conducted using an inductive 'bottom-up' approach in which there was no attempt to fit the data into an existing theory. (H. Smith, Moller, & Vossler, 2017, p. 564)

This brief description evidences that the authors have a clear theoretical position for their TA and have thought through *what* their data represent and how they are theorising language (we discuss different theories of language in Chapter Six). It also demonstrates that discussion of conceptual assumptions and underpinnings for TA does not *necessarily* have to involve deep complex theoretical debates (though sometimes these might be warranted). What is *most* important, is recognising and acknowledging a position, and one that is consistent with the analysis that follows. Note that although these authors do not cite theoretical literature in this quotation, we *do* recommend acknowledging the sources and context for your theoretical locating.

Rationalising your choice of reflexive TA needs to demonstrate that you understand *what* it offered and *allowed* you to do. In describing what reflexive TA offered for your project, try

ALERT Don't just provide a generic rationale for using TA; connect this to the purpose of your study.

to avoid simply citing its generic strengths (e.g. that it is theoretically flexible or accessible). Instead, explain *why* these are strengths for *your* research in particular; explain why it is a useful method *for your study*. You're aiming for a compelling – strong – rationale. In Table 5.1, we provide a series of different rationales we've encountered in published research, an evaluation of the strength of each – much like a website password-strength assessment[4] – and an explanation. Note that some combination of these different explanations could strengthen the rationale for TA. This can be evidenced in the examples in Table 5.2, which provides brief example rationales around the use of reflexive TA from published studies. Providing a particular and specific rationale for the use of TA demonstrates your *knowing* use of TA.

Table 5.1 Is my rationale for TA strong enough?

I used TA…	Strength	Explanation
To identify themes/patterns of meaning across the dataset	Medium – needs improvement	This explanation could be used to justify the use of any cross-case/pattern-based approach (see Braun & Clarke, 2013, 2021a); needs additional explanation for what in particular it allowed.
Because it is flexible	Weak – try again	Does not say why flexibility mattered for *your* research, and what aspects of TA's flexibility were important.
Because it is accessible	Weak – try again	Why does accessibility matter for *your* research? Practical/pragmatic rationales are rarely compelling unless design specific (e.g. because it provided an accessible method for the participant-co-researchers, none of whom had previous experience of qualitative research, to contribute to initial theme generation, see Braun & Clarke, 2021b).
Because I have used it before/I'm experienced in the method	Weak – try again	Although experience can bring depth to analytic insight, just being familiar with a method does not make it an inherently good one for your project.
Because it is widely used in my discipline/field of research	Weak – try again	This does not necessarily make it a good method *for your research question*. We acknowledge that it might aid publishability.
To allow for both inductive and deductive theme generation	Medium – needs improvement	Needs additional information that explains *why* both orientations were important, and what this aspect added to the analytic process.
Because it allowed themes to emerge from the data	Don't even try this one	Themes *do not emerge* in reflexive TA.
Because it allowed you to stay true to your participants' voices	Weak – try again	Data do not speak for themselves; themes do not passively capture meaning patterns pre-existent in the dataset.

---

[4]In the case of rationales for using reflexive TA, even 'medium strength' is not really good enough.

Table 5.2   Examples of rationales for (reflexive) TA from published research

Study overview	Rationale
Kjaran and Jóhannesson (2013) interviewed six current and former LGBT Icelandic secondary school pupils and used reflexive TA to explore how institutionalised heterosexism was manifest in secondary schools and how the participants responded to those manifestations.	Flexible application of TA meant analysis could be informed by themes in existing research on heterosexism; theoretical flexibility meant "the researcher… has considerable freedom to apply his or her theoretical framework, which in our case was queer theory" (p. 357).
Terry and Braun (2016) used 'critical thematic analysis' with qualitative survey data to explore how young men and women in Aotearoa New Zealand constructed the cultural meaning and importance of men's body hair and hair removal practices, and "to identify patterns within these constructions that highlight the relationships between new and existing ideals for masculine embodiment" (p. 16) in Aotearoa New Zealand.	TA was suitable for the analysis of a large dataset (584 responses) of qualitative survey data (a relatively novel data source, see Braun et al., 2020). TA's flexibility offered the possibility for an inductively-developed analysis, but which captured both semantic and latent meanings, and offered both descriptive and interpretative accounts of the data. Theoretical flexibility meant TA could be informed by critical discursive psychology (Wetherell, 1998) in the later interpretative stages of analysis, after three themes were developed, to explore the "rhetorical strategies deployed by participants to bolster arguments and establish the 'truth claims' of their commentary" (p. 17).
Hayfield, Clarke and Halliwell (2014) used reflexive TA in their research on bisexual women's experiences of social marginalisation and belonging, which drew on 20 interviews with self-identified bisexual women.	TA offered the possibility of an inductively-oriented experiential analysis that focused on patterned meaning. The theoretical flexibility of TA meant it could be informed by feminist approaches concerned with legitimising and 'giving voices' to the lived experiences of a socially marginalised group of women, while also locating these experiences within wider sociocultural discourses. TA allowed the authors to capture the "complex interactions between cultural discourses of bisexuality and […] these women's lived experiences of their bisexual identities and biphobia" (p. 358).

Depending on your context, there might be value in highlighting previous and successful use of TA in your discipline, research field or area, or in combination with your selected theory, or to analyse your chosen data collection method. But this is not always required. In *some* contexts, including some rationale or explanation for *why* you chose TA over a different method(ology) may be expected, but this is not a practice we advocate (see Box 5.1).

Suffice to say, we recognise method(ological) choice is informed by a range of factors including your teaching and learning context, what methods you learn, your supervisor's experience and feelings about different approaches, and student resources – including the books that are recommended to you or you have access to. These 'variables' wouldn't generally work as rationales for *why* a method was used – they haven't even made it into Table 5.1! What *is* vital for your rationale for TA is explaining what it offered your research *in particular*.

Describing what you actually *did* during analysis

As well as framing the rationale for why TA, you also need to explain *how* you did your analysis. What we want to emphasise here is the importance of writing about how you actually applied TA, rather than a more *generic* description of your process. We have read report after report, where the authors describe 'following the six phases of Braun and Clarke (2006)' and then list

====== **Box 5.1** ======

Should I explain why I used TA and not a similar method?

We should always justify the use of our chosen analytic approach. Some supervisors and examiners consider it good practice in a thesis or dissertation to *also* discuss *why* other approaches have been considered and rejected, or why the chosen method has been selected *over* other potential approaches. This is not something we recommend, but we are often asked *how* the use of TA should then be justified in a research proposal or report, especially given some degree of commonality of purpose between TA and other across-case approaches (see Braun & Clarke, 2021a). Why don't we recommend this kind of 'methodological survey' approach to method rationale? For a start, it risks allocating precious research time to comparisons of different approaches, at the expense of developing an in-depth understanding of what reflexive TA can offer. If you don't have a sound understanding of all the approaches you're 'rejecting' in favour of TA, there is a risk of mis-characterising these approaches. If you're doing this comparison at the behest of a supervisor it may be that the alternatives you present were not realistically on the table and aren't in fact credible alternatives to reflexive TA given the purpose, theoretical underpinnings and design of your research. More than this, we don't like this survey of methods approach because it risks inferring that there is always and only *one ideal* method for a research project – when this is rarely the case (see Braun & Clarke, 2013, 2021a). It also suggests that the student has been on a *quest* to seek and obtain this hallowed perfect method(ology). Finally, it's much more robust to provide a justification that shows understanding of the method used, what it offers, and how it was applied, that a thinner series of comparisons.

---

those phases, without providing any specifics of what this process looked like, *in practice*, for them. This is *not* the approach to aim for!

Imagine two different accounts of starting off on an adventure:

PRACTICE POINT   Make sure your method describes your analytic process, not the generic phases of reflexive TA.

> I caught the Heathrow Express to the airport, passed through immigration and security checks, and waited for boarding time. I then boarded the plane, found my allocated seat, listened to the pre-departure safety check, and perused the in-flight entertainment until I disembarked at my destination.

> The first part of my journey was smooth – whisked to Heathrow on the Express. At that point, things got a bit tangled; the airport was heaving, and finding my check-in and bag drop spot took longer than expected. Security objected to my trusty pocketknife, which I'd forgotten was in my hand-luggage. But I managed to negotiate going back out to send it home – I could pick up another when I landed. After that blip, smooth sailing through immigration and security, but then: a two-hour delay. Once on board – everyone a bit delay-grumpy – I found that I had a seat right at the back. Not great, but hello, a spare seat beside me. I could spread out. Joy! I settled in and was already dozing before we got to the safety instructions. What I expected to be an otherwise uneventful trip was anything but: the usual take-off delay at Heathrow, and then, four hours into the flight, we unexpectedly descended with a medical emergency, to the nearest airport. We sat on the tarmac for over three hours! By this point, I was starting to question whether I'd ever get here… Eventually, we took off again, and apart from a few bumps part way in, I slept most of it, and we landed smoothly. Exhausted, but excited, my adventure was about to begin!

The first of these offers a *generic* account. The second, a located, specific-to-the-moment, first-person version of *how things went*. This is akin to what we want to read in accounts of how you analysed your data using reflexive TA. Reviewers of papers might also ask for this, if you haven't provided it; likewise examiners. You can also think of this as a *gift* to others, so they have the opportunity to learn from how *you* did your TA (Trainor & Bundon, 2020). Box 5.2 provides a detailed methodological write up – of the kind we'd expect to be provided in a dissertation or thesis – from our former doctoral student Louise Davey. Note this is quite *long* compared to the typical description of analysis in a published paper – the latter format being far more constrained by word-limits (Levitt et al., 2018).

Box 5.2

An example of a student analysis process write-up, by Louise Davey

From Louise Davey's doctoral project exploring the impact of alopecia areata (AA), an appearance-changing hair loss condition, using both interview and survey data.

The Analytic Process

A six phase TA was undertaken to explore patterns across both datasets (Braun & Clarke, 2006, 2013; Terry et al., 2017). The six phases are distinct yet recursive, the reflexive nature of this approach to TA calling for repeated movements between the different phases in a spirit of inquiry and interpretation (Terry et al., 2017). I used both electronic and hard copies of the data over the course of my analysis and found that the movement between different media prompted in me new reflections, insights and interpretations. I also moved between different physical environments; sitting on the grass in quiet rural spaces, at my desk, in busy cafes and in the university library, among others. I was conscious that these changing spaces brought shifts in my mood and energy, shaping and colouring my analytic sensibility and interpretative responses to the data.

Most of the survey data were generated very quickly over the space of a couple of weeks following promotion of the study in the Alopecia UK online newsletter. With excitement and some trepidation, I immediately entered the familiarisation process that constitutes the first phase of analysis (Braun & Clarke, 2006). Because I had designed the project as a constructionist study, my initial analytic observations and interpretations were primarily deductive, shaped by discursive ideas so that I identified latent meanings underlying participants' words. I noticed multiple discourses of hair and hair loss in the data, yet alongside these intellectual or cognitive interpretations, I experienced strong emotional responses. I am conscious that the identities I occupy are multiple, overlapping and fluid, performed dynamically, in relation with the material world, the subjects I encounter and the body I occupy. I was therefore aware that some of what I was reading resonated with things I had heard from, or noticed in, the person in my life who lives with AA, and was mindful of the influence of my own subjectivities in my reading.

However, as I moved into the more systematic and rigorous second stage of analysis in which I began coding the data, I noticed that strong emotion was a pervasive feature of the accounts. I realised that the analysis needed to be able to capture both this semantic, affective quality, while allowing me to identify discourses and their operation in the constitution of subjectivity. By the time I had completed an initial coding of the survey data and started to undertake the interviews, it was clear to me that discourses and emotions were intertwined in the data, meeting, shaping and changing subjectivities in conscious and unconscious processes in which the visibility of hair loss and its signifying meanings were managed through a variety of strategies, including decisions about whether or not to camouflage hair loss. This prompted me to seek ways to capture all this complexity in a sufficiently coherent analytical frame. Butler's (1990, 1993, 1997) explorations of subjectivity through discursive and psychoanalytic concepts, accounting for the body through her theory of performativity, proved a helpful guide.

Just when I was ready to engage in systematic deductive coding of the full data corpus of interviews and surveys, shaped by the theoretical framework I have outlined, the *BJD* (*British Journal of Dermatology*) announced a qualitative special edition and issued a call for papers for qualitative research relevant to dermatology. Given the ethical responsibility I felt to fulfil my research objective of producing a study that was of relevance to diverse practitioners, this felt like too important an opportunity to miss. However, I was also aware that the Butler-framed analysis of subjectivity that I intended to undertake for my thesis was unlikely to speak to the *BJD* audience. My first supervisor and I independently coded the data from a broadly critical realist perspective (Madill, Jordan, & Shirley, 2000; Willig, 1999), identifying semantic and latent meanings and focusing on the **lived experience** of AA. We each then developed candidate themes, attending to socially produced meanings while staying close to the lived experiences described by the participants. We then met with my second supervisor to review and agree the final themes before producing the paper, which presented a critical exploration of meaning while 'giving voice' to the participants (Willig, 2013).

Having completed the paper (Davey, Clarke, & Jenkinson, 2019), I returned to coding of the data from a feminist poststructuralist position; both at this stage and as I developed the themes presented in the analysis section of this thesis, I was aware that the coding I had undertaken for the *BJD* paper was helping me to retain an empathic awareness of the experiences described by the participants. This helped me to engage in theoretical analysis of discourse and subjectivity without losing connection to the affective quality of their accounts. The process felt akin to working at relational depth with therapy clients; the theoretical and analytical tools operated alongside the empathic sensibility that is core to relational approaches to therapy (Clarkson, 2003; Kahn, 1997). As I worked through the coding of all the data, I moved into phase three of the analysis, identifying candidate themes and then collating relevant data extracts (Braun & Clarke, 2013). Phase four involved reviewing, revising, recoding and a lot of finding ways to "let things go" (Braun & Clarke, 2013, p. 234), a process that continued into and overlapped with phases five and six, where I defined and named themes and began writing up the analysis presented in this report.[5]

I subjected data from male and female participants to separate analyses at various points in the process of coding and theme development so that differences and similarities could be identified. This was especially important given the predominance of women among the participants. The overarching patterns presented in the themes apply to both male and female participants, but gendered discourses are a feature of the data and significant differences are noted and discussed as the themes are presented.

---

[5]Note that Louise's language here describing phases four and five reflects our original phase names, which we've since revised (as we discussed in Chapters Three and Four).

In Box 5.3, we offer another example of how to write about doing analysis that is around the length expected in a shorter journal article – using the childfree dataset analysis around the overarching theme of 'choice matters' (see Box 4.9 in Chapter Four if you want to remind yourself of the scope of this theme).

KEY CONCEPT Techniqueism refers to a preoccupation with methodological procedures or techniques, at the expense of theory, researcher subjectivity and reflexivity. It is similar to **proceduralism** or **methodolatry.**

An important aspect of the examples in Boxes 5.2 and 5.3 is that they acknowledge the *work* of the researcher in developing themes. In discussing your method, try to write in a way that avoids **techniqueism** – describe your active and situated process, rather than 'what the steps are'. Reflexive TA does not offer a technique you passively apply to your data to *extract* your analysis. Your themes *do not* emerge through application, but are developed through situated analytic practice. Write your method in a way that shows you recognise that reflexive TA offers a methodological tool to aid you in developing and interpreting patterned meaning, to give you a foundation for making certain claims about your data. Each phase involves deliberations and choices; the phases provide a framework for deep engagement as you make sense of your data. But this needs to be active, deliberate, and reflective. How you describe this matters: phrasing such as 'I did a TA...' or 'I employed TA...' evokes a fairly passive process; language like 'I used TA to...' evokes more ownership of the process, with you as "an active agent in the production of knowledge" (Trainor & Bundon, 2020, p. 3). Such language keeps the researcher *visible* in the analytic process. This is one of the reasons we prefer first person/active-voice language in reporting analysis – in contrast to the traditional third-person passive-voice of scientific scholarly reporting. Box 5.3 provides an example of such writing.[6] This is about capturing, and revealing, rather than concealing, "our methodological reflexivity[,] as being reflexive means never divorcing the 'products' of the research from the practices of research production" (Trainor & Bundon, 2020, p. 20).

PRACTICE POINT Using active first-person language when writing about your TA process keeps visible the active role of the researcher in producing the TA.

TELLING YOUR *ANALYTIC* STORY (THE RESULTS AND DISCUSSION SECTION)

In writing up the analytic part of your TA, your end-purpose is to tell an *overall* story, with conclusions drawn across the whole analysis. Themes need to be both fully developed in their own right *and* in relation to other themes. Think of a weaving together different strands to develop a singular whole. Those strands could be woven in different ways, but some ways do a better job of displaying and connecting the different strands than others. What you're

---

[6]Again, we recognise that this first person/active style of writing might not be possible within the requirements for your report.

━━━━━━━━━ **Box 5.3** ━━━━━━━━━

How we'd briefly write the analysis part of a methodology section, related to the overarching theme around 'choice'

Our critical, constructionist thematic analytic approach shifted during the analytic process between more inductive and deductive modes, and from an initially semantic to a more latent orientation. Through data familiarisation, we identified multiple points of potential analytic interest. Our coding initially produced a few hundred codes, but these often captured micro-differences in the dataset, and clustering easily reduced these to a more workable number. We initially clustered codes together into four potential broad patterns of meaning related to: choice; social responsibility; missing out without children; and good parents/bad parents (see our early mapping in Figure 4.2). For *this* paper, we focused on developing the analysis of the data connected to the provisional 'choice' theme, and noted initial patterns related to individual choice as unassailable, the right to choose, and choice as a sort of obligation. After review in relation to the codes, the coded data, and the full dataset, we became most interested in the latent ideas underpinning articulations related to choice, or the choosing person, and we shifted to developing a more theoretical and conceptual analysis around these ideas. We identified a logic around choice that appeared to reflect complementary yet distinctively different ideas related to choice, and we settled on an analytic structure with four themes. Each captured a different articulation of choice, with implications for how we can understand those who choose to be childfree. The themes were all encapsulated under an overarching theme of *choice matters*, which allowed us to emphasise the significant role choice played throughout the dataset.

---

doing in this section is providing the reader with examples of what you claim the data evidenced and what you think the patternings *mean*. Your data must be *interpreted* and connected to your broader research questions, *and to* the scholarly fields your work is situated within. This latter is sometimes forgotten, but is an important part of the task of (TA) scholarship. In doing research, you are not a lone voice shouting into a void, but part of a wider and connected network of voices.

> **ALERT** Don't forget to connect your analytic interpretation to the scholarly fields your work is situated in.

Introducing the analysis

It's good practice to give your readers an introductory *overview* of the analysis to come. Although it has likely been previewed in an abstract, it's been a while since the reader read that (if they did at all)[7]. At the start of this section,

> **PRACTICE POINT** Start the analysis section with a brief overview of your themes – in the form of a narrative description, a simple list, a table, or even a thematic map.

---

[7]It's conventional to treat abstracts and the main body of a report independently, so you shouldn't assume the reader has read the abstract.

give them the spoilers: let them know what to expect, albeit briefly. Often in reflexive TA, this takes the form of a summary paragraph or list of themes. For instance, in a paper exploring arguments against marriage equality, British psychologist Adam Jowett began the analysis section by listing the seven themes to be discussed:

> (1) marriage is by definition and tradition a union between a man and a woman; (2) marriage is designed as a framework for raising children; (3) if you allow gay marriage now, it will be polygamous and incestuous marriage next; (4) same-sex marriage would threaten the right to religious freedom; (5) same-sex couples already have equal rights; (6) changing the law to allow same-sex marriage would be undemocratic and (7) the government should focus on bigger priorities. (2014, p. 42)

The report of the study of bisexual women and marginalisation introduced in Table 5.2 named three themes and *very briefly* outlined the scope of each:

> This article reports three themes: Bisexual belonging?: 'There's nowhere to fit' captures the ways that these women felt that they did not belong in lesbian and LGBT (or heterosexual) communities. The dismissal of bisexuality: 'Well I think you should just make your mind up' and The sexualisation of bisexuality: 'Bisexuality's seen as this hypersexual identity' report how these women perceived their bisexuality to be misunderstood, marginalised, dismissed and misrepresented by both lesbians (and gay men) and by the wider culture. (Hayfield et al., 2014, p. 358)

A table also provides a useful way of previewing the analysis by presenting each theme along with a brief summary of the central organising concept and scope. We found a nice example of a summary table in a study of Welsh rugby fans' understandings of commitment to their favourite team (G. Hall et al., 2012): each theme was named[8] alongside a brief description of characteristics of the theme (see Table 5.3).

Finally, some people also use their final thematic map as a way of previewing the analysis to come, presenting something akin to the choice thematic map in Figure 4.7 in Chapter Four.

Table 5.3   Example of a theme summary table (from G. Hall et al., 2012, p. 143)

Theme	Characteristics
Affective loyalty	Strong emotional attachments that influenced psychological resistance to change
Involvement	Ideological behaviours in terms of effort to attend games and join in fanlike behaviour (e.g. jeering opposition and singing). Used to evaluate which fans were atypical fans (fair-weather fans, both in- and out-group) and which were exemplars of the fan base (die-hard fans)
Distinctiveness	The use of apparel to enhance acceptance as a fan of a specific team and also further maximise visual distinction from rival fans; avoid incorrect categorisation
Individualism	Two types of individualism; high levels of team-specific knowledge as a positive attribute and low levels of attendance and willingness to stick with the team through defeats or changes in personal circumstances (moving home) as a negative attribute

---

[8]We would have expanded the theme names for greater clarity, and to emphasise the fact they are not just 'topic summaries' but rather shared-meaning based themes (a risk with one-word names, that we highlighted in Chapter Four, is that they are taken as topic summaries).

Structuring the analysis section

The final analysis in TA combines data extracts and analytic narrative – the things *you* write, giving the reader your interpretation of the data and their meaning. We *very loosely* recommend a 50–50 balance of these two aspects: not too much data to suggest the analytic narrative aspect is underdeveloped (remember: data do not speak for themselves, which is why interpretation matters; see Chapter

> **PRACTICE POINT** A 50-50 balance of analytic narrative and data excepts in the analysis section provides a rough general guideline, but a greater proportion of analytic narrative may be required in a more latent/deductive analysis.

Seven); not too much narrative at the expensive of real data (as we discuss shortly, data extracts provide the foundational validation for your analytic claims). However, there is of course flexibility! More theoretical/deductive, or latent, or critical versions of TA might have a higher ratio of analytic narrative to data extracts (say 70:30). This is because such analyses often involve detailed analyses of data extracts (see Box 5.5) as well as locating the analysis theoretically. On the companion website, the papers by Anderson and Clarke (2019) and Beres and Farvid (2010) offer good examples of these two different data/analytic narrative ratios.

We are referencing a more *qualitative* reporting model here, where the 'results' and 'discussion' sections are combined, so your analytic narrative contains connections with, and develops the analytic points in relation to, other literature (e.g. see Beres & Farvid, 2010). We often use the heading *analysis* rather than results for such a section, as this highlights the interpretative work

> **PRACTICE POINT** A Big Q qualitative style of reporting contains an analysis section – rather than results or findings – in which the analytic narrative is connected to existing research and theory, and potentially also the wider context.

and active subjective role of the researcher. For the rest of this chapter, we discuss the analysis section of the TA report as if it was a combined 'results and discussion'. Despite our doing so, it is important to acknowledge that the combination isn't always appropriate (Box 5.4 contains pointers to consider if you wish, or are required,[9] to develop these sections separately). Furthermore, qualitative research *is* regularly reported in the more traditional scientific/quantitative format of a separate results and a discussion section (e.g. see Anderson & Clarke, 2019). In such cases, analysis still involves and requires *interpretation*, there's just more separation between reporting the data 'content' and the deeper interpretation of them. Note that if you're writing a thesis, you will usually also have a separate *general* discussion chapter, even if you contextualise your analyses in relation to existing literature when reporting each analysis. In longer reporting formats like theses, there is usually a need to draw out interpretation and conclusions *across* several different analyses.

---

[9]You might be required to have a separate analysis and discussion, for instance if a journal is particular in the format they require (see Opperman, Braun, Clarke, & Rogers, 2014).

======= **Box 5.4** =======

Writing separate results and discussion sections

The traditional scientific model of research report is to separate the results and discussion sections. It echoes an objective-scientist-ideal where you can – and should – separate out 'the (supposedly objective) findings' and what you as a researcher make of them. The implicit ideas this model promotes is one reason we find it problematic. But we recognise that this model is still firmly embedded in research reporting conventions, and in the expectations of many social and health sciences journals.

If you do write these sections separately, your manuscript will likely be a bit repetitive, and you'll have to determine whether the *interpretative work* of your qualitative analysis happens in both sections or primarily in the discussion.

There are two main ways to tackle the challenge of separate results and discussion sections:

- Report your themes in a more 'descriptive' way – 'describe' and 'show' the data content – and then locate the interpretative element of your report in the discussion. This style tends to involve using data extracts in a more illustrative way (see Box 5.5), and developing the analysis in relation to broader meanings across the dataset, rather than specific data extracts.
- Develop a more interpretative account of your themes in the results section, but then expand this with exploration of theoretical, scholarly and wider contextual interconnections and implications in the discussion section. In so doing, you could treat data extracts either illustratively, or analytically (see Box 5.5), or both. If writing in this way, a conclusion or longer 'general discussion' section[10] will often do some of the discussion work, such as reflecting on the limitations of your analysis.

One way we consider this separate results and discussion style working *poorly* in TA is where the results and discussions are effectively treated as separate entities, with little specific connection between the particular analytic points developed through engagement with the data, and the scholarly and other fields of knowledge and/or practice engaged with. In the worst cases, a discussion can almost feel like it could have been written without any data analysis at all. Given the importance of situating our analytic claims in reflexive TA – in relation to existing research and theory and wider relevant contexts (something we discuss further in Chapter Seven), such a practice is important to avoid. Another way we consider this separate approach working badly is where each theme is sequentially discussed in the discussion, rather than a broader, more integrative discussion of what the analysis tells us, overall. This particularly risks repetition of the results and a lack of analytic integration and depth.

---

[10]A general discussion is *particularly* important in dissertations and theses. For larger projects (e.g. full-year research Master's or doctoral projects), the general discussion might incorporate reflection across a number of differently focused analyses.

Both styles of analytic reporting – combined and separate analysis and discussion – can work with reflexive TA, and there is no inherently right or wrong approach:

- An *integrated* approach works *particularly* well when strong connections exist with existing research, and when the analysis is more theoretical or interpretative. Combination can also avoid repetition – drawing boundaries between the results and discussion, and avoiding repetition can be a challenge if reporting your analysis in two separate sections. If you're spotting lots of connections between your analytic 'results' and the existing literature, this suggests a more integrated approach would work best.[11]
- Two *separate* sections can work well for situations where a key goal is to produce clearly accessible implications or recommendations, as it might be in policy or practice related research. This format tends to be more typical in applied research, and more realist forms of reflexive TA. Also, if the connections between your analytic 'results' and existing literature are broader, perhaps related to your overall analytic conclusions or implications, then two separate sections might work best.

Selecting data extracts

Selecting which data extracts to include in your report is – surprise! – something that requires thought. The inclusion of data extracts in TA serves two main purposes: evidencing your analytic claims, and allowing the reader to judge the fit between your data and your understandings and interpretations of them. You should select a number of extracts (per theme) that most strongly and clearly evidence your analytic claims. Usually, you would select data extracts that evidence each of your key points in relation to each theme. You might select one to three extracts for each point, depending on the length of extract(s) and your analytic purpose – for instance, will you be using the extract to quickly illustrate something you're claiming, or will you develop a more detailed analysis around the extract? Depending on the level of *nuance* in your analytic argument, some of the points you make might not have associated data extracts. There are always word limits, and you don't want to circumscribe analytic depth by trying to illustrate *every* subtle variation with data.

Eight key tips for selecting good extracts are:

1. *Select vivid examples*: It's likely not all extracts will be particularly vivid, but aim to include the most compelling extracts (while also taking the next point into consideration). An example from the childfree dataset would be an excerpt from JOAS that succinctly suggests a dramatic revelation and experience through bold and clear language: "I never wanted kids… Then my first was born.. He was so perfect , such a miracle that I made a human wow! I thought I knew love but he showed me what it really felt to love someone with all the love I had." (The dataset on the companion website shows the full extract.)
2. *Select extracts across the range of data items*: Avoid the temptation to over-quote from one particularly articulate source. Although we often quote some participants or data items more than others, you're aiming to convince your reader that these patterns are evidenced *across* the dataset. For this reason, a balance and spread of extract sources is important.

---

[11]With the caveat that some outputs require a particular format or style.

3. *Select clear and concise extracts to illustrate analytic claims*: Data extracts that are clear, relatively concise, and not overly complex tend to work well, especially if using data in an illustrative way (see Box 5.5).

4. *Use longer extracts when treating data analytically*: More complex and longer quotations can work well when you're using data extracts in an analytic way (see Box 5.5).

5. *You want a range of quotations for each theme*: First, ones that evidence the central organising concept of the theme, then others to illustrate the different facets of the theme's expression.

6. *Avoid repeating extracts*: Only use the same extract more than once in exceptional circumstances – for instance, if it's a *brilliant* quotation that evidences *two* themes in a completely enmeshed way. (If you do so, it's good practice to acknowledge this, and refer the reader back to previous use.)

7. *Edit out unnecessary detail*: If you have an excellent data extract to use, but there's some irrelevant material in the middle making it longer than need be, remove the irrelevant text but indicate this with [...]. Imagine you ask a participant a question, they start to answer, then make an unrelated aside, then come back to the question. Its things like an aside comment that we're getting at here. Do *not* remove text which contradicts the analytic claim you are making. This is not about making the data fit *your* point. Consider this data item from CHCA in the childfree dataset (see Table 2.1): "Why do people assume that choosing to be childfree automatically means that you won't have children in your life? My partner and I have decided not to have kids for a range of personal, environmental and social reasons. But I am a Godmother, an aunt, an older cousin, and a friend to many children. Contrary to common misconception those who choose not to have kids are rarely lonely, just more self-aware. In many cases those who choose not to have kids have usually thought a lot more about that decision than those who reproduce." If you were making an analytic point related to *having children in your life*, it would be acceptable to edit the quoted excerpt to: "Why do people assume that choosing to be childfree automatically means that you won't have children in your life? [...] I am a Godmother, an aunt, an older cousin, and a friend to many children." Such editing allows the reader to access the meaning more easily, but does not remove material that contradicts the interpretations being made. But – not only does it need to be signalled (by [...]) in the quoted data excerpt itself, any practice of data editing needs to be described in the *method* section.[12]

8. *Clarify and contextualise extracts where necessary*: Similarly, sometimes meaning in an otherwise excellent extract might be *unclear* without some explanation or contextualisation. You can – indeed should – include needed clarifying information or contextualise the extract with the relevant information when you introduce it. For example, imagine you want to quote just *part* of a long anecdote a participant relayed in an interview. The part you want to quote contains an ambiguous reference to 'her' (e.g. 'I told her...'). In such instances, include clarification in square brackets within the quoted data (e.g. 'I told her [officemate]' or 'I told [officemate]'). Or it may be crucial for the reader's understanding of an extract – in terms of its literal meaning and/or significance – to explain where it came from in the data item (e.g. in response to a particular interview question, or following a challenging to someone's account in a focus group discussion).

---

[12]For transcribed audio data, removing elements from a quotation like hesitation or repetition generally does not need acknowledgement, but this should be described in the *method* in relation to how data were transcribed; likewise, for any added punctuation (see Braun & Clarke, 2013). There is guidance on transcription for reflexive TA on the companion website.

As data *do not speak for themselves*, analysis involves *you* making sense of the data, and clearly *telling the reader* what that sense-making is. The work your analytic narrative is designed to do is to combine showing the reader what meanings were 'in' the data, and what sense you made of those meanings.

Data extracts and your analytic narrative

Your analytic narrative needs to go *beyond* what is contained in the data excerpts you quote. The extracts you quote provide a structure for your analytic narrative, whether you use the data extracts as illustrations of a point you are making, or you discuss the specific analytic detail of the extracts. There are two typical ways data extracts are used in reporting reflexive TA: *illustratively* and *analytically*. Like much in reflexive TA, these are not the opposite points on a dichotomy, but form a continuum, and any one analysis might blend these different usages, or do one or the other.

Using data extracts illustratively

With an **illustrative use of data** extracts, your analytic narrative – the rich, detailed, interpretative account of the theme – tells a story about your themes, and their meaning and significance, without focusing on the *par-*

> **KEY CONCEPT** Using data extracts illustratively means using extracts to provide examples of your analytic points.

ticularities of individual data extracts. The analytic narrative would make sense without any instances of quoted data included.[13] Data excerpts are effectively *inserted into* this narrative, and provide *illustrations* or *examples* of the analytic points. They provide snapshots of data evidence to show the meanings you're claiming – and a basis for the reader to assess your interpretation of those meanings. As the narrative does not develop in relation to the *par-ticularities* of each data extract, you could, in theory, use any one of a number of extracts to illustrate each point. In this approach, you often find extracts presented after phrases like 'for example' or 'for instance' (see Box 5.5). This use is particularly common in *experiential* approaches to reflexive TA (for a more detailed discussion of experiential TA, see Chapters Six and Seven).

---

[13]If we saw an analysis with *no* data presented, we would have questions about the quality of the analysis. But in an illustrative use of extracts, the details of the specific extracts presented are not vital to *under-standing* the overall story of the analysis.

━━━━━ **Box 5.5** ━━━━━

Illustrative and analytic treatment of data extracts in reporting a theme

We will demonstrate the difference between an illustrative and an analytic use of a data extract, by coming back to *one* of the extracts we used in the theme based around a contradiction (*good and bad parents*) discussed in Box 4.7 in Chapter Four. We have developed an analysis around the *same* extract, first in an illustrative style, and then in an analytic style. The analyses we present are slightly different from each other and indeed different from what we offered in Box 4.7 (which offers another example of *illustrative* use of data). These varied analyses emphasise our point that there's no one *right* thing you should say about your data.

Illustrative use of an extract

Commenters regularly evoked the notion of 'fitness' – and thus 'unfitness' – to parent, and very occasionally referred to this explicitly (in the extract below, it appears as a "warrant of fitness") when talking about other people and their parenting. A dichotomisation between good/fit and bad/unfit parents was occasionally also invoked when commenters described *personal* characteristics or parenting practices, through which they positioned themselves either as good parents or bad parents. In relation to the latter, participants usually evoked a *potential* bad parent status, which they had managed to *avoid* – thus effectively situating themselves as *not*-bad-parents. For example, in the following extract, MIBE described a "serious" self-assessment process which led her to conclude that she would not be a good parent, and thus should not have children.

> I personally like the idea of being a parent but recognised very early on that I had too much of a temper, and that my moods were too up and down. I seriously looked at myself like giving myself a warrant of fitness for parenting, and declined the warrant. [...] I make an awesome part time, respite care mum, but I know my limits. There are so many amazing parents out there. Sadly there are also some appalling parents out there. My only judgement on the world is that I wish more men and women would give themselves a warrant of fitness before becoming a parent. It's such a huge responsibility, and it's for a very long time. (MIBE)

This idea of a dichotomy between good/fit or bad/unfit parents disrupted the idea that anyone is entitled to become a parent, suggesting that only those who will be good parents *should* have children. It also decontextualises parenting and makes it about individual psychology – as if good parenting is something that resides inside, in the character of the individual, and thus can be determined in advance. It takes away the myriad of contextual and situational factors, material, social, and cultural resources which contribute to parenting – both in the moment, and overall (Clarke, 2002). Furthermore, if parenting reflects internal characteristics, it's unlikely to change. One is either, simply, a good or a bad parent. That parenting might, in reality, reflect the intersection of the parent or parents, the child or children, and the various sociocultural, material and relational contexts of their lives, and change in relation to these, is obscured through the evocation of a good/bad parent dichotomy.

Analytic treatment of an extract

As well as commenting regularly on others' parenting, participants evoked an idea of *good parents* and *bad parents* in comments that related to themselves. They positioned their desires, and their material choices and practices, in relation to an either/or logic of good or bad parenting. Consider this extract from MIBE:

> I personally like the idea of being a parent but recognised very early on that I had too much of a temper, and that my moods were too up and down. I seriously looked at myself like giving myself a warrant of fitness for parenting, and declined the warrant. [...] I make an awesome part time, respite care mum, but I know my limits. There are so many amazing parents out there. Sadly there are also some appalling parents out there. My only judgement on the world is that I wish more men and women would give themselves a warrant of fitness before becoming a parent. It's such a huge responsibility, and it's for a very long time. (MIBE)

The category of unfit parent is widespread in the sociocultural context. It is gendered, racialised, heteronormative and classed (e.g. Breheny & Stephens, 2007; Clarke, 2001; Clarke et al., 2004; C. Thomas, 1997; Van Brunt et al., 2016; Ware, Breheny, & Forster, 2017), and is highly undesirable, reflecting a failure of what is often positioned as the most natural of relational duties for a woman – the care and raising of a child (Barnett, 2004). Although in this quotation MIBE claims a bad parent position, she also does so in a number of ways that resist the negative implications of such positioning. First, although she characterises herself as emotionally unstable ("too much of a temper", moods "up and down"), she also evokes a rational and logical self, not governed by emotions but able to surpass them. Her description positions her as highly self-aware, able to identify, separate out, and cast judgement on, different aspect of self, ultimately making a decision for the greater good rather than based in instinctive self-interest. She evokes the popular trope for difficult decisions of 'taking a long hard look at oneself' and the resulting outcome is one that goes against her personally "liking" the idea of parenthood. In this she evidences the rational choosing subject of neoliberal ideologies (Gill, 2008). Effectively, this neoliberalised, responsibilised account situates parenting as within the domain of *choice* in contrast to the domain of *affect* or *desire*. This suggests that everyone could, and ideally should, consider any and all implications around becoming and being a parent, and therefore choose to opt out if their fitness is in doubt. The extension of this logic obscures intense pronatalist normalisation, expectation and sometimes pressure, and risks placing *additional* blame on parents and non-parents for making a *wrong* choice.

MIBE also resists the negative associations of childless women as selfish and heartless (Clarke et al., 2021) or even 'child hating' in two ways: first through her initial description that she 'likes the idea of being a parent', and later through her self-characterisation as "awesome part time, respite care mum". In this later description, she also effectively claims a good parent position, albeit an occasional one, reducing any potential stigma around mental health or non-parenthood. In this brief extract then, MIBE effectively navigates a complex set of risky identities related to (non)parenthood, while reiterating in quite extreme terms, a dichotomy between "amazing parents" and "appalling parents."

Treating data extracts analytically

KEY CONCEPT Treating data extracts analytically means that you comment on and make sense of the specific features of a particular data extract in order to advance your analytic narrative.

For an **analytic treatment of data**, it's better to imagine the data extracts and your analytic narrative as knitted together. This is because here you focus on the specific detail *within* the quoted data extracts and you develop your analytic claims and overall narrative in relation to these. This type of ana-

lytic narrative produces a rich interpretative account that describes aspects of the overall patterning of the theme, but also provides a *particularised* analysis of elements of the patterning, in relation to the selected data extracts. With this style of analytic narrative, it would be impossible to simply *swap* one data extract for another, because your analytic narrative is developed *from* each extract. Likewise, removing the extracts would leave an analytic narrative that was somewhat meaningless, because the completeness and integrity of the narrative rests on the particular data extracts. This use of data extracts is more common in *critical* approaches to reflexive TA (for a more detailed discussion of critical TA, see Chapters Six and Seven).

Traps to avoid when reporting your analysis in reflexive TA

ALERT Data do not speak for themselves; you speak for data!

No matter which approach you take to combining data extracts and analytic narrative, you need to remember the mantra that data do not speak for themselves. This mantra is somewhat

built-in to an *analytic* treatment of data, but it is less obviously so for an illustrative use. When using data extracts in reflexive TA (especially in more *illustrative* mode) there are a few traps that are – fairly – easy to avoid; traps which would result in a weak analysis (we discuss quality in more depth in Chapter Nine):

- *Simply paraphrasing the data* – using different words to essentially say the same thing. To show what this looks like, in Box 5.6 we provide a paraphrased 'analysis' of the *same* extract we used in Box 5.5. Analysis doesn't *just* report data verbatim, or even summarise or paraphrase them. The so-called analysis in Box 5.6 goes no further than rephrasing and summarising what MIBE has stated. Interpretation is absent. Recognise that interpretation is your friend in avoiding the paraphrasing trap. When you're doing analysis with *interpretation* as your guiding principle, it's hard to (just) paraphrase or synopsise the data, because you have to focus on the *so what*, the question of what you think the data mean. But paraphrasing *can* creep in, so ask yourself whether your narrative goes *beyond* what is contained in the extracts you present and doesn't just summarise or paraphrase. This 'going beyond' might sometimes be fairly minimal, such as highlighting a key aspect and indicating why it's relevant, or it might do more, and interrogate and unpack what is said and what that means.

ALERT Don't paraphrase data! Explain what the data mean and why that is interesting and important.

- *Not analysing the data.* If, in a more illustrative treatment of data, you use multiple and often short extracts of data, seemingly reporting quite closely what participants said, analysis should still always move you *beyond* the data (unlike in Box 5.6). Even if you stay strongly inductive and close to the semantic meaning in your interpretation, analysis and its reporting is a process whereby you *interpret* data and organise them within a larger overarching conceptual framework and narrative.

- *Evidence of arguing with the data* – where your analytic narrative is not focused on interpretation so much as showing or describing why your participants or data are *wrong*.

- *Extracts that don't convincingly demonstrate your analytic claims.* Where either they do not support what it is you are claiming – you're overinterpreting – or, worse, suggest an *alternative* interpretation. Or, where there are so few extracts provided that the evidence for your analytic claim appears very thin.

> **ALERT** Don't argue with your participants/data – your role isn't to determine whether they are right or wrong, but to explain to the reader what is important and interesting about what they are saying.

These traps all come back to our key point: with reflexive TA, analysis effectively *uses data to make a point.* Your analysis is the 'answer' to a question, and so needs to be driven by the question 'so what?' What is relevant or useful here in addressing my question?

==================== **Box 5.6** ====================

Don't try this at home – paraphrasing your data

Some commenters claimed that they evaluated their own 'fitness' to parent and made a parenting choice based on the outcome. For example:

> I personally like the idea of being a parent but recognised very early on that I had too much of a temper, and that my moods were too up and down. I seriously looked at myself like giving myself a warrant of fitness for parenting, and declined the warrant. [...] I make an awesome part time, respite care mum, but I know my limits. There are so many amazing parents out there. Sadly there are also some appalling parents out there. My only judgement on the world is that I wish more men and women would give themselves a warrant of fitness before becoming a parent. It's such a huge responsibility, and it's for a very long time. (MIBE)

Here, MIBE describes her experience of wanting to parent, but as removing this as an option after evaluating her own mental health and deciding her temper and moods were too unstable. She suggests this practice should be standard practice for men and women before they decide to become parents, as there are too many bad parents doing a poor job of parenting.

Is 'thick description' something I should be aiming for?

Misperceptions abound around both TA and qualitative research, and both often get described in universalising ways. One claim you might hear is that your analysis should aim to provide **thick description**, so we briefly describe what this is and how it might apply in relation to reflexive TA analytic writing. Originating in ethnography but now in wider use, the concept of thick description is broadly understood as referring to analysis – and specifically an analytic *narrative* – that is richly contextualised and **interpretative** (Ponterotto, 2006). This is essentially how we conceptualise good reflexive TA reporting. However, we don't tend to use the term thick description, because some of the associated concepts are not ones that align with our conceptualisation of qualitative research, or are specific to different forms of qualitative research (see Ponterotto, 2006). One of the evocative aspects of thick description that Ponterotto described is that it positions the reader to be able to imagine or *feel* what's described in the data. *If* your TA is experientially orientated, that might be a useful image to keep in mind.

Although we don't suggest you should aim for 'thick description' as a named-practice, unless this particularly resonates in your disciplinary context/research field, the broad concept is a useful one to understand. For reflexive TA, one important writing-up practice often connected with thick description is *contextualising data extracts*. This refers not simply to helping the reader to understand the literal meaning of the extract (noted above), but, where relevant, providing context that helps the reader to understand the *significance* of the data and *assess your interpretation* of them (see Yardley, 2015). This might involve reflecting on the tone of an interview or describing a participant or their more general perspectives in some way. Or – for a dataset like the childfree comments – it might involve a rich account of the context in which the dataset was produced, as we did in Chapter Two. Providing context for extracts can be a way of disrupting the inference that meaning and experience exist independent of context, that there are decontextualised, universal truths. In adventure terms, it's like providing some context for the photos you present within the story you tell; it helps people make sense of and understand better what was going on. It importantly emphasises the situatedness of knowledge central to qualitative paradigms.

The flow of the story

Looking beyond the analysis developed around each *individual* theme, you need to consider theme *order*. This is another important part of telling the strongest story about your analysis. Sometimes flow might be easy to determine. Sometimes themes seem to 'build on' each other in an easily developed storyline. Sometimes it can be a challenge, such as when themes convey 'opposite' interpretations or meanings (e.g. parenting should be a rational choice; parenting is a natural evolutionary desire), as we discussed in Chapter Four. Which theme best comes first, to tell the best story? Good questions to guide the order in which you present your themes include:

- What is the logical flow here?
- Is one theme more central to the overall point, so needs to come first?
- Is one theme larger or more 'major' compared to the others – it might encompass more data and facets, or capture a particularly *salient* meaning – and so it makes the most sense to go first?
- Should certain themes go later, so the analytic narrative can make connections/build on analysis from earlier-presented themes?

This last question highlights that although themes are stand-alone entities, there are typically moments of interconnection between them. Qualitative data and datasets are often 'messy', and the analytic process in reflexive TA doesn't tend towards simple tidy demarcation. An extract of data, for instance, might convey the idea contained within two separate themes. Such interconnects provide useful clues to guide the order and flow of themes. If later themes can build on earlier ideas, flow can help both in avoiding analytic repetition – which can make research reports overly wordy and even boring – and developing analytic richness.

Should I use numbers to report theme 'frequency'?

Short answer and basic starting point: no! But it's more complicated, so we'll explain why, in general, we argue against the use of frequency counting in reporting themes in reflexive TA. We say in general, because sometimes there might be value in reporting absolute frequencies for concrete aspects of data – in the context of certain data collection methods (e.g. story completion, see Braun, Clarke, Hayfield, Moller, & Tischner, 2019; Clarke, Braun, Frith, & Moller, 2019). There are also discussions around how and where numbers might be useful within qualitative research practice (e.g. see Sandelowski, 2001). In reporting reflexive TA, we don't encourage a focus on frequency for a number of reasons:

> **ALERT** We generally advise against the reporting of theme frequency in reflexive TA because it's premised on assumptions that are not consistent with a Big Q qualitative framework.

- *There seems to be a remnant of quantification envy.* The reporting of theme frequency seems to represent an implicit re-articulation of the idea that numbers are more precise and better than general descriptions.
- *It buys into a logic where more is better.* But "counting responses misses the point of qualitative research" (Pyett, 2003, p. 1174). As we noted in Chapter Four, whether a pattern helps us elucidate a key aspect of understanding our research topic is not determined by how many people said it. To evoke your adventure again, something utterly transformative in your adventure might only be fleeting – that would not invalidate it as a key part of your experience or your story about it; something would be missing if you did not mention it, on return. Likewise, although common patterns can be valuable, infrequent ones might also be important in addressing the research question (Buetow, 2010) – as our 'choice' analysis in Chapter Four (Figure 4.7 and Box 4.9) illustrated. The fourth theme – *the 'real' victims* – was comparatively minor in frequency, but nonetheless an important part of the overall analysis of how choice operated.
- *Much qualitative data collection renders the use of simple counts problematic.* If data are collected from people, in an interactive way, they are subjective and situational, and each data item is not directly comparable to another. Participants in an interview, for instance, respond to non-identically-asked questions, in different interview contexts. We simply cannot assume that someone *not* reporting something (e.g. an experience, a perspective) means it is not *relevant* to that person, or not part of their life. Maybe they just didn't frame things that way, that time; maybe they forgot about an experience. This makes drawing absolute interpretations around presence or absence of a meaning circumspect at best.
- *Frequency and prevalence are not straightforward.* Nor is how important they might be analytically. How should we judge fairly brief *mentions* of something in most of the data items, compared to an in-depth and detailed focus on the same point in just one fifth of data items?

- *Critical qualitative research focuses on constructions rather than truths.* Critical frameworks that treat language in productive ways, as constructing the things they describe, rather than reporting on truth (see 'What do we think language does?' in Chapter Six), render this even *more* complex, because you're not simply looking for direct and explicated stating of an idea, or concept, and counting that as *evidence* for it.

Given all this, we argue that we should – in true *Big Q* fashion – embrace partiality, and refuse to nail down a final, absolute analysis. We recommend you continue to use the expressions common in pattern-based qualitative analytic reports – like 'many texts …' or 'a common theme…' or 'a majority of…' (see Braun & Clarke, 2013). If you *are* asked to provide some frequency – what do we recommend? If you can't persuade the editor/your examiner of the validity of your stance on frequency counts, we like the way book contributor Gareth Terry tackled this in his doctoral thesis about men and vasectomy in Aotearoa New Zealand. He gave some 'approximate' indicator of the number of interviews (out of a group of 17 participants[14]) that different descriptors related to:

> When a theme is discussed within this chapter, some quantifying language will be used to discuss its prevalence across the data corpus. It is important to note that these terms are not in any way attempting to 'count' the instances of a theme's occurrence (as per content analysis), but rather to provide some indication of the strength or consistency of a theme. Where the term 'many' is used, it refers to occurrences of the theme within at least 10 of the 17 'typical' participants' accounts. When I use 'most' or 'almost all', this will mean at least 12 to 14 occurrences are being referred to, and 'some' as six to eight. Terms such as 'commonly' and 'typically' or 'often' will more broadly refer to occurrences of the theme in anywhere between 10 and 17 interviews and 'occasionally' or 'uncommon' will refer to less than half of the participants. (Terry, 2010, p. 108)

Should I claim generalisability in reporting my TA?

The implication that TA ideally *would* generate statistically 'generalisable' knowledge is evidenced in published TA papers that either highlight or effectively apologise for lack of **generalisability** of their analysis. To quote just two of many examples:

> Given the small sample size, the findings are not generalisable. (Ford, Moodie, Purves, & MacKintosh, 2016, p. 7)

> The research involved a small sample size so the findings are not generalisable. (Muhammad, Milford, Carson, Young, & Martin, 2016, p. 39)

It may not seem at all odd that qualitative papers make such points. If you come to TA from a discipline dominated by, and a background or training in, quantitative/(post)positivist research, you'll likely have the spectre of generalisability haunting you (along with its similarly

---

[14]Gareth's overall doctoral project included interviews with 28 men; this analysis was based on a sub-set of 17 interviews.

popular sibling, reliability). Researchers overall seem to be deeply embedded in an ideology of statistical or empirical generalisability (Maxwell & Chmiel, 2014) as the aim and purpose of knowledge generation. It *is* hard to let go of the idea that value is ascertained by the

> **KEY CONCEPT** Generalisability refers to things we have identified in a specific 'sample' or context that have relevance for a wider population or context.

ability of our research to speak more widely and more generally than the specifics of our dataset or 'sample'. Indeed, the fact that qualitative researchers often use the language of *sample* evokes the idea that what we're looking at is a subset of a bigger whole (and, by implication, could be applicable to this bigger whole or population). Imagine flipping this around! Can you imagine a report of a factor analysis that effectively *apologised* for not providing a rich and deep analysis of people's subjective meanings? Or a report of a quantitative questionnaire that bemoaned its inability to capture the multi-faceted and contextually located texture of people's everyday lives, or the nuance of language use around the topic of interest? The strangeness of these inversions hopefully demonstrates why qualitative research apologising for lack of statistical generalisability is problematic. In making such apologies, certain norms or ideals around knowledge are evoked and effectively reinstated as the ideal (B. Smith, 2018; Varpio et al., 2021) – here, that research *should* be statistically generalisable.

So should you claim generalisability in relation to your TA? Some qualitative researchers have certainly argued for an exorcism of this spectre: a *let it go* reassurance that statistical or indeed any generalisability is *not* relevant to qualitative research. Many suggest we should turn to other criteria to talk about our research inferences beyond the boundaries of our dataset or participant group – such as some form of **transferability**, which is seen as more *qualitatively*-situated. These ideas have oft been repeated, including by ourselves. But the conversations around generalisability and qualitative research are more complex. Other qualitative researchers have taken a different stance, and argued for developing forms of generalisability grounded in the values of Big Q

> **KEY CONCEPT** Transferability refers to qualitative research that is richly contextualised in a way that allows the reader to make a judgement about whether, and to what extent, they can safely transfer the analysis to their own context or setting.

qualitative research (see Carminati, 2018; Hellström, 2008; Polit & Beck, 2010; B. Smith, 2018). Distinctly qualitative forms of generalisability have been proposed, in addition to transferability, which we overview in Table 5.4 (drawing on Smith's [2018] and others' work).

Overall, there are three broad issues at stake related to generalisability: wanting to say things beyond the specific; what we *mean* when we talk about generalisability; and whether we should just use some other concept to talk beyond the specific. Generally, in doing reflexive TA, we want to understand some issue or phenomenon, and we want to connect that to something broader. For instance, in researching body hair meanings and practices (e.g. Clarke & Braun, 2019b; Terry & Braun, 2016), we have wanted to extrapolate and consider broader inferences beyond the dataset and our specific analyses. In an analysis that explored how people made sense of male body hair, we made inferences about the meanings of male body hair in Aotearoa New Zealand culture in general. We suggested that "despite some greater shifts toward an idealisation of male hairlessness internationally [...] having at least

Table 5.4 Different types of *qualitative* generalisability

Type of generalisability (and key authors)	Brief description	Relevance to reflexive TA
Intersectional generalisability (Fine, Tuck, & Zeller-Berkman, 2008)	Exemplified by "work that digs deep and respectfully with community to record the particulars of historically oppressed and colonized peoples/ communities and their social movements of resistance, as well as work that tracks patterns across nations, communities, homes, and bodies to theorize the arteries of oppression and colonialism" (p. 174).	Applicable to reflexive TA with a concern for social justice, and particularly to the use of TA within community-based and participatory designs (Braun & Clarke, 2021b). Also applicable to experiential TA research that seeks to explore the lived experience of socially marginalised groups (e.g. wheelchair users, Black trans women).
Flexible generalisability (Goodman, 2008)	Originated in the discursive qualitative tradition. Discursive analyses are generalisable to the extent that they can show how a particular discursive strategy will often produce the same results. Several studies may be required to demonstrate that a discursive strategy achieves a certain function in a range of settings and when used by a range of speakers. Any generalisable discursive strategy is subject to change and unlikely to persist forever, because of the flexible nature of language.	Potentially applicable to constructionist and critical forms of reflexive TA, and particularly when constructionist and critical reflexive TA is combined with discursive approaches (see Box 8.5 in Chapter Eight).
Idiographic (Sandelowski, 2004), *analytical* (Chenail, 2010; Lewis, Ritchie, Ormston, & Morrell, 2014; Polit & Beck, 2010; Simons, 2014), and *vertical* (Stephens, 1982) generalisability.	All loosely capture the idea of building a deep interpretative and conceptually-oriented analysis that can contribute to wider knowledge. This type of generalisability occurs through conceptual or theoretical generalisability – for example, research generates a new concept or theory that has relevance for subsequent research.	Applicable to reflexive TA that is richly interpretative, particularly to more deductive/theoretical forms of reflexive TA.
Transferability, *inferential* (Lewis et al., 2014) or *case-to-case* generalisation (Chenail, 2010).	Describes research where the specific context, participants, settings and circumstances of the study are described in detail so the reader can evaluate the potential for applying the analysis to other contexts and settings. The burden of determining transferability is placed on the reader, but the researcher has to demonstrate 'sensitivity to context' (Yardley, 2015) in reporting their research to maximise the potential for transferability.	Potentially applicable to all forms of reflexive TA.
Naturalistic (Stake, 1995) or *representational* (Lewis et al., 2014) generalisability.	When the research resonates with the reader's experiences and/or they recognise similarities between the analysis and other research. As with transferability, the researcher must demonstrate 'sensitivity to context' (Yardley, 2015) in their reporting.	Potentially applicable to all forms of reflexive TA. 'Resonating with the reader's personal experience' is likely more applicable to experiential orientations.

some body hair is still considered a dominant expression of masculine embodiment" (Terry & Braun, 2016, p. 17). Similarly, in a paper using story completion data to make sense of male body hair removal, we noted:

> There were strong resonances between these stories and existing research on male body hair depilation, including survey self-report data, particularly Terry and Braun's (2016) qualitative survey data, from classroom exercises (Fahs 2012, 2013), media analyses (e.g., Frank 2014) and other analyses of popular cultural texts (e.g., Immergut 2002), and existing research on the construction of modern masculinities more broadly (e.g., Gill et al. 2005; Hall & Gough 2011). This suggests story completion is useful in capturing socially prevalent sense-making. (Clarke & Braun, 2019b, p. 110)

For those doing work around policy or in clearly applied areas, wanting to make more general claims will likely be a main driver in research. Likewise, those working for social justice will often want to speak beyond the specifics of any particular study. We like the claim from US social justice psychologist Michelle Fine and colleagues (2008, p. 174), that "inquiry that seeks to reveal the historic and contextual specificities of place and identity can shed light on the worldly effects of domination and resistance". Qualitative research can generate higher-level concepts and theories that have relevance beyond a particular setting or context (Polit & Beck, 2010). Indeed, *critical* qualitative research is often orientated to understanding and interrogating wider social meanings and consequences, through an exploration of a specific dataset; wider relevance is thus built in to critical frameworks at the same time as they often eschew simple claims of wider applicability.

Key in developing claims about the wider relevance of your analysis is finding a way to *retain* the contextualisation of data, and interpretation, that are central to qualitative paradigms. The common way statistical generalisability is used in quantitative research depends on a 'sample' that 'represents' a wider population. The understanding of knowledge generated from qualitative research as contextual is at odds with the idea that you can *simply* extrapolate to others (Polit & Beck, 2010). Put simply, context matters; we know people are situated beings. But does this mean we should limit ourselves exclusively to claims about our *specific* dataset or participant group? Generally, we agree with qualitative researchers who think the answer is 'no'.[15] A key task for qualitative authors is how we ensure "the readiness of [our] studies for reasonable extrapolation" (Polit & Beck, 2010, p. 1451) by readers, especially when the length of our report is constrained – by assignment word limits, academic regulations or journal word limits.[16] For writing up your TA, we recommend you carefully and specifically locate your participant group/dataset by not just describing demographic aspects (see Terry, Braun, Jayamaha, & Madden, 2021), but also (briefly) describing the contexts of data collection – such as norms and practices relevant to the data collection context. For a study on

---

[15]Approaches to 'synthesising' analyses across qualitative studies (e.g. Willig & Wirth, 2018) – some of which are using TA (which we briefly discuss in Chapter Eight) – are another way that 'broader generalisability' is being tackled beyond individual studies.

[16]Journal word limits are notoriously ungenerous, even in journals that welcome qualitative research, something that needs review (Levitt et al., 2018).

meanings around being childfree, as in our example dataset, this might include the historical, policy and demographic context of voluntarily not having children, intersectional analysis of parenthood and identity, as well as the wider discursive or representational status of not having children by choice (e.g. mainstream media representations and discourses of people who choose not to parent). This enables your readers to consider the 'fit' between your dataset and interpretations, and whatever contexts and datasets/groups they are interested in, or working with.

Given there are many variations in what generalisability can be, our answer to the question *should you claim generalisability?* is – naturally – it depends on *how* you conceptualise generalisability. Reflexive TA can in general be 'softly' generalisable, and can have relevance beyond the contexts studied. But critical engagement around this is important – as reflexive TA researchers, we should *not* frame the lack of statistical generalisability as a limitation of our research. We should also resist pressures from examiners, editors and others to do so (Braun & Clarke, 2021c). Instead, we should reflect on the ways in which the characteristics of our participant group/dataset, and the context and setting of our research, may have shaped or inflected our 'results'. And we should discuss the ways in which our results *might* be generalisable, knowingly and reflexively drawing on conceptualisations of generalisability theoretically consistent with the **philosophical assumptions** of our research.

> **PRACTICE POINT** Do your TA knowingly, and with integrity, and ensure the claims you make align with your overall frameworks for reflexive TA.

DRAWING CONCLUSIONS

Ever had that experience where you start telling a story, then realise it hasn't got a point, and so desperately hope that someone interrupts and saves the moment? Realising you don't have a conclusion to a story feels *wrong*. A good story doesn't just fizzle out. The same goes with writing up your TA – you need to draw some conclusions. Conclusions are the ultimate *so what* of the story. From the reader's point of view, it's like: *well we've stayed with you as you've told us about your adventure; what can we take away from it?* In more contemporary terms, your conclusions effectively offer a TL;DR (too long; didn't read) for the reader.

> **PRACTICE POINT** Conclusions are important to tell the reader why your analysis matters. You can draw conclusions in relation to a number of different domains.

We find it useful to think about the conclusions we might be able to draw in relation to six different domains – which we'll illustrate with examples from the childfree dataset:

1. Conclusions related to *the data and the analysis*. *What* do we know about this area that we didn't before, and what do we think the implications of that are? For instance, something that came across strongly in the childfree dataset was that the notion of fit and unfit parents was firmly embedded in people's sense-making about (not) having children, and that was used to legitimise and undermine choices to parent or not. The implications of this might be a persistent undermining

of those who choose not to have children simply because they do not want them, and an ongoing need for this group to rationalise their life choices.

2. Conclusions related to *existing scholarship and/or the discipline* you're working in. *What* does our study tell us that's new or different for our field or discipline? How might what we already knew be reinforced or validated by the similar understandings we've developed here? How can similar conclusions from different contexts or settings allow us to make claims about the broader relevance of *our* analysis? How does existing scholarship provide validity or foundations for the sorts of conclusions we draw from our analysis? For instance, we might conclude – alongside other literature – that the concept of individual choice is a deeply embedded one in westernised societies.

3. Conclusions related to *the method or methodology*. *What* does our use of this particular method(ology) reveal – in relation to the method itself, and/or in relation to the topic? For instance, our use of Facebook comments demonstrated that while usually fairly brief, they can provide a rich and even somewhat nuanced source of data. Facebook comments gave us access to diverse meanings as well as contradiction and tension. For instance, the seemingly straightforward concept of choice was used in many different ways, with many different meanings, throughout the dataset. If others have already claimed the value of such data for qualitative analysis, you can offer further evidence for the usefulness of a fairly new and exciting data source, and potentially contribute to the ethical discussion of the use of such data.

4. Conclusions related to *theory*. *What* might our story tell us about our theoretical 'takes' on the topic, the issue, or the analysis? For instance, our analysis suggested that in the domain of non-parenthood, neoliberal notions of choice seem to be only *one* conceptualisation of choice. Coming at the data with an analytic lens strongly influenced by neoliberalism as a theoretical framework (Gill, 2008)[17] would potentially obscure important nuance, and that choice reflected a wider range of philosophical and conceptual ideas than neoliberalism alone (see Box 4.9 in Chapter Four). This suggests that the influence of neoliberal thinking might be lower in this domain than some others; following on from this, we could explore what that might help us to understand about that theoretical framework, and/or theorising the meanings of voluntarily not having children.

5. Conclusions related to *practice*. *What* can we say about how people work or practice in an area, based on our data analysis? Our childfree dataset is not obviously applied, but we might suggest, for instance, that *mainstream media* and government agencies do not use the term child*less*, because it reproduces an already-pervasive deficit model of non-parenthood, that many people have to defend themselves against, and because people without their 'own' children often do have children in their lives. Or we might make suggestions for those working therapeutically with the childfree or those contemplating this: in order to work effectively with this client group, clinicians would need to understand the challenges that the childfree face in making, articulating and living out their choice. Therapists may need to support clients in developing strategies for managing pronatalist assumptions and expectations.

6. Conclusions related to *the wider societal context*. *What* might this mean for societal understanding, engagement or intervention? In our dataset, not having children appears still to be contested and problematic, despite being increasingly common. In our analytic conclusions, we might want to consider strategies to disrupt that, and promote a *different* narrative around not having children in the wider social context.

---

[17]As a framework for subjectivity, neoliberalism positions people to understand and experience life in terms of *individual* choices, actions and consequences. In this framework, agency and responsibility for making choices, and making the *right* choices, in life stops and starts with the individual (e.g. Gill, 2008; Gill & Orgad, 2018).

For any one research output, you are unlikely to draw conclusions in all of these domains, and there might be still *other* domains you consider. Conclusions related to data and scholarship (domains 1 and 2) are pretty standard expectations and are often combined. Whether or not method, theory and practice (domains 3–5) are relevant depends on overall design and purpose, and indeed the expectations relating to the context of your report. The wider context (domain 6) meshes in to questions of generalisability, and to what extent you feel comfortable and confident going *beyond* the scope of your dataset. In disciplines with stronger positivist-empiricist and specifically experimental traditions (such as psychology, our own blessed discipline), the acceptability or expectations around this vary hugely. Some conclusions are necessary, but understanding the purpose of your project and the context of reporting will guide you in what to include – for instance, if you're doing an applied degree such as a professional doctorate, conclusions related to practice (domain 5) will be vital. Our advice is to look for expectations in relation to the purpose of your output. Sometimes the expectations might be explicit. For instance, one of the journals we publish in, the US-based *Psychology of Women Quarterly*, invites authors to consider "practice implications" in their discussion (e.g. see Braun, Tricklebank, & Clarke, 2013). Other times, you might have to *deduce* this from skimming what a journal has published recently or, if you're conducting a student project, reading course guidance and asking for advice.

Finally, the drawing of conclusions involves not just a focus *backwards* to the data and what they say, but also an orientation *outwards*, towards other scholarship and contexts, and towards new or future research within the topic and field being explored. The conclusion to the story we tell is a key part of a conversation that each individual research project contributes to. It is, as noted earlier, one particular piece of work we're adding to a big, collective tapestry, and so we want our contribution to in some way at least acknowledge or not repeat sections of the tapestry that have already been completed.

REFLECTION AND EVALUATION IN YOUR WRITE-UP

Working from the premise that our analysis is both a *reading* of the data that needs to be defensible, and the premise that *no (TA) study is perfect*, or indeed ever *final*, reflection and evaluation is a very important part of qualitative scholarship. We've discussed the reflexivity part of the *process* of *doing* TA (in Chapter One especially). That process of being critically self-examining is also important for the process of *writing*. Here, we *briefly* mention including some kind of critical reflective evaluation as part of our written report.[18] The key take-home is that your written report should reflect back and consider what was gained and what was lost,

---

[18]This inclusion of some critical reflection in your (general) discussion is a separate issue from how much reflexive positioning you might include about yourself as researcher, earlier in a written report (often in a methodology section). Indeed, that is something we might return to, at this point in writing. Some reporting contexts, particularly those based firmly in more quantitative and positivist-empiricist traditions, do not necessarily like or allow such reflexivity within reflection and evaluation. So check out the values, expectations and limits for your report. If reflexive evaluation *is* possible, you might consider what you learnt about yourself, your research practice, and, if a practitioner, your applied practice, along the way.

by your decisions, choices and actions along the journey of your project – including but not limited to analysis. Imagine this like a coda to your adventure: you're safely back, and now have the space to reflect on what you did, the impacts that your choices and actions along the way might have had, and how you might do things differently (or better) next time. What were your highlights (study strengths) and low points (study weaknesses)? Thinking about these sorts of things – and writing them in to our papers – demonstrates good, thoughtful qualitative scholarly practice, *and* makes us better scholars by forcing us to be reflective. The discussion and guidelines in Chapter Nine will help develop your reflective evaluative skills.

> **PRACTICE POINT** Your discussion should include – if reporting conventions allow – some critical reflection on what you have learnt as a result of the choices you have made. Think of this as a gift to other researchers – what might they need to know before they embark on a similar study (e.g. in the same topic area or using the same methods)?

TELLING YOUR STORY *WELL*: THE VALUE OF THE EDIT

Telling a *good* story, and telling it *well*, takes practice. Storytelling is a craft. Likewise, writing a TA report is a craft, and to get a good end product, you need to hone and shape it from a rough and ready early rendering, into a skilfully crafted piece of work. This is akin to the differences between a story made up of a sequence of vlogs you posted quickly about your adventure, along the way, and a beautifully crafted short film about your journey, that you edited your vlogs into once you were back, and had time to pause and reflect on what story you were telling, how it flowed, what to emphasise, and where a meander sideways did or didn't make sense.

We cannot emphasise enough the value of the edit – or, more accurately, multiple edits. Unless you're an exceptionally unusual individual, good writing takes time, deliberation, and many edits. Time to move away (psychologically) can be useful in reviewing our writing, to see what does and (more importantly!) does *not* make sense. Input from others can also be really useful – but remember, *you* are the author of the story, and not all suggestions from others are good ones (this can particularly apply to reviewer suggestions, see Braun & Clarke, 2021c, and 'Managing quality during the publication process' in Chapter Nine). Finally, we find *reading our work aloud* – just to ourselves – is a helpful technique for identifying: bits of text that don't flow; ideas that are not expressed clearly; words that don't fit; sentences that are awkward or overly long. Hint: if you run out of breath before you finish a sentence, it is probably too long![19]

CHAPTER SUMMARY

In this chapter, we have focused on the final stages of finishing a reflexive TA analysis, emphasising the importance of maintaining a critically reflective and self-evaluative stance throughout. We have emphasised that the final part of doing TA is telling the story, and

---

[19]We only just managed to get through *this* sentence without running out of breath, as we read aloud for final book edits!

that *how* you tell the story matters. As part of this, we have noted the importance of writing and editing. We discussed and illustrated key considerations for each part of the analytic story, and provided examples for how you might construct different aspects of a reflexive TA research report. We discussed and illustrated different ways to treat data in analytic reporting, and explored some *thorny* issues in reporting TA: whether we should be using numbers in how we talk about theme frequency or prevalence, and whether claiming some sort of non-statistical generalisability is good practice. Finally, we emphasised the need for clear conclusions that draw out the implications of the overall analysis.

WANT TO LEARN MORE ABOUT...?

Writing is key in qualitative research, so if writing itself is a challenge, we recommend finding a guide to help develop your prose. Find what works for you. Two we like are:

Billig, M. (2013). *Learn to write badly: How to succeed in the social sciences*. Cambridge: Cambridge University Press.

Sword, H. (2016). *The writer's diet: A guide to fit prose*. Chicago, IL: University of Chicago Press.

For an accessible guide to **grammar**, we find this useful: Sinclair, C. (2010). *Grammar: A friendly approach* (2nd ed.). Maidenhead: Open University Press.

We recommend the excellent discussion of **editing** qualitative reports, which includes an example of hand-written edits on a page of a report, from: Woods, P. (1999). *Successful writing for qualitative researchers*. London: Routledge. The relevant chapter is Chapter Five, 'Editing'.

The American Psychological Association's **style guide** remains a very useful and popular general resource for writing and reporting guidance, including related to avoiding 'bias' in language. In addition to the weighty tome of their *Publication manual* (American Psychological Association, 2020), much guidance can be found online: https://apastyle.apa.org/.

Although we don't agree with everything in it, *Psychology of Women Quarterly's* **style guide** offers a lot of useful information regarding writing, correct word usage and grammar (but note there are variations in what is considered 'good' grammar and writing practice): https://journals.sagepub.com/pb-assets/cmscontent/PWQ/PWQ_Style_Guide.pdf

For a discussion on **reporting** qualitative research more generally, including a discussion of how to claim 'frequency', see: Braun, V., & Clarke, V. (2013). *Successful qualitative research: A practical guide for beginners*. London: SAGE – especially Chapters 11 and 13.

For an example of a TA paper that **treats data primarily illustratively**, related to the topic of our worked example, see: Bimha, P. Z. J., & Chadwick, R. (2016). Making the childfree choice: Perspectives of women living in South Africa. *Journal of Psychology in Africa, 26*(4), 4, 449–456.

For an example of a TA paper that **treats data primarily analytically**, related to the topic of our worked example, see: Hayfield, N., Terry, G., Clarke, V., & Ellis, S. (2019). "Never say never?" Heterosexual, bisexual, and lesbian women's accounts of being childfree. *Psychology of Women Quarterly, 43*(4), 526–538.

For a rich but also practical discussion of **generalisability** and qualitative research, see: Smith, B. (2018). Generalizability in qualitative research: Misunderstandings, opportunities and recommendations for the sport and exercise sciences. *Qualitative Research in Sport, Exercise and Health, 10*(1), 137–149.

ACTIVITIES FOR STUDENT READERS

Analytic writing activity: Practise writing about data descriptively versus analytically. Select data from one of the candidate themes in your 'men and healthy eating' dataset (from Chapters Two to Four) to work with. Discipline yourself to write one page of analysis where you treat the data *illustratively*. Make sure you have about 50:50 balance of data and analytic narrative. Repeat the exercise, with the same extracts, but this time write treating the data extracts *analytically*.

Doing this activity in a pair can be useful, as you can then feedback to each other on key traps – paraphrasing the data, (boring) repetition, *arguing* with the data, and going way beyond the data to draw indefensible interpretations.

Evaluating analytic claims activity: Identify a reflexive TA paper – for example, this one on disability disclosure at university: Blockmans, I. G. E. (2015). "Not wishing to be the white rhino in the crowd": Disability-disclosure at university. *Journal of Language and Social Psychology, 34*(2), 158–180.

Evaluate the author's methodological description, and then their analytic claims. Specifically, reflect on the following:

- Does the methodological description give you confidence in their analytic process?
- Do the analytic claims and interpretation seem *defensible* (we discuss this in more depth in Chapter Seven)?
- Does the author (or authors) locate their analysis in relation to the wider context and/or in terms of existing empirical or theoretical scholarship (for more discussion of how you do this, see Chapter Seven)?
- Do the analytic claims *resonate* with you – do they evidence some *naturalistic* generalisability? If so, why?
- Has the author (or authors) done a good job of providing some kind of *thick* description around interpretation, or providing a detailed locating of the dataset/participant group, so that specificity/transferability of the results can be assessed? Would you feel confident that you know enough about how the dataset or context might differ from your own location to make any claims about how the analysis might apply in your area?
- What sorts of *wider* claims – beyond the specifics of the dataset – does the author (or authors) make? Do you find these claims compelling? Why or why not?

Evaluating your own writing activity: Take a section of text that you have written for the analytic writing activity. Read it aloud and *record* yourself doing it (if you can bear that). Before listening to the recording, note down your reflection on:

- Places where you felt things didn't flow;
- Ideas that were not logically ordered;
- Points of repetition;
- Sentences that were clunky (the words didn't fall easily from your mouth) or unclear;
- Places you ran out of breath before the sentence ended;
- Any other points you noted about the writing.

Note: If speaking clarity is not easy for you, then you can adapt this exercise, either by asking someone *else* to read it aloud for you (digital readers are *likely* less effective, but could be worth trying if they're your best option), and record that reading. You could also try to listen to the voice 'in your head' – though we personally find this less effective for picking up textual clunkiness and lack of clarity.

Listen to the recording. Do you notice *additional* ways you would like to edit your text for precision, clarity, or even beauty? Beauty in writing *can* be a goal!

If you're teaching content related to this chapter...
Don't forget to check the companion website for a range of teaching resources:
https://study.sagepub.com/thematicanalysis

GOING DEEPER FOR TIP-TOP REFLEXIVE THEMATIC ANALYSIS

Theory, interpretation, and quality matters

6

A NOT-SO-SCARY THEORY CHAPTER
CONCEPTUALLY LOCATING REFLEXIVE THEMATIC ANALYSIS

Chapter Six overview

- **There's no such thing as atheoretical TA!**   157
  - o What sorts of theory are we discussing?   157
  - o Key basic starting points for TA and theory   158
- **The diversity of qualitative research: Revisiting some important conceptual divisions**   158
- **Let's get theoretical!**   163
- **What do we think language does? Three theories of language**   163
- **Introducing the 'ologies: The big scary theory**   166
- **Theories of reality: Ontologies**   167
  - o Realism   168
  - o Critical realism   169
  - o Relativism   173
  - o Do I really have to think about ontology for TA?   175
- **Theories of knowledge: Epistemologies**   175
  - o (Post)positivism   177
  - o Contextualism   178
  - o Constructionism   179
  - o Checking out the view from the houses of epistemology   184
- **Back to the confusion... Big Theory is contested terrain**   186
- **Theory as it's used: Some TA examples**   189

Two decades ago, US evaluation researcher Michael Patton observed that "those coming new to qualitative inquiry are understandably confused and even discombobulated by the diverse terminology and contested practices they encounter" (2002, p. 76). That still sounds about right – unfortunately. One of the deeply confusing elements is that qualitative research can be underpinned by very different, and sometimes contradictory, theoretical ideas. Many qualitative scholars like to write about these things – and often in ways that seem like a spiralling tornado of ideas and debates, fast moving, impenetrable, and somewhat terrifying. It doesn't need to be this way! We hope this chapter provides as gentle as possible an entry point into these complex ideas.[1]

> **KEY CONCEPT** Big Theory is so-called because it can be seen as the highest level of theory under which all other types of theory operate. Big Theory – or philosophical meta-theory – provides the foundations for our research.

This chapter is about what some might call **Big Theory**[2] – the conceptual ideas about data, and research that underpin everything we do. Such theory is like 'the oxygen' for our research, surrounding and in our practice, even if we don't think about it at all. Even if we don't *want* to think about it. And some of us don't. Although some people *are* excited, even energised, by Big Theory, for many others, such theory is *scary*... It conjures up the most obtuse and inaccessible philosophy ideas or classes that you just *can't* get your heard around, and that fear of failure. We've heard lots of people say 'I can't do theory'; we've seen many people want to avoid theory. We get it; we've been there!

With this chapter, we say *stuff and nonsense* to the idea that we can't do (big) theory – while at the same time acknowledging that some of these ideas *are* hard, and can be a bit counter-intuitive to grasp. This is especially the case if you've never trained in philosophy (which we haven't), and it's not part of your everyday common-sense and thinking about your life. But a useful starting point to dismantle any theory barrier you may anticipate ahead of you is recognising that we all *do* theory in our lives, even if we don't realise it. This is theory in the broadest sense, of having and using an explanatory framework for how and why things are.

> **PRACTICE POINT** Start to dismantle any fear of theory by recognising that in the broadest sense – as an explanatory framework – we use and 'do' theory all the time.

---

[1] It's important to acknowledge that we write this account of Big Theory from the point of view of our training in psychology. Each discipline has overlapping and sometimes divergent debates – further evidencing Patton's (2002) depiction of those new to qualitative research wading into a sea of confusion! Even if you're not from psychology or the social sciences, this hopefully provides a useful entry point from which to explore Big Theory within your disciplinary area.

[2] Our use of capitalisation for Big Theory both captures the sense of 'intellectual importance' some associate with theory at this level, but is also somewhat ironic; imagine us speaking this in a silly voice.

THERE'S NO SUCH THING AS ATHEORETICAL TA!

It is not unusual for researchers to assume that TA is atheoretical – an approach that needs no theory – instead of being theoretically flexible. Likewise, it's common for published TA research to not discuss the theoretical underpinnings or assumptions of this approach[3] – something that constitutes poor practice for reflexive TA (Braun & Clarke, 2021c). Researchers *always* make theoretical assumptions about reality, knowledge and language, even if they don't acknowledge these (Chamberlain, 2004; Malterud, 2016). Any analytic method contains theoretically embedded assumptions, whether acknowledged or not, when applied to the analysis of a particular dataset. This means TA

> **ALERT** TA cannot be conducted in a theoretical vacuum; we always make theoretical assumptions whether we are aware of this or not.

research, indeed all research, cannot be conducted in a theoretical vacuum. Even if theory isn't acknowledged, it's there, lurking, to bolster and/or undermine the validity of what you claim. Good reflexive TA needs both theory and explicit locating in terms of theory.

Theories sit behind all that we do when we're producing knowledge – whether it's when we're using TA to analyse qualitative data or doing structural equation modelling of quantitative data. Theory is really, really important to engage with, because theory is what gives TA or indeed any analytic approach both its analytic power and its analytic validity. Theory isn't a monster to run screaming from, but a beast to tame, and maybe even grow to love. To try to

> **ALERT** Theory provides TA with analytic power and analytic validity.

convince you of this, to show you it's not *so* scary, we start by situating our discussion of Big Theory in qualitative research, including TA, with a discussion of different orientations to qualitative research, which, themselves, delimit theory (see Figure 6.1).

What sorts of theory are we discussing?

We're not talking about **explanatory theory** (like various theories of health behaviour popular in health psychology),[4] but *bigger* ideas: about the nature of reality and what research gives you access to; about what constitutes meaningful knowledge; and about language and how it operates. Theory appears to be most needed when what we use goes *against* the norm or the common-sense, such as when we treat language as producing and constructing reality

---

[3]That there are lots of published TA papers in which the authors *don't* discuss their meta-theoretical assumptions, or seem confused about them, undoubtedly reflects both that discussions of theory in qualitative methodological literature are often not particularly accessible, *and* that understanding of key concepts can vary widely in the qualitative research field. Add to this a seeming willingness of methodological scholars and researchers to make definitive, but at times poorly informed, proclamations about *what qualitative research is*, and you have a recipe for confusion! But it doesn't need to be this way.

[4]We discuss explanatory theory and reflexive TA a little more in Chapter Seven, especially in Box 7.2.

through the ways it is used and describes objects (e.g. see Wetherell, Taylor, & Yates, 2001). But that is not the case. Even if you conceptualise these in a way that does not *seem* to need an explanation – for instance, you conceptualise language as a way for people to communicate their lived, emotional and psychological reality, arguably the common-sense view of language – your research is nonetheless theory-bound. It is nonetheless premised on particular assumptions about the relationship between language and reality.

Key basic starting points for TA and theory

Good TA will make theory clear and explicit, no matter which theories you deploy. For *now*, the most important things to know about theory and TA are:

- Theory is always there, whether in the background or the foreground;
- Theory *can* be complex and confusing when first encountered. Even decades on from our first encounters – we still find it confusing. Sometimes it's a bit like navigating a landscape in a thick fog, and getting completely disorientated;
- To start doing TA, you don't need to 'know it all' about theory – learning theory *first* isn't vital, but...
- To do TA well you do need to bring theory into your analytic process at some point, and know enough about it to be able to write about it in your report.

If you are new to theory, and new to qualitative research, we encourage thinking about qualitative research values (introduced in Chapter One) ahead of theory; it provides a gentler introduction to some more complex ideas. We briefly set the scene for our theory discussion by mapping some of the diversity of qualitative research.[5]

THE DIVERSITY OF QUALITATIVE RESEARCH: REVISITING SOME IMPORTANT CONCEPTUAL DIVISIONS

One of the most important things to understand about qualitative research it that it is not a *single* approach to research, with one single theory that underpins it. It is better thought of as an umbrella term for a variety of different approaches that share some assumptions in common. British psychologists Anna Madill and Brendan Gough (2008, p. 254) referred to a 'fuzzy set', clusters of methods that overlap, with some features in common. Some argue that qualitative research is best thought of as being underpinned by several **paradigms**, rather than just one – **(post)positivist, interpretive, poststructuralist** and radical is a common typology of different paradigms that can underpin qualitative research (Grant & Giddings, 2002; Lincoln, Lynham, & Guba, 2011).[6] Anna Madill's (2015) commentary

---

[5]Coming back to our discussion about mapping ('This is our mapping...' in our opening 'Scene setting'), this mapping of the diversity of qualitative research reflects our positioning as psychologists and our training in critical qualitative research. Not everyone would agree with our mapping – this latter point being a *major* theme around qualitative scholarship.

entitled 'Qualitative research is not a paradigm' captures this. The key point is that there are a range of different orientations and approaches, and the theories that underpin different approaches can be at odds with each other.

We have already (in Chapter One) introduced and discussed the distinction between experiential and critical orientations to qualitative research (e.g. Braun & Clarke, 2013; Reicher, 2000; Willig, 2013). We think this broad differentiating of forms of qualitative research is useful as a way of starting to think theoretically and conceptually.[7] These two broad orientations are a useful starting point because they require to some extent different ontological and epistemological assumptions – they delimit your possible theoretical orientations (and some design elements). The mapping in Figure 6.1 aims to demonstrate the layers of thinking and practice connected to theory, signalling why a 'critical' or an 'experiential' orientation can provide a useful starting point for theoretical engagement.

Experiential qualitative approaches are focused on meaning and experience, what people think, do and feel, and how they make sense of their realities. These orientations are often described in a way that resonates

> **KEY CONCEPT** An experiential orientation to qualitative research and TA centres the meanings and experiences articulated by participants.

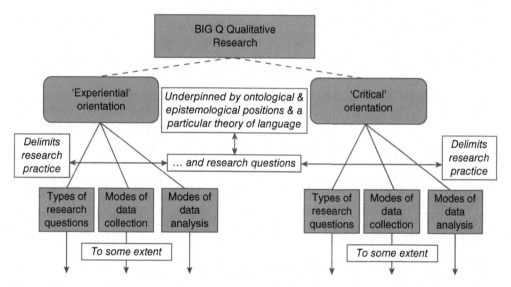

Figure 6.1   It's *all* connected: Qualitative orientation, theory, questions and methods

---

[6]The paradigms thought to underpin qualitative research are shifting and changing (e.g. Lincoln et al. [2011] added participatory). Newer paradigms – prevalent in some disciplinary areas more than others – that *potentially* radically re-shape the conceptualisation and practice of qualitative research – include so-called post-qualitative inquiry or posthumanism or new materialisms (Brinkmann, 2017; Lather, 2016; Lather & St. Pierre, 2013; Lupton, 2019; St. Pierre, 2021; Ulmer, 2017).

[7]Whether experiential and critical are two camps within one Big Q paradigm, or two different paradigms, is a debate for another book.

with what early qualitative researchers saw it offering: a way to 'give voice' to the 'rich tapestry' of people's lives. Experiential research is underpinned by a view of language as a tool for communicating meaning, offering a more or less transparent window into the psychological worlds 'inside the head', or social worlds 'out there'. Such research can be richly theorised and complex, but at its core retains a focus on participants' worldviews and frames of reference – a **hermeneutics of empathy**. Hermeneutics refers to the philosophy of interpretation – the assumptions that underpin how we make sense of and interpret data.[8] A hermeneutics of empathy is an analytic orientation grounded in seeking to understand and make sense of the reality captured in the data. Experiential research is *not* research that simply summarises participant data in a non-interpretative, untheorised way. Box 6.1 offers an example of experiential reflexive TA from our former student Rachel Graham.

> **KEY CONCEPT** A hermeneutics of empathy takes an interpretative orientation that seeks to stay close to participants' meanings and capture these in ways that might be recognisable to them.

> **KEY CONCEPT** Critical orientations to qualitative research and TA focus on interrogating patterns of meaning and the effects and implications of these.

Critical qualitative approaches are concerned with meaning-making, construction and negotiation, and with interrogating and unpacking patterns of meaning, often focused on the effects and functions of particular patterns of language use and meaning. Language is understood quite differently from experiential approaches – not as a means to convey truth or reality, but as an integral part of the way truth and reality are put together (see 'Theories of language' later in this chapter). Critical research is informed by a **hermeneutics of suspicion**, an analytic orientation that seeks to unpack and interrogate the truths and claims presented in the data. Critical versions of reflexive TA have quite a different task, then, from that of experiential reflexive TA. In Box 6.2, we provide an example from a former student, Matthew Wood.[9]

> **KEY CONCEPT** A hermeneutics of suspicion takes an interpretative orientation that interrogates and asks critical questions of the meanings in data and draws more heavily on the researcher's theoretical resources.

---

[8]A distinction is commonly made, based in the work of French Philosopher Paul Ricoeur (1970), between a hermeneutics of empathy and a hermeneutics of suspicion (Ricoeur, 1970; J. A. Smith et al., 2009; Willig, 2013, 2017), broadly mapping onto the distinction between experiential and critical orientations.

[9]Matt's 'familiarisation doodles' for this example of a critical TA study can be seen in Figures 2.1 and 2.2 in Chapter Two).

━━━━━ **Researcher Reflection – Box 6.1** ━━━━━

An example of experiential TA: African Caribbean women 'staying strong'? By Rachel Graham

My research for my counselling psychology professional doctorate thesis explored African Caribbean women's experience of distress in a context in which these women are expected to 'stay strong', within both Black communities and the wider society. Indeed, research has documented a prevalent 'strong Black women' (SBW) stereotype in the West, with origins in transatlantic slavery, which depicts and expects African Caribbean women to be resilient, self-reliant, self-sacrificing and nurturing of others (e.g. Beauboeuf-Lafontant, 2007). My interest in this area was formed by my own personal experiences as a Black woman – I would often slip into the SBW persona when faced with life difficulties and I knew countless other Black woman who did this. This personal experience combined with finding very little research on Black women and mental health in the counselling psychology literature led me to my research question: How does the SBW contextualise Black women's experiences and management of distress?

The field of counselling psychology in the UK emphasises the importance of people's subjective experiences and seeks to understand their inner worlds and constructions of reality (Strawbridge & Woolfe, 2003). This emphasis and my concern to provide a platform for the voices of Black women to be heard by mental health professionals meant I adopted a broadly experiential orientation in my research. This was underpinned by a critical realist ontology, reflecting my belief that reality is unattainable in its purest form because our perception of it is inescapably shaped by social context, language and social positioning (Danermark, Ekström, Jakobsen, & Karlsson, 2002), and an epistemological concern with the person-in-context (Ushioda, 2009).

I conducted five focus groups with a total of 18 African Caribbean women. My reflexive TA analysis of the data was informed by my philosophical positionings and Black feminist scholarship (e.g. Mirza, 1997). Analysis resulted in five intersecting themes that captured how the participants made sense of the SBW construct in relation to their experiences of managing distress. Two themes focused on the influence of the participant's social context in relation to the development of their beliefs about the SBW construct and strength more broadly: *Strength: A way to cope with racism* and '*Mad, Crazy and Weak': Mental health stigma in Black African communities.*

Three themes explored the impact of these beliefs on the participants' experiences and management of distress and the ways in which they concealed from others and minimised their distress, only confiding in selected others when their coping strategies failed to contain their distress: *Distress: My secret; Ultimate trust: Seeking support;* and *Minimising: A way of coping.*

Overall, my analysis demonstrated that the women's strength was brittle – it provided an outward appearance of strength, while concealing a multitude of emotional wounds and scars.

================ **Researcher Reflection – Box 6.2** ================

An example of critical TA research: Onward Gay Christian Soldiers?
By Matthew Wood

For my undergraduate research project in psychology, I examined the discursive positionings lesbian, gay and bisexual (LGB) Christians took up in the context of a 'battle' against religious homophobia. This was not exactly what I set out to explore! My broad interest was in the *experiences* of LGB Christians, particularly in relation to religious homophobia. Recognising the pragmatic difficulties of recruiting from such a specific group in a limited time frame (I had just under seven months to complete my research), I decided to use multiple modes for data collection, offering participants who lived nearby the choice of an interview or completing an online qualitative survey, and those further afield the online survey. This resulted in a sizeable participant group for an undergraduate project: of 21 men (N=14) and women (N=7), aged between 18 and 74 – all recruited through LGB Christian networks. Of these, 15 completed the survey and six participated in an interview.

My initial TA involved an inductive approach – and through this I identified that participants reported varying levels and forms of homophobia from the religious organisations they were or had been involved with. Then, in coding at a more latent level, I started to focus on the different strategies participants adopted for challenging the varying forms of religious homophobia they had encountered, and the ways they conceptualised themselves as doing 'battle' with the Church. For example: "there's a battle to be fought, and that battle's against…closed hearts and minds" (Franz, gay man, 44). Developing this as the central focus of my analysis meant I took on a *critical* approach to doing my TA, drawing on social constructionist concepts (Burr, 2015) and positioning theory in particular (Davies & Harré, 1990). I identified three main 'fighting styles' or positionings that the participants adopted in their 'battle' against religious homophobia, which I used as my themes:

1   an 'intellectual' position using theology and biblical scholarship as the 'weapon' of choice;
2   a confrontational and oppositional 'warrior' position demanding a recognition of homosexuality;
3   a conciliatory position, which sought change from within through sympathetic reasoning.

A critical perspective also enabled me to identify an essentialist discourse that participants drew on to make sense of their homosexuality, framing it as a 'gift from God'. Given the cultural visibility of the hymn 'Onward Christian soldiers', often associated with the Salvation Army, the title of my dissertation (Wood, 2016) seemed obvious!

A common feature of TA generally is **theoretical flexibility**. Specific types of TA are relatively fixed in terms of paradigmatic theory (which we elaborate on in Chapter Eight), but are more or less theoretically flexible beyond that. Reflexive TA is arguably the most flexible, and can be used across experiential and critical orientations. With reflexive TA, it doesn't *necessarily* help to think in purist terms. Much TA

ALERT Reflexive TA is arguably the most flexible type of TA and can be used across experiential and critical orientations.

research occupies positions of fluidity and messiness; divisions – as we've noted earlier – are often not binaries, but rather continua, and/or have scope for blurring. Reflexive TA that is primarily critical or experiential may seek to deploy aspects from the other broad orientation to gain additional insight into the data. Is this problematic? Sometimes, if theoretical tensions are not acknowledged, or there is a fundamental conceptual clash. Importantly, keep in mind that theory offers the basis and validity for what you're doing, analytically. If you're thoughtful and reflexively aware, and can *justify* a blended or partial approach, then go for it (Braun & Clarke, 2021c).

LET'S GET THEORETICAL!

Here we're not talking theory as an analytic tool, but rather, as noted above, theory as providing the conceptual basis for your whole project. These are philosophical meta- (big) theories, theories about reality and knowledge (the 'ologies or O&E stuff, Malterud, 2016), and also theories of language. Even how we understand language is theoretically informed!

Yes, this is complex, and understanding and awareness of ontological and epistemological positions,[10] and especially the ability to reflect on these, is something that develops over time and with experience. Don't expect this to all make sense straight away. If it does, great! Go and delve deeper. If it doesn't, keep coming back to it. Confusion is part of the process with theory, for most of us. *We* still suffer confusion around theoretical ideas and concepts, even after decades of thinking, writing and working as qualitative scholars. This chapter will give you a basic idea of the different aspects you need to know about to navigate successfully through the messy swamp that is theory! We start with theories of language, as they map well to the experiential/critical orientations we've already discussed, and some understanding of language theories is useful for *really* grasping ontological and epistemological variation.

> **PRACTICE POINT** Ontology and epistemology are complex! Be patient with yourself if you struggle with this – pretty much everyone does, some are just afraid to admit it... It takes time to develop a clear(ish) sense of your Big Theory positions.

WHAT DO WE THINK LANGUAGE DOES?
THREE THEORIES OF LANGUAGE

The distinction between experiential and critical qualitative approaches hinges – in part – on how language is conceptualised (Reicher, 2000). For *experiential* researchers, language is a tool for communicating experience in a relatively straightforward way. People might forget

---

[10]Another 'ology name and concept you might come across is axiology, which is used to refer to the researcher's values and ethics, and how these inform the research process. We don't discuss axiology as such. Instead, we focus on the concepts of subjectivity and reflexivity, which we introduced in Chapter One, and which encompass similar territory.

ALERT For experiential researchers, language is a tool for communicating meaning – the words we collect from participants communicate something about their thoughts, feelings and beliefs.

or conceal details, reinterpret past experiences through the lens of the present (Braun & Clarke, 2021d), or struggle to find words to express themselves, but none of these shift the fundamental assumption that language reflects people's thoughts, feelings and beliefs. Researchers working in this tradition conceptualise language as a transparent window onto the psychological and social landscape of meanings 'under the skull' or 'out there' in the world. In experiential research, 'out there' meanings can encompass the social norms and expectations that shape and constrain individual experiences and are reflected in the way people talk about their lives. By contrast, *critical* qualitative researchers view language as something active, as creating meaning, rather than simply reflecting it. In critical qualitative research, we don't look *through* language to the realities it provides access to, we look *at* language itself and the realities it creates.

ALERT For critical researchers, language isn't simply a conduit or a communication tool, but a social practice, one of the main ways in which humans and societies create meaning and realities.

KEY CONCEPT Mind-independent truths are truths that exist separately from our ability and attempts to know them.

KEY CONCEPT Mind-dependent truths are truths that cannot exist without the knower.

Influential British cultural theorist Stuart Hall's (S. Hall, 1997) demarcation of three different theories of representation provides a very useful and accessible mapping – translating representation to language works just as well. Hall distinguished between reflective, intentional and constructionist theories of representation:

- *Reflective*: language reflects the true nature of something – it's like a mirror; it reflects back to us the truth of things. Reflective conceptualisations of language are realist; a material reality independent of language is assumed to exist and to be revealed through language. These conceptualisations assume the existence of **mind-independent truths**.
- *Intentional*: language is used to convey the speaker's unique perspective on things, *their reality*. This maps to some extent onto what are sometimes called 'standpoint' theories (see Harding, 2004; Naples & Gurr, 2014) – we understand things uniquely; we use language to convey our truths.[11] Intentional conceptualisations of language move away from universal meanings and locate meaning within the person; a **mind-dependent truth**.
- *Constructionist* conceptualisations treat language as social and meaning as more malleable and flexible. Meaning is created or constructed in and through language, and in and through language use, the *ways* we talk and write about things. Language here is understood as symbolic, and powerful, rather than neutral; as active, rather than passive.

---

[11]The critical realist, contextualist, phenomenological and, to a lesser extent constructivist, theoretical frameworks we discuss in this chapter are loosely underpinned by intentional theorisations of language.

Your conceptualisation of language shapes the claims you can legitimately make about data. This means it is absolutely *crucial* to your analysis – although the chances are that unless you're working in some kind of broadly critical space, you might not have thought about it. Box 6.3 provides an example of data from one of Ginny's studies, showing two potential 'readings' of the data; one based on a conceptualisation of language as intentional and one on language as constructionist.

> **PRACTICE POINT** Understanding your theory of language is vital, as it shapes the claims you can legitimately make in your analysis (connected to 'O&E stuff').

=== **Box 6.3** ===

Theories of language applied to data

Consider the following short extracts from two focus group discussions collected for Ginny's study about heterosexual sexual health (Braun, 2013):

Sally: …there's this whole romantic thing of you know of what sex is and condoms certainly, what you are saying before, there's nothing romantic about a condom you know.

Jenna: Yeah, they're just so annoying and like you know half the time they're just going to like come off or like rip or something, it's just like why (laughs) if it's going to rip we may as well just not use one anyway and just have proper sex without annoying things.

If we treat language as intentional, we would look at what personal subjective realities are being conveyed here. Both Sally and Jenna reveal a dislike of condoms, and a potential non-use of condoms. Their reality is of condoms as annoying, unromantic, and dysfunctional. This frame for language fits with postpositivist and contextualist epistemologies, and critical realist ontologies, which we discuss shortly.

If we treat language as constructionist, we wouldn't be interested in thinking about condoms as having an inherent truth, or the participants' experiences as real or true. We wouldn't ask, for instance, whether Jenna *really* experiences condom failure about 50% of the time, and therefore start to wonder whether or not she's using them 'correctly'. Instead, we would explore what reality is being *created* in these stories. What 'nature' is ascribed to condoms? For instance, unsuited to the task; effectively something that works in opposition to coitus (which is interesting, because condoms are designed only for intercourse). And then we might ask, well what 'nature' is ascribed to intercourse and heterosex more broadly? This constructionist approach doesn't aim to find the inherent truth about objects or experience, so much as examine what 'versions of events' are told, and then consider the implications of those versions.[12] This approach fits constructionist epistemologies and relativist ontologies, and perhaps some critical realist ontologies too.

---

[12]Ginny's analysis of this heterosexual sexual health focus group data, which drew on both TA and critical discursive psychology – see Box 8.5 in Chapter Eight – developed this latter approach (see Braun, 2013).

Language is centrally connected to ontological and epistemological thinking and practice, as different ontological and epistemological positions are underpinned by these different – sometimes quite contradictory – conceptualisations of language.

INTRODUCING THE 'OLOGIES: THE BIG SCARY THEORY

The terms **ontology** and **epistemology** (the 'ologies) refer to the **philosophical/ meta-theories** that underpin *all* research. This 'O&E stuff' (Malterud, 2016) can seem *separate* from the actual process of doing research, head-melting theory that has little practical importance. Nothing could be further from the truth, as they are deeply connected to research practice. For research practice, they inform: what is ideal; what is permissible; and what doesn't make sense. But the terms themselves are off-putting, and strike fear into many – we hope to take some of the fear out of these terms (and theory more broadly) and equip you to confidently define and discuss the philosophical and theoretical assumptions underpinning your use of TA, and conduct TA reflexively and theoretically knowingly (Braun & Clarke, 2021c). As noted above, whether your research orientation is broadly experiential or critical narrows down the range of 'ologies that might underpin your research quite a bit.

> **ALERT** Your use of TA needs to be located with regards to ontology and epistemology.

What *are* ontology and epistemology about? The standard one-line definition is that ontology refers to theories about the nature of reality or being, and epistemology to theories about the nature of knowledge and knowledge production. We find even these a bit inaccessible, so a more simplified way of putting it is: ontology is about *what* it is that we think we can know and epistemology is about *how* we think we can know it (each with a series of rationales and explanations for why). We'll come back to explaining more in the sections that follow, but ontologies and epistemologies are connected, and ontological positions tend to give rise to particular epistemological positions. These two in turn give rise to a choice of potential methodologies and methods (which the flowchart in Figure 6.1 illustrates).

> **KEY CONCEPT** Ontology relates to the nature of reality or being; theories of what exists/is real.

> **KEY CONCEPT** Epistemology relates to knowledge, theorising what it is possible to know and meaningful ways of generating knowledge.

> **KEY CONCEPT** Paradigms can be thought of as the overarching value or belief systems that encompass big theories – our ontological and epistemological positions. In the messy swamp of theory, positions like (post)positivism are regarded as both paradigms and epistemologies.

We find it useful here to come back to the notion of paradigms, defined as "basic belief systems" (Guba & Lincoln, 1994, p. 107) and value systems (Guba & Lincoln, 1982) that encompass meta-theoretical – the ontological, epistemological and methodological – assumptions in which our research practice is embedded. US Education academics Egon Guba and Yvonna Lincoln

(1994) argued for an 'order of influence' where ontology supersedes epistemology, and epistemology supersedes methodology, an approach we think is useful to understanding the relationship between these theoretical aspects.[13] What's important is ensuring that the different philosophical and theoretical assumptions underpinning your use of TA are harmonious and coherent (Chamberlain et al., 2011), and that they work together. Although we imagine most qualitative scholars would agree with the notion of conceptual and design coherence –

> **PRACTICE POINT** Your paradigm, ontology, epistemology and methodology should generally fit together and be harmonious and coherent.

dubbed 'fit' or, more recently, 'methodological integrity' (Levitt et al., 2017), and discussed in various guiding texts (e.g. see Braun & Clarke, 2013; Willig, 2013) – not all do.[14]

THEORIES OF REALITY: ONTOLOGIES

All researchers make assumptions about the nature of reality, and the nature of 'being' – whether this is done knowingly or not. At the most basic, this comes down to the question of whether or not we assume (aka theorise) a reality that exists separately from our research practice, that we can use our research to know and understand. *Very* simply put, there are three answers to this question of 'is there a reality that exists separately from our research practice?':

- 'Well of course there is' – this is captured by an ontological position known as **realism**.
- 'Definitely not, how naïve are you?' – this is captured by a position known as **relativism**.
- 'Um yes but also no' – this is captured by a position known as **critical realism**, which is mostly ontology, but things all get a bit messy (see the more detailed discussion in Box 6.4).

---

[13]Often scholars argue that ontology *delimits* or produces epistemology. But it is of course more complicated than a simple causal chain, and even that idea is contested. Some argue that ontology and epistemology are less deterministically connected, even separate. For instance, see some of the discussion in critical realist writings such as Maxwell (2012b) and, for a more complex discussion, Pilgrim (2014). Others – including in the area that's now called post-qualitative inquiry (St. Pierre, 2021) – talk of **onto-epistemologies**, a term we quite like as it captures an enmeshed blurriness. But we are trying to keep things as simple as possible, so won't use that term here.

[14]*Not* all qualitative researchers do agree with the principle of design coherence. For instance, authors of an approach called 'consensual qualitative research' have argued for combining constructivism – understood as a belief in "multiple socially constructed realities" with a simultaneous concern with a "participant's 'lived experience'" (Stahl, Taylor, & Hill, 2012, p. 24) – and postpositivism – an approach that acknowledges that "an objective truth exists, [but] only an approximate understanding of that truth can be attained" (Stahl et al., 2012, p. 23). Similarly, Guest et al. described their 'coding reliability' approach to TA (discussed in Chapter Eight) as comprising "a bit of everything – grounded theory, positivism, interpretivism, and **phenomenology** – synthesized into one methodological framework" (Guest, MacQueen, & Namey, 2012, p. 15). These combinations sit theoretically uncomfortably for us as Big Q qualitative researchers.

Realism

The cult US TV show *The X-Files* famously claimed 'the truth is out there' – if they searched in the right ways and in the right places, agents Mulder and Scully would, eventually, discover the truth about the existence of extra-terrestrial life. A realist ontology takes a similar position: it conceptualises a knowable reality, which can be uncovered in an accurate and an objective way. It's a truth that is waiting to be discovered; such knowledge needs to be untainted by the influence and subjectivity –

> **KEY CONCEPT** A realist ontology assumes a knowable world, a truth waiting to be discovered.

'bias' – of the researcher. In a pure – sometimes called **'naïve'** – view of realism, the truths we discover will be *independent* of the tools we used to discover them, which includes our minds as researchers and our actions in doing research. This is captured by the core idea of **'mind-independent truth'** (Tebes, 2005). Realism is often associated with traditional science (and there is a particular version of realism called scientific realism[15]), and the idea(l)s of time and context-free generalisations, and cause and effect laws and models (Guba & Lincoln, 1994). But realism as an ontology is far more pervasive than just in science. It appears within qualitative research. It also forms a large part of dominant common-sense ways of thinking about the world, especially in westernised nations. If that's your context, and you've never thought much about the nature of 'reality', chances are realism will seem natural, and even unquestionable. After all, you can bang a table, make a sound, hurt your hand, and know it's a table (Edwards, Ashmore, & Potter, 1995)!

When realism informs TA, the researcher can be conceptualised as an archaeologist digging in the dirt to discover hidden treasures (Braun & Clarke, 2013), a farmer harvesting crops, or someone walking along a beach collecting shells or other objects (Braun & Clarke, 2016). The data we find or gather will represent a reality that's there to be uncovered. The task of a realist thematic analyst is to accurately and objectively represent the content of their data – this logic underpins 'coding reliability' TA in particular (see Chapter Eight). But many TA researchers, using different TA versions, describe their approach, typically focused on participants' experiences, perspectives and sense-making, as realist, as about capturing individual subjective perceptions of real true phenomena. The presumption of both explicitly *and* implicitly realist versions of TA is that data, such as, "interview accounts provided by participants [...] reflect personal experience (as long as appropriate steps have been taken to minimise participant 'reactivity')" (Gough & Lyons, 2016, p. 235).

> **ALERT** A purely realist approach doesn't align well with the Big Q orientation of reflexive TA. A critical realist approach works better.

From our position as Big Q qualitative researchers, we are troubled by the idea of **simple** or **pure realism**. A pure realist position seems hard to marry to an understanding of data and meaning as contextual, and a recognition and valuing

---

[15]According to Madill et al. (2000), scientific realism assumes that although the scientific method is imperfect, it *can* access true representations of the world and is the best method for doing so.

ofsubjectivity within the research process. When your focus is on 'mind-dependant' truths (Boghossian, 2007) – which it usually is with TA – we think at most one can claim a *critical realist position*. The term critical realism (which we discuss next) highlights something ironic: that realism itself is not a singular approach! What we have outlined here is best described as **naïve realism**, which assumes that the world is as it appears to be.[16] This has been dubbed a 'correspondence theory of truth' (Madill et al., 2000), that the world corresponds perfectly to what we see when we look at it. Like looking at the world through a clear, modern glass window pane (see 'Checking out the view from the houses of epistemology', below).

Critical realism

Scholars who subscribe to 'pure' realism have been positioned as guilty of what is termed an 'ontic fallacy' (Pilgrim, 2014): of confusing their representations of reality *with* reality. In contrast to the naïve realist correspondence theory of truth, critics argue that reality and representations of reality are *not* one and the same. Enter critical realism! Critical realism offers what we might consider a contextualised version of realism, or you could call it the 'having your cake and eating it too' position – a bit of ontological realism with a side of ontological relativism, and epistemology all smooshed together. No disrespect is intended by that description – we like cake, and we like eating it! Critical realism is, in some ways, the most confusing ontological position to artic-ulate. But as critical realism seems to be the most popular big-theory position for reflexive TA,[17] we have tried to provide as simplified and accessible a description here as possible that covers some key basics. Box 6.4 *introduces* the complexity, including the question of whether it is 'just' an ontology.

> **KEY CONCEPT** Critical realism can be understood as combining ontological realism (the truth is out there) with epistemological relativism (it's impossible to access truth directly) to provide a position that retains a concept of truth and reality but recognises that human practices always shape how we experience and know this – human practices can be said to give rise to perspectival and contextual truths.

Critical realism is *realist* in the sense that it broadly postulates a reality that exists independent of a researcher's ideas about and descriptions of it. But – and here's where critical realism

---

[16]We have changed our position slightly on realism from the one we took in our original writing on TA (Braun & Clarke, 2006). In that paper we discussed realist approaches to TA. Now, having thought more about the assumptions embedded in reflexive TA (Braun & Clarke, 2019a), we think *critical* realism is more appropriate as an ontology.

[17]Although critical realism has become popular, various qualitative methodologists (e.g. Denzin & Lincoln, 2005) have questioned its value for qualitative research, suggesting that it is simply positivism/ foundationalism in disguise, and effectively a way to sneak realism in by the back door.

[18]Although critical realists don't endorse the existence of multiple realities, a distinction is made between 'transitive reality', bound up with human practices (such as science or research), and 'intransitive reality', which continues independent of human practices (such as gravity) (Pilgrim, 2014).

differs from pure or **simple realism** – our experiences and understandings of reality are theorised as *mediated* by language and culture. Our experiences are not pure internal-to-us truths, but rather are socially located (Pilgrim, 2014). Like with simple realism, reality is viewed as singular – critical realists do *not* endorse the idea of multiple realities, and truth is not the troubled concept it becomes with relativist positions (see below).[18] However, critical realism conceptualises different perspectives on, and interpretations and representations of, or possibilities for, this singular reality, or truth. Language and culture are important systematic influences. US qualitative methodologist Joseph Maxwell (2012b, p. 9) explained the influence of language and culture on reality thus: "language doesn't simply put labels on a cross-culturally uniform reality that we all share. The world as we perceive it and therefore live in it is structured by our concepts, which are to a substantial extent expressed in language." Here, language and culture don't simply offer an obfuscating 'layer' between us as researchers and the reality we want to know, like a voile or net curtain across an otherwise clear window, obscuring our ability to see what's out there. Maxwell's view is somewhat more fundamental; there's no way around or outside language and culture; you cannot identify a simple 'additive' distortion to reality that these provide.

Where a critical realist view of the influence of language and culture differs from a *relativist* view (discussed next), is that reality always delimits what is possible: "these constructions are theorized as being shaped by the possibilities and constraints inherent in the material world" (Sims-Schouten, Riley, & Willig, 2007, p. 127). No matter how much language and culture may be understood to influence and construct our reality (Sims-Schouten et al., 2007), the material world has an ontological status that is independent of, but only ever accessible in relation to, human representations, language and discourse. For some critical realists, reality encompasses not just the natural or biological world, but human meanings and emotions (Maxwell, 2012b). Crucially, the qualitative researcher is part of the world they want to understand; they cannot stand outside of the human and social reality they are observing through their research (Pilgrim, 2014).

━━━━━━━━ **Box 6.4** ━━━━━━━━

Some of the complexity of critical realism

There are lots of different variations of critical realism;[19] the term 'critical realism' is also interpreted and used in lots of *different* ways. Critical realism was popularised in the writings of the English philosopher Roy Bhaskar in the 1970s (1975, 1979) and has evolved since then. Critical realism is sometimes framed as a 'third way' between (realist) positivism and relativism (Bergin, Wells, & Owen, 2008). Others frame it as *superseding* both realism – often reframed as 'naïve' realism – and relativism/radical constructionism. The latter is

---

[19]There are even different names for critical realism! Other names you might come across that capture a similar position include 'subtle' realism (Hammersley, 1992) and 'complex' realism (Clark, 2008).

associated with a denial of an independent reality, linguistic reductionism, and attending to only the transitive aspects of reality; those associated with human practices. Some frame critical realism as something like the progeny of realism and relativism, taking the best of both approaches and combining them into an über-meta-theoretical position (Alvesson & Sköldberg, 2009).

For some, then, critical realism collapses the traditional distinction between ontology and epistemology – and the idea of a somewhat hierarchical relationship with ontology preceding epistemology. But some critical realists argue *against* such an "ontological/epistemological collapse" (Lincoln & Guba, 2000, pp. 175–176), the conflation of ontology and epistemology (dubbed the 'epistemic fallacy'), or the folding of the two into each other, so they are reflections of each other (Maxwell, 2012b). They reject this collapse (and particularly the conflation of realism and positivism), and argue for the importance of *distinguishing* ontology and epistemology. Particularly, they argue for critical realism as combining ontological *realism* (the belief in an independent reality) and epistemological *relativism* (a rejection of the possibility of having 'objective' knowledge about the world, and an acknowledgement that all knowledge is partial and incomplete, interpretative and provisional) (Maxwell, 2012b). We told you defining critical realism was tricky!

As an ontological position for qualitative research, critical realism has been used to underpin everything from experiential research focused on participants' experiences and perspectives, to social constructionist and discursive research (Willig, 1999). So, what does taking a critical realist position mean for reflexive TA? It means your data don't provide you with a clear and direct reflection of reality. Instead, you access a *mediated* reflection of reality. What you access is your participants' perception of (their) reality, shaped by and embedded within their cultural context, language and so on, or a particular representation of reality (Willig, 2013). Participants bring you a located, interpreted reality (the data), which you then interpret via TA. This interpretation inescapably takes place through the lens of your cultural memberships (which we discussed in relation to familiarisation in Chapter Two, and explore further in Chapter Seven). The goal of a critical realist TA is to provide a coherent and compelling interpretation of the data, grounded in, or anchored by, the participants' accounts, that speaks to situated realities[20], and the limits and constraints of the world participants exist within. A critical realist TA might consider how the material world and social structure shapes and constrains people's sense-making and might also situate their accounts in the materiality they have to negotiate and manage (Sims-Schouten et al., 2007). For an example of what a critical realist approach offered a project that spoke both to 'reality' and the social production of reality, see Box 6.5, where our student Lucy Cowie describes her Master's project.

PRACTICE POINT Reflexive TA, from a critical realist approach, provides access to situated, interpreted realities, not simple, decontextualised truths.

---

[20]We use the term 'situated realities' instead of the singular 'situated reality' to capture the way in which critical realist analysis and thinking, while realist at its core, captures and acknowledges that the experience of reality is different for different people in different contexts.

Coming to critical realism, by Lucy Cowie

I am a young Māori/Pākehā[21] woman, and during my time at university I had often witnessed opposition to ethnicity-specific equity (ESE) programmes. ESE programmes are designed to restore equality for indigenous, under-represented, or marginalised populations within the university (and in wider society) by adding supports that are responsive to their social and cultural needs. In New Zealand, ESE programmes often take the form of 'affirmative action' or 'targeted admission' in to university (Mayeda, Keil, Dutton, & Ofamo'Oni, 2014). For instance, a number of programmes have entry spaces reserved for Māori and Pasifika students, and scholarships that only Māori and Pasifika students can obtain, in order to address ongoing social and financial marginalisation. ESE programmes also provide safe, culturally-responsive spaces once students have entered their studies. For example, in the university-wide Tuākana programme, Māori and Pasifika students can access further support, or attend workshop groups made up of only Māori and Pasifika students.

I am fully supportive of ESE programmes, and I have been involved myself as a Tuākana, as a recipient of targeted scholarships, and as a participant in a group for Māori and Pasifika postgraduate psychology students. However, when I've heard opposition to ESE programmes, I've had difficulty responding. I felt guilty about the times I hadn't responded at all or had responded without making any difference to the opponent's ideas. Furthermore, when I started my Master's, it was really important to me that my project addressed a social justice concern and be useful for working towards positive social change. Thus, I chose to explore how people talk about ESE programmes for Māori and Pasifika students at The University of Auckland (UoA) and, specifically, to focus on how people who are *supportive* of ESE programmes respond to negative comments or opposition to the programmes. I started the research hopeful that my participants would have insights into *how* to respond to opposition to ESE initiatives, which may lead to useful intervention (and resolve the frustrations I'd experienced).

My approach was informed by Kaupapa Māori research principles, centred around research as done by, for, and with Māori. Kaupapa Māori research (meaning research with a Māori approach) is a response to research and policy about Māori issues often being done 'to' Māori rather than 'with' Māori (L. T. Smith, 2013). Key pillars of Kaupapa Māori research include self-determination for Māori, doing research that supports the collective good, and fostering respectful relationships. In my project this meant, for example, providing food and a thank-you gift for research participants, space in the interviews to share *whakapapa* (extended family connections, which are important to belonging and identity), and extensive consultation in order to focus on the benefits of the research to Māori.

I decided to recruit participants of any ethnicity, to avoid *inadvertently* suggesting that challenging anti-ESE statements should be the responsibility of the Māori and Pasifika students who are the recipients of such programmes. I interviewed 20 students from across the UoA about their experiences of responding to anti-ESE expressions. Participants' experiences seemed to mirror mine in many ways, and participants did not offer any 'magic bullets' for responding to anti-ESE statements as I had (naïvely) hoped. Although the interviews were *personally*

---

[21]Māori refers to Indigenous people in Aotearoa New Zealand; Pākehā refers to those of European descent.

beneficial – their stories made me realise that I wasn't alone in finding it difficult to respond – they quickly presented a new set of challenges for the analysis. Overall, participants tended to say that although it was important to respond to anti-ESE statements, it was incredibly difficult to do so, and shouldn't really be the responsibility of students anyway. So, my analytic challenge was representing their views and experiences while also disrupting the idea of personal responsibility for responding to anti-ESE arguments.

Using reflexive TA, I developed five themes that structured participants' talk around responding to anti-ESE statements. These went beyond simply reporting the participants' experiences, to capture how they made sense of 'the problem' and their location in relation to it:

Damned if you don't (respond to anti-ESE sentiment) outlined the ways that participants suggested that there was a strong moral imperative to challenge opposition to ESE, with silence representing complicity and a failed moral duty to improve the world.

Anti-ESE sentiment does harm explored how participants positioned anti-ESE sentiment as damaging, particularly to Māori and Pacific students.

Don't be angry, be rational outlined how participants framed anger as a justified, yet unhelpful, emotion to express in discussions of ESE. In comparison, rationality was positioned as a positive way to discuss ESE.

It's an uphill battle described the ways that participants positioned responding to anti-ESE expressions as unlikely to be successful and almost futile, even if done within the constraints of rationality described in the previous theme.

Whose responsibility is it anyway? explored participants' accounts of who is responsible for challenging anti-ESE sentiment and the suggestion that the *University* needs to do more to support Māori and Pacific students.

I originally intended to use TA with a social constructionist lens, inspired by discursive work around language and racism (e.g. Augoustinos & Every, 2007; Tuffin, 2008). However, throughout the interviews and early analysis, this sat uneasily with the power of participants' experiential stories, and critical realism (Madill et al., 2000) appeared to be a better fit for the project. Like realism, critical realism assumes that there is a knowable world or 'truth' to be discovered that is independent from human structures (Madill et al., 2000). However, a critical realist position also advocates that this 'truth' is obscured by both subjectivity and processes that produce knowledge (Braun & Clarke, 2006). Critical realism allowed me to centre the 'lived experiences' of my participants in experiencing and responding to anti-ESE statements (experiences that were often highly distressing), while *also* allowing me to highlight some of the cultural and social resources and understandings that underpinned their accounts. TA within critical realism meant I could meet two aligned goals: supporting participants in resistance to anti-ESE sentiment, while also recognising the ways that the context structures and limits this resistance.

Relativism

Relativism is an ontological position (and also an epistemological one, but more on that later) that radically departs from the ontological 'common-sense' of realism, and even

> **ALERT** Relativism does not subscribe to the notion of a singular reality that exists independent of human practices.

critical realism and the assumption that there is a singular reality or truth. Relativism conceptualises reality as the product of human action and interaction and does not subscribe to the notion of a singular reality that exists *independent* of human practices. Reality and truth are contingent, local and multiple. Relativism can be described as an **anti-foundationalist** ontology, in that the idea of an ultimate foundation for and of truth/reality is rejected. In realism (both simple and critical), an assumed singular reality provides a *foundation* for the knowledge produced, a bedrock for experience. It is the 'thing' we are getting at when we seek knowledge about something. With relativism, we cannot assume *anything* beyond, beneath or behind that which we're seeking to understand. This difference between foundationalist and anti- or non-foundationalist ontologies is profound and important – in the latter, there is no final arbiter of truth, the truth is what is developed from an analysis, supported by the data and all the scholarly processes involved to demonstrate and evidence the claims.

> **ALERT** In relativist TA, there is no final arbiter of the 'truth' of your analysis.

Relativism ties people in knots in all sorts of ways and produces lots of critiques and reactions (e.g. Parker, 1998). Two of the most common have been about morality and materiality. Materiality refers to the idea that if you're taking a relativist position, you're denying the material world. Morality refers to the idea that if you subscribe to relativism, you lose any basis for morality. Such critiques have been thoroughly refuted (Edwards et al., 1995). It's also important to recognise that there are different *kinds of* relativism and adopting ontological relativism doesn't mean adopting moral or material relativism (Burr, 1998). When we're talking about research, relativism relates to how we imagine the knowable world (psychological, social, affective, behavioural, etc.), and, fundamentally, what we think we can justify in terms of knowledge claims (here relativist ontology merges with relativist epistemologies such as **constructionism**).

> **PRACTICE POINT** With relativist reflexive TA, you offer a reading of your dataset, showing what sorts of realities are produced and constructed.

A relativist ontology for reflexive TA only makes sense for critical orientations, because your analytic task is more subjective, situated and anti-foundational. In doing relativist reflexive TA, your task is to offer an inevitably and thoroughly partial 'reading' of your dataset, showing how participants/texts make sense of (their) reality and 'bring certain realities into being'. That sounds confusing, so let's make it a bit more concrete by going back to the childfree dataset we used in Section One. A relativist analysis might ask, 'What are the realities about 'being childfree' that are evident within the comments?' Being childfree is framed in terms of deficits, responsibilities, freedom, failure, and many other ways (our analysis examples in Chapters Five and Seven discuss this). A relativist analysis doesn't frame one of these as more *real* or *true* than the others. This is because there is no singular or even situated reality of 'being childfree' that the data are (implicitly) compared with. The only meanings that matter for the analysis are those related to the dataset. Analysis tends to be concerned with the consequences and implications of such meaning-making rather than with conceptually tying them back to some ultimate meaning of being childfree. That is not to say the analysis would not be located and grounded by context – it would, because meaning is context-dependent rather than free-floating – but there is no foundational truth that anchors it and provides its validity. Analysis will always be a 'reading'. Your account of your data is not 'true' or 'accurate', but should persuade of the reader of the sophistication and utility of your account, telling them about your meaning-making and why it matters.

> **PRACTICE POINT** Your task in relativist TA is to provide a convincing account of the meanings of the dataset, and explain why these meanings matter.

Do I really have to think about ontology for TA?

If we haven't already convinced you of the answer to this, let us be clear: yes! As noted, ontology always lurks in the background and within the process and 'outputs' of the TA research you do. We think it's helpful to realise that thinking about ontology connects to the purpose of your project. But more importantly, it connects to *practice*, and to ensuring not only that you produce a coherent analysis, but that you understand what it is you're doing, and why you're doing it. To help with this decision-making, we've produced an overview and comparison of what a (naïve or simple) realist (small q) TA and relativist (Big Q) TA might look like (see Table 6.1), to highlight the differences between these types of TA (adapted from Carter & Little, 2007; Patton, 2002). These are somewhat caricatured 'extreme' cases. There is more blurriness than a two-type comparison suggests (including critical realist TA research, which dips in and out of the different columns).

THEORIES OF KNOWLEDGE: EPISTEMOLOGIES

Epistemological positions reflect assumptions about what constitutes meaningful and valid knowledge and how such knowledge can (and should) be generated. Epistemology is really about what we think it's possible to know – and, therefore, how we should go about trying to know it. Epistemology is deeply connected to ontology.[22] Before we get onto common epistemological positions in research, it's useful to recognise that we do consider and use epistemology in our everyday lives, even if we don't think in these terms. 'Fake news' aside, we draw on sources of information to inform our actions, judgements, choices, and so on. For many of us, 'science', or at least empirically generated knowledge, is the most valid and other sources are questionable at best, spurious at worst.[23] Is our own personal experience of something *valid* knowledge, in the face of science that disputes or contests it? Do we treat faith and religion as providing valid knowledge and truth – that then guide our understanding and our practices in the world? Do we understand people not as separate individuals (as tends to be the case in Anglo-western contexts), but as deeply interconnected to others (alive and ancestral) and to land and place (as is the case for many Indigenous peoples)? Do we believe astrology (western or Chinese variations) has anything to offer our understanding of why we are the way

---

[22]In our mapping of Big Theory, as noted earlier, epistemological positions flow from ontological positions, and both constrain the whole research endeavour within certain logics (see also Figure 6.1).

[23]The concept of epistemic power (and correspondingly, epistemic violence – see Box 7.3 in Chapter Seven – and epistemic resistance) highlights the connection between knowledge legitimation and social and political organisation (e.g. Collins, 2019).

we are? Or say a friend says to you, 'Sunscreen is bad, and you shouldn't use it'. Would you trust that? Would it depend who that friend was? What if you read it on Reddit? Or on Goop? What if you saw a story on the BBC? What if the much-esteemed journal *Science* published an article that gave evidence the chemicals in sunscreen damage more than the protection they offer? This is the stuff of epistemology: what modes of information do we trust as real, true, valid sources of information? And how can such knowledge be generated?

Table 6.1 Realist and relativist TA: An overview comparison

Questions	(Simple) Realist TA	Relativist TA
What overall paradigm?	Small q qualitative; (post)positivist epistemology.	Big Q qualitative; non-positivist epistemology.
What is the research goal?	To understand reality in a way that is as accurate as possible. Another researcher should be able to replicate the results in the same or a similar setting.	To explore meaning in context. The researcher should allow the unexpected to happen, be open to multiple ways of making sense and observe how people use language to create meaning.
What sort of knowledge is possible?	Truth through objective knowledge production. It is possible to access participants' real thoughts and feelings, but you need to be alert for deception, inconsistency and error. Objectivity is idealised.	Objective knowledge is not possible, and there is no single truth to discover. Knowledge is contextually located and produced within relationships and interactions; meaning will be different in different times and contexts.
In research with participants, how should the researcher relate to participants?	The researcher is ideally a neutral conduit for the delivery of information; they should avoid introducing bias and inaccuracy into data collection, by approaching it in a non-leading, unobtrusive, depersonalised, consistent way.	The researcher is understood as *part* of the data production process, and they 'co-create' the meanings with participants. The researcher should 'be themselves' when interacting with participants, work to establish trust and 'rapport', respond *in situ* as appropriate, and be reflexive.
In research with participants, how are participants viewed?	As offering their experiences and perspectives to the research, which aims to report their thoughts and feelings accurately – to get inside their heads; to 'walk a mile in their shoes'.	As subjective, situated producers of meaning – in their own lives and during data collection. Not as conduits of information.
How are data conceptualised?	Data provide access to reality, they reflect participants' feelings, thoughts and beliefs; although subject to the vicissitudes and vagaries of memory and so on.	Data reflect meanings *co-constructed* by the participant and researcher, in a particular context. They don't reveal a single underlying truth, but located sense-making.
What is the purpose of researcher reflection?	To set aside assumptions and prior knowledge to avoid influencing the research.	To reflect on their role in the process of knowledge creation; a research journal provides a tool for ongoing reflection throughout the research process.
How is quality conceptualised?	Accuracy and reliability of observations and interpretations is valued; inter-coder reliability measures this.	Criteria specific to the qualitative tradition are prioritised (Yardley, 2015). Reflexivity is key to quality control.
What steps can the researcher take to ensure quality?	Asking participants to check their transcripts for errors; triangulating data sources; using a codebook for coding and multiple trained coders; testing for inter-coder reliability and resolving coding inconsistency through consensus; seeking participant confirmation of the results.	Engaging in thorough and persistent reflexivity, including through a reflexive journal; allowing time for thoughtful and creative data engagement, including approaching the analytic process in a rigorous and systematic but recursive way (and keeping records); returning to the full dataset as the analysis develops.
How should the research be reported?	Written in the objective scientific third person.	Written in the first person; the researcher should write in their own voice and tell *their* story. Creative outputs are possible.

Within the realm of qualitative research, epistemology is about what knowledge is *possible* and how you go about getting that. Epistemological positions broadly align with the ontological positions described, of realism, critical realism and relativism. Three commonly utilised epistemologies in qualitative research across the social and health sciences are **(post) positivism, contextualism** and constructionism.[24]

(Post)positivism

The dominant epistemological framework across the sciences and social sciences is now undoubtedly postpositivism, an approach that has evolved – in response to critique – from the previously dominant scientific approach of positivism.[25] Guba and Lincoln (1994, p. 108) dubbed positivism the "received view", the beliefs and values that have dominated science of all stripes for several centuries. The

> **KEY CONCEPT** Positivism was the dominant epistemological framework underpinning scientific research for several centuries. It assumed an objective reality and the possibility of generating objective knowledge about this through the appropriate application of scientific methods.

associated norms and values are often (implicitly) treated as 'the natural order of things', the way *good and proper research* should be conducted.

Positivism relies on (a simple) realism, where reality exists *independently* of human efforts to know and understand it (Burr, 1998). A relatively straightforward relationship between the world and our perception of it is assumed. For the positivist researcher, researcher and participant are assumed to be *separate* entities and the researcher can potentially investigate the world without influencing it (Guba & Lincoln, 1994). Research is about capturing a reality that pre-exists the research, is 'out there' in the world. Good *data* capture this reality and allow it to be known and understood. The task of the researcher is to gather data, like harvesting crops, and systemise them, with the ultimate aim of creating true, objective knowledge following a rigorous scientific method – in which the researcher's values and biases are prevented from influencing the research process (Willig, 2013). *Good* data provide the basis for empirically-grounded conclusions, generalisations, theory testing and theory generation.

Most researchers who work in this tradition would now label themselves and their approach *post*positivist – an unreconstructed positivist is a rare beast these days. Importantly, the addition of 'post' captures conceptual 'refinement', but otherwise retention of the inherent logic and values of positivism. This is not a radical departure from positivism or

---

[24]Carla Willig (2013) similarly described three epistemological positions, but included phenomenology (rather than contextualism), alongside positivism and constructionism. Phenomenology aims to produce knowledge about the subjective experiences of participants. We think phenomenology could be *broadly* considered a contextualist approach.

[25]Critiques of positivism have been varied from theoretical, methodological, conceptual and other grounds, including political, for example: "positivism is not only epistemologically and ontologically flawed; it is also co-responsible for many of the social ills and political catastrophes of the world" (Patomäki & Wight, 2000, p. 213).

KEY CONCEPT Postpositivism is now the dominant framework underpinning scientific research and represents a refinement of positivism – objective knowledge remains the goal but observation is acknowledged to be imperfect and influenced by the researcher's values and culture.

a diametrically opposed epistemology. This refinement includes recognition that our observation cannot be pure and perfect – and indeed a 'view from nowhere' (Haraway, 1988). All observations are selective, and our perception of the world is partial; reality can only ever be understood imperfectly, and from a situated position. What is not up for debate is that objective knowledge is the ideal – and it is desirable to *strive for* objectivity, even if objectivity is recognised as ultimately impossible (Guba & Lincoln, 1994). In this way, positivism broadly retains a "master narrative" status (Nadar, 2014), even in much qualitative research. This leads to research practices designed to aim for, and to demonstrate, objectivity – such as measures of coding reliability in some forms of TA (which we discuss in Chapter Eight) – that only make sense within these 'small q' frameworks.[26]

Contextualism

Contextualism offers an epistemology more compatible with Big Q qualitative researching, in that while it retains a sense of truth, it emphasises the ambiguous, context-contingent nature of language and meaning, the dependence on theory and interpretation for 'data' to have meaning and 'make sense', and the political-ideological nature of research (Alvesson & Sköldberg, 2009; Madill et al., 2000). Associated with the work of the US philosopher Stephen Pepper (1942), the central metaphor of contextualism is the "human act in context" (Tebes, 2005, p. 216). In

KEY CONCEPT Contextualism views knowledge, and the human beings who created it, as contextually situated, partial and perspectival.

more basic terms, humans cannot be separated out from, and meaningfully be studied in isolation from, the contexts they live in and that give meaning to their lives. With contextualism, multiple accounts of reality are possible; one account is not necessarily invalidated by a conflicting account, but some accounts may be more valuable and persuasive than others (Madill et al., 2000). This means knowledge is often evaluated in terms of its utility rather than its accuracy.

---

[26]Like in much of the 'O&E stuff', there is considerable variation in how postpositivism is used, understood, and, indeed, what research it is conceptualised as relevant for. Some scholars frame postpositivism as aligned well with qualitative research of certain traditions (e.g. Morrow, 2007) – such as more experiential approaches – whereas others situate postpositivism as (more) appropriate for quantitative research (e.g. Ponterotto, 2006). We view (post)positivism as the practical or 'working' philosophy for much mainstream psychology – capturing and underpinning the assumptions psychologists make about what constitutes reality, meaningful knowledge and the like when conducting and writing about their own research, and reviewing and evaluating others' research. One can, and some do, dispute the influence of positivism in psychology through considering philosophical texts and statements (see Robinson, 2021; Shadish, 1995). But *our* interest is always with theory is as something we practice, we 'do' – knowingly and unknowingly – through our research, not with abstract philosophical discussions.

In a contextualist epistemology, knowledge *cannot* be separated from the knower, and the researcher's values and practices inevitably shape the knowledge they produce. The researcher and participant are 'in relationship', co-producing meaning, rather than two independent entities. Contextualism requires a reflexive researcher (Madill et al., 2000; Tebes, 2005), though not to 'weed out' sources of contamination or 'bias' and control them. Such reflexivity considers the researcher's role in shaping meaning and renders visible *to the reader* some of the contexts of the research that shape the knowledge produced. Knowledge produced through research is viewed as local, situated and provisional (Madill et al., 2000; Pettigrew, 1985), with 'results' dependent on the contexts of the research, and the inter-pretative engagement of the researcher. Data analysis is acknowledged to be partial and subjective, but data provide some grounding for results, and perhaps reveal something of the underlying logic of social practices. In this sense, there is a 'something' behind the contextually-produced accounts we gather for analysis. For Madill et al., "the onus on researchers is to make their relationship to the material clear and to ground analysis in participants' own accounts" (2000, p. 17).

Hopefully it's no surprise that contextualism broadly maps onto a critical realist ontol-ogy. Similar to the way that critical realism occupies a position somewhere 'between' realism and relativism, contextualism offers something of a 'middle ground' between epistemologies of (post)positivism and constructionism (Henwood & Pidgeon, 1994), and has been characterised as 'weak constructionism' (Kitzinger, 1995). Social influences are acknowledged, but the thorough-going anti-foundationalism of constructionism is circumvented through a concern for 'truth', albeit a provisional, contextual and liminal truth (Braun & Clarke, 2013).

Constructionism

Constructionism inverts the normative relationships between research, language and knowl-edge: constructionism is founded on the premise that research practices *produce* rather than *reveal* evidence (Willig, 1999). The researcher is not like a farmer harvesting crops, or an archaeologist or detectorist searching to uncover treasures in the ground; she is like an artist or maker, a composer, a storyteller, creating *something* with her tools and techniques, skills and cultural resources. But what this something might be is bounded and has to 'make sense' within existing systems of meaning. The work might surprise, shock or subvert, but is none-theless comprehensible for what it is (art, craft, music, a novel). Because constructionism offers an epistemology so counter to common-sense ideas about research and knowledge, we explain it in more detail and with a bit more theoretical context than postpositivism and contextualism.

In (post)positivist and contextualist epistemologies, *language* is understood to reflect a reality that is separate from it, be that an 'objective' reality or the perspectival 'realities' of individual participants. In constructionism, as previously noted, language becomes an entirely different beast. It is not a neutral conduit for some separate experience or truth; it does not more or less accurately describe these. Instead, language is understood as 'doing things', sometimes described as 'bringing realities into being'. Take clothes as an analogy. We typically think of clothes and adornment as an expression of some 'inner' identity, such as our gender, music tastes, subcultural alignments, values, and so on. But do clothes reveal a truth, or do they produce a truth? US feminist philosopher Judith Butler (1990) theorised clothing as one of the dominant ways in which we understand and 'live out' *gender*. Butler argued that when it comes to gender, clothes are not an expression of an inner gender identity, but one of the ways in which ideas and a reality around gender are produced (or 'done'). Butler theorised gender not as inner reality, but as a social production, which needed constant (but often unrecognised) work. With clothing, we *create* and *reinforce* a sense of binary gender difference. In this theorising, Butler inverts the conventional presumed relationship between clothing and gender. Social constructionists do something similar with language –

ALERT A focus on language is central in constructionist versions of reflexive TA.

they theorise that ways of talking and writing *create* realities, rather than simply *reflect* them. This means that a focus on language is central to constructionist research.

There is no one version of (social) constructionism (Madill et al., 2000), but US psychologist Ken Gergen's work (e.g. 1973, 2015) has been hugely influential in how it's understood and used. Gergen cites *major* influences on the development of social constructionism as including:

ALERT Constructionism isn't a single approach, so make sure if using this epistemology that you specify your particular approach.

- The postmodernist intellectual and cultural tradition;
- Swiss linguist Ferdinand de Saussure's linguistic theory, which gave rise to the field of semiotics (the study of systems of communication);
- French literary theorist Jacques Derrida's deconstructionism, which drew on semiotic theory;
- The sociology of scientific knowledge – US and Austrian sociologists Peter Berger and Thomas Luckmann's (1967) *The social construction of reality* is a landmark text; and
- The Austrian-British philosopher Ludwig Wittgenstein; his book *Philosophical investigations* (1953) is often described as the most important philosophical treaty of the 20th century.

KEY CONCEPT The term **poststructuralism** describes a set of non-realist/relativist theoretical traditions. These situate meaning as multiple, socially-constructed and connected to wider systems of power.

Others (Holstein & Gubrium, 2011) also cite the French poststructuralist philosopher Michel Foucault as another major influence.[27] This is a long list of complex terms and Big Theory ideas developed by intense-looking, now-dead western-dwelling White men (Google them, you'll get what we mean). Gergen (2015) does also include reference to feminist, Marxist and postcolonial theory, but overall (White, male) western theory predominates. Box 6.6 presents a brief discussion on using TA within

---

[27]Foucault's more accessible texts include *Discipline and punish* (1977) and *The history of sexuality (vol. 1)* (1978).

============ **Researcher Reflection – Box 6.6** ============

Beyond western ontologies and epistemologies: Using TA in the context of Indigenous knowledge frameworks, by Jade Le Grice and Michelle Ong

Concepts, theories, and methods developed and 'discovered' in western social science research are often assumed as universal. However, Indigenous scholars (often trained in western research approaches) have argued these knowledges, and the methods utilised to generate them, function to justify colonising practices and Indigenous exploitation (Enriquez, 2013; L. T. Smith, 1999). In the Philippines, great social unrest during the 1970s led to the inception of Sikolohiyang Pilipino – Indigenous Filipino psychology (Paredes-Canilao & Babaran-Diaz, 2013). Social scientists from various disciplines questioned the dominance and uncritical application of social theories and methodologies taken from western (specifically, US) contexts; such a practice was identified to produce knowledge that was incorrect, irrelevant, or even detrimental to Filipinos (Enriquez, 1976). In New Zealand, settler-colonial invalidation of Māori knowledge, culture, and language inculcated Māori resistance to ensure its survival in the promotion of Māoritanga in the 1960s and 1970s (L. T. Smith & Reid, 2000), educational initiatives through Kura Kaupapa in the 1980s (L. T. Smith, 1992) and further initiatives that centred Māori self-determination, including research, known as *kaupapa Māori* (L. T. Smith & Reid, 2000).

An important area of Indigenous research is expanding the theoretical and methodological toolkits for Indigenous academics and practitioners. Innovative research methods have been developed from Indigenous worldviews and cultural practices, including methods of data collection pakikipagkwenuthan (Orteza, 1997), kōrero mai (e.g., Pitama, Ririnui, & Mikaere, 2002), and methods of analysis pārākau (Lee, 2009), thought space wānanga (L. T. Smith et al., 2019), and wairua (Moewaka Barnes et al., 2017). TA is another useful addition to the Indigenous researcher's toolkit for its theoretical flexibility and systematic guidelines for doing analysis, which allow for the nuanced use of Indigenous knowledges, theories, concepts, and practices in data analysis. TA can accommodate a broad range of approaches: from realist ontologies where the aim of the project might be to represent Indigenous people's experiences, to poststructuralist ontologies that engage more critically with the ways that power and language combine to inform knowledge that is produced about Indigenous people.

Jade utilised TA in her PhD study of Māori and reproductive decision-making (Le Grice, 2014; Le Grice & Braun, 2016, 2017; Le Grice, Braun, & Wetherell, 2017). This was initially conceptually/theoretically driven through attending to how participant accounts drew from mātauranga Māori (Māori knowledge) associated with whanaungatanga (people and their relationships with one another), whakapapa (ancestral relatedness across past, present, and future generations) and wairua (spirituality). More fine-grained analysis was data-driven, and subthemes were derived from recurrent patterns in participant accounts. This was a useful method for attending to how participants practised mātauranga Māori in contemporary life, resisting colonial-informed racialised social and discursive formations.

In Michelle's study on ageing Filipina migrants (Ong, 2015; Ong & Braun, 2016), TA allowed for an analysis that straddled poststructuralist views on language and an attention to culturally-shared notions of women's ageing and migration. TA's systematic process and theoretical flexibility were key to achieving an understanding of Filipina migrants' meaning-making around ageing that was sensitive to differences in the women's individual contexts and that made clear

(Continued)

connections between these individual contexts and a larger, more globalised context. Michelle hopes that such an analysis adds to the voices being raised against migration policies (in both home and host countries) that view people entirely in terms of their economic potential, and that her study spurs more interest in power, language, and subjectivity within Sikolohiyang Pilipino.

In conclusion, TA can be flexibly orientated to attend to Indigenous researchers' questions of analytic interest. It can be utilised to investigate the interrelation of Indigenous concepts within a holistic understanding of Indigenous knowledge and worldviews, and honed to attend to patterns of cultural practice, and resilience, within everyday lives. TA can also attend to interstices of power, constituted through intersectional diversity (as to gender, sexuality, age, ability, religion, among others), and the complexity of lived experience among Indigenous people. This wide analytic scope has considerable potential to align with Indigenous research objectives to produce decolonising and liberatory knowledge, and achieve social justice.

KEY CONCEPT Indigenous knowledge frameworks is a collective term for the diverse theoretical and methodological approaches to knowledge developed by Indigenous researchers and people, based in their worldviews. These provide alternatives to the globally dominant westernised colonial knowledge systems.

two **Indigenous knowledge frameworks** (Māori and Filipino), which disrupt an ontology/epistemology separation, but have some alignment with critical theories. Indigenous knowledge frameworks are becoming more widely discussed in scholarly contexts and gaining more 'institutional' acceptance around the world, as populations whose knowledges have been oppressed and suppressed through processes of colonisation re-take control over research agendas and research practice (Denzin, Lincoln, & Smith, 2008; L. T. Smith, 2013). There is, still, a long way to go (and, yes, we appreciate the irony of including our discussion in a separated-out box).

Constructionism has two challenges for both comprehension and practice. As we've already noted, it is 'counter-intuitive' to many, and it is associated with lots of complex, daunting terminology and theories.[28] Although we're both fans, we recognise these challenges can be immensely off-putting. But there are really good, comparatively accessible accounts of constructionism (e.g. Burr, 2015; K. J. Gergen, 2015), and you don't need to read all the books mentioned above to do social constructionist TA effectively (we certainly haven't, and like to think we manage!). Reading such texts would no doubt *deepen* your understanding of social constructionism, but start with the more accessible ones.

What unites most forms of constructionism is an understanding of knowledge as historically and culturally constituted; knowledge is situated and tied to human practices – it is 'socially constructed'. Constructionism overlaps with contextualism but goes further, rejecting the

---

[28]There is also irony in an intellectual tradition concerned with how certain ideas gain legitimacy over others, being primarily associated with the intellectual outputs of highly privileged social groups – White western men.

notion that there is any anchor or foundation for knowledge, which determines its ultimate truth. Constructionists also view pretty much everything as a social construct – science, technology, reproduction, sex (as in sexed-bodies, as well as sex-as-acts), homosexuality, the unconscious, food and eating, physical activity... You name it,

> **ALERT** Kitzinger (1995) described approaches like contextualism as constituting a form of 'weak constructionism' in contrast to social constructionism's 'strong' or 'radical' constructionism.

constructionist scholars have deconstructed it! They have shown how what we 'know' a particular thing *is*, doesn't reflect some true nature, but is a product of human practices, located in particular cultural and historical contexts. These things are without essence or ultimate (natural) foundation. This doesn't mean that we don't *live* as if things like sex, eating and reproduction aren't real – of course we do! It means that we cannot 'find' – and therefore there cannot *be*– any 'reality' of sex, eating or reproduction outside of human practices, which give rise to the meanings and understandings we work with, and act in relation to.

This makes constructionism, like relativism, an anti-foundationalist approach – no essential or material foundation for knowledge is assumed. There is no reality outside of human practices (that we can access). Not only can we only know about reality in and through our human practices (Madill et al., 2000), this is the reality that is taken to *matter*. People worry, again, about the material world, the tables we can bang. But like with relativism, it's not about a denial of this. As well-known US social constructionist Sheila McNamee explained: "there is no denial of a physical or material world by any social constructionist [...] There is a physical world, but the physical material world is meaningless until we name it. And so we can't step out of discourse. We're always in some discourse. We can't step out of language. That is part of the human condition" (quoted in Efran, McNamee, Warren, & Raskin, 2014, p. 11).[29]

Constructionist TA is concerned with exploring what or how reality has been 'made' (constructed), and usually what the implications of this are. Constructionism is still an *empirical* tradition for knowledge production, involving generating data and analysing them.[30] You might also come across the term constructi*vist* – we explore whether this is the same thing as constructionist in Box 6.7.

================== **Box 6.7** ==================

Is constructivism just a different name for constructionism?

Ah, the tricky questions! We have used the construc*tionism* in this section, but the term construc*tivism* is also used in the qualitative methodological literature, sometimes interchangeably with constructionism. Differences in terminology sometimes reflect disciplinary divergences –

(Continued)

---

[29]Sheila McNamee, with Ken Gergen and feminist constructionist researcher Mary Gergen (e.g. 1988, 2017), was among the founders of the Taos Institute in the US (www.taosinstitute.net/), an organisation with a global network committed to advancing social constructionist ideas and practice.

[30]The researcher is recognised as active in the process of data generation; if collecting data from people, meaning is understood as co-constructed between the researcher and the participant, rather than extracted from participants by researchers (Guba & Lincoln, 1994).

such as when sociologists use constructivism and psychologists use constructionism to refer to broadly the same tradition. Some argue that constructionism and constructivism actually capture *different* theoretical traditions, not just disciplinary differences in terminology. But the meaning of these terms is often contested and confused; there is no universal agreement on what these different theoretical traditions are, and within each, there is (again) a range of *different* perspectives.

There have been numerous attempts to map the terrain of constructivist research (e.g. Chiari & Nuzzo, 1996); here we map out *our*[31] understanding of the differences *between* the constructivist and constructionist theoretical traditions. In our mapping of the qualitative terrain, construc*tivism*, like construc*tionism*, is concerned with the production of meaning (by people), but often has a more individual and psychological orientation than construc*tionism*. The latter focuses more on social (e.g. collective, relational) meaning-making, even if individually expressed or accessed (see Burr, 2008; Crotty, 1998; K. J. Gergen, 2015; McNamee, 2004; Raskin, 2002). This focus has led to critiques of constructionism as emptying the person of psychological content (Burr, 2008), and associated critiques of an absence of personal agency within some constructionist analysis. In psychology, constructivism is particularly associated with the personal construct psychology (PCP) of George Kelly (1955), and the later work of Maturana (1988) and others, often described as radical constructivists (to distinguish their approach from PCP). In sociology, constructivism seems more associated with theoretical traditions (such as labelling theory, symbolic interactionism and script theory) that we'd identify as *precursors* to social constructionism, rather than as social constructionism *fully realised* (some sociologists no doubt argue that these traditions *are* constructionist). As we said, it's a mess and definition is perhaps a fool's errand.

So is constructivism just constructionism by another name? Sometimes, when people use it that way. But really no. We do not regard them as the same, although there are synergies. When it comes to qualitative research, both constructivism and constructionism acknowledge the active role of the researcher in knowledge production, but constructionism goes further. People use the term constructionism precisely to indicate their rejection of the 'individualist' accounts of constructivists (Raskin, 2002). We think constructivism is more aligned to critical realism than the relativist ontology associated with constructionism. But, given the different 'takes' on constructionism (Madill et al., 2000), as well as constructivism, it's important to demarcate the particular *version* of constructionism or constructivism that informs *your* work.

Checking out the view from the houses of epistemology

It's difficult to conjure a metaphor that adequately captures these epistemological positions – (post)positivism, contextualism and constructionism – and the differences between them. But let's use the example of being in a house, looking through a window at some flowers.[32]

---

[31]Our understanding of the differences between constructivism and constructionism is not shared by *all* qualitative researchers.

[31]Don't think too hard about the metaphor; it's bound to unravel at some point.

For each, we will consider: (1) what foundation can there be for the knowledge you gain; and (2) what type of knowledge – from objective to situated – is possible.

In the *house of positivism*, you walk or roll yourself over to the windows in the main living room. The window has curtains you pull open and you have a clear view, through clean, modern glass, out on to the garden. You see some beautiful blue flowers in the garden. Your friend Asha comes into the room and looks through the windows; they also notice the blue flowers. You can open the door that goes out into the garden, and *touch* and *smell* the flowers, confirming what your observations from inside the house told you was there. You take a photo and post to Instagram with #BlueFlowers. In this house of positivism, you can access an objective reality directly, through the clear glass of the windows. Observable reality is the foundation for knowledge and objective knowledge is possible.

In the *house of postpositivism*, you can see into the garden through the windows, but the door is locked so you can't go out into the garden. And somewhat annoyingly, the windows have a pink colour tint over them. You're sure the flowers are blue, but your friend Asha insists they're purple. Your other friends Bina and Zahra come and look out of the window; both also decide the flowers are blue. Given this, you feel confident the flowers *are* blue. You take a photo through the window and post to Instagram with #BlueFlowers. In the house of postpositivism, the clear glass that positivism relies on becomes somewhat obscured by the 'filter' of cultural and personal perspectives and values. It's impossible to access reality directly, unmediated by these values (though you wish you could). You strive for objectivity, recognising there will always be some level of uncertainty about whether your determinations ('results') actually are the absolute uncontaminated truth. An almost-observable reality is the foundation for knowledge, and slightly-situated-but-hopefully-still-objective knowledge is possible.

In the *house of contextualism*, you, Asha, Bina and Zahra are in different rooms, all of which look out over the garden, but from a slightly different position. Furthermore, no one has a clear window: your window is covered in a pink tint; Asha's in bubble wrap; Bina's with a net curtain they can't remove; and Zahra's is streaky coloured glass. The flowers still look blue to you, but everyone else thinks they're a different colour. The door is locked so there's no way to check the colour and determine which colour the flowers are. You agree to disagree. You still take a photo, filter it to look *extra* blue, and post to Instagram with #BlueFlowersAreTheBest. In the house of contextualism, there is no clear glass, but clear glass is not the ideal. Everyone is viewing what they see from a perspective. You can only access people's subjective perceptions and interpretations of their realities, and these are shaped by their values and context; there is no direct access to an objective, universal, acultural, ahistorical, decontextualised reality. Within contextualism, *situated* knowledge is what is possible, and although some foundation in a separate reality is assumed (there *are* flowers growing in the garden), this is not accessible nor of interest.

In the *house of constructionism*, you might not even think you're in a house! As you enter the hallway you're suddenly covered in glitter. A note stuck to the wall tells you that this is invisibility glitter, and you notice your hand disappearing. Before you have a chance to 'freak out', you move into a room with closed curtains. Embroidered text in the curtain reads: *Welcome to the house of constructionism! Don't turn around, even if you hear a noise. Draw the curtains to reveal ... a window? a mirror? You won't be able to tell – but does it matter?* While you're pondering this, you think you hear other people move into the room, who also stop and stay. You decide to cheat and have a quick peek behind you, but find you can't turn around. So you pull back the curtain, and... You see a crowd of people looking towards you – you're not there (thanks invisibility glitter!). Is it the crowd of people behind you, reflected? Or a different crowd, on the other side of a window. You reach forward to touch the surface, but there's just empty space. You try to ask, 'is anyone here?', but your voice makes no sound. Your head starts to spin, and you try to take some photos to capture your experience. When you leave, you don't even know if it was 'real'. When you meet up with Asha, Bina and Zahra later to compare notes, you find that each of you has had a *different* experience of what was in the house, what you saw, and what you took away from it. You've no way of determining that one of these is truer than the others. Your photos don't reveal much, but you post a blurry, multi-coloured photo on Instagram with #TheTruthsAsISawThem #TheTruthIsNotOutThere #TruthIsWhatWeMakeIt. In the house of constructionism, there is nothing to provide an *anchor* for the (shifting) observations you make of the world. There is *no* observable reality that can and should provide a foundation for knowledge. Knowledge is gained, but all knowledge is situated and partial. The world that matters (the world to understand) is the world we're in, the world we *can* observe from our positions, and the world we shape as we move through it.

BACK TO THE CONFUSION... BIG THEORY IS CONTESTED TERRAIN

PRACTICE POINT Don't expect to 'conquer' theory immediately. If it's confusing or frustrating – rather than exciting – give yourself a break and focus on something different. Come back to it another time; try looking at different sources. You will get there.

We have come to the end of our whirlwind journey through Big Theory. If your head feels like it's going to explode, or you're feeling frustrated ("I don't get it"), don't worry. It is complex and it is confusing. Take a deep breath. Stare out of the window for a while. Go for a walk, roll or ride. Take a nap. Meditate... Do something to shift focus. But *don't* give up. Revisit this chapter again when you're in a different headspace. Read other sources particularly relevant to *your* research – both topic and field. You *will* get there!

Our aim in this chapter has not been to provide a definitive overview of philosophical/meta-theories that all qualitative researchers would agree with. We concur with Michael Quinn Patton that "there is no definitive way to categorise the various philosophical and theoretical perspectives that have influenced and that distinguish types of qualitative inquiry" (Patton, 2002, p. 79). Rather, we have aimed to provide a broad mapping of the 'ologies, avoiding as much specific 'jargon-ish', disputed and baggage-laden terminology (P. L. Berger & Luckmann, 1967) as possible, while remaining recognisable to many qualitative researchers in the social and health sciences. But it inevitably reflects *our* standpoint and training as (critical) psychologists (e.g. Braun & Clarke, 2019a, 2021d; Braun, Clarke, & Hayfield, 2019; Lainson, Braun, & Clarke, 2019).

What makes discussing the 'ologies particularly confusing is that researchers can use the same terms to mean different things – sometimes reflecting disciplinary differences, sometimes simply irregular use. Furthermore, constructionism, realism and critical realism are regarded by some as ontologies and by others as epistemologies,[33] and by others still as encompassing *both* ontology and epistemology. As previously noted, some authors refer to *multiple* qualitative paradigms (e.g. Grant & Giddings, 2002; Madill, 2015); others prefer to imagine one qualitative paradigm, but with different 'camps' or orientations within it – us included (Braun & Clarke, 2013). We refer to a *qualitative* paradigm; other terms include an interpretative (Malterud, 2016) or naturalistic (Lincoln & Guba, 1985) paradigm. People vary hugely on what they regard as the 'radical' alternative to the dominance of positivist-empiricism. For some, it's social constructionism (K. J. Gergen, 1999; Kitzinger, 1995).[34] Some designate the much newer player of *post-qualitative enquiry*, originating in US education research (e.g. Lather, 2016; Lather & St. Pierre, 2013; St. Pierre, 2021), as an approach that moves beyond positivist/realist accounts; it encompasses a mode of practice we'd understand as falling firmly within a *qualitative* paradigm. Add into the mix the wide range of developing Indigenous knowledge frameworks (e.g. Denzin et al., 2008; Enriquez, 2013; L. T. Smith, 2013), and you start to grasp how this is a messy, shifting, complex domain, and one that continues to evolve. Somehow that is *perfect*, because for us (and many others), good qualitative research does not *shut down* or *singularise* meaning, does not search for a singular truth, but rather values situated and variable knowledges.

But where does that leave you, learning about these approaches and trying to understand and plot a way through this complex and confusing terrain? Unfortunately, to be a good qualitative researcher, crossing your fingers and hoping for the best *isn't* the solution! If you've got a good grasp of what we've covered here, do you need to go deeper? Are you surprised that our answer is 'it depends'? If your understanding of ontology and epistemology encompasses what we have written in

> **PRACTICE POINT** Always check your local guidelines for expectations relating to dissertations or theses!

this chapter, and you're doing a dissertation or (Master's) thesis, you'll *probably* get by – but *do* check the expectations and requirements in your local context.[35] To be crystal clear – we

---

[33] As an example of this variability in how theoretical frameworks such as realism are classified in the world of 'O&E stuff', we have categorised realism as an ontology, but Madill et al. (2000) presented it as an epistemology.

[34] Constructionism, with its 'suspicious' orientation to texts, representation, and meaning-making, has also been challenged from the start by other critical non-positivist scholars, for obscuring certain aspects of knowing and being, related to embodiment/materiality, and feelings or affect. An 'affective turn' within the humanities and social sciences has been one attempt to 'capture' and explore such aspects that have been 'left out' of 'suspicious' constructionist analyses (e.g. see Moreno-Gabriel & Johnson, 2020).

[35] If something in your local requirements seems really at odds with the principles of Big Q qualitative, do question it with a supervisor. Sometimes generic guidelines for student research are written for an implicitly quantitative/positivist empiricist project, and expectations may be at odds with a qualitative paradigm. You may not 'win' any dispute, but it's worth asking!

are not advocating that this is the level you should *aspire* to, but rather describing what we regard as often-acceptable practice. The one exception is for *critical* qualitative research, where a richer knowledge of the precise ontological andepistemological underpinnings of research is often expected. We encourage reading further, once you've determined a general onto-logical/epistemological position for your research – which may, also, change, as a project progresses, as Lucy's work in Box 6.5 showed. Further reading is particularly important for more advanced research degrees (e.g. doctorates) or research for publication. You don't need to be an expert in philosophical meta-theory to do good reflexive TA, but it's useful to know something about the assumptions that underpin and inform your practice and conceptualisation of TA.[36]

In TA research, theoretical confusion can result from following proscriptions for alleged universal good practice, without considering the ontological and/or epistemo-logical assumptions underlying such practices. As we discuss further in Chapters Eight and Nine, practices like **consensus coding**, measuring **inter-coder reliability**, and **member checking** or **participant validation** (where participants are asked to check the 'accuracy' of the analysis) are often presented as good practice for *all* forms of qualitative research. But all of these prac-tices are infused with assumptions about the nature of reality and meaningful knowledge (Varpio, Ajjawi, Monrouxe, O'Brien, & Rees, 2017). The concept of *theoretical awareness* is an important concept that needs to inform your TA for good practice and can avoid what we call 'positivism creep' (see Box 9.1 in Chapter Nine). Theoretical awareness means having an understanding *that* your prac-

> **KEY CONCEPT** The concept of theoretical awareness highlights the need for researchers to have some understanding of the theoretical assumptions that inform their TA research. Theoretically aware TA is TA in which research is practised in alignment with these theoretical assumptions.

tice is informed by (big) theory and you need to consider and conduct your research in accordance with these theoretical assumptions. It also means ensuring an overall theoretical conceptual and practice-based coherence for any particular project you do (Braun & Clarke, 2021c).

In our own work, we are mostly relativist-constructionist in orientation. But we dabble in critical realism-contextualism, and often supervise students who want to work within these traditions (as well as others, see Box 6.6). Being effectively polyontological and pol-yepistemological (poly = many) doesn't trouble us, as long as we're coherent with what we do *in each analysis*. What troubles us is when it gets messy *within* a particular analysis (Braun & Clarke, 2021c). In mentioning our personal orientations, our goal is to make *visible* the assumptions that *inevitably* shape our engagements with qualitative methods (Braun & Clarke, 2019a; Braun, Clarke, & Hayfield, 2019; Lainson et al., 2019).

---

[36]As we discuss in Chapter Eight, the assumptions underpinning different versions of TA can vary quite considerably.

THEORY AS IT'S USED: SOME TA EXAMPLES

Only a minority of published TA research demonstrates a use of theory that is knowing, reflexive, and clearly articulated – what we hope you aspire to! We end this chapter with some discussion of what theory looks like in practice, since it's always there, even if 'invisibly'. Table 6.2 provides an overview of a selection of TA projects that draw on different ontological and epistemological frameworks, as well as other theory. The table illustrates the variation in terminology around Big Theory noted previously. The description of each study encompasses both how the authors articulated their theoretical positions and use of theory, and, in places, our interpretation of their unarticulated theoretical assumptions. We also include 'smaller' theory in the table – **political theories** such as queer theory or feminism, and explanatory concepts or theories that might be associated with a particular discipline or object of study (see Box 7.2 in Chapter Seven). The latter includes the idea of 'implicit bias' or, more broadly, concepts such as attitudes and body image (all from psychology), that have seeped into cultural common-sense. Sometimes such theories can – unfortunately – get treated as if they are not theoretical, without an ontological and epistemological basis, as theoretically-neutral or trans-theoretical, instead of concepts that are embedded in a particular theoretical tradition and require a cluster of assumptions for coherence. For good theoretical practice, we encourage theoretical reflexivity at all levels of theory.

Table 6.2   Some varied use of theory in published TA research

Research example	Methodology/ methods	Big Theory	Small(er) theory	How is (small) theory used?
The subjective experiences of British Muslim gay men in gay social spaces, particularly the impact of frequenting such spaces on identity processes (Jaspal & Cinnirella, 2012).	Interviews with 20 British-born self-identified gay Muslims of Pakistani heritage.	Realist epistemology; reflective view of language. Participants' talk assumed to be a fairly reliable representation of their cognitions; focus on subjective experiences, meanings and motivations.	Identity process theory (IPT) (Breakwell, 1986) and the concept of identity threat (and the use of coping strategies to alleviate identity threat).	'Quasi-deductive' – theory used to add theoretical depth to data analysis. Also, data analysis used for developing theory – advancing and developing IPT.
How women involved in the US women's movement in the 1970s make sense of their feminist identities (McDougall & McGeorge, 2014).	Interviews with 14 women who were involved with the 1977 US National Women's Conference.	Postmodern feminism (Allan & Baber, 1992) – that assumes experiences are socially located and shaped.	Feminist phenomenology (Dahl & Boss, 2005) which assumes knowledge is constructed, and events can have multiple meanings for different individuals.	Design of the interview guide. And as a guiding lens embedded in the analytic process: "feminist [TA] involves coding the data with an awareness of gender-based oppression and how women's ways of being and identities have been marginalized in society" (p. 82).

(Continued)

Table 6.2 (Continued)

Research example	Methodology/ methods	Big Theory	Small(er) theory	How is (small) theory used?
How do children with a visual impairment experience their physical self-concept in physical activity and sport? (de Schipper, Lieberman, & Moody, 2017)?	Interviews with 6 children aged 9–11 years with a visual impairment of some kind.	"A social constructivism paradigm which acknowledges that subjective meanings are formed through interactions with others and historical and social norms in the lives of individuals" (p. 57).	Hermeneutic-phenomenology (Henriksson & Friesen, 2012); the physical self-concept (PSC) model (Fox & Corbin, 1989; Shavelson, Hubner, & Stanton, 1976)	Interview guide based on the PSC; hermeneutic phenomenology influenced a bottom-up analytic approach; the PSC provided a framework for segmenting data/ analysis; the PSC model's hierarchical structure provided a framework for reporting.
Institutional heterosexism in Icelandic upper secondary schools and how LGBT students respond to its manifestations (Kjaran & Jóhannesson, 2013).	Interviews with 6 former and current LGBT students from secondary schools in and outside of Reykjavík	Unclear – language treated as intentional (reflecting participants' thoughts and feelings) but reference to heterosexual, heterosexist and homophobic discourses circulating within, and shaping, the school environment. Seems most aligned with critical realism.	Queer theory (Jagose, 1996); the concept of heterosexism (Pharr, 2000).	Queer theory informed: (a) the conceptualisation of the research as providing a platform for LGBT students to articulate their experiences; (b) the conceptualisation of sexuality and gender as fluid; and (c) was used as an analytic tool, including using themes from earlier research (e.g. DePalma & Atkinson, 2010) to inform analysis.
Hospital-based nurses' beliefs about hand hygiene (White et al., 2015).	Five focus groups (N=27 nurses) conducted in three large urban public teaching hospitals in Queensland, Australia.	Realist.	Theory of planned behaviour (TPB) (Ajzen, 1991) and particularly the belief base framework of TPB.	TPB informed the development of the focus group guide; the beliefs component of TPB provided a framework for the coding and analysis of the data, and the presentation of the results.
How do young urban Aboriginal women in Vancouver understand their participation in a recreation programme that aimed to enhance their lives (Hayhurst, Giles, Radforth, & The Vancouver Aboriginal Friendship Centre Society, 2015)?	Participatory action research framework; interviews and photovoice activities with 11 young women participants in the programme; a 'sharing circle' with 7 of the young women (participants produced a summary of issues discussed).	Indigenous (non-western) frameworks that aimed to prioritise Aboriginal girls' everyday knowledges and practices of subject-making and intercultural engagement, and explore how these are impacted by powerful neo-colonial discourses.	Feminist post-colonial theory (Darnell & Hayhurst, 2013); a post-colonial feminist approach to girlhood studies (De Finney, 2010); feminist participatory action research (Reid & Frisby, 2008); and decolonising methodologies (Swadener & Mutua, 2008).	Theoretical commitments informed the use of a participatory methodology and the data analysis.

CHAPTER SUMMARY

In this chapter we introduced you to some of the complex and deep-level theory that is always part of doing TA, or indeed any empirical research. We explicated two broad frameworks for Big Q qualitative researching – an experiential or a critical orientation – and introduced three different theories of language that more or less align with these. We emphasised that being clear on your theory of language matters because it determines what you can and cannot claim on the basis of textual data. We then introduced the (related) ontologies (theories of reality) and epistemologies (theories of knowledge) that are common across the social and health sciences. These, again, provide a conceptual foundation for any TA that you do. We ended by emphasising the importance of acknowledging and reflecting on the theoretical assumptions that inform your use of TA.

WANT TO LEARN MORE ABOUT...?

For an accessible introduction to the theories and concepts *underpinning qualitative research* in the social sciences, for readers new to qualitative research, see Chapter 2 in: Braun, V., & Clarke, V. (2013). *Successful qualitative research: A practical guide for beginners*. London: SAGE.

For another psychology-based and accessible discussion of the *theoretical underpinnings of qualitative research*, see Chapters 1 and 2 in: Willig, C. (2013). *Introducing qualitative research in psychology* (3rd ed.). Maidenhead: Open University Press.

For an excellent introduction to the *theoretical foundations of qualitative inquiry*, and particularly positivism and postpositivism, constructionism, the 'interpretivist' paradigm and critical theory (Marxism, feminism and poststructuralism), see: Crotty, M. (1998). *The foundations of social research: Meaning and perspective in the research process*. London: SAGE.

For an accessible and lively discussion of the *paradigms underpinning qualitative research*,[37] and comparing them to the positivist paradigm that typically underpins quantitative research, see: Grant, B. M., & Giddings, L. S. (2002). Making sense of methodologies: A paradigm framework for the novice researcher. *Contemporary Nurse, 13*(1), 10–28.

---

[37]Their mapping (for the field of nursing and midwifery research, and drawing on the work of US education researcher and feminist methodologist, Lather, 1991) is not quite how we'd map things. Interpretative broadly maps onto what we call experiential qualitative, and we prefer constructionist or critical to their use of poststructuralist, as these terms are broader and more inclusive. We're not sure if interpretative and poststructuralist traditions constitute separate *paradigms*. We don't regard radical research as a *separate* paradigm, either, but rather as something that cuts across both interpretative and poststructuralist (their terms) paradigms. These differences illustrate how contested Big Theory is!

A more challenging, but nonetheless hugely rewarding, text on the **theoretical underpinnings of Big Q** qualitative inquiry is: Alvesson, M., & Sköldberg, K. (2009). *Reflexive methodology: New vistas for qualitative research* (2nd ed.). London: SAGE.

To understand more about the **theories of language** discussed in this chapter, we recommend going back to this classic: Hall, S. (1997). The work of representation. In Hall, S. (Ed.), *Representation: Cultural representations and signifying practices* (pp. 13–74). London: SAGE.

For an introduction to a wide array of **Indigenous knowledge (and critical) frameworks** within qualitative research, see: Denzin, N. K., Lincoln, Y. S., & Smith, L. T. (Eds.). (2008). *Handbook of critical and indigenous methodologies.* Los Angeles, CA: SAGE.

For an excellent and key discussion of **'decolonising' methodologies and Indigenous research**, we recommend: Smith, L. T. (2013). *Decolonizing methodologies: Research and Indigenous peoples* (2nd ed.). Dunedin, NZ: University of Otago Press.

For a great exploration of **how we 'do' epistemology** through our methodological choices and approaches to research, see: Carter, S. M., & Little, M. (2007). Justifying knowledge, justifying method, taking action: Epistemologies, methodologies, and methods in qualitative research. *Qualitative Health Research, 17*(10), 1316–1328.

One of the more accessible accounts of **critical realism** and its value for qualitative inquiry that we have come across is this book from a US education researcher: Maxwell, J. (2012). *A realist approach for qualitative research.* Thousand Oaks, CA: SAGE.

For a more challenging but compelling account of **critical realism**, particularly for doctoral students and researchers working in applied fields, see: Pilgrim, D. (2014). Some implications of critical realism for mental health research. *Social Theory & Health, 12*(1), 1–21.

For an accessible and engaging 'invitation' to **social constructionism** from one of the key figures in the social constructionist movement, see: Gergen, K. (2015). *An invitation to social construction* (3rd ed.). London: SAGE.

For a shorter and fairly accessible introduction to **social constructionism**, see: Burr, V., & Dick, P. (2017). Social constructionism. In B. Gough (Ed.), *The Palgrave handbook of critical social psychology* (pp. 59–80). London: Palgrave.

If you are really struggling to shake off the shackles of positivism, this account of the **essentialism vs. social constructionism debate** in relation to lesbian and gay psychology is a really good entry point: Kitzinger, C. (1995). Social constructionism: Implications for lesbian and gay psychology. In A. R. D'Augelli & C. J. Patterson (Eds.), *Lesbian, gay, and bisexual identities over the lifespan: Psychological perspectives* (pp. 136–161). New York: Oxford University Press.

For an accessible discussion of how ***positivism often problematically lingers*** in some of the concepts widely referenced in qualitative research, see: Varpio, L., Ajjawi, R., Monrouxe, L. V., O'Brien, B. C. and Rees, C. E. (2017). Shedding the cobra effect: Problematising thematic emergence, triangulation, saturation and member checking. *Medical Education*, 51, 40–50.

ACTIVITIES FOR STUDENT READERS

Theoretical assumptions exercise: Think about who you are as a researcher, and the assumptions and perspectives you bring to the research process, particularly about the fundamental questions of the nature of human existence and the structure of reality (Crotty, 1998), and how we can create meaningful knowledge about the world. Try to identify your assumptions about human existence, reality and knowing. Reflect on, and write notes on, these questions:

- Why does research matter? What is its purpose?
- What is the nature of reality? Do you think there is an objective and singular reality that exists independent of our minds, our ways of knowing it? Or do you think realities are created in and through human practices?
- What is the researcher's *role* in the research process? Do you think they discover/harvest meaning or play an active role in meaning creation?
- How best can we generate knowledge about the world? Should we strive for objectivity, or regard subjectivity as a strength?
- What role do the researcher's values play in the research process?
- Following this, try to determine what ontology and epistemology best reflects the answers you gave to these questions. Does that surprise you? How do you feel about this? What would holding these positions mean for research practice in TA, and the sorts of knowledge you could generate?

Theoretical detection exercise: Find a recently published TA paper in your discipline/field of research, or use one of the papers made available for this exercise on the companion website. Try to identify the philosophical meta-theoretical assumptions informing the paper. In doing this, look at those explicitly acknowledged by the authors, and those you can 'detect' from reading the paper – NB that these *might* contradict the explicitly acknowledged assumptions. Broadly speaking, try to determine if the paper is realist, critical realist or relativist? Postpositivist, contextualist or constructionist? Is the theory of language informing the data analysis reflective, intentional or constructionist? Is the paper an example of experiential or critical TA? Is there any evidence of confusion around Big Theory? From this exercise, do you feel the paper offers a theoretically *coherent* use of TA?

If you're teaching content related to this chapter…
Don't forget to check the companion website for a range of teaching resources:
https://study.sagepub.com/thematicanalysis

7

SO *WHAT*?

THE IMPORTANCE OF INTERPRETATION IN REFLEXIVE THEMATIC ANALYSIS

Chapter Seven overview

- Doing interpretation during theme development   197
- What is interpretation?   199
- Interpretation needs to be defensible!   201
- Different modes of interpretation for reflexive TA   203

  o From more descriptive to more interpretative modes of analysis   203
  o Experiential to critical orientations in interpretation of data patterns   204

- A deductive orientation: Working with existing theoretical concepts in doing
  interpretation   208
- Locating data within the wider context   211
- Minimising harm in interpretation: Ethics, politics and representation   214

Time to tackle interpretation! Interpretation, or more specifically *doing data interpretation*, is something people can find daunting. Although this chapter is located in Section Two, interpretation is something that is – or should be – embedded into the analytic process in reflexive TA (Section One), rather than being a separate optional add-on. Interpretation is not some *mystical* process, but instead involves "doing what human beings do"[1] (J. A. Smith, 2019, p. 171). At the most basic, interpretation is simply the act of making sense of something. That said, it is sometimes (incorrectly) assumed to be a process that people *implicitly* understand, or it is just not explained well. Our aim in this chapter is to discuss what interpretation involves, the different ways it can be *done*, and demonstrate *how* it is done, and done *well*, building on our discussion of (big) theory in Chapter Six, as theory always grounds and delimits data interpretation. Because interpretation, like theory, is important throughout the reflexive TA process, we have located this chapter in Section Two to avoid suggesting it's a compartmentalised practice that only informs certain phases of reflexive TA.

Reflexive TA has sometimes been *misinterpreted*[2] – potentially through our not being clear enough in our initial writing – as a purely descriptive method, as if it offered a way of simply conveying information from point A (data collection) to point B (report), like a delivery drone who picks up an order from an Amazon warehouse, and drops it at your home. Far from it! Even more-descriptive accounts of data, which stay close to participant or text meanings, both *require* and *reflect* interpretative work. Qualitative analysis is *always* an interpretative activity. You are *not* a magician; meaning is not self-evident or just sitting in data, waiting for your flourishing reveal. If you start to think about interpretation *as* integral to doing (thematic) analysis as breathing is to living – and that's how we believe it is useful to conceptualise it – then you start to appreciate how hard it is to talk about interpretation as a *separate* process and practice (though we are doing so pragmatically, here). For us, the language of *analysis* already includes interpretation built-in, as a taken-for-granted aspect.[3]

> **ALERT** All forms of reflexive TA require interpretative work on the part of the researcher – making meaning of data is an interpretative activity.

---

[1]This quotation about interpretation as an essentially human practice comes from the developer of **interpretative phenomenological analysis (IPA)**, Jonathan Smith, talking about IPA processes, but it aligns with our point here.

[2]Reflexive TA has also been used as a descriptive method, despite our intention, which Janice Morse recently described as a form of "incomplete inquiry" (2020, p. 4). Morse warned against (such) "weak research that 'signifies nothing', simply theming for the purpose of theming" (2020, p. 4).

[3]Language might also contribute to confusion about the role of interpretation in qualitative research, as there are many different ways words like 'analysis' and 'interpretation' get used. Although early qualitative scholars framed a qualitative paradigm – in contrast to the empiricist tradition – as an *interpretative* one (for instance, in discussing quality, Yvonna Lincoln [1995] described "the entire field of interpretative or qualitative inquiry", p. 275), this isn't necessarily reflected in language used in qualitative reporting. Carla Willig (2017) suggested that qualitative researchers may have taken up the term analysis in preference to interpretation to describe what we do, to better align *with* the empiricist orientation that dominates the social sciences, as a way of rhetorically claiming validity. Within a quantitative positivist-empiricist tradition, a differentiation *between* doing statistical analyses and then interpreting the meaning of the results of those probably makes sense. But, in qualitative analysis, we feel analysis and interpretation are better understood as felted together, as impossible-to-separate strands.

Interpretation in reflexive TA is both part of the analytic process, and embedded in its outcome ('the analysis'), and we focus on both aspects in this chapter. There are different *forms* of interpretation that represent different *outcomes* connected to different approaches to reflexive TA (introduced in Table 1.2 in Chapter One) – from more descriptive to more interpretative modes, and from more experiential through to more critical takes on data. We discuss and illustrate both of these continua. Interpretation should always be tied to *context*, and we also discuss what it means to do interpretative work informed or directed by theory, as well as locating analysis within wider contexts. This connects to the ethics and politics of representational practice, or how we do interpretative work with integrity. We end this chapter with a discussion of the ethics and **politics of representation**.

DOING INTERPRETATION DURING THEME DEVELOPMENT

It's easy to conceptualise research and analysis as *revealing the truth* about something. Even if you understand truth-telling as your *purpose* with qualitative analysis (which it is for some approaches), we find a truth-telling framing unhelpful in developing an *interpretative* orientation for analysis. Our task is *not* to stand up in court and 'tell the truth, the whole truth, and nothing but the truth'. Instead, we like Michael Quinn Patton's (1999, p. 1205) description that the analytic "task is to do one's best to make sense out of things". Instead of conceptualising your analytic task as one of discovering, distilling and revealing the essence of the data, we suggest it's better to imagine you're *telling a story* in a way that aims to *make sense of* what's going on. A story that gives the audience (a reader, a listener) a clear *take-home message* – one that includes an indication of *why they should care* about the story you've just told them. This means you have to be clear what the take-home messages

> **PRACTICE POINT** Conceptualise your analytic task as one of storytelling rather than truth-telling – to acknowledge the role of interpretation in making sense of data.

> **ALERT** Your analysis needs to give the audience a take-home message: what does this mean and why does it matter?

you want the audience to leave with *are*, and you have to be clear on *why* you think those particular take-home messages, those *interpretations*, are valid *and* important. This is why analysis cannot simply be a compilation of quotations of data, the meaning of which is treated as self-evident (we discuss processes for quality TA in Chapter Nine). Analysis needs a strong *authorial* narrative, which takes the reader *beyond* the data (as discussed in 'Telling your analytic story' in Chapter Five). Data extracts provide the reader with the tools to *evaluate* your analytic narrative and interpretative claims.

Interpretation starts during *familiarisation* (Chapter Two) – though it's quite likely you will have already started interpreting the data, if you've been engaged in data collection. During familiarisation, or data collection, you often make observations or have ideas about things that are going on – the sorts of things you record in your familiarisation notes. Interpretation at that stage is tentative and should be recognised as such – don't cling tightly to early interpretations, assuming you've noticed everything and made sense of the data in the best way.

In general, the interpretative process for TA operates most strongly as you move from coding into theme generation, development and refinement (Phases three to five), and is honed in and through writing (including final writing up in Phase six). Interpretation needs to operate in concert with your research question – even if the particulars of that question aren't yet refined (as we discussed in 'What's my purpose here? Settling on a research question' in Chapter Two). Just as there are endless patterns we *could* focus on, it is the ones that *matter* most in addressing our research question that become part of our developing analysis, so interpretation needs to be anchored to the research question(s) and purpose of a project. Our research question(s) and purpose, alongside our dataset, provide the foundation for our interpretation; wider contextual elements provide the scope for it (discussed later in this chapter). A key practice point is to stay orientated to your research question – orientated, but not shackled, as it is not fixed.

> **PRACTICE POINT** Stay orientated to your research question during the interpretative analytic process to avoid losing sight of your analytic focus and purpose.

Asking questions in relation to the patterns you're developing, and the implications of them, can be useful in helping to develop an *interpretative* analytic orientation, one that moves beyond describing semantic content. During phases three to five, examples of the questions *we* might ask include:

- What assumptions are part of this pattern of meaning?
    - Assumptions on the part of participants or expressed within the dataset?
    - Assumptions that *I* might be making as I make sense of the data?

- What wider meanings or ideas does this pattern rely on?[4]
- *Why* might this pattern of meaning matter?
    - Might it matter more, or less, to certain people?

- What are the implications of this pattern?
    - For any participants?
    - For the issue at hand?
    - For the academic knowledge of the field?
    - For society? Both overall or for particular groups within a society?

> **PRACTICE POINT** Asking questions of yourself and your analysis is a useful tool for 'going deeper' into interpretation.

This isn't an exhaustive list of questions you could ask, so much as starting suggestions for how you might orientate to thinking about patterns in the dataset, and why those patterns might matter. Such questions are useful to think about for *each* potential developing theme, and for your overall analysis – the *story* that addresses your research question.

---

[4]This idea – that patterns rely on other meanings or ideas to make sense – might be hard to grasp. Let's briefly explore this with the themes of 'choice' from the childfree dataset (see Box 4.9 in Chapter Four for the summary of 'choice' themes). For parenting to be imagined and framed by the logic of *choice*, and thus be the strongly patterned meaning in the dataset it was, certain other meanings related to how we think about individual people and their lives have to exist. An example of this could be that people can and should make life-choices based in *individual* (or couple) wants or needs, rather than wider family or community wants and needs. In asking this question about what wider meanings a pattern relies on, we are trying to 'denaturalise' some of the ideas that are normalised and embedded in our worlds.

WHAT IS INTERPRETATION?

Interpretation is one of the most obvious *and* the most opaque ideas in analysis, vital to the task, but hard to describe, and even harder to codify as a practice. In general, we try to avoid loose, glossy meme-like phrases such as *to be human is to interpret*, and yet interpretation is something deeply embedded in human psychological activity. Interpretation, at its most basic, is sense-making activity, and we engage in it all the time. It's what we do when we encounter the stimuli in our worlds. We try to make sense of what each stimulus represents, what it means, often without any conscious effort or intent. Interpretation is the 'so what' process that accompanies our identification of what something *is*; it might even shape our identification of *what* that something actually is. Interpretation, then, is essentially a process of making sense of what is going on – in data, in the case of qualitative analysis – why that might matter and what the implications might be.

> **ALERT** Interpretation is the essentially human activity of working out what is going on.

Already this is sounding more cryptic than it needs to, so let's translate this into a concrete example from our everyday lives. Imagine you receive a text-based message. For most of us, text-based communications (e.g. SMS, DM) have become mundane and commonplace, perhaps our most common form of non-face-to-face communication. We recognise the stimulus for what it is easily and without thought. We read the brief message: "Sorry I can't meet later". Brief, yes. But far from simple, when it comes to interpretation! Those five words (without emoji or punctuation) could be interpreted in so many different ways. Depending on how we make sense of the message, our reaction might be anything from an affectively neutral response, to relief, or frustration, happiness, sadness, or concern. Our making sense will be shaped by what we bring to this process and the wider context of the message.

Interpretation is the meaning-making we engage in, and it does not occur in a vacuum, it's not fixed, and it's not self-evident from a stimulus itself. Some general key points about interpretation:

- *Interpretation depends on us* – on our psychology, our affect, our values and politics, and the assumptions and ideals that permeate our take on the world (the sorts of things we interrogate with reflexivity; do go back to Chapter One if you need a refresher). Some of these are temporal and shifting – for instance, our mood in the moment (imagine you're feeling misanthropic when you get the message, after witnessing a good friend experiencing some threats and abuse online) or the immediate context of our lives (imagine you're feeling overstretched and have more on your plate than you can manage). Some are more deeply embedded. For instance, as (White, middle-class) feminists, we both have a tendency to immediately notice things and explore meaning through gendered lenses. We identify gender in descriptions of events or encounters, where others might not, and it feels 'natural' to do so. We note our Whiteness and class privilege specifically, as it allows a particular (seemingly neutral, but far from it; DiAngelo, 2018) *gendered* lens in contexts of White dominance and privilege.
- *Interpretation depends on context.* What meanings or implications we make about a stimulus inevitably reflect context, both the immediate and wider context. Imagine that text is from your boss, and your immediate work context is one of precarity. You'd planned to meet to talk about your getting further work for the company. Or the message is from

an old and dear friend, but who nonetheless has a history of making plans and then cancelling on you at the last minute. Perhaps it's from a colleague you know has a chronic health condition, that impacts them in variable ways. Each of these contexts would steer your interpretation (combined with your psychology) in a different way. In relation to *analysis*, Rachel Graham's

> **ALERT** The wider context of data shapes our interpretation of their meaning.

reflections in Box 1.3 (in Chapter One) highlighted that how you might read and make sense of British-based African Caribbean women's accounts of their lives depends not only on your positioning, but also on an understanding of the sociohistorical and contemporary context of racism in (and beyond) the UK (Akala, 2018; Eddo-Lodge, 2018).

- *Interpretation brings together all our knowledge related to the subject or object at hand.* For a text message, that would include any previous communication we've had with the sender, and the thought and preparation that went into whatever was planned. Interpretation becomes our *best guess* at what is going on in relation to these aspects. In relation to *analysis*, our own experiences combined with our academic substantive and theoretical knowledge can help us go beyond a semantic reading of our data, especially if it gives us a *different* reading of what is going on than the explanations offered by participants or in the text. We discuss an example of this in Box 7.1, related to our student Sophie Sill's work on heterosexism and homophobia in women's competitive team sport in Aotearoa New Zealand.

- *Not all interpretation holds up to scrutiny.* This is not an 'anything goes' situation. Interpretation needs to be *defensible.* A worried conclusion that your boss is going to fire you would need more contextualised justification than just the message. A concerned conclusion that your colleague might be going through a bad patch would be justified through your contextualised historical understanding of the impact of their condition on their health, and how it constrains

> **ALERT** Not all interpretation is created equal. Interpretation needs justification. Some interpretation is justifiable; other interpretation is unwarranted.

their life. In relation to *analysis*, your interpretation is never just based on the dataset. While the dataset grounds it, scholarly knowledge, theory, ideology, politics and all sorts of other factors can come together in how you make sense of meaning – and even the meaning patterns you notice.[5] Your argument for what those patterns *mean* needs to be discussed in relation to the aspects that lead you to a certain interpretation. To give a scholarly example: we have done quite a bit of work on body hair meanings and practices (Braun et al., 2013; Clarke & Braun, 2019b; Jennings et al., 2019; Li & Braun, 2017; Terry & Braun, 2013a, 2016; Terry et al., 2018). In that work, we theorise and understand body hair removal as a *gendered practice* rather than simply individual choice – yet the latter is often the predominant explanation for body hair removal by participants or in the data. We frame hair removal as gendered for several reasons – including that this is an interpretation supported by existing research and theory, and the feminist lens we bring

---

[5]Some refer to this form of interpretative practice, informed by theory, ideology and politics etc., as *strong interpretation* (Chamberlain, 2011).

to interpreting the data and the wider sociocultural context of body hair and embodiment. We also interrogate why participants predominantly frame hair removal in terms of individual choice – not to 'argue with' participants and show why they are *wrong*, but to explore why such an interpretation of hair removal makes sense in our contemporary context and what implications it has. Good analytic practice requires that we explain our interpretative tools and contexts for understandings to convince the reader of *our* interpretation. The question is, *why* should we be believed. More on all this in a moment.

The key take-away is that for us as qualitative researchers, interpretation is *inevitably* subjective (we reiterate, this *isn't* a problem), and there is no absolute, singular, correct interpretation. (Conversely, we *will* argue that interpretation can be wrong in various ways.) Our framework for reflexive TA – with phases and processes for rigour, including revisiting the whole dataset, and the requirement for being an active thinking researcher who *makes choices* – provides tools to facilitate a thorough and data-connected interpretation. When it comes to interpretation, try not to be guided by the question 'am I doing this *right*?' so much as by the questions 'are there good *grounds* for what I'm claiming?' and 'am I ignoring some inconvenient "truths"?' If you can answer yes to the second, and no to the last, you're well on your way to a defensible interpretation.

> **ALERT** Interpretation is inherently subjective; and this is okay! There is no 'correct' or singular interpretation of data.

> **PRACTICE POINT** Try to let go of anxiety about doing interpretation 'correctly' and instead ask yourself whether there are good grounds for the claims you're making about your data.

INTERPRETATION NEEDS TO BE DEFENSIBLE!

As interpretation goes beyond the data, the challenge, or balancing act, nicely captured by UK-based critical psychology scholars Carla Willig and Wendy Stainton Rogers, is:

> to go beyond what presents itself, to reveal dimensions of a phenomenon which are concealed or hidden, whilst at the same time taking care not to impose meaning upon the phenomenon, not to squeeze it into pre-conceived categories or theoretical formulations, not to reduce it to an underlying cause. (2008, p. 9)

As qualitative researchers, we need to keep asking whether our interpretation has moved *too far* from the data. *Too far* is of course one of those vague concepts that can produce an instant sense of anxiety: how do I know if I've

> **PRACTICE POINT** Ask yourself whether your developing analysis has moved too far beyond the data.

gone too far? Sorry! As we've already noted, finality, permanence and correctness are not hallmarks of reflexive TA, nor of the entire field of Big Q qualitative researching. So you do have to try to settle in to some degree of uncertainty to conduct qualitative research effectively (the challenges and some strategies around this were discussed in Boxes 4.3 and 4.4 in Chapter Four). Practically, this question is about making sure that you're not shaping the data to tell *your* story, or smoothing over complexity to (mis)represent the stories in the data. In writing this, we get a mental image of the 'ugly stepsister' in the fairy-tale *Cinderella*, trying to force her foot into the glass slipper. Despite the very questionable gender politics of Cinderella, the image evokes well the idea of (mis)using data to tell *your* story, rather than telling *your* story *of the data*. Don't try to make the data fit your narrative; don't be the 'ugly stepsister'!

> **PRACTICE POINT** Don't force the data into the story you want to tell.

We've put this section early in this chapter, because it signals what you're aiming for with interpretation. We as researchers need to do the work to show how our interpretation is *defensible*, in light of the intersection of: (a) our topic, existing knowledge and the wider context that surrounds it; (b) the dataset that we're working with; (c) the theoretical frameworks we're working with; (d) our individual position(s); and (e) the processes we've engaged in to develop that interpretation – sometimes individually, sometimes in a research team, sometimes with the community the research connects with. In doing so, we have to convince our audience that we haven't come to the data with our interpretation pre-formed, and that it has developed *through* our analytic process. This is the case no matter whether our analysis is more inductive or deductive, more developed through a hermeneutics of 'empathy' or 'suspicion' (see Willig, 2017). It's tempting to think 'suspicious' or deductive interpretation needs more care, because such interpretation more obviously goes *beyond* the voices of participants. But, as we will argue and show later in the chapter, it applies to *all* interpretation (see Fine & Torre, 2004). Let's come back to our tendency for a *gendered* analysis: as tempting as it is, we don't stomp around shouting 'that's gendered!' at everything we encounter,[6] without giving it deeper thought. Without asking ourselves what that might mean, and if, and how, gender plays out, and plays out in particularly classed, and/or raced ways.[7] Instead, we use our gendered *lenses* as a kind of signal to look at and think about something, more deeply and critically, in a *particular* way; to ask questions that locate gender as a key component to consider. We strive to use it to open up, rather than close down, meaning-making.

What is defensible depends on context, and your task as analyst is to show how and why you believe your interpretation has validity. To come back to our text message example: imagine

---

[6] Well, maybe we *sometimes* do this, and with lots of swearing, but only in the privacy of our own homes. It's not analysis like we're talking about in reflexive TA.

[7] Coming back to our point earlier about the intersections of gender, race and class, it would be easy for us as White middle-class feminists to simply stop at gender in our analysis, and not consider how race and class are also key elements in how we view and understand the world. Over the last few years in the westernised world, the *failure* of White feminists to acknowledge that their feminism reflects their situated *and* privileged positioning *as White* has been a cause of tensions within feminism (e.g. Cargle, 2018). Such critique is *not* new; what is new(ish) is the ways it has become more key to 'everyday feminism'.

it is from your unreliable friend, and your reaction is to shout, swear, and be tempted to throw your phone across the room. Someone who witnesses your response tells you that you're overreacting (which annoys you more!), but your response, in context, seems justifiable to you. It reflects the history that precedes the text, the rich context that grounds your response. The person judging your reaction doesn't know that, unless you explain to them. To make your reaction *defensible* to the person you are with, you have to explain to them *why* that particular reading makes the most sense to you, and why it matters, effectively providing a rationale for your reaction. If you explained that to the person with you, and they then agreed your reaction *wasn't* an overreaction, you've shown your interpretation is defensible. That's not to say that your reaction is the only one possible! It is *not* about saying you are *right* or no other reading is possible. It is about convincing someone else that the reading you've offered makes sense and matters.

DIFFERENT MODES OF INTERPRETATION FOR REFLEXIVE TA

But what does *interpretation* actually *look like* in practice? In the next sections, we discuss interpretation across different forms of reflexive TA. These different forms of TA serve quite different purposes – so although interpretation is a somewhat universal practice, the outcomes of interpretative analytic work can look quite different, depending on what it is you're aiming to do. What mode of interpretation is appropriate comes back to your research purpose, research question, and the audience(s) you're addressing with your analysis.

From more descriptive to more interpretative modes of analysis

As we've noted, all reflexive TA needs to involve interpretation. But your analyses can be situated somewhere along a continuum from primarily offering description (e.g. of an experience, such as of what it is *like* to be childfree, or of a concept, such as pronatalism) to interrogating, unpacking, and even theorising (e.g. the assumptions underpinning the ways people describe being childfree); the more interpretative end of the continuum. Even within a more descriptive mode of interpretation, we'd still characterise the interpretation involved as "com[ing] from the researcher and [. . .] informed by insights from theory and other related research" (Chamberlain, 2011, p. 50), and an understanding of the wider context.

> **ALERT** Analysis always involves interpretation but it can be primarily descriptive, in the sense of 'staying close' to the data, to participants' sense-making, or primarily interpretative, in the sense of bringing in the researcher's conceptually informed lenses to interrogate the ideas expressed.

In the worked example analysis of the childfree dataset, the contradictory theme *good and bad parents* (see Box 4.7 in Chapter Four) offers an example that is fairly *descriptive* but also deeply interpretative. The theme describes a pattern that is evident at a quite semantic level (even *if* the idea of a contradictory theme is somewhat conceptual). In so doing, it provides a descriptive account, and one that would be easily recognisable to someone reading the dataset for themselves. However, our analysis is interpretative, because we don't stop at the point of identification of this pattern – instead, we ask *what are the implications of this pattern?* We also located our analytic interpretation of this pattern within the wider societal context to consider such implications (see 'Locating data within the wider context', below). Similarly, our student Louisa Davey's critical realist TA around alopecia areata (hair loss; see Box 5.2 in Chapter Five) not only reported a range of meanings associated with hair and hair loss *for* the participants, but asked what these meaning patterns then meant in terms of people's lives, and also healthcare interactions and practice (Davey et al., 2019).

Our worked example analysis developed within an overarching theme of *choice matters* (see Box 4.9 in Chapter Four) offers an example from the interpretative end of the 'more descriptive to more conceptually interpretative' spectrum. This end of the spectrum often aligns with more critical, constructionist and latent approaches within reflexive TA. Our analysis was developed through our interrogation of the *logics* of choice within the dataset. Instead of stopping at reporting that 'choice' was important in how people made sense of being childfree, our analysis brought a range of conceptual/theoretical tools to the interpretative process, as we sought to parse out the different *logics* of choice within the dataset. In doing so, we identified that there were quite different frameworks or understandings of choice at play, associated with bigger Anglo-western systems of meaning. Our analysis went far *beyond* a direct reporting on recognisable patterned dataset content, to ask question about what might be at stake when we talk about parenting within choice frameworks. Why might this meaning and interpretation matter?

More interpretative analyses can *matter* in a range of ways. They can matter through the contribution they make to theoretical discussions or understandings (see commentary by Beres & Farvid, 2010, on the companion website). They can matter through providing deeper or more complex understandings of what is *at stake* for some kind of practice or policy development. For example, Ginny's analysis of 'national identity' explanations of sexual health risk in Aotearoa New Zealand provided access to meaning-making with direct consequences for how sexual health promotion should be framed, to increase uptake of the message (Braun, 2008). They can matter through providing a nuanced explanation for what might be going on, when more descriptive accounts just don't *quite* feel like they're getting to the heart of things (see Box 7.1, p. 206).

Experiential to critical orientations in interpretation of data patterns

The more descriptive to more interpretative modes overlap with broad takes on the data – whether your analysis is based in a more experiential or critical framework for qualitative researching (Braun & Clarke, 2013). As we discussed in Chapter Six, an experiential orientation to TA grounds it within the meanings and life-worlds of the participants or within the meanings of the data. Critical orientations to TA tend to take more researcher-directed interpretative frames, or an interrogative approach, where interpretation is not entirely determined by data-based meanings (Braun & Clarke, 2013; Willig, 2017). Each position is based in different epistemological and ontological frameworks and allows us to make quite different claims, different *types* of interpretation.

Often, interpretation based around *participant* meaning might seem obvious or straight-forward, and that focus might continue to be the basis on which your analysis develops and is 'completed'. Or it might prove to be a step in the journey towards a quite different take on things. To come back to our adventure analogy, imagine you've now returned home and are starting to write a story of your trip. You have loads of photos, social media posts, as well as a journal and other bits and pieces you picked up along the way. You start to write and find that as well as a description of what you did, you can identify and describe some key patterns across the diverse experiences. You're pretty happy with this first attempt, and people are interested in it – you get it published in an online magazine you admire. But your curiosity has also been piqued, and you start to read other stories, and consider different information. In doing so, your position shifts... You read a critique of the colonial gaze and neocolonialism in and through travel (S. E. Smith, 2014), and although it's a bit uncomfortable, you wonder if you might inadvertently have reproduced these ideas in how you've written up your experience. You read around gender politics in the region, and reflect on how your sex/gender may have shaped not only how you've told your story, but the very experiences you had in the first place (Kugel, 2013). You start to reflect and ask *different* questions about the ways you have understood your journey. Going back to all the evidence of your trip, you read and make sense again with new questions at the forefront of your mind. Questions such as: what sorts of things need to be in place for me to have this experience, and to interpret it in this way? What sorts of assumptions does it rest on? What (problematic or not) ideas am I inadvertently reproducing in how I've told this story? These sorts of questions – and others – help you to develop a differ-ently nuanced and more complex understanding, including an interrogation of how you are making meaning about your journey. And, as a result of this, your account of the trip may change.

This is analogous to what can happen in reflexive TA, as a researcher shifts from a more experiential to a more critical orienta-tion within the scope of a developing analysis. Sometimes, you might develop one more expe-rientially-orientated analysis, and then move on to a *new*, more critically-orientated one (as our former student Louise Davey did, see Box 5.2

> **PRACTICE POINT** Your analytic orientation can shift from more experiential to more critical through your engagement with the data, resulting in your settling on one analysis. Or you can offer multiple interpretative 'takes' on the data.

in Chapter Five). Instead of a worked example from the childfree dataset to demonstrate this, we use the analysis of one of our students, Sophie Sills, developed for her Master's project, as it nicely illustrates this shift and change. Sophie's initial *experiential* interpreta-tion left her feeling that *more* needed to be said, to make sense of the data. This feeling was based on her experiences and scholarly knowledge. So she shifted her interpretative lens to a *critical* one, to address the nagging questions. Box 7.1 briefly summarises this project, Sophie's research question(s) and her developing analysis.

================================ **Box 7.1** ================================

Shifting from an experiential to critical orientation to build analytic depth

The analytic development of themes within the Master's research project[8] of one of our students, Sophie Sills illustrates key points in this book:

- Not getting too attached to themes early on, as your analysis might radically change (as emphasised in Chapters Three and Four);
- Shifting across more inductive/experiential and more theoretically-informed approaches to TA (discussed in Chapters Three and Six);
- The value of reflexivity in analysis (a key concept, see Chapter One).

Sophie's research explored the experiences of queer participants in competitive women's team sports. Having played competitive team sports herself for many years, and identifying as queer, Sophie was an *insider* in the research area in several ways (see 'Minimising harm in interpretation', below). Her experience suggested there were many ways that implicit norms, assumptions and expectations of heterosexuality (heteronormativity) and more explicit forms of discrimination and marginalisation (heterosexism, homophobia and biphobia) played out in this area. The research literature also indicates sports as a site in which these operate (e.g. Carless, 2012; Gough, 2007; Lenskyj, 2013; Norman, 2012; Willis, 2015; Wright & Clarke, 1999), despite a wider sociocultural context in which *liberal tolerance* has come to dominate discussion around sexuality (e.g. Clarke, 2005; Ellis, 2001; Gough, 2002). Sophie was interested in exploring the experiences of players, including around discrimination and marginalisation, in order to improve the situation, such as by developing resources and guidelines for clubs and coaches.

Sophie interviewed 31 people (most face-to-face, some via *Skype*) who identified as lesbian, gay, bisexual, queer, pansexual, asexual, aromantic, and unsure, who played across a wide range of sports, and at levels from international to local competition. Some were interviewed individually, and others in small groups or pairs, giving her a very large participant group for a research Master's project (see Braun & Clarke, 2013). Following transcription, Sophie embarked on reflexive TA, and her process through different thematic iterations illustrates the twists and turns the analytic path can take. Sophie's participants' stories – her data – could be read multiple ways, and indeed, this is how Sophie's analysis developed.

The first iteration produced robust patterns that spoke to participants' views and experiences around inclusion and marginalisation. Participants identified incidences of heterosexism or homophobia, but also suggested these weren't that bad, and that they can or did put them aside, that it didn't affect them. Or, that it was their own responsibility 'to deal' – to *not* be affected by it. A simple reporting of such 'results' suggests that queer participants in women's competitive team sports don't really experience much homophobia or heterosexism, and it doesn't affect them *too much*. And that reading isn't *wrong*.

But Sophie wasn't satisfied with that reading – in a way that aligns with the notion of *naturalistic generalisability* (which we discussed in Chapter Five; see B. Smith, 2018), it didn't ring true enough. She then had to grapple with questions of *why not?* and *what was missing?* from that analysis. Switching to a more suspicious hermeneutic, and going deeper into a

---

[8]Sophie's Master's project involved one calendar year of full-time, research-only study.

more theoretically- and contextually-informed analytic mode, she asked questions about *how can these data make sense?* and *how can I make sense of these data?* Her focus shifted from capturing experiential truth, to asking how and why might truth be made – and made in certain ways. Sophie's final analysis examined how participants talked about and accounted for their experiences in women's team sport. She particularly focused on experiences that could be described as heterosexism or homophobia, in contexts of apparent liberal tolerance, a neoliberal emphasis on individual responsibility, and an emphasis on the value of 'the team' as an effective *single unit* within sports culture.

Sophie generated five key themes: *It's not so bad*; *I can take it*; *No I in team*; *Each to their own*; and *It's my own making*. These theme names have echoes of some of the key patterns captured in the first analytic iteration, but the analysis went far beyond reporting and interpreting experience. *It's not so bad* captured an overall tone in which experiences that *could* be described as heterosexism were often downplayed, dismissed, or not framed as such. Through rejecting common portrayals of queer people as victims, and drawing on ideas of the tough athlete, participants' talk framed themselves as strong and able to *take* any heterosexism. Participants often framed themselves as good *teammates* by suggesting they put others before themselves; in this context, questioning heterosexism becomes almost selfish, and disruptive to a *team* environment. Participants regularly drew on a discourse of *liberal tolerance* to describe their experiences in sport. Connecting to neoliberal individualism, some participants implicitly framed (avoiding) heterosexism as the individual's responsibility, and positioned themselves as making the correct choices, or acting in the right ways, to avoid being targeted by heterosexism (this latter theme resonates strongly with the worked example of TA we offered in Braun & Clarke, 2012).

The more 'empathetic' or surface analysis, which took the participants' accounts at face value, suggested there wasn't much that's problematic for queer participants in women's team sports; the more interpretative, contextualised, and theoretically-informed 'suspicious' analysis told a different story. This critical analysis was not intended to negate the stories participants told, but rather to use them as a starting point for a deeper understanding of what might be at stake when people say heterosexism doesn't really affect them. The participants' talk, which Sophie read in relation to, and resisting, a narrative of heterosexist victimhood, makes sense if we consider the broader sociocultural contexts of the participants' lives and experiences, and the context of team sports.

This example highlights the value of TA in producing analyses that illuminate our understanding of a particular issue, but which, instead of *revealing the truth*, can be regarded as critical interpretations arising from a context and a relationship. Between ourselves as researchers, our participants (if we have them), the data and our engagement with them, our theories around analysis, existing scholarship in the area, and any communities we might be working in/with.

As this example shows, the interpretative focus for experiential and critical TA is *quite different* (see Willig, 2017). We want to be *very clear* that we are not claiming that critical analyses are *better*, in some decontextualised way, than experiential analyses. This is not the case – both critically- and experientially-orientated work can be done poorly, or it can be done well, and again, it also comes back to fit with purpose. Part of doing analysis well is being clear you understand what it is you're doing.

ALERT Critical TA is not inherently better – more sophisticated and cleverer – than experiential TA! You should select the approach that best fits your purpose and not worry about trying to do something 'clever'. Seriously! ☺

A DEDUCTIVE ORIENTATION: WORKING WITH EXISTING THEORETICAL CONCEPTS IN DOING INTERPRETATION

Theory is one of those words that garners reactions that range from delight to fear and loathing. Theory is often misunderstood, and maybe because of that often simply ignored, in doing TA (Braun & Clarke, 2021c). But, as discussed in Chapter Six, theory is everywhere, and "even without great theoretical awareness, underlying theories will always be present, leading the researcher's gaze" (Malterud, 2016, p. 121). To do *good* interpretative reflexive TA, you need to understand this, and be explicit around theory, and where and how theory informs the analysis.

ALERT To really get to grips with interpretation in reflexive TA, you need some understanding of the meta-theoretical positions – the 'ologies – that underpin and give validity to your interpretative practice.

In Chapter Six, we discussed Big Theory, theory at a philosophical or meta level – the ontological and epistemological positions we're working with. We can understand data in quite different ways, and the ways we theorise them determine which sorts of interpretations hold validity, and which don't. For instance, we can treat text as simply a conveyance for experience or opinion – in the childfree comments, we'd treat the views expressed as *reflecting* the opinions of the people who posted them. Alternatively, we can theorise our data as constructing rather than simply reporting realities and truths, and we might explore how the very concept of 'being childfree' is *constructed* in the dataset – what particular nature is ascribed to it.

ALERT In reflexive TA, a deductive orientation involves using existing theory and concepts to develop your interpretation of the data.

Another way theory comes into play in doing TA is through theory-driven analysis, where interpretation utilises existing theory to guide the developing analysis. This captures analysis that is strongly informed by existing theoretical constructs (e.g. heterosexism and heteronormativity) or a wholesale theory (e.g.

Foucault's theory of sexual ethics or identity process theory). In such strongly *deductive* or *theory driven* reflexive TA, you, as researcher, deliberately seek to explore, or develop your analysis in relation to, one or more pre-existing ideas or frameworks. You do not have to know this in advance! As was the case with Sophie Sills' analytic process (which we discussed in Box 7.1), sometimes early in the interpretative development, it may become clear that a more theoretically-informed analysis can tell a richer, more complex, and more useful story.[9] Box 7.2 offers a quick overview of some of the forms of theory that might inform your interpretative analytic process.

---

[9]This use of theory for analytic interpretation is not simply a process of bringing literature in as you tell a rich, connected analytic story (discussed in Chapter Five).

━━━━━━ **Box 7.2** ━━━━━━

Explanatory theory in reflexive TA

The whole process of interpretation – sense-making – *relies* on enmeshed layers of theory. When working in a theoretically-driven way in TA, when working with explanatory theory, Big- or meta-theoretical positions provide the all-encompassing theoretical framework for interpretation. Big Theory (which we discussed in Chapter Six) is not *separate* from the sorts of theory we discuss in *this* box and *this* section. Rather, Big Theory permeates it all, like the air we breathe: mostly we don't notice it, and we're often unaware of it, but it's constantly there.

Other types or levels of theory include:

- The theory that informs our interpretation practices in *broad conceptual* ways, such as theories related to phenomenology (Langdridge, 2017), discourse (Wiggins, 2017), or affect (Moreno-Gabriel & Johnson, 2020; Wetherell, 2015).
- Explicitly *socio-politically inflected* theories that you draw on to make sense of the possibilities and boundaries for understanding and experience within the material, symbolic, and power organisation of our worlds – our immediate and broader contexts. Such frameworks include various feminisms (Collins & Bilge, 2016; McCann & Kim, 2013), postcolonial (Said, 1994) and decolonisation theories (G. Adams & Estrada-Villalta, 2017; L. T. Smith, 2013), crip theory (McRuer, 2006), queer theory (Sullivan, 2013), and many more.
- Theories that are more specific – you might call them *lower-level theories* – theories that focus on exploring or explaining a specific topic, mechanism or process. Within the mainstream of our discipline of psychology, this includes popular theoretical frameworks like social cognition (Carlston, 2013), and identity process theory (Jaspal & Breakwell, 2014). In mainstream psychology, this level of theory is often equated *with* theory, full stop; ontological and epistemological assumptions are rarely discussed.[10]

Theory is harder to notice if our explanatory frameworks are effectively the common-sense ones, the dominant or normative ones, because they are then shared or assumed by many, and frequently are invisible to us – just like the air we breathe. The trick is to recognise that theory is *operating* in all sorts of ways, even if it's not explicated. Our best practice guidance is to try to be as clear as we can about the assumptions that inform, and validate, the interpretation we do in reflexive TA – and to use reflexivity as a tool for striving to recognise *and interrogate* these.

Sometimes you will have a sense *in advance* (or early on) that you want to develop a theory-directed analysis. What you want to do with your interpretative work might be predominantly located and framed – at least *initially* – by ideas derived *not* from the data themselves, but from ideas already at play in the wider social or scholarly context. These ideas will direct your interpretative engagement with your data. One of the papers we reproduce with reflective commentary on the companion website provides an example of

---

[10]As we've noted, absence of *discussion of theory* should not be equated with absence of theory. Even if theory is not discussed at other levels, it's still there (Malterud, 2016).

this sort of TA. The authors, Melanie Beres and Panteá Farvid, who had separately worked on projects related to heterosexual casual sex in Canada and Aotearoa New Zealand, recognised their datasets provided a rich context to explore their joint interest in a theorical and practical construct called sexual ethics, connected to how people develop ethical and non-harmful (physical) intimacies (e.g. Carmody, 2008). Beres and Farvid (2010) sought to explore and understand sexual ethics meaning-making in and through their datasets related to casual heterosex. In this sort of theory-directed interpretation, your conceptual and theoretical ideas, then, explicitly guide the sorts of ways you engage with the data (sometimes even how you collect the data), and the interpretations you develop in relation to this.

> **ALERT** Theoretically-driven or deductive reflexive TA is not about testing hypotheses.

There are two important points to note here. First, this is *not* the same as quantitative hypothesis testing. Theory-directed reflexive TA is not aiming to prove (or disprove) a theory or hypothesis. You don't *apply* a theory to the data to *test* if the data evidence it. 'Deductive' reflexive TA offers a theoretical *exploration* of qualitative data, and remains embedded within a framework of openness and situated meaning connected to Big Q research values (discussed in Chapter One). This

> **ALERT** Theoretically-driven or deductive reflexive TA is not about massaging or selecting the data to fit a pre-existing theory.

approach is *not* about massaging your data to fit into your preconceived notions, or telling a partial story of the data that fits with a pre-existing theory or concept. Rather, this analytic orientation recognises and acknowledges the conceptual ideas we (always) come to data and a project with, and gives them greater analytic priority in our interpretative processes than in inductive-orientated analyses.

When working with data in this more theoretically-informed or directed way, the following guidelines will help you to avoid (inadvertently) shoe-horning the data to fit an existing idea, and to demonstrate how you have avoided this pitfall:

- *Work from a curious, open and questioning position when engaging with data more theoretically.* For instance, understand your task as exploring *how* a theory or concept is evidenced – and *not* evidenced – within the dataset, rather than one of merely *identifying* it in the dataset.
- *Always keep your interpretations tentative.* Don't only seek affirming evidence, solidifying your analysis early on.
- *Keep asking which data aren't fitting with the developing interpretation, and, importantly, in what ways they aren't fitting.* This is about ensuring that the interpretative frames you're bringing to the data aren't obscuring a different story, a fuller story, or one that may be more important to the topic. Is your conceptual framework *limiting* what you are able to say about the data, in ways that provide either an impoverished analysis, or one that only gives a partial view? Reflect on the gains and losses connected to your particular theoretical lens.
- *Always be wary of imagining your reading as the right or the only one possible from the data.* Because interpretation is inherently subjective there is always potential – in theory at least – for multiple readings of data.

Our take-home message is that theory is unavoidable, when it comes to interpretation and analysis in TA, and it need not be scary (see Chapter Six). Recognising that theory informs the whole endeavour is a useful starting point for being explicit *and reflexive* about how theory informs the analysis – at all levels. Knowing to avoid simply laying theoretical constructs over the top of the data patterns, and always, always being tentative in taking a deductive orientation, will set you up well for doing more theoretically-driven TA.

LOCATING DATA WITHIN THE WIDER CONTEXT

It is good practice in reflexive TA to locate your interpretation within the wider context. This is not about providing a factual summary of the context of data collection, so much as treating your data and your participants (if you have them) as embedded in contexts that have inflected the data. Much as your interpretation is similarly inflected

> **ALERT** In reflexive TA it is good interpretative practice to locate your data in their wider context. This acknowledges that the sense we make of data is shaped by the contexts of its production, both immediate/local and wider.

by *your* positions. Too often we read analyses that describe a topic as if it happened in Anycountry – a mythical place, but all too often, actually the US or the UK. Similarly, we read about experiences of a participant group as if they were Anypeople – again, a mythical people, but all too often actually White people from high consumption westernised countries. These experiences or perspectives are written about as if they're universal and don't need to be situated, don't need to be considered as partial and contextual – but they inevitably are that. If you speak from a position of societal or cultural dominance, from a position that is *the norm*, you are not *automatically* treated as 'speaking from a position' and thus having a requirement to name or particularise the issue or perspective you're capturing in your analysis. This connects with politics and representation (which we discuss next) but also ties to an *important* analytic practice of locating your interpretation in the wider context. By that, we mean that the particulars of the participant group/dataset, and the context of the research, are described or considered in interpreting the data, and making claims about them. Not to do so is to produce not only a poorer analysis, but to also reduce the reader's ability to consider and evaluate things like the *transferability* of your study, the applicability of your analysis to *their* context (see Yardley, 2015).

> **ALERT** Situating data within the wider context is part and parcel of doing quality reflexive TA, and of facilitating transferability and demonstrating sensitivity to context (Yardley, 2015) – two quality markers.

Interpretation can *locate* the data at different levels, and orientate to various aspects of the wider context. These various aspects, none of which is entirely separable from each other, include, but are not limited to:

- *Ideological aspects* – such analysis would interpret the data in light of prevailing broad meaning-making frameworks – ideologies – that form the dominant common-sense of society. An example of an ideologically-located analysis would be consideration of neoliberal ideology, and how it shapes what is experienced, what is desired, and what is imagined (e.g. Chen, 2013; Gill, 2008; Scharff, 2016). In relation to the childfree dataset, we have noted that the idea of *individual choice* was prevalent. An analysis that just treated choice as an obvious explanation – common-sense! – would fail to locate the analysis in ideological context, where individual choice and responsibility have become core neoliberal logics about how individuals, and indeed society, operate. Another level of ideological locating could be to discuss your analysis in light of gendered or racial politics around the topic at hand. In relation to parenting, for instance, the experience of non/parenthood is deeply enmeshed with race, gender and sexuality (Clarke et al., 2018; Le Grice, 2014); it is not separable from them. For example, in a context where motherhood is expected and normative for straight women, but not-expected and less common for lesbian women, the experiences of childfree lesbians will be shaped by this differing societal context (see Clarke et al., 2018). Again, an analysis around being childfree that failed to explore how meaning connected to such ideologies would leave big gaps.

- *Political aspects* – such analysis would interpret the data in light of contemporary and/or historical political arrangements and governance. Political here could be big-P, formal government-related politics and practice. Or it could encompass small-p politics, related to the structuring, organisation, and operation of power within society, leading to differently-organised potentialities and marginalisations for different groups. An analysis around *being childfree* that located interpretation in relation to politics might interrogate how different viewpoints or meanings contrasted with, or reflected, the current political governance of parenthood and non-parenthood. The possibility to be childfree, and the sense-making around those who are, is likely vastly different in countries characterised by pronatalist politics than in those with more ambivalent or even restrictive politics (e.g. Sweden's pronatalist versus China's strict population planning laws),[11] or in a context where abortion is relatively accessible compared to tightly circumscribed or illegal, or deeply contested,[12] like it is in the US. In a different way, reference in the childfree dataset to concepts like taxation and to the future of society provide entry-points ripe for a politically-located analysis, where having children is framed as a political rather than just personal act. For instance, countries like Sweden have utilised political policy related to parenting and childcare as part of a pronatalist position, to encourage increased childbirth and parenting (Kramer, 2014).

- *Historical aspects* – such analysis would interpret the data with a longer-term view of meaning, politics and ideology in society. Such analyses seek to recognise continuances from the past in terms of available meaning, as well as departures and disjunctures. Around a topic like being

---

[11]The differences between pronatalist and more permissive political contexts and the possibilities and sense-making these allow for around being childfree, were starkly illustrated for Ginny one time, when she used the childfree dataset to teach TA in Iceland. The idea of 'parenthood as choice', which was prevalent in the dataset, was surprising to the students. This led to an unexpected – for Ginny – discussion of the rarity of not having children, for women especially, in Iceland, and a possibility for deeper interrogation and reflexivity around this in developing an analysis, for the students.

[12]Given potential shifts and changes in policy, data and interpretation need to be considered in relation to the *timeframe* for data collection. Meaning and possibility might vary quite considerably from decade to decade, or even year to year, especially in places where politics or policies can change rapidly.

childfree, an analysis might explore how an idea like selfishness seems to be *less* prevalent in the dataset than we might have expected, based on older analyses, and speculate as to why this might be. Or in a context like Aotearoa New Zealand, how is the historical and ongoing impact of colonisation a crucial interpretative context for making sense of the differential meaning-making around parenting, connected to race and Indigeneity. Māori parenthood, for example, has a long history of negative representation and being deemed *a problem* (Le Grice, 2014; Ware et al., 2017), that would likely inflect data related to discussions of (non)parenthood, in both obvious and subtle ways.

- *Material aspects* – such analysis would interpret the data in light of material conditions in which people's lives are embedded. For a topic like the choice to be childfree, how might affluence/poverty be part of sense-making around this? Or an analysis might explore whether the *material* possibilities around parenting, such as through a wage-related *motherhood penalty* and *fatherhood premium*, shape the choice to be childfree (Cooke, 2014). Or it might ask how the material possibilities for reproductive autonomy in a local context intersect with the options or choices that individuals articulate as available to them? For instance, in a context absent of reproductive control for women, such as where access to contraceptives is limited, is being childfree even imaginable as a *choice*?
- *Policy aspects* – such analysis would bring policy, contemporary and/or historical, to bear in the interpretation of data. For instance, policy and legislation related to reproductive autonomy and decision-making, including abortion, potentially provide important contexts for interpreting data related to the childfree choice. Policy concerns around promoting child-welfare might provide an important context from which to interrogate questions of how people make sense of those who are childfree. In the childfree dataset, for instance, the notion of *good versus bad parents* played out in multiple ways. Such concepts don't arise from nowhere; they are deeply embedded within, and both challenged and reinforced by, policy and practice related to parenting and child welfare. This sort of contextualising is particularly important for analyses that seek to speak to policy development. Note that it is particularly important to watch out for the trap of 'arguing with the data' (see Table 9.2 in Chapter Nine) when doing policy-inflected interpretation, because you might easily be drawn into comparing policy and data, and reporting on ignorance of policy or 'facts' (such as demographic data about rates of childlessness), or misunderstandings of these.
- *Discourse aspects* – such analysis might explore the discursive 'conditions of possibility' (Gavey, 2018) in and through which the data need to be interpreted, to make sense. Discursive locating means exploring what discursive formulations of the topic, and of society more generally, are at play in the dataset, and how understanding these might add to our analysis. For instance, useful questions might be – how are raced, gendered, classed, ableist, heteronormative discourses of motherhood evidenced in discussions about those who are childfree (Hayfield et al., 2019)? How might such discourses delimit attempts to create social change towards equality of possibility to be childfree? What fractures in, and resistances to, dominant discourses are also evident in the dataset?

As noted, these levels are, in practice, often deeply connected. In separating these different aspects out, we're seeking to draw attention to various options for locating the analysis in relation to the wider context, rather than suggesting these should be undertaken either discretely or sequentially. Nor are we suggesting that all of these are important always. Definitely not! What the specific mesh of contextualising will look like depends

PRACTICE POINT Which contexts are relevant to a specific analysis will be shaped by the purpose of the research.

on the particulars of each project. At the risk of sounding like the proverbial broken record, the locating that is relevant depends on your research question!

MINIMISING HARM IN INTERPRETATION: ETHICS, POLITICS AND REPRESENTATION

Discussing interpretation, Carla Willig noted that "the process of interpretation poses significant ethical challenges because it involves a process of transformation" (2017, p. 282).

ALERT Interpretation is never neutral or objective, it always happens from a position and therefore the power structures in the wider society always contextualise our interpretative practice.

There is no simple or pure description; we always interpret from a position – or, perhaps more accurately, an aggregate of positions. This means interpretation is inevitably a *political* act. We hope that by now it does not seem *surprising* that we end a chapter on interpretation with a discussion related to the politics and ethics of representation. A "concern for representing participants" has been described as "perhaps the most significant ethical dilemma we face" as qualitative researchers (Swauger, 2011, p. 500). Ethical codes highlight our professional obligation to protect people from harm through the

KEY CONCEPT Representational ethics relates to the potential for our analyses to harm our participants/the social groups represented in our data.

misuse or misrepresentation of our research (e.g. British Psychological Society, 2018). As ethical qualitative researchers, we need to think about the **representational ethics** and politics of our analyses.

As we've discussed, reflexive TA research is a process of meaning-*making* and meaning-*telling* – not just summing up the things people said. Simply put, representational ethics is a question of how we tell a story that does *not do harm*.[13] But – no surprise! – there are different layers to thinking about representation, ethics, politics and harm. Two interconnected strands of the ethics and politics of representation relate to:

- *Participants in our research*: how do we tell a research story that remains *true* to participants' stories, without simply repeating what they say? We don't have to tell a story that our participants would *agree* with, however. Telling that kind of story can feel ethically troubling,[14] especially if you are doing more *critical* versions of TA (Weatherall, Gavey, & Potts, 2002), but remember these two elements:

---

[13]Telling a story that does not do harm in the ethical sense; we have an ethical obligation as researchers to protect research participants from harm.

[14]To some extent, feeling ethically troubled by telling a story our participants might disagree with relies on the idea that telling participants' stories would not reproduce *harmful* accounts – for instance of fat-phobia, heterosexism, transphobia, misogyny, or racism. This feeling rests on an assumption that our participants' experiences are somehow good and right. It also seems to rest on an assumption that we will be doing *experiential* research, reporting our participants' experiences and perspectives (discussed in Chapter Six). *Critical* qualitative research is very different – for example, interrogating the political operation of (harmful) discourse is vastly different from seeking to 'honour lived experience' (for some interesting discussions, see Billig, 1978; Blee, 1998; Flood, 2008; Scully, 1994; Throsby & Evans, 2013).

- First, our purpose in doing reflexive TA is to tell a story of patterned meaning, based on a *range* of data and participants. It is not to provide a case-study of a single person's experience. This means there will be elements of the analyses we present that are both familiar *and* unfamiliar in different places, to different participants, that sometimes resonate with their own views and experiences, and sometimes don't. Second, our task is one of *interpretation*, of *making sense of* what our *data-set* (not just an individual participant) tells us, based on the skills and wider knowledge we bring to the process (Chamberlain, 2011; Willig, 2017). We are not simply a refining *sieve* that the data pass through on their way from the participants to the report. Depending on the form of reflexive TA we undertake, our analysis will be closer to, or further away from, data meanings as expressed by participants.

- Regardless, we have an important ethical responsibility to ensure, first, that participants understand the *purpose* of the research and the *broad* form of the *likely* analysis we will undertake (*likely*, because sometimes this changes *a lot*). For example, you might tell participants that you intend to report the reoccurring patterns in people's experiences across all of the data and offering some observations about what these experiences might mean in the wider context. (Note we do not mean you need to tell the participants exactly what the analysis will be before you've done it; that would be impossible!) Second, that we don't undertake interpretation in a way which patronises or somehow belittles participants. For example, in doing a critical analysis related to *compensatory kids* in the childfree dataset, we would have to take care that we did not inadvertently position participants who articulated this idea as somehow misguided, or ignorant. Our focus instead should be on *the idea* and what it can tell us about the wider meanings of being childfree.

- This concern for negative impacts on *individual* participants relates to the wider communities that participants are members of, and how the stories we tell about participants might be harmful or beneficial to these wider communities. For instance, in a project Ginny contributed to examining sexual coercion among men who have sex with men – members of a marginalised community – the research team were concerned about the potential for negative impacts on both the participants *and* the wider community (Braun, Schmidt, Gavey, & Fenaughty, 2009; Braun, Terry, Gavey, & Fenaughty, 2009; Fenaughty et al., 2006; Gavey, Schmidt, Braun, Fenaughty, & Eremin, 2009).

- *The wider society.* This considers the implications for members of the community or communities that participants are part of, just noted, but also how our representational practices might work for – or against – a more socially-just society. At the broadest level, this is about taking care that our research does not reinforce existing negative stereotypes of communities or groups.[15] For instance, making sure that your interpretation does not uncritically reinforce the idea that women who do not have children *are* selfish – even if the women you interview reiterate that idea! Or perpetuate racist stereotypes that frame Māori mothers as irresponsible and even dangerous as parents (Le Grice, 2014). This is about recognising that in our societal contexts, different interpretations have different consequences, depending on who the participants are, and indeed who *you* are, as the researcher. Researcher identity is part of the issue of representation and ethics and connects to various positions of social marginality and privilege (see Box 7.3).

---

[15]The potential for negative impacts on the participants and the wider community of men who have sex with men was something Ginny and her co-authors explicitly tackled in their reporting from the men and sexual coercion project (e.g. see Braun, Terry, et al., 2009).

Box 7.3

Interpretation across difference: Power, privilege and positioning

Here we introduce three useful concepts related to interpretation and analysis – though they also connect more broadly to research design and research practice before, and after, analysis. These concepts are insider/outsider positions, the Other, and **intersectionality**. Each is relevant and important to consider in relation to interpretation, ethics and politics, but frames or approaches these in slightly different ways.

The concept of insider and outsider is the most straightforward. We are an *insider* researcher if we are a member of the group we are studying, and an *outsider* researcher if we are not a member of the group we are studying. But identity is messy, and we are often a complex mix of *both* insider and outsider (e.g. Hayfield & Huxley, 2015; Hellawell, 2006; Obasi, 2014; Paechter, 1998, 2013; L. T. Smith, 2013), and sometimes insider or outsider identities shift and change. It's often assumed that being an insider researcher is simply better (inviting trust or bringing an insider advantage; Clarke, Ellis, Peel, & Riggs, 2010), and that it confers a more ethical position. But any position raises challenges and complexities (e.g. Wilkinson & Kitzinger, 2013).[16] From the point of view of *interpretation*, it is important to recognise the position(s) we speak from in relation to insiderness and outsiderness, and engage in reflexivity in relation to understanding, interrogating and acknowledging how this has shaped our research processes (see Hellawell, 2006). But it's not so simple…

A framework of insider/outsider risks obscuring the social reality that not all identities are created equal – and that although there is considerable variation in the privilege afforded to any individual member of a certain social group, social *groupings* overall vary in their level of privilege or marginalisation within society. How much insider and outsider positions matter can vary along these lines of privilege and marginalisation. For instance, when researching Māori reproduction and parenting for her PhD, book contributor and Aotearoa New Zealand Indigenous psychologist Jade le Grice was an *insider* in working with a marginalised Indigenous population in a settler-colonial country.[17] On another important dimension of the project, Jade occupied a *partial outsider* position, as she was *not* a biological parent, although had atawhai children (a partner's children she temporarily nurtured as her own during a relationship) while writing her PhD (this evokes an insider/outsider position that can – sometimes quickly – change).

In relation to Jade's project, her insider and outsider positions were ones of different significance to society. Another useful concept to make sense of the ways power is inflected through

---

[16]If you are an outsider considering conducting research with a socially marginalised group, look for discussion and guidance on conducting appropriate and sensitive research with your participant group. See, for example, guidance for conducting research with trans participants (N. Adams et al., 2017; Vincent, 2018) or discussion related to the *possibility* of non-Indigenous researchers being involved in research with Indigenous populations (e.g. Came, 2013; V. M. Carpenter & McMurchy-Pilkington, 2008).

[17]This designation of Jade as an insider researcher is, however, too simplistic, as insider and outsider positions are more complex than just being members or not of broad social groups, especially where marginalised and oppressed populations are concerned (L. T. Smith, 2013). As Jade reflected on in her PhD (Le Grice, 2014), a simplistic notion of insider-as-Māori was complicated by her own experiences, in a colonial context where Indigenous access to community and identity has been suppressed in all sorts of ways. In such oppressive colonial contexts, being able to feel you have an 'authentic' Indigenous identity can be challenging (e.g. Borell, 2005).

societally-significant differences is 'Otherness' or 'The Other'. A concept of *the Other* has been theorised and described within various scholarly traditions, from western philosophy to postcolonial studies to feminism. Typically, the term the Other is used to describe a person or persons who belong to a social *group* that is marginalised or otherwise outside the dominant norms (e.g. who, in westernised nations, is female, Indigenous/a Person of Colour, working class/poor, LGB+, disabled, trans or nonbinary). It captures privilege and disenfranchisement and does so through theorising the individual *within* current and historical societal organisation and structures of power.

Theorising Otherness is not *just* about insider or outsider status, but about power. Issues relating to **representing the Other** capture, in the words of British feminist psychologists Celia Kitzinger and Sue Wilkinson, "whether, and how, we researchers should represent members of groups to which we do not ourselves belong – in particular, members of groups oppressed in ways we are not" (Kitzinger & Wilkinson, 1996, p. 1; see also Rice, 2009). For reflexive TA researchers focused on participant lived experiences and/or sense-making, the politics and ethics of representing the *Other* is an important consideration. Simply *avoiding* research that might involve representing the Other is not the simple solution. As the majority of academic researchers come from positions of some social privilege, just researching as insiders would perpetuate inequity, where knowledges and experiences of those socially marginalised or invisiblised remain hidden. At the same time, the notion of typically relatively privileged, White, middle-class researchers benignly 'giving voice' to participants from social marginalised groups – and neglecting to interrogate Whiteness and the lives of the privileged – has rightly been problematised (e.g. Clarke & Braun, 2019a; Fine, 1992).[18]

The concept of **epistemological violence** has been developed to capture the way *interpretation* of data from or related to, and subsequent *representations of*, the Other, can do harm (L. T. Smith, 2013; Teo, 2010, 2011). The closely related concept of **epistemic violence** evokes *harm* related to *knowledge* and discourse, connected to systems of power and oppression (see Spivak, 1988), and epistemic *exclusions* through who gets to be a legitimised knower (e.g. Ahmed, 2000; Ymous et al., 2020). Any research involving representing the Other needs to be undertaken with great care, *without* assumptions of entitlement to ask any questions and make *any* interpretations with *any* populations, and *with* reflexivity.[19]

In talking about representing the Other there is a risk that a singular dimension of identity is decontextualised and treated in a *simplified* way. Although there is value in focusing on broad

(Continued)

---

[18]Although we've already also unpacked the idea of simply 'giving voice' from a research practice point of view, this discussion relates more to the ethics and politics of the notion. Despite criticisms, there remains a qualitative tradition orientated to giving voice (e.g. MacKenzie, Huntington, & Gilmour, 2009). The ethics and politics of this are different depending on how 'consciously' and 'reflexively' such research is undertaken, from what positions the researchers speak, and whether the research is informed by community-based or **participatory research** principles and practices.

[19]See Norris (2015), for an example of a reflective engagement with the complexities of Otherness in research using TA; for still-thought-provoking discussions of the politics of representing women's experiences, see classic texts from Fine (1992) and Kitzinger and Wilkinson (1996).

categories – such as women, or disabled people – there is *much* variation between people within social categories (as our brief discussion of Jade's positioning noted). Some frameworks theorise discrimination or privilege in 'additive' terms – with concepts like 'double discrimination' (e.g. Fairchild, 2002). Within an additive framework, bisexual Black men, for example, would experience 'double' discrimination – as bisexual *and* as Black. Each form of marginality a person experiences can be conceptualised as a box, and like a box each is separate and self-contained. If a person has more than one box, these are stacked on top of each other – theoretically, the person with the highest stack is the *most* marginalised. But this model over-simplifies how systems of marginalisation work as these often cannot be simply parsed out. How might we theorise these differently to capture the way different systems intersect and shape each other, and to capture social privilege? Intersectionality can offer a valuable approach for tackling this challenge. A concept with a long history in US Black feminist thought and activism dating back to anti-slavery campaigns (e.g. Combahee River Collective, 1995; Truth, 1851), intersectionality came to prominence through the work of US Black feminists such as Kimberlé Crenshaw (1991), who coined the term (see also Brah & Phoenix, 2004; Carbado, Crenshaw, Mays, & Tomlinson, 2014; Christensen & Jensen, 2012; Collins, 2019; Collins & Bilge, 2016; Marfelt, 2016; Overstreet et al., 2020).

Intersectionality theorises discrimination and social marginalisation outside of simple additive models and instead captures both experiences of social disadvantage (e.g. Black and bisexual disadvantage) and *privilege* (e.g. male, abled, and thin privilege), and theorising these as almost two sides of the same coin (e.g. racism and White normativity don't just disadvantage people of colour, they also privilege White people). It particularly captures the ways in which different forms of privilege and disadvantage intersect. For example, different systems of marginality and privilege – around race and gender say – are not separable, instead they *inextricably* shape the meaning and experience of each other. The Black anti-slavery and women's rights activist Sojourner Truth's (1851) famous 'Ain't I a woman?' speech, delivered in 1851 at the second annual Women's Rights Convention in Akron, Ohio, is often used to powerfully highlight the racialisation of dominant constructions of femininity in the US at the time:

> That man over there says that women need to be helped into carriages, and lifted over ditches, and to have the best place everywhere. Nobody ever helps me into carriages, or over mud-puddles, or gives me any best place! And ain't I a woman?

In this popularised version of Truth's speech,[20] womanhood is not some universal category that applies to all, and Blackness cannot simply be 'added' to it, to provide a fuller definition of some generic category of woman. Instead, this account reveals Whiteness and femininity as felted together so they cannot be disentangled from each other.

Intersectionality has been widely taken up within certain disciplines – though not as much in our discipline, psychology, as one might expect (Phoenix, 2006). But we should note: the uptake of intersectionality in social sciences has been critiqued, with the concept being transformed into a way of 'capturing complexity' – at the level of the individual – rather than

---

[20]The popular – claimed 'true' – version of her speech appears to be anything but. Instead, it's been described as a revised version of a (problematic) account of her original speech (see Overstreet et al., 2020). Two versions of the speech can be compared on the website: www.thesojournertruthproject.com/.

addressing oppression and power at the sociostructural level (e.g. Cole, 2020; Overstreet et al., 2020).[21] In terms of interpretation within reflexive TA, what might intersectionality offer or mandate? At the most basic, a way of engaging with participant data that is nuanced and contextualised, and incorporates privilege and marginalisation into our sense-making. That recognises the locatedness and partiality of what we claim. Coming back to questions of ethics, politics and practice, it requires reflexivity to recognise our interpretative work is always going to be partial and imperfect and reflects *our* situatedness. Some useful reflections on the challenges of implementing intersectionality theory in empirical research include Bowleg (2008, 2017), Cole (2009) and Phoenix (2006).

Part of the wider context for research is language, and the way it can often unintentionally marginalise. Therefore, it is important to consider the language you use, and how it might convey stigma, or might marginalise. A good *starting* guideline is to work with the language people themselves use.[22] For instance, if someone uses a gender-neutral personal pronoun *they*, do not misgender them by using she or he when referring to them in any publication. Mainstream psychology's publication 'bible' – the American Psychological Association's (2020) *Publication manual* – includes useful guidance around avoiding bias through language, related to a wide range of marginalised social identities. But beware: language shifts as context changes, and sometimes *quite* rapidly. The types of terminology that make it into publishing guides – like the *Publication manual* – might become out of date before the guide is updated. They also likely represent a more mainstream take on language and its consequences than those working at the forefront of social justice might prefer. For instance, in the UK, BME/BAME – Black and minority ethnic/Black, Asian and minority ethnic – is currently the dominant *mainstream* language for people and communities of colour, but there are numerous critiques of the problematic assumptions embedded in

> **ALERT** Language matters! Think carefully about the language you use to describe social groups, especially marginalised groups, and groups to which you do not belong.

---

[21]A focus on complexity rather than oppression in using intersectionality has also been argued as a way Black women or Women of Colour – the original focus of the theory – have been marginalised or 'erased' in the application and development of intersectionality studies (e.g. Alexander-Floyd, 2012; Cole, 2020).

[22]However, even the notion that you should start from the language people use themselves is more complicated, and needs to be approached cautiously. If you're not an insider to a community, it's important to be mindful and reflexive around a sense of entitlement to use insider terms (as illustrated by debates about the appropriateness and/or appropriation of slang terms like *woke* and *bae* – coming from African-American cultures – or *yas kween* and *throwing shade* – coming from US Black and Latinx, queer, drag cultures – being adopted by liberal straight White people (Tremeer, 2019). Even what terms are valued or used can be contested *within* communities.

such mainstream terminology (Gabriel, n.d.). What might be *best practice* isn't always easy to identify, especially if you're not connected to a community or activist context. For instance, around disability, you can find advice to use 'person first' language – such as 'person with a disability' – with the intent of not defining someone by their disability. You can also find advice to use 'disabled person' to capture the way people are disabled *by society* rather than being inherently disabled themselves (which person first language arguably implies). Our advice: look for recent advice around best practice, and especially from respected scholars or activist organisations. But, if you're working with a marginalised population, educate yourself around what is at stake with language, and reflect on your positionality in the project (see Box 7.3).

Being reflexive, asking questions about the social locations we're reading our data from, what values might be embedded in that reading, what we might be noticing and *not noticing*, and how our readings might impact those affected by our project (e.g. our participants, or social groups represented in the data) is crucial for engaging in the interpretative process in an ethical way.

CHAPTER SUMMARY

This chapter has focused on *interpretation* – one of the key elements of the analytic process in reflexive TA, and in qualitative analysis more widely. We described what interpretation is and explored different ways interpretation can be approached in reflexive TA. We discussed modes of analysis that are *more* descriptive through to modes that are *more* interpretative, as well as more *experientially* orientated to more *critically* orientated analysis. We considered the different ways theory can provide a framework for, and even guide, the interpretative process. We emphasised the need for interpretation to be *defensible*. To be defensible, interpretation needs to be grounded in the dataset, but also located, and we explained a number of different ways such locating can be achieved. We finished up by discussing ethics, reminding ourselves that analysis is a political act, and therefore important for ethical consideration. Our interpretation needs to consider how we represent participants in the stories we tell.

WANT TO LEARN MORE ABOUT...?

For a really excellent discussion of **interpretation**, located within but applicable beyond psychology, we recommend: Willig, C. (2017). Interpretation in qualitative research. In C. Willig & W. Stainton Rogers (Eds.), *The SAGE handbook of qualitative research in psychology* (2nd ed., pp. 274–288). London: SAGE.

As a starting point for reading around **ethics** and qualitative research, including **representation**, see: Swauger, M. (2011). Afterword: The ethics of risk, power, and representation. *Qualitative Sociology, 34*(3), 497–502.

For a broader discussion of the complex issues around **ethics**, particularly related to critical research, see: Macleod, C. I., Marx, J., Mnyaka, P., & Treharne, G. J. (Eds.). (2018). *The Palgrave handbook of ethics in critical research*. London: Palgrave Macmillan.

For an introduction to **intersectionality theory and practice**, this book offers a rich discussion: Collins, P. H., & Bilge, S. (2016). *Intersectionality*. Malden, MA: Polity.

For a longer discussion of the **politics of research and knowledge, including Indigenous research and decolonisation**, we recommend this excellent book: Smith, L. T. (2013). *Decolonizing methodologies: Research and indigenous peoples* (2nd ed.). Dunedin: University of Otago Press.

For a paper which nicely illustrates **the value of time and distance for developing richer interpretative insights**, see: Ho, K. H., Chiang, V. C., & Leung, D. (2017). Hermeneutic phenomenological analysis: The 'possibility' beyond 'actuality' in thematic analysis. *Journal of Advanced Nursing, 73*(7), 1757–1766.

We reflected on **time in qualitative research and analysis** in a recent chapter: Braun, V., & Clarke, V. (2021). The ebbs and flows of qualitative research: Time, change and the slow wheel of interpretation. In B. C. Clift, J. Gore, S. Gustafsson, S. Bekker, I. C. Batlle & J. Hatchard (Eds.), *Temporality in qualitative inquiry: Theories, methods and practices* (pp. 22–38). London: Routledge.

For an example of **interpretation at the more descriptive/experiential end of the reflexive TA spectra**, focused around the topic of 'childfree', see: Bimha, P. Z. J., & Chadwick, R. (2016). Making the childfree choice: Perspectives of women living in South Africa. *Journal of Psychology in Africa, 26*(4), 449–456.

For an example of interpretation at the **more theoretical/critical end of the reflexive TA spectra**, focused around the topic of 'childfree', see: Graham, M., & Rich, S. (2014). Representations of childless women in the Australian print media. *Feminist Media Studies, 14*(3), 500–518.

ACTIVITIES FOR STUDENT READERS

Located interpretation activity: Use the healthy eating and men dataset you worked with in Chapters Two to Five, and select one of the themes you developed. With this theme, try to develop an interpretation that is located within the wider context. Select *one* of the contextual elements we discussed (i.e. policy, ideology, etc.). Do some research to gain more understanding of the wider context relevant to the theme. For instance, if you were to choose *policy*, you might both Google healthy eating policy from the UK (where the dataset comes from), *and* search for academic studies on healthy eating policy. Then, further develop your analysis of the theme related to what you have learned. Use this information to contextualise and rationalise the claims you're making about the data in the theme, and to discuss why the theme you've identified matters. For example, your reading around policy might have helped you to notice different ideas or assumptions related to your theme, which have implications for how and why you understand this theme as important. In doing this task, you will be (re)writing the story of the theme developed so far – focusing on the *so what* in your interpretative story.

Reflect on representation: Reflexively consider your identities and practices in relation to the healthy eating dataset you've compiled (e.g. are you a man? Do you come from the same social and cultural location as the stories? Do you consider yourself a healthy eater?). Ask yourself in what ways what you're noticing in the data, and the interpretations you're making, might be inflected – strongly or partially – from these positions? Ask yourself what you might be missing. If you're doing this as a classroom activity, the next step would be to discuss your reflections and developing analysis with a classmate, and explore whether you can use the different perspectives you each bring to develop the analysis and/or your insight further.

If you're teaching content related to this chapter…
Don't forget to check the companion website for a range of teaching resources:
https://study.sagepub.com/thematicanalysis

8

ONE BIG HAPPY FAMILY?

UNDERSTANDING SIMILARITIES AND DIFFERENCES BETWEEN REFLEXIVE THEMATIC ANALYSIS AND ITS METHODOLOGICAL SIBLINGS AND COUSINS

Chapter Eight overview

- **A brief and partial history of 'thematic analysis'**   224
- **Variation across TA approaches: Core concepts**   228

  - Coding: Process and/or output?   229
  - What is a theme?   229
  - Researcher subjectivity (reflexivity)   232
  - A process of theme development or identification?   232

- **Mapping the main members of the TA family: Our tripartite clustering**   234
- **Coding reliability approaches: Small q thematic analysis**   237

  - What do we think is problematic about coding reliability approaches to TA?   238

- **Codebook approaches to TA (MEDIUM Q)**   242

  - Template analysis   242
  - Do we perceive any problems with template analysis?   244
  - Framework analysis   244
  - Do we perceive any problems with framework analysis?   246
  - Challenges with using codebook approaches in general   246

- **So is reflexive TA the *best* approach to TA?**   247
- **But wait... there's *even* more? Other approaches to TA**   247

  - The use of TA for qualitative evidence synthesis   250
  - 'Off-label' TA: *Combining* TA with other approaches   254

The question of what TA is might seem simple: it is a method of qualitative analysis, widely used across the social and health sciences, and beyond, for exploring, interpreting and reporting *relevant* patterns of meaning across a dataset. It utilises codes and coding to develop themes. But this simple description belies complexity, contestation, and even *contradictory* renderings – and that's before we even get into the myths and misperceptions that muddy the water! We love this description by Canadian sports researchers Lisa Trainor and Andrea Bundon (2020) that TA "simply cannot be simplified; it is a complex and beautiful method with so many options" (p. 1). Nonetheless, we regard our task in this chapter as demystifying as much as we can, while retaining complexity. We aim to provide a contextualised and nuanced account of what TA *is* and offer some clarity about where the method came from, the different versions of TA that *currently* exist (with the caveat that this is a changing domain), and some different ways core concepts are understood and practised.

Before our discussion about the history and variety of approaches to TA, we want to clear up a few misunderstandings or myths about TA. These are myths that we regularly encounter everywhere: from published papers to manuscript reviews, classroom questions to examiner reports. In Table 8.1 we summarise a myth or misunderstanding about TA, and provide a brief response. All the misunderstandings are discussed in much more depth in various places throughout this book, including in this chapter. This flying visit into the land of 'what TA is not' sets you up well for a longer and more engaged visit into the land of 'what TA is'.

A BRIEF AND PARTIAL HISTORY OF 'THEMATIC ANALYSIS'

We are not historians, but our exploration of the history of TA for various publications shows many different meanings associated with the phrase 'thematic analysis' – and many claims for its origin. German qualitative methodologist Uwe Flick (2014a) argued his development of **'thematic coding'** in the 1990s pre-dated the development of TA, but it seems that both TA and thematic coding have been in use since at least the 1980s. Another claim is that TA developed from, and is a variant of, grounded theory (e.g. McLeod, 2011). The origin of

---

[1]We actually got to 11. But we kept the title at ten, as a bit of ironic self-mockery and a gentle poking of fun at the idea that researchers choose qualitative methods because they can't handle numbers or statistics!

[2]To address a question we get regularly, yes, TA is a suitable analytic method at all levels of student research, including doctoral (Braun & Clarke, 2021b).

Table 8.1 Don't believe everything you hear! 10[1] claims about TA that are actually wrong

Myth or misunderstanding	Our response
1. There is *a* singular method called TA.	TA is not a singular method; there are many different versions of, and approaches to, TA. Some are idiosyncratic to one researcher/team; some are widely used. The differences between approaches can be significant.
2. TA is *not* actually a distinct method but a set of generic analytic procedures (e.g. Flick, 2014a; Pistrang & Barker, 2010).	This feels a bit like 'splitting hairs'. TA (in different versions) *is* a widely used method in its own right and offers a robust and coherent method of data analysis.
3. TA is *only* a very 'basic' or unsophisticated method (e.g. Crowe, Inder, & Porter, 2015); it needs another method to bring interpretative depth (such as grounded theory).	The sophistication – or not – of the analysis depends on the use of the method, not the method itself.[2] TA can be used to produce a sophisticated, nuanced, insightful analysis, just as other approaches such as grounded theory can (likewise, all analytic approaches can produce poor quality analyses if used badly).
4. TA is only a summative or descriptive method (e.g. Aguinaldo, 2012; Floersch, Longhofer, Kranke, & Townsend, 2010; Vaismoradi, Turunen, & Bondas, 2013).	TA should be used to do more than provide data summary or data reduction. A more descriptive analysis is only one of the many types of analysis TA can produce. Descriptive analyses can't just be data reduction, as even descriptive approaches involve interpretation by an inescapably subjective researcher.
5. TA is only an inductive method.	TA works very well for producing inductive – or data-driven – analyses; it also works well for producing latent and deeply theoretical analyses.
6. TA is only an experiential method (e.g. Flick, 2014a; 2014b).	TA can work well for research seeking to understand people's subjective experiences or perspectives. Some versions – including reflexive TA – work equally well for *critical* qualitative research and the analysis of data that doesn't centre on "subjective viewpoints" (Flick, 2014a, p. 423).
7. TA is only a realist or essentialist method.	TA can be essentialist or realist, but some versions – including reflexive TA – can also be constructionist or critical.
8. TA is atheoretical (e.g. Crowe et al., 2015; Flick, 2014a; Vaismoradi et al., 2013).	That TA is *independent of* an inbuilt theory (making it more method than methodology) has meant some interpret this to mean theory can be ignored. This is a mis-reading; theory must be considered, as it's always there, even if not articulated. In TA, the researcher must select the theoretical and conceptual assumptions that inform their use of TA. Although most approaches to TA claim to be theoretically independent or flexible, some approaches are more flexible than others, and all reflect broad paradigmatic assumptions that shape the analytic procedures and the conceptualisation of core constructs such as the 'theme'.
9. The proper way to do TA is…	There are many variations of this myth, which claim a particular methodological tool or technique is something that *all* TA should do (e.g. consensus coding; early theme development). The various variations of TA often have distinctive techniques for doing TA, reflecting their quite different conceptual foundations.
10. There are no guidelines for how to do TA (e.g. Nowell et al., 2017; Xu & Zammit, 2020).	There are many guidelines for how to do TA, including many from us on how to do reflexive TA!
11. It's difficult to judge the quality of TA.	This ranges from claims that researchers 'bias' the research, to the bizarre suggestion that TA researchers 'leave out' inconveniently disagreeing data (Aguinaldo, 2012), to the claim that there aren't good discussions of quality and standards from which to judge quality. There are!

TA has also been credited to philosopher of science Gerald Holton (1973) in his analysis of 'themata' in scientific thought (Joffe, 2012). However, there is a longer, diverse application of the term. For instance, in the 1930s, musicologists used it to describe a particular kind of analysis of musical scores (Calvocoressi, 1931; Kinsky & Strunk, 1933). In the 1940s, sociologists named their method for analysing mass propaganda TA (Lazarsfeld & Merton, 1944), and anthropologists debated and established principles for the TA of cultural systems (e.g. Cohen, 1946; Opler, 1945). In the 1940s and 1950s, psychoanalysts used the term to refer to techniques for analysing the results from projective tests like the Rorschach ink blot test (e.g. Harrison, 1943; Winder & Hersko, 1958). Some researchers early in the history of TA used the term TA interchangeably with '**content analysis**' to describe their analytic techniques, and many others continue to do so (see Braun & Clarke, 2021b). The use of the term 'thematic content analysis' is still relatively common (e.g. Brewster, Velez, Mennicke, & Tebbe, 2014; J. Green & Thorogood, 2009). British-based psychologist Hélène Joffe (2012) proposed that TA *developed from* content analysis, and this does seem to be the most satisfying explanation for how TA came about.[3]

> **ALERT** The most satisfying explanation for the origins of TA is that it developed from qualitative refinements of content analysis.

Some of the older instances of TA resemble its use in the contemporary social and health sciences context. For example, Dapkus (1985) described her TA approach in a study of the human experience of time as an adaptation of a phenomenological procedure[4] outlined by Colaizzi (1978). She discussed processes of coding and theme development that resulted in three major categories summarising participants' experiences. Dapkus built in procedures for establishing reliability and accuracy in coding – through use of multiple coders – a practice both used and rejected by different contemporary versions of TA (see the next section 'Variation across TA approaches').

> **ALERT** There are many, many different versions of TA – most have some characteristics in common but otherwise diverge – often widely – in procedures and underlying philosophy and research values.

The development of idiosyncratic approaches to TA by individual researchers seems to be a common feature of the history of TA. In researching different approaches, we stopped after identifying more than 20 different versions of TA, some of which are widely used,

---

[3]We say *seems* to be the most satisfying explanation for how TA came about, because understanding precisely how TA developed is an almost impossible task. The analysis of text is undertaken in many different academic disciplines, often with different versions of content analysis and TA that have developed across several decades, and in some cases centuries – content analysis has been used since the 19th century in some disciplines (Downe-Wamboldt, 1992).

[4]Phenomenology is the study of first-person personal experience (see Allen-Collinson, 2016). We increasingly encounter interpretative phenomenological analysis (IPA) being treated as the default or *definitive* phenomenological analytic approach in psychology and those choosing to use TA within a phenomenological framework are sometimes asked to justify 'why not IPA?' It's important to note, then, that TA has a history as a phenomenological method that pre-dates the development of IPA.

and some less so.[5] More widely-used procedures for TA began to be published in the 1990s – sometimes called TA, sometimes using different terminology. One of the first was US psychotherapy researcher Jodi Aronson's (1995) very brief outline of a four-step process of: (1) data collection and transcription; (2) identification of data relevant to pre-identified patterns (coding); (3) theme development; and (4) contextualising the themes in relation to existing literature. Other notable and frequently cited procedures from around that time include those outlined by US psychologist Richard Boyatzis (1998), '**template analysis**', outlined by British psychologist Nigel King (1998), drawing on the work of Crabtree and Miller (e.g. 1999), and '**framework analysis**', developed by British applied policy researchers Jane Ritchie and Liz Spencer (Ritchie & Spencer, 1994).[6]

Publication of methods for TA continued into the 2000s, with guidelines from British psychologists Hélène Joffe and Lucy Yardley (Joffe, 2012; Joffe & Yardley, 2004), US public health researchers Greg Guest, Kathleen MacQueen and Emily Namey (2012), as well as our own first TA publication (Braun & Clarke, 2006). In that paper, we described TA as "a poorly demarcated and rarely acknowledged, yet widely used qualitative analytic method" (p. 77). This reflected a long history of methodological practice where a TA was produced without a *defined* TA approach, or a specific set of procedures, being referenced. Indeed, it was not uncommon to read a description that suggested some variation of '**themes emerged**' from the data (e.g. Ebright, Urden, Patterson, & Chalko, 2004; Parasuraman, Zeithaml, & Berry, 1985).

Our original claim of TA being "rarely acknowledged" no longer applies. Overall, TA *is* now commonly acknowledged; TA has become a widely used and acknowledged method, usually with sources cited from a flourishing methodological literature – though not always accurately (Braun & Clarke, 2021c). TA does, unfortunately, still remain "poorly demarcated" however, with a wide variety of descriptions of the method (e.g. B. L. Peterson, 2017). Some of the confusion and mis-citing occurs because TA, despite a common name, is not a single method. There are still numerous instances of authors describing an *overall method* that mixes elements from quite different orientations. Currently, we regard a tripartite division

> **ALERT** TA remains poorly demarcated – in large part because the diversity of TA approaches seems poorly understood.

between clusters of similar approaches to TA the most useful way to differentiate the field. Fugard and Potts (2020) described TA as a family of methods. We like this imagery – we've used it for our chapter title! You can imagine each 'cluster' as a branch of a family tree descended from an original pair of parents – each cluster made up of one sibling or cousin, and their collected family members.

---

[5]We don't cover *all* of the different TA approaches we identified in this book.

[6]Although not explicitly labelled as TA, the qualitative analytic procedures outlined in the mid-1990s by US education researchers Matthew Miles and Michael Huberman (1994) are also often used or identified as a method for doing TA (e.g. B. L. Peterson, 2017).

Before we discuss this tripartite categorisation, we outline and clarify some core concepts that vary across different approaches to TA.

VARIATION ACROSS TA APPROACHES: CORE CONCEPTS

TA methodologists generally view TA as having the flexibility to be implemented with a more inductive orientation or a more deductive orientation. Similarly, most acknowledge that coding and theme development can capture meaning across a spectrum, from manifest or semantic to latent or implicit meaning (e.g. Boyatzis, 1998; Braun & Clarke, 2006, 2013; Joffe, 2012). But there are also some important differences across the various TA methods. These connect to the extent to which an individual method is embedded within qualitative research values or a qualitative paradigm. In Chapter One, we briefly introduced the idea that the term 'qualitative research' describes a range of research practices – from the use of qualitative techniques of data collection and analysis within a postpositivist paradigm (small q qualitative) to the use of these within a qualitative *paradigm* or Big Q qualitative (see Madill & Gough, 2008). As discussed in Chapter Six, (post)positivism is the paradigm that generally underpins quantitative research. It emphasises objectivity and the possibility of discovering universal truths independent of the methods used to discover those truths. A qualitative *paradigm* emphasises the multiple and contextual nature of meaning and knowledge and researcher subjectivity as a resource for research (Braun & Clarke, 2013). To make the landscape of TA extra confusing, TA researchers don't always acknowledge *which* conceptualisation of qualitative research underpins their research or they seem to draw on a '**mash-up**' of both understandings, often without awareness or discussion (see Braun & Clarke, 2021c).[7]

ALERT TA approaches sit on a spectrum from Big Q reflexive to small q postpositivist.

In Big Q or 'fully qualitative' research, processes tend to be flexible, interpretative, and subjective/reflexive. Big Q rejects notions of objectivity and context-independent or researcher-independent truths, and instead emphasises the contextual or situated nature of meaning, and the inescapable subjectivity of research and the researcher (Braun & Clarke, 2013). Small q qualitative or 'qualitative positivism' (Brinkmann, 2015; W. L. Miller & Crabtree, 1999) often involves a more structured approach to data collection and analysis, guided by concern to: (a) minimise the researcher's influence on the research process – conceptualised as 'bias' – and (b) achieve accurate and

---

[7]Big Theory is a complex and often messy terrain in qualitative research (as Chapter Six showed). It's often not about simple dichotomies. Some of the theoretically-informed practice dimensions across which TA methods and techniques vary, reflect lines between two end points, rather than either/or binaries. Where this variability becomes problematic is where values and practices *conceptually* at odds with a paradigm are introduced *unknowingly* and without justification (Braun & Clarke, 2021c). Our colleague and TA co-author Nikki Hayfield memorably dubbed such conceptually messy mash-ups "confused q", following Kidder and Fine (1987).

objective results. Such aspirations and practices are *incompatible* with a Big Q approaches. These conceptual and practice-based differences inform our tripartite clustering of TA methods. TA methods typically differentiate between coding – *the way to* your destination – and the theme – *the destination*. But that general agreement covers much variation, both at the level of concept, and process. Before we move on to discuss our tripartite clustering, we provide a refresher by revisiting and expanding on some of the fundamental conceptual and practice points we made in Chapters Two to Four.

Coding: Process and/or output?

Coding is a *process* common across TA and indeed many other qualitative analytic approaches. Through close data engagement, data meanings are tagged with code labels. Within some approaches to TA, coding is only conceptualised as a *process* – the process through which themes *are identified*. The point of coding is to find evidence for themes. Within other approaches, including reflexive TA, the 'code' exists as an analytic entity in its own right, a 'product' that results from early phases of analytic development. Coding is not just the process *for* theme development; coding is the process for generating codes and code labels, and tagging data with code labels. For methodologists like us who view a code as an analytic entity

> **ALERT** Conceptualisations of coding as a process vary: from finding evidence for already determined themes, to generating codes – from which themes are later developed.

and output, codes are conceptualised as the 'building blocks' of analysis – themes are develop from codes, and thus represent a second 'level' of data analysis (we discussed this in-depth in Chapter Three).

What is a theme?

Richard Boyatzis's definition of a theme is widely cited: "a theme is a pattern [...] that at the minimum describes and organises possible observations or at the maximum interprets aspects of the phenomenon" (1998, p. vii). This singular definition belies the use of two vastly different conceptualisations of 'themes as patterns', which we first discussed in Chapter Four. We conceptualise themes as *patterns* of meaning (e.g. concepts, ideas, experience, sense-making) that are underpinned and unified by a central idea (see Table 8.2). This central idea, concept or meaning that unites or holds a theme together is sometimes quite explicitly expressed (a 'semantic' theme) and sometimes quite conceptually or implicitly evidenced (a 'latent' theme). In the latter instances, the data that evidence the patterning of the theme might appear quite disparate.

US nursing scholars Lydia DeSantis and Doris Ugarriza (2000) identified several key features of themes, which are a good fit with how we conceptualise themes. Themes:

- Are actively produced by the researcher, they don't "spontaneously fall out" (p. 355) of data;
- Are abstract entities, often capturing implicit meaning 'beneath the surface' but can be illustrated with more explicit and **concrete data**;
- Unite data that might otherwise appear disparate, or unite meaning that occurs in multiple and varied contexts;
- Explain large portions of data, and are built from smaller meaning units (codes);
- Capture the essence of meaning;
- Are different from data *domains*, but can explain and unite phenomena within a domain; and
- Are recurrent.

Another important characteristic of this conceptualisation of the theme, identified by US theatre professor and qualitative methodologist Johnny Saldaña, is that it is "an *outcome* of coding [...] not something that is, in itself, coded" (2013, p. 14). Like the code, the theme is also conceptualised as an **analytic *output***, distinct and developed from smaller meaning units (codes).

> **ALERT** Themes are predominantly conceptualised in two different ways: as topic summaries or as patterns of shared meaning underpinned by a central organising concept. Understanding this distinction is key for doing good (reflexive) TA.

But there is a second prevalent way 'theme' is used in TA. Such 'themes' do *not* fit the conceptualisation of a theme we've just described, and so, as noted in Chapter Four, we call these 'topic summaries'[8] (see also Connelly & Peltzer, 2016). This name evokes what such 'themes' effectively capture: the diversity of responses to a topic, issue, or area of the data repeatedly spoken or written about. Topic summaries do not evidence meaning organised around a central idea or concept that *unites* the observations; instead, the analysis reports 'everything that was said about X'. Sometimes these topics reflect the very questions participants were asked to respond to during data collection (e.g. the main interview questions). For these reasons, topic summaries have been characterised as instances of poorly realised or underdeveloped analysis (Braun & Clarke, 2006; Connelly & Peltzer, 2016). Topic summaries typically focus on surface-level or descriptive meaning. They are often named with a single term that captures the topic or focus (e.g. 'emotional', 'behavioural', 'diagnosis', 'cognitive', 'body' and 'intersubjective', in Floersch et al., 2010) or are rather general (e.g. 'Perceived risks and benefits associated with conventional cigarettes versus e-cigarettes', in Roditis & Halpern-Felsher, 2015).

These two main uses of a 'theme' – and thus what the analytic 'endpoint'[9] of TA is – are fundamentally different conceptualisations (Table 8.2 provides a contrast from two published papers). Topic summaries are most common in applied research and in disciplines and fields without a strong tradition of qualitative research. But they can and do

---

[8] One of our students dubbed the 'topic summary' conceptualisation of a theme a '**bucket theme**': the researcher effectively puts 'everything that was said' about a topic into the bucket and that becomes the 'theme'.

appear everywhere. What is confusing for those reading TA, learning TA, and doing TA, especially without a background steeped in qualitative research training and experience (Braun & Clarke, 2019a; Braun, Clarke, & Hayfield, 2019), is that what counts as a theme is rarely articulated. Only rarely is any other way of conceptualising themes acknowledged. This means that the 'theme' is often undertheorised in published TA studies (Braun & Clarke, 2021c). Furthermore, you can easily find two published studies that report using the same version of TA, but where 'what counts as a theme' has been conceptualised in totally different ways.[10]

Table 8.2   Shared-meaning themes vs. topic summaries

An example of 'themes' as topic summaries	An example of themes as shared-meaning patterns
Bacsu et al.'s (2012) research on healthy ageing among rural populations in Canada involved interviews with 42 senior women and men living in rural communities. Eight 'themes' in line with their stated focus on "the support systems that exist for rural seniors at both the personal and community level" (p. 79) were reported: housing; transportation; healthcare; finances; care giving; falls; rural communities; and support systems. Each theme was relatively short (roughly 200 to 600 words) and provided a summary of what participants explicitly said in relation to each area. Take 'housing': the main thrust of this topic summary was that many participants identified housing as important and discussed what type of housing best met the needs of seniors; participants also expressed concerns about a lack of appropriate housing. In presenting this 'theme', two illustrative data extracts from participant interviews were provided alongside analytic commentary (the other themes had between two and five data extracts). The theme was contextualised in relation to existing literatures.	Gareth Terry's research with Ginny on the meanings of male body hair (based on over 500 responses to an online survey; Terry & Braun, 2016) reported three themes: (1) men's body hair as natural; (2) men's body hair as unpleasant; (3) men's 'excess' body hair as needing to be managed. The themes were long (between roughly 1600 and 1900 words, with at least 13 data extracts each). Each focused on a core idea explicitly and implicitly evidenced. Theme 1 captured the way male body hair was often described as natural for men and "a dominant expression of masculine embodiment" (p. 17). As well as reporting overt statements about the naturalness of male body hair, the authors discussed underlying assumptions connected to naturalness – such as that men *should* be hairy and women 'hairless' and that men's embodiment is biologically located (natural) and women's is socially located (worked upon and produced). The authors explored how these gendered assumptions were naturalised and essentialised in the participants' accounts. Theme 2 reported a meaning contradictory to theme 1 – men's body hair as unpleasant. Theme 3 focused more conceptually on the way participants implicitly managed the tension between these contradictory conceptualisations of male body hair: Men's body hair was *natural*, yes, but a concept of *excessive* hair evoked disgust; such 'excess' hair should be managed (reduced).

[9]Remembering, as emphasised in Section One, that the 'endpoint' in TA is not a clear destination, but the point at which the analysis has been developed and is good enough.

[10]Some published studies conceptualise themes in a way compatible with the version of TA they have used; others in incompatible ways, such as when authors use topic summaries in claimed-reflexive TA studies (Braun & Clarke, 2021c). Reports mostly evidence one or other conceptualisation of a theme, but we do sometimes come across reports with a mix of topic summaries and shared meaning themes. Something we've also encountered is shared meaning only being evident at the level of the subtheme. In such papers, subthemes are typically not used sparingly (as we advised in Chapter Four). Rather each topic summary encompasses several 'subthemes', which are often one-dimensional and closer to codes.

Researcher subjectivity (reflexivity)

Big Q research can be considered reflexive research, where knowledge is situated, and inevitably and inescapably shaped by the processes and practices of knowledge production, including the practices of the researcher (Finlay, 2002a, 2002b; Gough, 2017). Research within a qualitative paradigm *values* reflexivity, subjectivity, and indeed the contextual, partial and located nature of knowledge (as discussed in Chapters One and Six). Within postpositivist or small q research, such elements are framed as bias or even as a contaminant; their impact needs to be managed and minimised. Across the varieties of TA, there are quite different concerns at play related to subjectivity, connected to what counts as the 'best' kind of knowledge. Relating to paradigmatic locations, this ranges from (ideally) bias-free, accurate and reliable knowledge at the small q/postpositivist end of the spectrum, through to situated and contextualised, subjective knowledge at the Big Q end of the spectrum. These epistemological positions produce distinct 'quality' practices, such as: (a) trying to manage the potential for researcher subjectivity to 'bias' and distort **coding accuracy**, through consensus coding and measuring **inter-coder agreement**; to (b) the researcher using a reflexive journal to reflect on their assumptions, and acknowledging the situated, partial and subjective nature of coding (see Chapter Nine for more on quality).

> **ALERT** Conceptualisations of researcher subjectivity vary from framing it as bias with the potential to distort the 'accuracy' of coding through to viewing it as an essential resource for analysis.

A process of theme development or identification?

Finally, we want to note that there are differences across versions of TA in terms of the conceptualisation of the *process* and language of theme *development* or *identification*. This language differentiation matters, and the way the process is viewed matters, because it connects to deeper understandings of what researchers conceptualise as, and how they seek to generate, patterned meaning. This also connects to what counts as conceptually coherent and quality practice (see Chapter Nine). TA practice can broadly be conceptualised in two ways: (a) a process where the researcher *identifies* existing-in-the-dataset patterns of meaning; (b) a process where the researcher, as a situated, subjective and skilled scholar, brings their existing knowledges to the dataset, to *develop* an understanding of patterned meaning in relation to the dataset. These fundamentally different conceptualisations of the TA process are demarcated in Box 8.1.

Process A is most aligned to small q qualitative – a process for coding is required that rigorously and robustly *identifies* themes in a reliable way. Themes are effectively analytic 'inputs' that coding provides the evidence of. Process B is most aligned to Big Q qualitative – practices for coding and theme *development* need to reflexively grapple with researcher subjectivity, with theme development positioned as an *active* process. Themes are best conceptualised as 'outputs' of this analytic process.

> **ALERT** Depending on how the process of theme creation is conceptualised, themes can be understood as inputs into the analytic process, developed early on, or outputs from the analytic process, developed later on.

Box 8.1

How do I get my themes in TA? Two different conceptualisations of the process

Process A (theme identification; themes as inputs)

Data >> identification of themes >> coding for theme identification (as evidenced in the dataset)

Process B (theme development; themes as outputs)

Data >> coding to explore and parse meaning >> theme development and refinement (from codes and dataset)

This active process of reflexive engagement with data for theme development is captured by a phrase we have become (in)famous for: *themes do not emerge*. This is not our original idea. Instead, it reflects a wider critique of the inference that analysis is a passive process of discovery. The notion that themes passively emerge from data also denies the active role the researcher plays in developing and reporting themes (Taylor & Ussher, 2001). We still love this description, that the language of 'themes emerging':

ALERT Get the badge; sing along – themes don't emerge, themes don't emerge!

> Can be misinterpreted to mean that themes 'reside' in the data, and if we just look hard enough they will 'emerge' like Venus on the half shell. If themes 'reside' anywhere, they reside in our heads from our thinking about our data and creating links as we understand them. (Ely, Vinz, Downing, & Anzul, 1997, pp. 205–206)

During the writing of this book, Victoria posted a query on Twitter for a 'spoken word inter-view' we were preparing for about the development of reflexive TA (see Braun, Clarke, & Hayfield, 2019). After one query related to such passive language for theme development,11 another Twitter user posted a response related to their experience of theme development, which perfectly captured the active, engaged, and occasionally frustrating process of theme development in reflexive TA (see Figure 8.1).

---

[11]For our discussion related to this query around alternatives to passive 'themes emerged' language, see Braun et al. (2019).

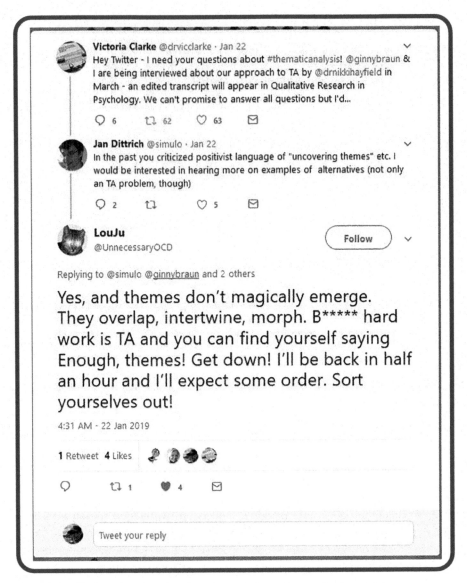

Figure 8.1 Themes do not emerge!

MAPPING THE MAIN MEMBERS OF THE TA FAMILY: OUR TRIPARTITE CLUSTERING

These differences between the various varieties of TA matter, both conceptually, and for doing good TA. Although we understand the sentiment behind the suggestion that "it is crucial that researchers are not precious about 'their' ways of working with thematic analysis" (Brooks, McCluskey, Turley, & King, 2015, p. 206), we cannot *entirely* agree, as it risks suggesting that the differences between versions of TA aren't *that* significant. From our perspective, they *are*.[12] Having clarified the core ideas, concepts and process that vary across different forms of TA, we now outline *our* tripartite typology for classifying forms of TA, based on what we regard as characteristic philosophical assumptions and analytic procedures.[13] These three clusters are:

- **Reflexive TA** – capturing approaches situated within a Big Q framework.
- **Coding reliability TA** – capturing approaches situated within a small q framework.
- **Codebook TA** – capturing approaches situated within what we characterise as a MEDIUM Q framework.

Table 8.3 provides an overview of the three main types of TA, drawing on examples from one main author, and how they conceptualise key elements. We note there is variation within each of these types, and expand the discussion in the next sections.

Our goal is not to promote reflexive TA as the *best* TA, suitable for any and all purposes – although we will explain why we believe it is the best TA approach for a 'fully qualitative' orientation to research. Our goal *is* to lay out some of the key ways in which the various TA approaches differ, as well as how they are similar, to inform more *knowing* use of the method. To date, there is much problematic use of TA, which often seems to result from the unknowing mixing of elements from small q and Big Q approaches (Braun & Clarke, 2021c). UK social psychologist Stephen Reicher, discussing quality criteria for qualitative research, wrote of the "serious danger of papering over cracks that are nearer chasms" (2000, p. 3)

> **ALERT** There are tensions between small q and Big Q approaches to TA; they are not complementary and cannot simply be combined without carefully thinking through the underlying conceptual clashes.

across different *qualitative* approaches and orientations. This idea of 'chasms' captures the point that some of the differences between various forms of TA are not just minor quibbles over process.

Reflexive TA offers the comparison point for our discussion of the other versions of TA. If you need a quick refresher on the values and processes of reflexive TA, we encourage you to revisit Chapter One, and especially Box 1.1. That chapter situates and explicates the values that inform 'our' approach to TA, which undoubtedly inflect both our descriptions and assessments of other approaches to TA.

---

[12]Our caution in fully endorsing this statement from Brooks et al. (2015) also reflects a context where these conceptually significant, if not fundamental, differences don't seem to be fully understood by the wider community using TA (Braun & Clarke, 2021c).

[13]In many of our earlier publications on TA, we only distinguished between small q and Big Q TA (e.g. Braun, Clarke, & Terry, 2014; Braun et al., 2016; Clarke et al., 2015; Terry et al., 2017). After being asked how our approach to TA related to approaches like template and framework analysis, in more recent publications we have distinguished between three main types of TA, adding in 'MEDIUM Q' TA (e.g. Braun, Clarke, Hayfield, & Terry, 2019; Clarke & Braun, 2018).

Table 8.3 Comparing TA: A quick overview of different forms of TA

Approach	Reflexive (Braun & Clarke, 2006)	Coding reliability (Boyatzis, 1998)	Codebook (Template analysis; N. King, 2012)
Big Theory (see Chapter Six)	Closer to a method than a methodology. Theoretically independent or flexible – with a wide range of theoretical positions possible: critical realist; relativist; constructionist.	Not its own method(ology); a process used as part of many qualitative methods. Theoretically flexible, but claimed flexibility limited by postpositivist assumptions.	A technique (method) not a methodology. Theoretically flexible or independent – realist, critical realist (phenomenology), constructionist (broad patterns of discourse only).
What is a theme? (see Chapter Four)	Patterned meaning across dataset. Relevant to the research question. United by shared idea/concept. Can have semantic or latent focus. Themes *actively generated* by the researcher, not discovered.	A pattern that describes and organises meaning; potentially also interprets. Can be identified at the manifest (directly observable) or latent (underlying) level. Themes *identified* by the researcher.	Recurrent features of data relevant to the research question. Themes reflect data topics (e.g. intergenerational issues), rather than storied, conceptual patterns. Themes *created* by the researcher, not discovered.
What is a code/coding? (see Chapter Three)	Coding is an organic and evolving process of noticing potentially relevant meaning in the dataset, tagging it with a code, and ultimately building a set of codes from which themes are developed. Codes (analytic 'outputs') have 'labels' that evoke the relevant data meanings. Can focus on meaning from semantic to latent levels.	Coding is a *process* to identify themes using a predetermined set of codes, organised within a codebook. Codes (analytic tools) are developed *from* themes, as a way to identify each theme. Codes and themes are sometimes used interchangeably (e.g. thematic codes).	Coding is a *process* to identify evidence for patterns (themes). Codes (analytic tools) are labels applied to data to identify it as an instance of a theme. Codes can be descriptive and interpretative. Codes and themes are organised hierarchically, and sometimes laterally, into a layered template that guides coding for theme identification.
Analytic orientation	Works for more inductive ('bottom up') to more deductive ('top down') orientations.	Inductive or deductive; inductive the "least frequently used [...] and probably the least understood" (p. x).	A middle-ground: can be used inductively, but mainly deductive(ish), with a priori themes tentative, and can be redefined or discarded.
Analytic process	Organic process; starts from familiarisation; coding and recoding; theme development, revision and refinement in relation to the coded data and then the full dataset. Themes as analytic 'outputs'.	Development of themes and codes from prior theory and research or inductively; construction of codebook; application of codebook to data by multiple coders to find evidence for themes; testing coding reliability. Themes as analytic 'inputs'.	Some a priori themes developed first from interview guide/literature; coding to evidence these and other themes; themes and codes refined after some *initial* coding; development and refinement of template; coding guided by template for final theme development. Themes as analytic 'inputs' – but they can also evolve and new ones can be developed, so can also be 'outputs'.
Researcher subjectivity (see Chapters One, Two)	A resource to be utilised; the researcher is both active and positioned.	A 'risk' to the validity and quality of the analysis. Needs to be 'controlled' and minimised.	Acknowledged and accepted. Reflexivity encouraged.
Quality (see Chapter Nine)	Deep questioning data engagement and a systematic, rigorous analytic process. Analysis moves beyond summary or paraphrasing. Researcher reflexivity and explication of choices.	Multiple independent coders. Inter-rater reliability. Reliability conceptualised as consistency of judgement in applying codes to identify themes.	Participant feedback. Audit trails. Multiple researchers code and compare. Measures of inter-coder reliability not recommended.

CODING RELIABILITY APPROACHES: SMALL Q THEMATIC ANALYSIS

The approaches to TA we call coding reliability are united by adherence to (post)positivist notions of reliability and a sometimes-implicit, sometimes-explicit, aim of seeking unbiased, objective truth from qualitative data. Although claimed as theoretically flexible, such approaches are delimited by the values of this broader paradigm. These approaches to TA typically share with *codebook* approaches a more structured coding practice than in reflexive TA. Coding is guided by a tool – a **codebook** or **coding frame**. In coding reliability forms of TA, the coding process culminates in a measure of 'coding reliability', which is used to assess the 'accuracy' or 'reliability' (hence the name 'coding reliability') of the coding process.

> **ALERT** Small q TA is underpinned by (post)positivist conceptions of reliability.

Coding in small q TA is conceptualised as a *process*, but codes themselves are not typically conceptualised as an analytic entity, an analytic output that is *distinct* from a theme. For instance, Guest et al. (2012) are unusual in defining 'code' but their definition demonstrates this blurriness: "A textual description of the semantic boundaries of a theme or a component of a theme. A code is a formal rendering of a theme" (p. 279).[14] Procedures in small q TA centre on the development of a codebook or coding frame, which is used to code for instances of themes (typically topic summaries). This of course means themes are developed before coding and are conceptualised as analytic inputs (as well as outputs – what is reported). The codebook typically consists of a definitive list of codes. For each code, there is a label, definition, instructions on how to identify the code/theme, details of any exclusions, and examples (Boyatzis, 1998).

> **ALERT** The code is not a distinct analytic unit in coding reliability TA.

> **ALERT** A codebook, which lists and defines codes/themes and provides instructions on how to apply them, is an essential component of coding reliability TA.

The codebook tends to be developed in one of two ways: (1) deductively from pre-existing theory or research; or (2) inductively, following data familiarisation. For a deductively-derived approach, the codebook is developed independently from the data, requiring little or no engagement with the dataset prior to coding. It is then 'applied' to the dataset – the researcher decides which sections of data are instances of particular codes/themes. Thus, the coding process conceptually represents a search for 'evidence' for themes. Such an approach echoes

> **ALERT** Codebooks can be developed inductively following data familiarisation or deductively from existing theory or research.

---

[14]Because a distinction between codes and themes is not always made or clear in coding reliability TA, and the terms are often used interchangeably, we sometimes use 'code/theme'.

the scientific method – a researcher starts with a theory, develops hypotheses (themes) and conducts an experiment (coding) to test (find evidence for) the hypotheses (themes). For an inductively-developed codebook, the researcher familiarises themselves with some (or occasionally all) of the data and then creates a codebook to be applied to the whole dataset to identify evidence of themes. Inductive approaches to codebook development in small q TA were originally described as the "least frequently used [...] and probably the least understood" (Boyatzis, 1998, p. x), but more recent texts have emphasised "inductive analyses, which primarily have a descriptive and exploratory orientation" (Guest et al., 2012, p. 7).

Such inductive orientations to codebook development retain a similar 'evidencing' ethos to deductive approaches, and a concern for 'accuracy' in coding. To this end, small

> **ALERT** Quality procedures in coding reliability TA centre on the need for accurate and reliable coding. The 'threat' researcher subjectivity poses to reliability is managed through the use of multiple coders, measuring inter-coder agreement and consensus coding.

q approaches emphasise the need for multiple coders to apply the codebook to the dataset. These coders are ideally 'blind',[15] in the sense of having no prior knowledge of the topic area and/ or not being informed of the research question. The conceptual framework for multiple coders is one of consensus – whereby two or more coders coding the same piece of data in the same way is evidence of 'accuracy' and therefore quality. 'Coding reliability' – a measure of the extent of agreement between different coders – is a key quality requirement. After multiple researchers have independently coded the data using the codebook, the level of 'agreement' between the coders will be calculated using one of a number of statistical tests (see O'Connor & Joffe, 2020; Yardley, 2008). Such assessments of inter-coder agreement determine whether coders applied the same code(s) to the same segments of data to a sufficiently high level that coding can be considered to be reliable. If a sufficient level of agreement is *not* reached, resolution occurs through recoding.[16] One of the key rationales for such quality procedures is that the *subjectivity* that individual researchers bring to data collection has to be managed. Overtly conceptualised as 'bias', researcher subjectivity is a threat, not a resource, for small q TA.

What do we think is problematic about coding reliability approaches to TA?

There is nothing inherently 'wrong' with coding reliability approaches to TA! As long as your TA project is done in a way that is conceptually coherent, the analytic practices align with your purpose and framework, and the whole process is undertaken with integrity (see Braun & Clarke, 2021c, and Chapter Nine). That acknowledged, these approaches are not for us.

---

[15]We use the problematic ableist term 'blind' here, but with scare quotes, because it is the predominant one used to describe research processes where the coder does not have access to key information that is theorised as otherwise distorting their judgement.

[16]In theory, coding disagreements are resolved through recoding, but, in practice, it is rare for anything other than high levels of coding agreement to be reported.

Various elements of small q TA approaches, and a postpositivist-inflected 'discovery orienta-tion' for analysis, have been critiqued from a range of perspectives, including from the Big Q orientation we occupy. We outline some of these critiques now.

By prioritising postpositivist conceptions of reliability, small q approaches mandate assumptions and practices at odds with quali-tative research values (e.g. Grant & Giddings, 2002; Kidder & Fine, 1987; Madill & Gough, 2008). Consider this statement: "the need for

> **ALERT** Coding reliability approaches have a coherent internal logic, but it's one that is fundamentally incompatible with Big Q qualitative research values.

full agreement among coders is designed to help minimise the effects of experimenter bias because it reduces the influence of any one coder over the assignment of codes" (Heath, Lynch, Fritch, McArthur, & Smith, 2011, p. 600).[17] To value a coding process and outcome, wherein different researchers achieve the same outcome (identical coding) using the same measure (codebook), you have to assume that themes are *in* the data, waiting to be found by the researcher (N. King & Brooks, 2018). Language matters, as we've noted before, and can reinforce this idea. For example, Boyatzis defined a theme as "a pattern *found in* the infor-mation" (Boyatzis, 1998, p. vii, our emphasis). The idea here is, effectively, that the truth of meaning lies *within* the dataset, and the researcher is merely the conduit for revealing it.[18] This idea is a popular one. For instance, the QDAS giant NVivo (see Box 3.3 in Chapter Three) has the phrase "what is your data trying to tell you?" front and centre of their home-page (along with other problematic messages; see Braun & Clarke, 2021d). Elsewhere we have described this 'discovery' (or 'researcher-as-archaeologist') approach to theme devel-opment as underpinned by a conceptualisation of themes as "diamonds scattered in the sand waiting to be plucked-up by a lucky passer-by" (Braun & Clarke, 2016, p. 740), similar to "fossil[s] hidden in a rock" (N. King & Brooks, 2018, p. 220). Themes are implicitly concep-tualised as entities that pre-exist the analysis; analysis is about identifying or finding these themes *in* the data. This conceptualisation is problematic for many qualitative researchers, not only because it rests on a whole set of – rarely acknowledged – theoretical assumptions, but because it renders researcher subjectivity at best invisible and at worst problematic.

Take the claim that coding is better, that is, more accurate or objective, when two or more coders agree. The main concern here is to control for subjectivity. For example, in their 'thematic content analysis' of interview data exploring women's engagement in community leadership, Bond et al. noted that: "all interviews were consensus-coded by two or three researchers, two of whom by design were unfamiliar with, and therefore presumably unin-fluenced by, previous research examining community leadership" (2008, p. 52). Knowledge of previous research is positioned here as a potential contaminant, something that risks

---

[17]The language "effects of experiment bias" is a good hint that this paper by Heath et al. (2011) is embed-ded within postpositivist research values.

[18]It's important to acknowledge here, as we noted in Chapter Two, that people's thinking, writing, and use of language also shifts. We have shifted from 'searching for themes' to 'generating initial themes' for instance, because of some of these very concerns that 'searching for' evoked a passive discovery mode (Braun & Clarke, 2019a; Braun, Clarke, & Hayfield, 2019).

distorting a researcher's coding. The idea that coding can be distorted depends not only on a realist idea of singular truth, but also on idea(l)s of 'discovery' of that truth. Within coding reliability TA, coding is conceptualised as something that can be accurate (finding diamonds) or not (finding glass from broken bottles). Furthermore, instead of conceptualising researcher subjectivity – including their pre-existing knowledge of the topic – as *valuable*, it is viewed as a potential barrier to good coding.

Another critique relates to the codes themselves and the limiting of analytic depth. The types of codes amenable to use within structured codebook approaches, including measurement of coding agreement, are often relatively **coarse**, superficial, or descriptively concrete. The critique US qualitative nursing researcher Janice Morse made over two decades ago *still* applies: "maintaining a simplified coding schedule for the purposes of defining categories for an **inter-rater reliability** check [...] will simplify the research to such an extent that all of the richness attained from insight will be lost" (Morse, 1997, p. 446). We'd also ask: can '*un*knowledgeable' coders effectively add such depth, insight and creativity? Moreover, as Irish and British psychologists Cliodhna O'Connor and Hélène Joffe (2020) highlighted, there are only so many codes coders can hold in their working memory. The more codes there are in the codebook, the lower inter-coder agreement is likely to be. Limits of 30–40 (MacQueen, McLellan, Kay, & Milstein, 1998) and even 20 (Hruschka et al., 2004) codes have been recommended *to facilitate agreement*, which, depending on the size of the dataset, effectively rules out more fine-grained and nuanced coding. For us, this reveals a key problematic of approaches to coding that prioritise consensus (inter-coder agreement): uniformity is valued over depth of insight.

> **ALERT** From our perspective, coding reliability procedures often result in themes that are relatively superficial and underdeveloped.

Given a close conceptual connection between codes and themes, coding reliability approaches also often produce *themes* that are relatively superficial and – in our view – 'underdeveloped' (Connelly & Peltzer, 2016). Such underdeveloped 'themes' are, in practice, often simply topic summaries (see Table 8.2 and Chapter Four), with each providing a summary of patterns in participants' responses to a particular topic. These topics sometimes map *closely* onto data collection questions. As an example, the following three 'themes' were reported in a focus group study of anorexia patients' perspectives on a group intervention for perfectionism: (1) perceived benefits of the group; (2) nature/content of the group; (3) suggested improvements. These themes very closely mapped onto the questions asked in the focus groups (Larsson, Lloyd, Westwood, & Tchanturia, 2018). Given a close mapping between themes and data collection questions, with themes as topic summaries, it is not surprising that a "good consensus" between two independent coders was achievable. But what potential depth and richness of meaning is lost?

> **ALERT** One of the things we find most troubling about coding reliability TA is that the values underpinning it are rarely articulated and explicitly acknowledged.

From our Big Q perspective, there are many troublesome practices in small q TA, but perhaps the most troubling is when the values that underpin it are not articulated or acknowledged. For some, any differences between qualitative and quantitative data/analysis are not 'chasms' so much as gentle brooks, not paradigmatically incommensurate. Guest et al., for instance, argued that it is "not true" that "qualitative research methods are difficult to reconcile with a positivist approach" (2012). Key coding reliability TA authors have described TA as an approach that can 'bridge the divide' between quantitative and qualitative (or positivist and interpretative) research (Boyatzis, 1998; Guest et al., 2012; Hayes, 1997; Luborsky, 1994). Boyatzis evocatively described TA as "a translator of those speaking the language of qualitative analysis and those speaking the language of quantitative analysis" (1998, p. vii).[19]

What such definitions rely on (sometimes implicitly) is *one type of* qualitative orientation, with the 'chasm' (Reicher, 2000) between different orientations *within* qualitative research elided. In our view, TA 'bridges the divide' by relying on a limited and indeed impoverished definition of qualitative research, as tools and techniques (small q), rather than an *expanded* definition, in which qualitative research provides both a philosophy and techniques for research (Big Q). Indeed, most small q authors implicitly conceptualise TA within realist and experiential ('empathic') frameworks, while the possibility of critical ('suspicious') orientations (Willig, 2017) is not even acknowledged. What *particularly* troubles us is that the limited conception of qualitative inquiry that underpins small q TA is not acknowledged *as* limited, or often even as situated and partial.

> **ALERT** Coding reliability TA can only 'bridge the qualitative/quantitative divide' by offering a limited conceptualisation of qualitative research as merely providing tools and techniques.

But more broadly, we are *very troubled* by the way good practice in *small q* TA is often equated with good practice in TA and qualitative research more generally. For instance, through the inclusion of multiple coders in qualitative 'quality checklists' (O'Connor & Joffe, 2020). Ryan and Bernard (2003) claimed analytic validity "hing[es] on the agreement across coders", and noted "strong intercoder agreement also suggests that the concept is not just a figment of the investigator's imagination" (p. 104). In promoting inter-coder reliability as an implicitly or explicitly 'universal' – rather than paradigm-embedded – marker of quality, researcher subjectivity becomes problematically conflated with poor quality analysis, and the inference that subjective knowledge is necessary flawed. Reader, it is not! We suspect this embracing of such 'good practice' guidelines reflects their easy-alignment with the positivist-empiricism that dominates much methodological training, and the wider under-valuing and lack of training of qualitative research across many disciplines. Indeed, it's not uncommon for researchers using Big Q TA to be asked by journal reviewers and editors, and thesis examiners, to include discussion of coding reliability measures in their report or explain *why* they were not used (Braun & Clarke, 2021c).

> **ALERT** It is problematic to assume coding reliability quality measures are relevant for all types of TA; they are not!

This, to us, is just a more particularised version of having to justify *qualitative* over *quantitative* research approaches – something far less common than it used to be, thankfully! What seems to underlie the equation of coding reliability with good quality coding, in all forms of

---

[19]This notion of 'bridging the divide' may be why (small q) TA seems to hold particular appeal for mixed methods researchers.

TA, is a failure to appreciate the divergent paradigmatic assumptions that underpin different TA approaches, and a general lack of understanding of the qualitative paradigm.

From our standpoint as Big Q researchers, small q approaches do not allow for the very things that are essential to producing good quality *qualitative* analysis (we discussed qualitative values in Chapter One, and will focus on quality in Chapter Nine). However, there *is* a logic to small q TA that is consistent with its postpositivist leanings, even if these are rarely explicitly acknowledged.

CODEBOOK APPROACHES TO TA (MEDIUM Q)

> **ALERT** Codebook approaches combine Big Q qualitative research values with a more structured approach to coding and early theme development. The more structured approach often reflects the pragmatic demands of applied research.

There are several approaches to TA that sit somewhere *between* reflexive and coding reliability varieties, and combine values from a qualitative paradigm with more structured coding and theme development processes. Reflecting this combination, we suggest such approaches are effectively a 'MEDIUM Q' approach, and use the term 'codebook' to collectively describe them. Like coding reliability, the analytic process centres around the development of some kind of codebook or coding frame and so involves a more structured, less open and organic approach to analysis than in reflexive TA. Coding reliability is, however, not encouraged – or even *discouraged* (see N. King, 2016) – and thus researcher subjectivity is not problematised, but recognised and even valued. The codebook or coding frame, developed deductively ahead of analysis or inductively after (some) data familiarisation and coding, serves as a tool to guide data coding and/or a way of mapping or charting the coded data. Again, themes are often conceptualised as 'analytic inputs', identifiable early in the analytic process – even if evolution of these is possible.

This cluster of approaches often goes by names other than 'thematic analysis', including **matrix analysis** (e.g. Cassell & Nadin, 2004; Miles & Huberman, 1994), framework analysis (e.g. Ritchie & Spencer, 1994), **network analysis** (e.g. Attride-Stirling, 2001) and template analysis (e.g. N. King, 1998). We recognise these different approaches vary, but to us, the differences between these approaches are less significant than what separates them from other approaches in our tripartite TA differentiation. We discuss codebook approaches further in relation to first template analysis and then framework analysis, as these are two of the more commonly used and well-defined codebook approaches.

Template analysis

Template analysis was developed by British psychologist Nigel King and colleagues (Brooks et al., 2015; N. King, 1998, 2004, 2012, 2016; N. King & Brooks, 2016, 2018), drawing on the work of Crabtree and Miller (1999). It is framed as a 'middle ground' approach to TA (N. King, 2012). Template analysis offers a set of techniques rather than a methodology. Template analysis is positioned as theoretically 'independent' and flexible, and able to be used across realist and critical/'subtle' realist (Hammersley, 1992) approaches (Brooks et al.,

2015), as well as with (some) constructionist approaches to qualitative research. King has suggested that template analysis is suitable for use in constructionist research focused on broader discursive patterns (N. King, 2012; N. King & Brooks, 2018).

Some aspects of template analysis seem to retain the 'postpositivist sensibility' that informs small q TA. Template analysis ostensibly combines a "high degree of structure" *and* flexibility (N. King, 2012, p. 426), although flexibility here *is* constrained compared to reflexive TA.[20] The main differences between reflexive TA and template analysis centre on how codes and themes are conceptualised and how the analytic process unfolds. In template analysis, codes can be descriptive and interpretative (N. King, 2004), a distinction that echoes that between manifest/descriptive and latent/conceptual coding in other types of TA. Codes are effectively tools for the identification of

> **ALERT** Template analysis and reflexive TA overlap in various ways – the primary differences relate to when themes are developed (earlier or later), how they are (implicitly) conceptualised (topics or themes) and the nature of the coding process (more- or less-structured).

themes. The analytic process centres on the development of a coding frame – the template – and the generation of a final hierarchal coding/thematic structure through the application and refinement of the template in relation to the whole dataset. The template offers a way of hierarchically mapping patterned meaning, and moving from broader to more precise meanings; multiple layers evidence refinement. One trap for novice researchers is to become overly focused on the details of the template; King (2012) has cautioned that the template is a tool for, and not the purpose of, analysis.

> **ALERT** The template is a tool for, not the purpose of, analysis, in template analysis.

Although the template can be generated entirely inductively, template development usually combines deductive and inductive processes. So-called **a priori** codes might be identified ahead of data engagement, as 'anticipated themes' developed from literature or interview questions. Coding of usually a subset of the dataset also contributes to developing an initial template or a priori codes/themes (Brooks et al., 2015). 'Openness' comes in as the template is developed and refined through full dataset coding. This approach has been described as offering efficiency, especially when working with larger datasets (N. King, 2004) and some facilitative structure to those new to qualitative analysis. With this dual a priori and data-based theme development approach, themes sit somewhere on a spectrum from analytic inputs to analytic outputs. In fitting with a qualitative paradigm, King (2012) has cautioned that themes are not hidden in the data waiting to be found, and are not independent of the researcher. Yet there may be a risk of settling themes too early on, and using coding simply as the means to identify those. Unlike reflexive TA, template analysis does not involve two levels of analytic work – coding *and* theme development – and two distinct analytic entity outputs – codes *and* themes. Rather the terms code and theme are often used interchangeably, echoing the conflation of these terms in small q TA.

---

[20]King (2004) has noted that template analysis is not well suited to a less-structured analytic approach.

Do we perceive any problems with template analysis?

In the conceptualisation of template analysis, no. The structured-but-flexible approach may offer a useful entry-point into qualitative-values-informed TA, especially for researchers who are working in teams of mixed experience or are new to qualitative research. It is advocated as useful for applied research (Brooks & King, 2012), which may sometimes have such research team characteristics. The differences between template analysis and reflexive TA may reflect the applied psychology roots of template analysis, and the **neo-positivist** (Duberley, Johnson, & Cassell, 2012) assumptions common in applied fields (Clarke & Braun, 2018). That said, there are elements of the approach that we feel *risk* foreclosing analysis, and undermining depth of engagement, and thus the potential of the method to deliver rich, nuanced analyses of the topic at hand.

There is a risk that an emphasis on developing apriori codes/themes – especially if strongly connected to data collection questions – reduces open, organic interpretation and thus results in foreclosure of analysis. Themes potentially become conceptualised as analytic inputs that evidence is *sought* for, rather than *products of* the analytic process, where understanding of patterning and relationships deepens and changes through the analytic process. We specifically identify the use of interview questions as 'themes' as an instance of a weak analysis – because no analytic work has been undertaken (Braun & Clarke, 2021c). There is also a risk that instead of themes, what is produced are topic summaries of data collection questions. For example, the 'themes' reported in template research on UK managers' conceptions of employee training and development (McDowall & Saunders, 2010, p. 617) – "conceptualisations of training and development"; "training and development decisions"; "evaluation of outcomes"; "relationship between training and development" – *closely* reflect the headings in the interview schedule.

> **ALERT** The dominance of (post) positivism in many fields no doubt gives appeal to the structured elements of template analysis. But it's precisely these elements, combined with early theme development and the potential for topic summary themes, that risk an underdeveloped analysis – if the researcher lacks a good understanding of Big Q research values.

Finally, there is a risk that the *meaning* focus of Big Q research is lost through an overemphasis on mapping structure and hierarchy. From our perspective, many different levels around themes can undermine a rich nuanced understanding. Although this is advocated for in template analysis as a way to capture richness, it risks evoking the production of a quantitative-relational-model, where the focus is on relationships between 'variables', rather than on depth of meaning. In reflexive TA, the production of many themes/levels usually reflects a superficial analytic process and a failure to identify underlying patterns and concepts (Braun & Clarke, 2013). Therefore, our concern with template analysis is that *if* it's treated as a technique to apply, without a good understanding of overall qualitative values and processes, it risks a thin and underdeveloped analysis (Connelly & Peltzer, 2016).

Framework analysis

Framework analysis offers another example of a codebook approach that is similar to TA (Gale, Heath, Cameron, Rashid, & Redwood, 2013; J. Smith & Firth, 2011). Developed in the

UK in the 1980s with an initial focus on applied policy research (Ritchie & Spencer, 1994; see also Ritchie, Spencer, & O'Connor, 2003; Srivastava & Thomson, 2009),[21] the method has been described as particularly useful for research where the objective is clear and known in advance, timeframes are tight, a dataset is large, and it is conducted in teams, including teams with varying levels of qualitative research experience (Parkinson et al., 2016). The method emphasises the importance of 'audit trails' to map analytic development – a widely used qualitative quality measure (see Chapter Nine) – and for analytic transparency (Gale et al., 2013; Leal et al., 2015; Ritchie & Spencer, 1994). Indeed, other forms of TA have been critiqued for 'subjective' results and a lack of transparency in how the themes were produced, as well as for taking data out of context and the potential for misinterpretation (J. Smith & Firth, 2011). This latter critique connects to what is a key differentiator of this particular approach from other TA approaches: retaining focus on individual cases within an approach that focuses on themes across cases. Using the framework, researchers can compare data not just across, but also within, cases. This dual focus is identified as a key strength of framework analysis (Gale et al., 2013).

The method's key characteristic is the development of a (data reduction) framework. Like the template in template analysis, this framework is a *tool for* analysis, not the endpoint of analysis. Themes form the basis for this framework. Like other codebook approaches, themes – often closer to topic summaries than shared meaning themes – are developed fairly early in the analytic process from (some) data familiarisation, and the data collection topics/questions. Coding is primarily a process for identification of 'themes'. The framework is a data matrix with *rows* (cases or data items, such as an individual interview) and *columns* (codes) making *cells* of summarised data (Gale et al., 2013). The coding frame (data matrix) developed from this process is then applied to the dataset, indexing instances of themes. Once the framework is finalised, processes of mapping (of themes, relationships, etc.) and interpretation complete the process. Researchers need to hold in mind a clear distinction between "'identifying a framework' (for the purpose of sifting and sorting) and 'mapping and interpretation' (for the purpose of making sense and understanding)" (Parkinson et al., 2016, p. 117).

> **ALERT** In contrast to coding reliability TA, where the codebook is used to measure the accuracy of coding, in codebook approaches, the codebook – the template, framework or matrix – is used to chart or map the developing analysis.

Framework analysis is not aligned with a *particular* theoretical approach (Gale et al., 2013; Parkinson et al., 2016) and can be utilised inductively or deductively – although induction is often circumscribed by highly focused aims and objectives (see also N. King, 2012; J. Smith & Firth, 2011).

---

[21]Framework analysis is now also popular in health and nursing research (e.g. Gale et al., 2013; Leal et al., 2015; Parkinson, Eatough, Holmes, Stapley, & Midgley, 2016; Pope et al., 2006; J. Smith & Firth, 2011; Swallow, Newton, & Van Lottum, 2003; Ward, Furber, Tierney, & Swallow, 2013).

Do we perceive any problems with framework analysis?

Again, the simple answer is *no*. Framework analysis is clearly a good 'fit' with the purpose and goals of applied policy research, especially if the outcomes of research are clearly defined in advance of data analysis. For instance, it has been used to address very practical and concrete questions related to the *implementation* of particular policy and to identify the factors that were helping or hindering that process (e.g. around care for people with intellectual disabilities and mental health problems; M. Kelly & Humphrey, 2013). With focused and applied questions, the structured approach undoubtedly has pragmatic appeal as it offers clear guidelines to achieve your research purpose. But we do have cautions about what some aspects of this method might evoke, both in process and outcome, from a Big Q perspective. The method itself has been acknowledged as a compromise of some qualitative principles by key authors (Ritchie & Lewis, 2003). For those doing research in social and health sciences areas, we suspect framework analysis is appealing *because of* its neo-positivist elements (the codebook; a topic summary approach to themes).

We also have questions about the translation of this method out of the policy analysis context to health and other social research, and how it might delimit a fuller Big Q qualitative research practice in those fields. We share Parkinson et al.'s concerns that the structured analytic process may inadvertently encourage researchers to view the analytic stages as "mechanical steps to follow", producing "unthinking'" data engagement (2016, p. 125). Parkinson et al. raised a potentially analytically important difference, between the qualitative data gathered in policy/healthcare research and data in psychological (and related social science) research. The former fields tend to work with data that are "more concrete or factual". Psychological data often focus on "experience, narrative or discourse", aspects which are less suited to a structured analytic approach. With the latter, they found "that the less clear, more ambiguous and subjective aspects of the data could not be summarized as easily during the indexing stage" (2016, p. 128).

ALERT As framework analysis was designed for use with relatively concrete data, the more abstract or experiential data generated in other fields – including our home discipline of psychology – may prove challenging to analyse using a framework approach.

Challenges with using codebook approaches in general

From our perspective, codebook approaches, including template analysis and framework analysis, carry risks of mechanising and delimiting analytic and interpretative processes, in a way which constrains the Big Q potential of these approaches (as some authors acknowledge; Ritchie & Lewis, 2003). These risks are not *inherent* in the method, but perhaps enabled by the structure(s) they offer to support analytic development – particularly for researchers who might not have good conceptual, paradigmatic,

ALERT Applied qualitative methodologists have argued that topic summaries cannot easily be translated into actionable outcomes, and applied research requires the reporting of fully realised themes to have clear implications for practice.

or theoretical grounding in qualitative research values (as might be the case with some applied research teams). Codebook approaches *are* commonly used in applied research – indeed have often been developed specifically *for* applied research – and sometimes are promoted as the *best* TA method for applied research. But if these approaches do (inadvertently) produce topic summaries more than conceptually founded patterns of meaning, translation into **actionable outcomes** – with clear implications for practice – is arguably compromised (see Connelly & Peltzer, 2016; Sandelowski & Leeman, 2012). Sandelowski and Leeman argued that:

> knowing the difference between a theme and a topic is foundational to the crafting of accessible findings. For example, writing that trust, confidence, and symptoms were themes discerned in interviews with persons concerning their adherence to a treatment regimen conveys nothing thematic because these words as yet convey no idea concerning what researchers found out about trust, confidence, and symptoms in relation to treatment adherence. (2012, p. 1409)

SO IS REFLEXIVE TA THE *BEST* APPROACH TO TA?

Despite the concerns or questions with different versions of TA we've just noted, what we're *not* saying is that reflexive TA is the best approach and the one that everyone should use![22] We think reflexive TA is the most 'fully qualitative' member of the family, and thus most suitable for those who want to explore deep, complex, nuanced meaning and understanding. But most important is ensuring alignment of your chosen method with your goals and purpose (Braun & Clarke, 2021b). Each type of approach to TA comes with a number of limitations and constraints, alongside advantages. In Table 8.4 we briefly summarise what each type offers, and what some of the challenges are. The table includes both the original authors' and our own assessments.

ALERT Reflexive TA is the best approach to TA! Only joking! Of course we think it's a good approach, but it only makes sense to use it if your research values align with the values underpinning reflexive TA. Our overriding concern is that whatever TA approach people use, it aligns with their research values and they use it knowingly.

BUT WAIT... THERE'S *EVEN* MORE? OTHER APPROACHES TO THEMATIC ANALYSIS

As nice and tidy as a tripartite clustering of TA approaches might be, it doesn't fully contain the diversity of the field. There is a range of other approaches – some idiosyncratic, some more widely used – that effectively *do* TA in some way. These include approaches called 'thematic coding' (Box 8.2), which use grounded theory coding techniques to do TA, and approaches to

---

[22]Indeed, in response to email or Twitter questions about the use of reflexive TA, or in reviewing research claiming to use reflexive TA, it's not uncommon for us to suggest another approach as more suited to the aims and purpose of the research.

Table 8.4 A quick summary of *advantages* and *challenges* for different forms of TA

Approach	Reflexive (Braun & Clarke, 2006)	Coding reliability (Boyatzis, 1998)	Codebook (Template analysis; N. King, 2012)
What they offer	Theoretical flexibility (but Big Q). Potential for analysis from inductive to deductive. Works well from experiential to critical approaches. Open and iterative analytic process, but with clear guidelines. Development of analytic concepts from codes to themes. Easy to learn but requires a 'qualitative mindset' and researcher reflexivity. Works especially well for a single researcher; can be used with team research. Works with wide range of datasets and participant group sizes.	Theoretical flexibility (but small q). Potential for analysis from inductive to deductive (but fully inductive rare). Focused on experiential approaches. A highly structured analytic approach, which might seem reassuring to new qualitative researchers. Potential to 'speak within' the language of postpositivist quantitative research. Potential for 'hypothesis testing' (deductive TA). Requires research team (more than one coder) for reliability.	Theoretical flexibility. Can be used inductively or deductively, but typically occupies a middle-ground between these. Particularly suited for experiential approaches, but can be used critically. *Structured* and systematised, but flexible, techniques for data analysis can be helpful for new qualitative researchers. Structured process offers some efficiency in analysis. Useful for exploring perspective of different groups. Can be used by single researchers or teams. Fairly easy to learn. Works well with larger datasets.
What can go wrong?	Failure to discuss theory to locate the use of the method. Analysis not grounded in qualitative values, or in broader theoretical constructs. Failure to explicate the particular way(s) the method has been used. Use of topic summaries instead of themes. A too fragmented and particularised analysis, presenting many themes and a complex thematic structure without depth of interpretation. Absence of interpretation; simply descriptive summaries.	Failure to discuss (big) theory or conceptual frameworks for the analysis. Inconsistency of judgement in coding data. 'Bias' from the researcher affecting the coding and identification of themes. No data interpretation; simply descriptive summaries.	Failure to discuss theoretical or methodological orientation. Codebook (the template) treated as *purpose* of analysis; lack of development of themes during data engagement. Overemphasis on (hierarchical) thematic structure at the expense of depth of meaning. No data interpretation; simply descriptive summaries.

Box 8.2

Thematic coding

Thematic coding was particularly common before TA was widely recognised as a distinctive method, but remains used and discussed in methodological texts (e.g. Ayres, 2008; Flick, 2018; Rivas, 2018). Like TA more broadly, thematic coding has often been presented as a generic technique for qualitative analysis, that informs many different analytic approaches, centred on the development of "a framework of thematic ideas" (Gibbs, 2007, p. 38) about data. Most authors describe more inductive and more deductive orientations as possible, and encourage (some) openness around coding and the evolution of analytic ideas throughout the coding process. Rivas (2018) emphasised an increasingly interpretative approach as the analysis progresses. Some make a distinction between data-driven (descriptive) codes – close to the respondent's terms – and concept-driven (analytic and theoretical) codes (e.g. Gibbs, 2007). Gibbs emphasised the importance of a flexible approach and warned researchers "not to become too tied to the initial codes you construct" (2007, p. 46).

German psychologist Uwe Flick's description of thematic coding (e.g. Flick, 2014a, 2018) bears similarity to codebook types of TA, with some delimiting of analytic focus before the analysis, and an emphasis on analysis at the level of individual data items in turn, before moving to developing an overall thematic patterning.[23] The method typically involves the use of *ground theory* techniques, sometimes in combination with techniques from TA, to develop themes from data (the purpose of TA) – rather than the categories and concepts associated with grounded theory analysis (see Birks & Mills, 2015; Charmaz, 2014). Thematic coding is definitely not intended to develop a grounded theory, but grounded theory techniques like line by line coding, constant comparison, and memo writing feature in various accounts of thematic coding. Its use thus evokes the use of 'grounded theory' techniques to *do TA* that we have critiqued elsewhere (Braun & Clarke, 2006, 2013).

Does it matter that researchers use techniques and concepts from grounded theory to produce something akin to TA, especially *now*, when there is a well-developed range of methods for TA? We think it does, but it is important to interrogate such reactions. We should ask: is suggesting people 'should use TA to do TA' actually methodolatry (Chamberlain, 2000), a preoccupation with the purity of method, or proceduralism, "where analysts focus on meticulously following set procedures rather than responding creatively and imaginatively to data" (N. King & Brooks, 2018, p. 231)? We don't *think* it is, because we concur with such critiques. Promoting rigid rules for good practice, insisting on 'one true way' of applying a method, thereby avoiding thinking, theory and taking reflexivity seriously, can lead to qualitative research that is rather limited: often merely descriptive/summative; with little or no interpretation of the data; implicitly peppered with postpositivism; and lacking depth of engagement, thoughtfulness and creativity. As this book evidences, we advocate for creativity, and thoughtful reflexive practice in qualitative research (Braun, Clarke, & Hayfield, 2019). But we also advocate for *clarity*, and for knowing *why* you're doing what you do. With thematic coding, we have concern when the use of grounded theory to do 'TA' does not evidence a knowingness, and when there isn't a clear and strong rationalisation for why these (grounded theory) procedures are used to generate themes rather than the categories and concepts associated with a grounded theory. Productive debate about method requires that researchers use techniques knowingly and are able to clearly articulate the assumptions underpinning them (Braun & Clarke, 2021c). We've not *yet* been convinced of the value of thematic coding and what it offers that is *distinct* from TA.

---

[23]This sequential focus on individual data items and then overall patterning echoes the analytic process in interpretative phenomenological analysis (J. A. Smith et al., 2009).

TA developed specifically for use with visual data (Boxes 8.3 and 8.4). There are also a number of – mostly idiosyncratic – approaches that defy easy categorisation in our typology, because they combine elements of the different types, often problematically. Some of these approaches are positioned as refinements of TA. These include, among *many* others, *systematic text condensation* (Malterud, 2012), *saliency analysis* (Buetow, 2010), and a *hybrid approach* to TA (Swain, 2018). The usefulness of a seemingly endless proliferation of different approaches to TA, especially if developed without reference to existing and established approaches, is debatable. If methodologists locate their development in relation to the existing approaches and explain what their approach offers that is new and distinctive, then such methods can be assessed for additional or new value; but often, these approaches fail to do that. If you use any of the more idiosyncratic approaches, it is important to understand where they fit in the terrain of TA, what assumptions they make, and what they consequently offer and constrain.

Whereas we feel thematic coding orientates backwards, to how TA used to be conducted, the visual approaches to TA we highlight orientate *forwards*, to an 'emerging' area – the use of TA on *visual*, rather than textual, data. As this is a new area, there is no definitive guide for doing reflexive TA on visual data. We provide a brief synopsis of British social psychologist Kate Gleeson's (2011) early and thoughtful work in visual TA (see Box 8.3), and a commentary and methodological discussion from Scottish psychologist Matt Sillars, who is exploring using TA for analysing photographs (in Box 8.4).

The use of TA for qualitative evidence synthesis

We first learnt that reflexive TA was being used for qualitative evidence synthesis when people sought advice in workshops and over email on doing qualitative synthesis. Although we don't have the expertise to advise on using TA for that purpose, our curiosity *was* piqued. We started to explore qualitative evidence synthesis (Paterson, 2012), and particularly **thematic synthesis**, which draws on TA, and briefly describe them here. Thematic synthesis is the process of integrating the results of multiple qualitative studies (J. Thomas & Harden, 2008). Broadly speaking, it is part of the **systematic review** tradition (a type of literature review following a specific protocol and methodology; see Boland, Cherry, & Dickson, 2017; Higgins & Green, 2011). The synthesis involves the amalgamation of qualitative research reports ('primary research reports') that relate to a specific topic, by identifying the key concepts that underpin several studies in a particular area of research. Some argue that what distinguishes qualitative evidence synthesis from the more traditional *narrative* literature reviews is that the synthesis 'goes beyond' the content of the original studies to make "a new whole out of the parts" (Cruzes & Dybå, 2011). It does so by providing new concepts, theories or higher-level interpretations. A distinction is often made between thematic synthesis and TA – the latter involves the identification of important or common themes in a body of research and summarising these under thematic headings (e.g. Garcia et al., 2002).

Like TA as a primary research method, TA as a tool for qualitative evidence synthesis can be 'inductive', grounded in themes identified in the literature, or deductive, evaluating particular themes through an investigation of the literature (Dixon-Woods, Agarwal, Jones, Young, & Sutton, 2005). Both TA and thematic synthesis are examples of a more aggregative

======= **Box 8.3** =======

Polytextual TA for visual data analysis

Kate Gleeson (2011, 2021) developed what she called *polytextual thematic analysis* for analysing visual data, drawing on Hayes' (1997, 2000) reflexive approach to TA. Her approach was firmly Big Q and aimed to capture recurring patterns in the form and content of visual images. The process she outlined centred on "viewing the pictures repeatedly while reading and considering various cultural images and texts that enable their interpretation" (2011, p. 319). Gleeson's process involved 11 steps:

1. Viewing the images repeatedly and noting potential (proto-)themes and the features of the image that evoke the themes;
2. Reflecting on the effects the images have on you and describing these in your notes;
3. For all recurrent proto-themes, compiling the relevant images and reflecting on whether the theme is distinct;
4. Writing a brief definition of the proto-theme;
5. Identifying all instances of the proto-theme across the data items;
6. Once again, compiling relevant material for each proto-theme, revising the definition of the theme if necessary and considering elevating the proto-theme to a theme (NB: this means it has been repeatedly checked and considered; it does not mean it is fixed and finalised), compiling your notes on the elements of the various images that best illustrate each theme;
7. Continuing to identify themes until no further distinctive themes are developed;
8. Reviewing the theme definitions and considering their distinctiveness, redefining themes if necessary to highlight the distinctiveness of each theme;
9. Exploring whether the themes cluster together to form higher order themes;
10. Defining the higher order themes and considering all themes in relation to them;
11. Finalising the themes that best address the research question and will constitute the basis of the write-up.

Gleeson argued that this approach allowed for the comparison of different sets of images. She illustrated her approach by comparing two different calendars featuring images of people with Down's Syndrome.

Conceptually and methodologically, Gleeson's approach seems very similar to reflexive TA, as it encompasses: data familiarisation; different *levels* of analytic engagement (themes and higher order themes – we think these broadly map on to codes and themes in our approach); clustering lower order analytic units into higher order analytic units; writing theme definitions; processes of review (in relation to the coded data); and reflection on the relationship between themes, and the distinctiveness of each theme.

(and [critical] realist) approach to qualitative evidence synthesis, one that involves combining the results of primary research into themes to produce a general description of the relevant phenomena; the results are treated in insolation from their contexts. Thematic synthesis can also lean towards the more interpretative (even constructionist) approaches to qualitative evidence synthesis, that produce a new model or theory, and that consider the contexts of the primary research (Dixon-Woods et al., 2006; Paterson, 2012).

Researcher Reflection – Box 8.4

How I use TA on visual data, by Matt Sillars

'Visual methods' is a catch-all term for a wide range of approaches that all use the 'visual' as data, to elicit data, to interpret a social phenomenon or to capture an experience (Banks & Zeitlyn, 2015). Visual methods have a long history in the social sciences, especially within anthropology and sociology (Prosser, 1998). Interrogating the visual has often been thought problematic by those focused on word-orientated methods, such as interviews, but increasingly it is finding a valued place in the social and health sciences (e.g. Glaw, Inder, Kable, & Hazelton, 2017; Harper, 2012; Reavey, 2012; Rose, 2014). I am interested in exploring the way towns and cities are complex social environments, with discourses of power and inequality potentially evidenced by the street furniture, architecture, road layouts and so on. My analysis of a photograph of Inverness Castle and town centre (see Figure 8.2) illustrates the value of TA for analysing visual data.

My analytic approach is guided by semiotics, which offers the researcher a way of deconstructing images and breaking them down into sets of ideas (for an accessible introduction, see Thwaites, Davis, & Mules, 2002). The basic unit of semiotics is the 'sign', which can be anything that communicates meaning. A simple example would be that in the UK, the 'dress' codes for girl/boy stereotypes communicate an (assumed) gender of a child very quickly to an observer through symbols. Skirts, trousers, shoes, hairstyles and so on are symbols/signs which are combined in larger sign systems, forming paradigms that we interpret very effectively. As communication requires that the people involved all have common ground in order to understand each other, it is, by its nature, a reflexive process, where meaning is constructed through a social process, rather than being a fixed property (Chandler, 2017).

Figure 8.2   Image of Inverness Castle with white grid lines overlay (photo by Matt Sillars)

My visual TA process: I would normally work with a set of images, in the same way an interviewer would be working across a set of transcripts, but I describe my process here with reference to a single image of Inverness Castle in Scotland, the sort of image you may find on a postcard (see Figure 8.2). Research images can be 'found' in print, in participants' photo collections or taken by the researcher themselves. Treating the image as I would a transcript, I can begin to apply the key stages of reflexive TA, especially phases one and two – familiarisation and generating codes.

Familiarisation: I place the image in the centre of a large piece of paper – leaving lots of margin space for making notes, in the same way that a transcript may be annotated. I begin to work around it in detail, paying close attention to the sides and corners; details here are often missed as the centre of an image is seductive and can 'trap' the eye. To help me look carefully, I often use a grid overlay and work cell by cell across the image (see Figure 8.2). As I work, I compile, in the wide margin, a comprehensive list of features I have observed (see Figure 8.3). In this way I am not in danger of being selective and missing out any details, however small. For example, note the house on the far right of the image, almost out of frame.

Generating codes: Connecting the margin notes to the relevant parts of the image with clearly drawn lines is important (see Figure 8.3). This echoes the process of basic initial 'coding' of a transcript through the use of highlighter pens if working in hard copy, and ensures that the relevant information is made clear and is preserved, as it will be referred to at the reporting stage. Even the most obvious features, such as the water and the sky, are listed. It is very easy to

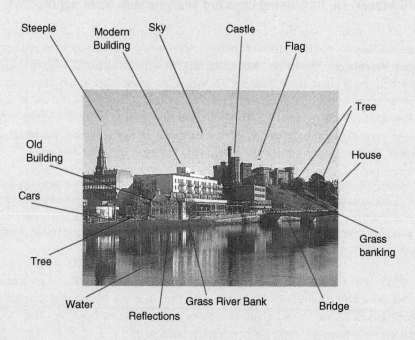

Figure 8.3   Initial analysis of photograph (grid lines omitted for clarity)

(Continued)

overlook the more obvious elements – often I don't see the wood for the trees! It is also possible to use software packages, such as NVivo, that cope well with images, and allow sections of a photograph to be isolated and coded using key words or phrases.

Theme development and review: These phases function in a similar way to analysing textual data, clustering together codes to produce initial themes, and revising and developing these to more effectively describe the social processes I am trying to make sense of. Here, basic (early, descriptive) themes may become developed and refined through review and reflection. In my analysis of Inverness Castle, the key paradigms of commerce, tourism, heritage, transport are obvious on the surface, but the signs also combine to inform me about the changing nature of towns and cities. The standard 'paradigm' of the city, focused on a central business district, less concerned with people than profit, is challenged here by the way that the river and the green spaces operate. The commercial buildings exist, but they are mediated by other elements. Thus, tensions may be explored thematically as the analysis develops.

Reflection: Visual TA allows the researcher to develop different ways of thinking about the social world and our experience of it. We can build thematic models that may illuminate concepts that are not as clearly evidenced in other approaches. On its own, or as part of a qualitative approach using multiple methods, the visual has a key role to play in social research.

'Off-label' TA: Combining thematic analysis with other approaches

Finally, we also briefly note the increasingly common 'mashing-up' of TA with other analytic approaches, to produce distinct 'hybrid' approaches.[24] In addition to engaging in 'academic **bricolage**' (Kincheloe, 2001) blending TA with elements of discourse analysis (see Box 8.5), researchers are combining TA with a range of other approaches, including idiographic approaches such as **narrative analysis** (e.g. Palomäki, Laakasuo, & Salmela, 2013; Ronkainen, Watkins, & Ryba, 2016) and case study research (e.g. Cedervall & Åberg, 2010; Gadberry, 2014; Manago, 2013). We are excited by (reflexive, aware, knowing) usages of reflexive TA in ways that we did not imagine or anticipate! In qualitative research:

> methodological elements can be combined and novel approaches can be taken in order to advance and improve existing methodological approaches. We do not dissuade such hybridisation. Rather, we argue that it needs to occur knowingly and purposefully and be rooted in a sound understanding and reporting of the compatibility of different philosophical underpinnings and practical applications. (Bradbury-Jones et al., 2017, p. 11)

For us, what's important is that such '**mash-ups**' and methodological mixes represent intentional, reflexive choices on the part of the researcher, not the unknowing combining of different types of TA, or TA and grounded theory procedures (see Braun & Clarke, 2021c). Theoretically-unknowing blending is problematic because it:

---

[24]An approach that also captures the concept of 'mixing' different approaches – but in somewhat a different way from what we mean here by mash-ups of TA and other methods – is methodological pluralism (e.g. Frost & Nolas, 2011; Shaw & Frost, 2015). In such qualitative studies, a number of different analytic approaches are used to analyse the same dataset – what is valued in methodological pluralism is the different 'takes' different approaches provide.

can compromise the application of methodological rigor to data analysis and challenge the validity of qualitative research findings. The uncritical blending of methods threatens to result in a product that Morse (1991) describes as a "sloppy mishmash" rather than good science. (DeSantis & Ugarriza, 2000, p. 351)

So perhaps the take-home message is a question and an answer: (Q) can I 'break the rules' and do things differently with TA? (A) yes, but if you do, make sure you do so knowingly. This *is* an adventure, but you need a solid (theoretical) foundation for knowing which 'rules' can be

> **ALERT** If you feel there is need to 'break the rules' with TA, make sure you know why you're doing it, and provide a justification for your novel use of TA.

broken, and which are important to retain. Innovation for innovation's sake isn't the point. A robust process that will generate important and rich(er) understandings is the point.

▰▰▰▰▰ Researcher Reflection – Box 8.5 ▰▰▰▰▰

Combining TA and discourse analysis, by Gareth Terry

The construction of themes to tell a story about a qualitative dataset gels nicely with my love of patterns and synthesis. Reflexive TA offers huge potential for richness of analysis, describing similarities and differences across a dataset (Terry, 2016, 2021; Terry & Braun, 2011a, 2011b). Sometimes, though, some feature, or the complexities of an extract or theme, stand out and demand a different type of engagement – for instance, looking at the patterned ways language is used by individuals to accomplish particular ends (an 'action orientation'; Potter & Edwards, 1999). One way to attend to these features is to combine reflexive TA with insights from other approaches, which provide tools and techniques for interrogating more fine-grained details of language and discourse. I have used reflexive TA in combination with insights from critical discursive psychology (e.g. Terry & Braun, 2009, 2013b, 2016), or applied a poststructuralist lens to data (e.g. Terry & Braun, 2012), and labelled this hybrid approach as 'critical thematic analysis' in my writing.

Sometimes I will simply follow the standard phases of reflexive TA, and then enter into a second level of analysis – informed by a discursive approach – with extracts I want to treat analytically (as discussed in Chapter Five). At other times, the inclusion of other approaches occurs simultaneously with the phases of reflexive TA. Becoming thoroughly immersed in the data and generating lots of rich latent codes will often lead to insights about a particular extract or set of extracts. At times, fitting with a poststructuralist DA approach (e.g. Gavey, 1989), the themes I construct will show some evidence of discourses that shape and produce people's accounts. In which case, I will attempt to map out the implications of this shaping, and the types of positions made available (e.g. childfree people are 'selfish'; Terry & Braun, 2012). At other times, I will examine the sense-making tools that people use, drawing on the 'canon' of texts associated with discursive psychology to help understand the patterns in rhetoric and talk more generally (e.g. Terry & Braun, 2016). There are also times when I do both (e.g. Terry & Braun, 2013b). For me, what differentiates a *critical* TA from a wholesale shift into poststructuralist discourse analysis or critical discursive psychology is that the primary attention of the analysis is still towards the construction, interpretation and reporting of themes. This means that you get to tell a rich story about a given dataset, as well as identifying and drawing out specific discursive features of interest.

CHAPTER SUMMARY

All methods and approaches have limits, things they cannot do, purposes they cannot fulfil, and the same is true of TA, both generally, and in relation to specific iterations. In this chapter, we've provided a description of the field of TA *as we understand it, at this time*. We started with a short contextualising history of the use of the term and the likely origins of the method. We then outlined some the key domains where different forms of TA often vary in a systematic way: (1) the role coding plays within the analytic process, and the very idea of what a 'code' represents; (2) the conceptualisation of a theme – as a pattern of shared meaning unified by a central idea, or a 'topic summary'; (3) the extent to which researcher subjectivity is recognised and valued or managed-as-a-risk; and (4) the process for analysis, including around whether themes are analytic 'inputs' or 'outputs'. We then described three main TA siblings, clusters of approaches to TA which are located in different places on a spectrum of TA: *reflexive TA* approaches offer a fully Big Q approach; *coding reliability* approaches are firmly small q; and somewhere between these, *codebook* TA approaches have something of each – and can be understood as MEDIUM Q. Despite a shared framing of TA as method, not methodology, these positionings inherently delimit the method in certain ways. We finished the chapter by exploring additional (idiosyncratic) variations or applications of TA that don't fit tidily within our tripartite clustering, including 'thematic coding', the application of TA to visual data, systematic evidence synthesis, and methodological mash-ups. Some of the questions and critiques we raised around different approaches to TA are conceptual, related to Big Q qualitative values; some reflect poor enactments of a method. Reflexive TA is no exception, but, to us, remains the only form of TA *fully* compatible with a Big Q orientation.

WANT TO LEARN MORE ABOUT...?

For an explainer on **our tripartite typology** of different approaches to TA, have a watch of (or listen to) 'What is Thematic Analysis?' on Victoria's YouTube channel: https://youtu.be/4voVhTiVydc.

For a commentary on how our understanding around **reflexive TA** has shifted and changed, and **what we'd revise from our 2006 paper**, see: Braun, V., & Clarke, V. (2019). Reflecting on reflexive thematic analysis. *Qualitative Research in Sport, Exercise and Health, 11*(4), 589–597.

As a starting point for reading more around **template analysis**, Nigel King's website offers a quick entry point to the method: https://research.hud.ac.uk/research-subjects/human-health/template-analysis/

For a more detailed discussion of **template analysis**, see: King, N., & Brooks, J. M. (2016). *Template analysis for business and management students*. London: SAGE.

For guidelines for **framework analysis**, see: Ritchie, J., & Lewis, J. (2003). *Qualitative research practice: A guide for social science students and researchers*. London: SAGE.

For a discussion around **framework analysis** related specifically to health research, see: Smith, J., & Firth, J. (2011). Qualitative data analysis: The framework approach. *Nurse Researcher, 18*(2), 52–62.

If you want to find out more about **coding reliability forms of TA**, see: Boyatzis, R. E. (1998). *Transforming qualitative information: Thematic analysis and code development.* Thousand Oaks, CA: SAGE.

For an **applied orientation to coding reliability TA**, see: Guest, G., MacQueen, K. M., & Namey, E. E. (2012). *Applied thematic analysis.* Thousand Oaks, CA: SAGE.

As a starting point to explore **using TA with visual data**, we recommend: Gleeson, K. (2021). Polytextual thematic analysis for visual data: Analysing visual images. In P. Reavey (Ed.), *A handbook of visual methods in psychology: Using and interpreting images in qualitative research* (pp. 536–554). London: Routledge.

ACTIVITIES FOR STUDENT READERS

Critical evaluation of TA in published research: Find a paper that reports on data analysis with TA. Feel free to choose your own, or select one of these two (available on the companion website):

For beginners to critically evaluating published TA, we suggest: Buchanan, K., & Sheffield, J. (2017). Why do diets fail? An exploration of dieters' experiences using thematic analysis. *Journal of Health Psychology, 22*(7), 906–915.

For a more challenging evaluation activity, we suggest: Matthews, E. J., & Desjardins, M. (2017). Remaking our identities: Couples' experiences of voluntary childlessness. *The Family Journal, 25*(1), 31–39.

Determine whether a *particular* form of TA (coding reliability, codebook or reflexive) is used and cited, or not. Or is there evidence of some 'mash-up' of different approaches to TA? If a mash-up, is this explicitly acknowledged and discussed? Next, identify *how* the authors conceptualised codes/coding and themes, based both on what they said about them (if anything), and what they actually *did* in the analysis. Identify how they handled the question of researcher subjectivity. Having critically evaluated the method of the paper – how it was conceptualised and used and reported – decide whether you think this offers an example of Big Q, MEDIUM Q or small q (or, indeed confused q) qualitative research. Explain why you think that is.

If you're teaching content related to this chapter…
Don't forget to check the companion website for a range of teaching resources:
https://study.sagepub.com/thematicanalysis

9

GETTING YOUR OWN HOUSE IN ORDER

UNDERSTANDING WHAT MAKES GOOD REFLEXIVE THEMATIC ANALYSIS TO ENSURE QUALITY

Chapter Nine overview

- **They did *what?* Common problems we encounter in TA work!**   260
  - o   Premature closure of the analysis   266
- **Strategies for ensuring quality in *your* TA research**   268
  - o   Reflexive journaling   270
  - o   Talking about your data and analysis with others   271
  - o   Allowing time for your analytic insights to fully develop   272
  - o   Working with an experienced supervisor, mentor or co-researcher   273
  - o   Making sure themes are themes, and naming them carefully   274
  - o   Drawing inspiration from excellent examples of published research   274
  - o   Demonstrating quality through an electronic or paper trail   275
- **Managing quality *during* the publication process**   275
- **Are *generic* qualitative quality criteria and strategies useful in TA research?**   277

Within social justice and activist movements, the idea of 'getting your own house in order' has been used to evoke *personal* responsibility for dealing with your own, or your community's, understanding and action, among those with privileged identities – for instance, White individuals and communities (Howard, 2020), rather than, as is more common, asking those marginalised or minoritised to do the work for you. In this chapter title, we evoke it to highlight that it's 'on us' to ensure we do *quality reflexive TA*.[1]

So, how do you know if your reflexive TA is any good? This question is one we are familiar with because we hear it a lot, especially from people who are new to TA. It's one that can cause considerable stress and anxiety. It partly connects to the absence of a rigid *formula* for doing reflexive TA – as we discussed in Section One, the process is reflexive and questioning, and far from rigid. Likewise, how you do TA varies, connected both to the plethora of different types of TA (discussed in Chapter Eight), and a wide range of different conceptual bases for analytic practice (discussed in Chapter Six). To make matters even more confusing, there is an increasingly wide *variety* of evaluative tools for qualitative research, and it's not unusual for people to make declarative statements about 'what quality is' (sometimes sensibly, sometimes problematically, sometimes in contradiction of each other). This messy context can make it *hard* to feel that you have a grasp of what you're supposed to be doing, and what counts as good – or good enough. This chapter is here to help!

The key to quality in TA is: (a) understanding *good* practice, and (b) understanding *problems*, or poor practice, so that you can recognise and avoid them (through a). This chapter synthesises material from the rest of the book, to help you to understand what good and poor TA practice looks like, discuss what sorts of evaluative criteria *can* be useful, and give you resources and suggestions to facilitate good practice on your part. The resources we provide here will also help you to evaluate the quality of TA research more generally – whether that's for a university assignment centred on critiquing an example of TA research (if you're a student), or for marking and examining assignments, dissertations and theses (if you're an academic). The companion website has an additional chapter for academics, 'Teaching, supervising, and examining for quality TA', which provides tips for teaching, supervising and assessing for quality TA.

THEY DID *WHAT?* COMMON PROBLEMS WE ENCOUNTER IN TA WORK

What is bad practice and consequent good practice in reflexive or indeed any TA? If you've read the book sequentially, we hope you have a *pretty good idea* by now, since we've covered this throughout. But, unfortunately, there is *quite a lot* of TA research that evidences what we regard as problematic practices (Braun & Clarke, 2021c). Therefore, being as clear as possible about poor – and, just as importantly, good – practice and outputs is essential. Some problems reflect poor analytic practice; some result from unreflexive mash-ups of elements from different types of TA (on the latter point, see Chapter Eight).

When critically evaluating TA, it's important to recognise the particular characteristics of the type of TA being claimed and used. We begin our consideration of quality by overviewing the strengths (or opportunities) and limitations (or challenges) of *reflexive* TA (see Table 9.1; developed and extended from Braun & Clarke, 2006).

---

[1]In doing so, we acknowledge that quality isn't entirely under your own control – that others, such as reviewers and editors (and teachers, supervisors and examiners) are key players in facilitating or diminishing quality TA. We acknowledge this, and the challenges that can ensue, by including a section on 'Managing quality during the publication process'.

Table 9.1 Strengths and limitations of reflexive TA

Strengths or opportunities

Flexible with regard to theory, research question, data collection method, dataset size and generation strategy, and analytic orientation (inductive-deductive, semantic-latent, experiential-critical) and purpose (descriptive-interpretative, in-depth examination of selected data domains versus rich description or interrogation of meaning across entire dataset). This means it has potential for wide ranging application.

Status as a *method*, rather than a theoretically informed and delimited 'off-the-shelf' methodology. This means researchers must actively engage with questions of underlying theory and philosophy; knowing and reflexive use of TA is crucial for quality.

An accessible 'starter method' for those new to qualitative research.

Can highlight similarities and differences across the dataset.

Can generate unanticipated insights.

Allows for social as well as psychological interpretations of data.

Useful for experienced qualitative researchers seeking to produce complex, nuanced, sophisticated and conceptual analyses.

When used within an *experiential* framework, results are accessible to an educated general public.

Easy to incorporate into ethnographic and participatory designs; theoretical flexibility avoids theoretical tensions and contradictions.

Flexibility and accessibility make it a useful method for **community research** designs, where participants are co-researchers and contribute to data analysis; also useful for designs where participants are invited to reflect on the resulting analyses or these are returned to participants.

Can be used to produce analyses with actionable outcomes and that can inform policy development.

Limitations or challenges

Flexibility and wide range of potential applications can lead to 'analytic paralysis', especially for those new to qualitative research.

The researcher *must* engage with theory before data analysis or risk theoretical assumptions and concepts being unknowingly and unreflexively imported into the analysis.

Flexibility with regard to theory and analytic orientation and purpose means it is difficult to formulate precise guidance for higher-level (more interpretative) analysis. As with many other qualitative approaches, doing TA involves 'craft skills' that are difficult to distil into recipe-like guidance.

Limited interpretative power if not used in combination with a particular theory or concepts.

Cross-case orientation means the complexities and contradictions in the accounts of individual participants can be difficult to retain/capture in the analysis (especially in research with larger samples).[2]

Can't be used for a fine-grained analysis of **language practice** (see also N. King & Brooks, 2018).

As a fun way of signalling some of these, we created a reflexive TA bingo card for you to use at TA presentations or when reading reports of a TA (see Figure 9.1). Bingo has become a trope for spotting 'bad practice' in numerous contexts, including corporate presentations and meetings ('... bullshit bingo'; conference bingo). Although our Reflexive TA Bingo card is silly, and some of the squares (e.g. pronunciation of Braun) are *not* indicators of quality practice (!!), the card is intended as a tool for evaluative thinking when engaging with reports of TA – and specifically *reflexive* TA. Do take it to conferences – virtual or in person ones; you can download a PDF from the companion website – though maybe don't declare 'bingo' if you do check all the boxes!

---

[2]The loss of contradiction and complexity in individual accounts through focusing on patterns *across* the dataset has been dubbed the "fragmentation of accounts" by King and Brooks (2018, p. 232), this may or may not be an issue depending on your research question and focus. It can potentially be addressed by presenting selected case studies for presentation in your report, or combining TA with other forms of analysis (such as narrative analysis) as we touched on in '"Off-label" TA' in Chapter Eight).

Reflexive Thematic Analysis
B I N G O

Mentions inter-coder reliability	Implicitly (post)positivist TA (not acknowledged)	More than 3 levels of themes	Mention of a lack of (statistical) generalisability	Messy mix of realism and constructionism
Unacknowledged social cognitions (e.g. attitudes or body image)	Themes are thin – just a single idea (a code)	Themes do not have a central organising concept	"Themes emerged"	Data collection stopped at "saturation"
Use of passive voice	No reflexivity	**Thematic Analysis**	Only Braun & Clarke 2006 cited	Mention of "bias"
Clarke spelled as Clark (no e)	More than 6 themes	No theory of language – treated as window to truth	Themes are topic summaries	Very few participants quoted/over-quoting of one or more
Implicitly realist TA (not acknowledged)	Braun pronounced BRAWN (not Brown)	Mismatch between extracts and analytic claims	Use of a codebook	Data are just paraphrased without interpretation

Figure 9.1 Reflexive TA bingo (spot the problems, win the prize![3])

We provide a more serious summary of common problems we encounter in TA research (Braun & Clarke, 2021c; see also Connelly & Peltzer, 2016; DeSantis & Ugarriza, 2000) in Table 9.2, and also list concomitant good practice.[4] We have organised these into

---

[3]There is no prize other than satisfaction in knowing that you are able to spot bad practice in TA!

[4]Table 9.2 is designed as a useful easy reference guide for key things to look for in evaluating TA for assignments, or for marking/examining assignments or dissertations and theses (further resources for the latter can be found in the online only chapter, 'Teaching, supervising, and examining for quality TA', on the companion website).

weaknesses in the analysis and interpretation of data, that is, weaknesses in the *application* of TA; conceptual confusion both about TA and about qualitative research more broadly; and an unknowing and unreflexive engagement with TA.[5] Although our primary focus is reflexive TA practice, many of these issues are not limited *just* to (claimed) reflexive TA outputs – and so the table has use in TA evaluation more generally. We also want to note a *word of caution* related to critically evaluating others' research. It's easy to be judgemental of others; harder to hear judgement of ourselves. Keep the notion of kindness and generosity in mind as you evaluate. Not everyone is the deeply informed TA practitioner that you are becoming!

PRACTICE POINT Be kind and generous when critically evaluating others' research.

Table 9.2 Common problems and good practice in (reflexive) TA research

Problems in TA	Good practice
Analysis not fit for purpose	
Analysis fails to address, or only partially addresses, the stated research question (e.g. the focus of the analysis has shifted from the original intent but the research questions or aims have not been revised to reflect this).	Research question revisited in light of the developed analysis. The analysis clearly and fully addresses the research question.
The analysis does not cohere with the claimed theoretical and philosophical assumptions; there is a disconnect between the claimed assumptions and the enactment and reporting of the analysis.	The research exhibits good conceptual 'fit' and 'methodological integrity' (Levitt et al., 2017). The TA approach coheres with the theoretical assumptions of the study. The analysis as reported matches the theoretical positions declared.
The theoretical assumptions guiding the analysis are not explicated; the analysis is treated as atheoretical. Theoretical assumptions and concepts are imported unacknowledged and unknowingly into the analysis.	The researcher clearly explicates the philosophical and theoretical assumptions underpinning their use of TA, and the analysis enacts and reflects these. The use of TA is theoretically knowing and reflexive.
Weak or underdeveloped themes (evidence of premature analytic closure)	
Use of data collection questions as 'themes'; simply summarising what participants said in relation to each question (topic summaries as 'themes').	Themes are not limited to data collection questions and evidence thoughtful, reflective analytic work that develops and interprets patterns – sometimes beyond semantic content.
Use of topic summaries as themes.	Themes cohere around a *shared* central organising concept. An individual theme does *not* report 'diverse' meaning in relation to a topic, unless contradiction is the focus of the theme or diverse meaning at a semantic level is underpinned by a unifying latent concept.

(Continued)

---

[5]As we noted in the 'Design interlude', having 'good enough' data is also an important starting point for quality TA.

Table 9.2 (Continued)

Problems in TA	Good practice
Only *summarising* what participants said; little or no analytic (interpretative) work undertaken beyond summarising the data content.	Analysis goes *beyond* data summary (data 'reduction') to *interpret*, and to explain the significance of the data, in relation to the research question.
Themes are poorly named (e.g. one-word theme names). The theme names convey little information about the essence or central concept of the theme.	The theme name (usually a brief phrase) captures something of the theme essence or central concept, orienting the reader to what is to follow. Data quotations might be used for (some) theme names, perhaps slightly paraphrased and with an explanatory sub-title.
Using existing disciplinary concepts as theme names. Data are simply summarised within an *existing* concept or framework (this is *particularly* problematic in analyses described as inductive).	Existing theoretical concepts are employed knowingly and reflexively, as tools to enrich the analysis, not as delimiting boundaries for it. What the analysis contributes to the existing literature, how it extends and develops this, are clearly articulated.
Too *many* themes: Themes are thin and scrappy, containing few or even only one analytic observation; confusion between codes (single facet) and themes (multiple facets). Discussion of themes lacks depth and detail.	The number of themes is appropriate and each theme is presented in depth and detail; the boundaries between themes are clear. Six or fewer themes reported in an 8,000-word report. Themes are coherent and focused and capture *significant* patterns of meaning.
Too *few* themes: Themes are long and overly complex; lack coherence, focus and boundaries.	Although themes are unified by a central concept, they are not limited to one analytic observation (single facet) but capture a cluster of related observations (multiple facets).
Analysis is overly *fragmented* – many different levels of themes reported.	There is a *maximum* of three theme levels – overarching themes, themes and subthemes – and judicious use of the latter to highlight a facet of the central concept.
Analysis is thin – themes are underdeveloped.	Analysis is thick and tells a rich interpretative story that goes beyond simple description.
Too much overlap *between* themes.	Each theme is distinct, but the themes work *together* to tell an overall story about the data in relation to the research question.
Too little relationship between themes. Themes appear completely unrelated; themes do not tell an 'overall story'.	The relationship between the themes is clearly evident or explained.
Themes are not internally consistent or coherent, appearing to lack a central underpinning concept.	The purpose or focus of each theme is clear. Themes are underpinned by a central organising concept.
Weaknesses of interpretation (in presented analysis)	
Data are interpreted in a contextual vacuum; failure to situate data within relevant (social, political, policy, etc.) contexts.	The data are contextualised and located within relevant contexts, including, where appropriate, the wider social context.
Themes consist of headings, one or two sentences of framing analytic narrative and a long string of data extracts. Analytic narrative is largely absent or underdeveloped.	Themes consist of a fully developed and rich analytic narrative, with data extracts embedded. The analytic narrative is (ideally) thoughtful, insightful, compelling, nuanced and multi-faceted.

Problems in TA	Good practice
Analysis evidences 'arguing with the data' or 'taking sides' – disagreeing with some participants by citing evidence to show their beliefs are mistaken; being overtly judgemental or critical of *participants'* perspectives in experiential TA.	The researcher's orientation to the data is that of curiosity and making sense of meanings, rather than judgement. The researcher explains what is interesting or important about the data, in relation to the research question and the relevant contexts.
Paraphrasing rather than interpreting data. The analytic narrative simply repeats what the participant said in slightly different words.	The analytic narrative explains the relevance of data content.
No analysis is done. The data are left to 'speak for themselves', sometimes framed as the researcher not intervening in participants' accounts. The researcher assumes the meaning and significance of the data are obvious.	The researcher *explains* to the reader what meaning they make of the data, and the relevance and significance of this.
Relationship between data and analytic narrative	
Connection between data extracts and analytic claims unclear or absent. Data extracts do not convincingly or compellingly illustrate what is claimed.	Good 'fit' between data extracts and analytic claims. The selected extracts are vivid and compelling.
Too many or too few data extracts used. At the extremes, no data extracts to illustrate analytic claims/the theme consists of a sentence or two of analytic commentary, then a string of data extracts.	Good balance between data extracts and analytic narrative – the precise proportion depends on the type of analysis undertaken, but generally the analysis will consist of at least 50% analytic narrative.
Several data extracts are presented to illustrate *minor* analytic observations. One or no data extracts are presented to illustrate *major* analytic observations.	Major (complex) analytic claims are well illustrated with relevant data extracts. Minor analytic points are merely noted or illustrated with one extract or a few very short extracts.
Failure to consider other obvious interpretations of the data in a way that undermines the convincingness of the analysis.	If there are other (fairly obvious) interpretations of the data, these are considered. The researcher makes a case for why their interpretation is compelling, perhaps drawing on evidence from elsewhere in the dataset or existing literature.
Insufficient evidence of patterning of themes *across* the dataset. Evidence for themes undermined by over quoting a small number of data items and failing to quote extracts of data from *across* the dataset.	The researcher carefully selects data extracts from across the dataset, including a variety of participants/data items, to demonstrate patterning *across* the dataset. Multiple extracts from one (particularly articulate and expressive) participant or data item are balanced by extracts from across the other data items.

Having presented these commonly evidenced problems, we now discuss issues related to the *premature closure of analysis* in a bit more detail, as this is an area that people particularly struggle with. We follow this with a range of strategies you can use to facilitate good practice!

Premature closure of the analysis

Although we emphasised throughout Section One that there is no *final destination* with TA, and you make a decision about when your analysis is 'good enough', there are ways in which analysis might be foreclosed – effectively 'stopped too soon'. This is what the concept of premature closure of analysis captures: the researcher stops their data analysis at the level of superficial results (Connelly & Peltzer, 2016). In TA, this plays out in a number of ways. We discuss three here: the way themes are conceptualised; lack of interpretative engagement; and uncritical use of theoretical concepts.

> **ALERT** Premature closure of analysis happens when the researcher stops analysing their data when they have produced only superficial results, capturing the most obvious meanings in the data.

Confusing topics and themes: Connelly and Peltzer (2016) argued that premature closure is often related to a confusion between categories (or data *topics*) and themes (discussed in Chapters Four and Six). How do you know if you're doing this? Connelly and Peltzer suggested that a topic can usually be labelled with one word (e.g. stigma; gender), whereas a theme generally requires a longer and more nuanced label to capture its essence (see also Sandelowski & Leeman, 2012). Premature closure related to topic summary 'themes' can also happen when data collection questions (e.g. interview or qualitative survey questions) are used as 'themes', with each theme effectively consisting of summaries of participant responses to interview questions (e.g. Lorch et al., 2015). It might seem reasonable to know the diversity of views around a topic, and there might indeed be some use in this. But some have argued that "knowing the difference between a theme and a topic is foundational to the crafting of accessible research findings" (Sandelowski & Leeman, 2012, p. 1407), and actionable or usable research results in *applied* research (see also Connelly & Peltzer, 2016). We would add that it is also vital to high quality (reflexive) TA practice.

> **ALERT** Topic summaries are often the result of researchers treating their data collection questions as themes and summarising participant responses to each question.

Lack of interpretative engagement with the data: Superficial analyses can also reflect a lack of *interpretative* engagement with the data. If the explicit goal of analysis *is* to produce a surface reporting of what participants said, then that is one thing. Occasionally this *might* be the intentional analytic goal, especially when the data are more concrete. But more typically, this seems to reflect underdeveloped analysis. The data themselves are not analysis. Analysis for reflexive TA is the result of a (subjectivity-inflected) *interpretation of* data by the researcher. Reporting a large number of themes is also suggestive of premature closure and a superficial engagement with data. DeSantis and Ugarriza (2000) argued that reporting too many themes is equivalent to giving the reader unanalysed data; it precludes any meaningful interpretation of the analysis, and dilutes the unifying function of a theme. *Interpretative* engagement with data is key for high quality reflexive TA.

> **ALERT** Reporting a large number of themes, and subthemes, is a 'red flag' for premature closure.

Uncritically using existing theory and concepts: Premature closure can also occur when pre-existing (disciplinary) concepts and terminology – 'small' theory – are used to provide a structure or framework for the analysis.[6] Such concepts and terminology must be defined and used *knowingly* and *reflexively*; without this, the use of such concepts can result in a superficial analysis, one that risks simply recycling existing knowledge instead of developing new understandings related to the dataset and context of the research (Connelly & Peltzer, 2016). Such analyses might not be understood or positioned as 'deductive', but they effectively are that, if reading and interpreting the data is guided and constrained by (the unknowing use of) such concepts. One important question too rarely addressed is whether the researcher's engagement with the data was limited rather than expanded by their – explicitly acknowledged or not – favoured theory. This is an important question for all analysis; what we bring inevitably shapes the scope of our possible sense-making and our interpretative lens. At worst, the use of pre-existing theory results in an analysis that 'fits into' the theoretical framework. Theory merely provides a framework for presenting the data. To avoid analytic foreclosure, reflexive awareness and critical self-questioning around theory are essential. The paper and reflexive commentary by Melanie Beres and Panteá Farvid (2010) on the companion website provide a nice example of theory used to open up and enrich analytic engagement and interpretation (see also 'A deductive orientation' in Chapter Seven).

> **ALERT** There is a real risk that working deductively and using pre-existing (small) theory can result in an impoverished analysis – merely fitting the data into the existing theoretical framework. Reflexivity, and interrogating how you're engaging with the data and the theory in the analytic process are key to avoiding this problem.

> **PRACTICE POINT** Ask yourself: (how) are implicit ideas or theories – often these are disciplinary-embedded and even invisible ones – shaping and limiting my engagement with the data?

As discussed in Chapters Six and Eight, what's key in choosing – and using – an analytic approach is conceptual coherence and 'fit' (see Braun & Clarke, 2021b, and Design Interlude). Does this method, and this version of it, suit your purpose? We find Levitt et al.'s (2017) concept of *methodological integrity* useful for thinking about quality. Methodological integrity captures alignment and coherence in research design and procedures, research questions and theoretical assumptions, so that a research project

> **KEY CONCEPT** Methodological integrity characterises research in which theoretical assumptions, research questions, research design, and methods are all in conceptual alignment.

---

[6]In our discipline of psychology, for instance, concepts such as 'social support' and 'body image' are commonly used in TA research. These theoretically embedded concepts have a long history within the discipline. But have also acquired colloquial and common-sense meanings, and their meaning is rarely reflected on and discussed in the TA reports in which they are used. This unreflexive and unacknowledged use risks analytic foreclosure.

produces a trustworthy and useful outcome. Methodological integrity requires a *thoughtful, reflexively aware* researcher, something we have argued is vital for quality TA practice. As we discussed in 'Scene setting', our approach to TA is *not* like a baking recipe that must be followed *exactly* for the outcome to be successful. Doing good quality TA is far more about *sensibility* than strictly following procedure or technique. This is not to say that procedures are redundant; rather, following procedures 'to the letter' is no guarantee of quality.

STRATEGIES FOR ENSURING QUALITY IN *YOUR* THEMATIC ANALYSIS RESEARCH

How can you avoid the common problems we have detailed in this chapter? In our original paper on thematic analysis (Braun & Clarke, 2006), we developed a 15-point quality 'checklist' for TA (reproduced in many subsequent publications). We know this was popular as a quality measure – we repeatedly get requests to reprint it in theses and dissertations. Such checklists can be useful, but *only* if they are accompanied by thoughtful engagement and understanding. Without this, checklists *risk* evoking 'dos and don'ts' and 'right and wrong' ways to do TA – rules to be obeyed. The items on our checklist – which we've slightly *updated* in Table 9.3 – centre on ensuring a rigorous, systematic and *reflexive* analytic process.

KEY CONCEPT The concept of theoretical knowingness captures the practice of engaging with and deploying theory deliberatively and reflexively in our research.

Remembering that we conceptualise TA as an adventure, not a recipe (Willig, 2001), our recommendations for ensuring quality in reflexive TA centre on ways to foster depth of engagement, researcher reflexivity and **theoretical knowingness**.

For us, quality depends *not* on notions of consensus, accuracy or reliability, but on immersion, creativity, thoughtfulness and insight. It depends on moving beyond the obvious or superficial meanings in the data – unless your purpose is expressly and knowingly to focus on these. As "it takes much effort, time, and reflection to develop the craft of TA" (Trainor & Bundon, 2020, p. 20), we emphasise time as a key resource for reflexive TA research. British social psychologist Brendan Gough and New Zealand health psychologist Antonia Lyons referred to "the (slow) craft of doing high quality [qualitative] research" (2016, p. 239). We have similarly emphasised the importance of the "slow wheel of interpretation" to high quality qualitative research (Braun & Clarke, 2021d). For Gough and Lyons, "creative thinking, theorising, imagination, patience are all essential to high quality research and thus to the production of new and different knowledge" (2016, p. 239). We heartily agree! In this section, we discuss a series of strategies that can help you to maintain a curious and open stance, to keep your adventurous spirit alive, and encourage fresh perspectives on your data:

- Reflexive journaling;
- Allowing plenty of time for your analysis;
- Gaining insights from others (e.g. peers, supervisors, co-researchers);

- Naming themes carefully;
- Drawing inspiration from good published examples;
- Demonstrating quality through an 'audit trail'.

Table 9.3 Our 15-point checklist for good *reflexive* TA – version 2022

No.	Process	Criteria
1	Transcription	The data have been transcribed to an appropriate level of detail; all transcripts have been checked against the original recordings for 'accuracy'.
2	Coding and theme development	Each data item has been given thorough and repeated attention in the coding process.
3		The coding process has been thorough, inclusive and comprehensive; themes have not been developed from a few vivid examples (an anecdotal approach).
4		All relevant extracts for each theme have been collated.
5		Candidate themes have been checked against coded data and back to the original dataset.
6		Themes are internally coherent, consistent, and distinctive; each theme contains a well-defined central organising concept; any subthemes share the central organising concept of the theme.
7	Analysis and interpretation – in the written report	Data have been *analysed* – interpreted, made sense of – rather than just summarised, described or paraphrased.
8		Analysis and data match each other – the extracts evidence the analytic claims.
9		Analysis tells a convincing and well-organised story about the data and topic; analysis addresses the research question.
10		An appropriate balance between analytic narrative and data extracts is provided.
11	Overall	Enough time has been allocated to complete all phases of the analysis adequately, without rushing a phase, or giving it a once-over-lightly (including returning to earlier phases or redoing the analysis if need be).
12	Written report	The specific approach to thematic analysis, and the particulars of the approach, including theoretical positions and assumptions, are clearly explicated.
13		There is a good fit between what was claimed, and what was done – i.e. the described method and reported analysis are consistent.
14		The language and concepts used in the report are consistent with the ontological and epistemological positions of the analysis.
15		The researcher is positioned as *active* in the research process; themes do not just 'emerge'.

Reflexive journaling

> **ALERT** Don't just take our word for it! Reflexive journaling is widely recognised as a quality strategy for Big Q qualitative research.

Canadian nursing scholar Lorelli Nowell and colleagues describe a reflexive journal as a "self-critical account of the research process" (2017, p. 3), documenting the researcher's own thoughts about the developing analysis and their conversations about it with others. We initially discussed reflexive (or reflective) journaling in Chapter One, but come back to it here as an important technique for ensuring *quality* (see Connelly & Peltzer, 2016; Nowell et al., 2017). Reflexive journals invite and encourage an ongoing, embedded process of reflection about your research practices and assumptions *throughout* the research process (Nadin & Cassell, 2006), rather than a sporadic and compartmentalised engagement with reflexivity. Use the journaling process to reflect on how your assumptions and responses might delimit your engagement with the data, and to open-up new and alternative interpretative possibilities. In journaling for quality TA, we encourage you to reflect on the prior *knowledge* and *assumptions* you bring in to the research and how these might shape your interpretation of your data.[7] This is an important tool for avoiding 'positivism creep' – the inadvertent (re)appearance in Big Q TA of positivist assumptions (see Box 9.1, and Chapter Six), that those of us with a background in a positivist-dominated discipline are particularly vulnerable to. Try to get distance from how you are making sense of your data and reflect also on your *emotional* responses to the data (and to any participants) – go back to Box 2.2 in Chapter Two, for an example of this in practice. To function as a *reflexive* journal, it needs to be a space where you question and push yourself, rather than a space to simply record your thoughts (see Cunliffe, 2004, 2016).

========= **Box 9.1** =========

Check yourself! Avoiding 'positivism creep' by developing a qualitative sensibility

Something very common in both student and published TA research in many disciplines and research fields, particularly those in which (post)positivism dominates, is 'positivism creep'. By this we mean positivist assumptions slinking into the research, unacknowledged by the authors (Braun & Clarke, 2021c). We come back to reflexivity – and specifically reflexivity around the disciplinary values, assumptions and norms you are embedded within (Wilkinson, 1988) – as a vital tool here, ensuring you undertake (reflexive) TA in a knowing way. Similarly, developing a thorough-going qualitative *sensibility* is key to avoiding positivism creep. A qualitative sensibility (discussed in Chapter One) is a qualitative 'head-space' or orientation, a way of thinking about research underpinned by a deep-seated and almost 'intuitive' sense of the ethos of Big Q qualitative inquiry, which connects to bigger questions of ontology and epistemology (which we tackled in Chapter Six).

---

[7]Keeping a reflexive journal for TA is similar to a process called memo writing in grounded theory (see Birks & Mills, 2015), although reflective or reflexive journaling is a freer, much more open process.

Talking about your data and analysis with others

Talking with others about your data and/or your developing analysis can be useful for clarifying your analytic insights and deepening your engagement with your data (it can also be a tool for reflexivity; Nadin & Cassell, 2006). For us, engagement with others always *adds something* to our analysis – even if it's only validation that we're noticing something useful. More typically, the questions that others have, or their different 'takes', can help us to deepen our interpretation. Alongside formal mentorship and supervision (discussed next), talking and presenting to peers and others can be effective tools for developing the richness and quality of your analysis.

Forming a peer data analysis group: Simply talking to others (e.g. course peers) informally about your data and analysis can be a useful way of immersing yourself in your data or clarifying your analytic insights and 'take'. To develop this into a more structured process, if you are in a situation where this is possi-

> **PRACTICE POINT** Data analysis groups were integral to our PhD research. We found them an invaluable way both to develop our own analyses, and to learn about the process of qualitative analysis more broadly.

ble, consider organising a peer data analysis group, where you meet regularly with a small group of peers to discuss your data or developing analysis.[8] If you don't have others in your context who are also working on TA or other qualitative analyses, we suggest looking for virtual support – for example, using hashtags such as #PhDChat and/or #AcademicChatter on Twitter can function as an entry point to a network of people who might want to engage for mutual benefit.

Presenting your analysis (informally and formally): we appreciate that many dread the idea of public speaking, but because presenting a *preliminary* analysis can be so productive and helpful, we encourage you to do this. We mean something more formal than peer data analysis groups, where you have developed a presentation for a specific audience. Such presentations

> **PRACTICE POINT** Presentations can be hugely anxiety provoking – we've been there – but because they are so useful, we encourage you to 'feel the fear and do it anyway'. Such presentations can function as great preparation for any oral exam your research degree might require.

range from those to local research groups to those at conferences or seminars. Putting together a presentation is useful for analytic development, as the questions you need reflect on (What are my key analytic insights and points? What is my overall argument? What does this contribute? Why might this matter?) are useful in ascertaining how clearly you understand what your analysis might have to offer – even when this is still *in progress*.[9] It can be particularly helpful to do this before you are too settled on your thematic structure – especially presenting to research groups – as people's questions can make you want to change tack or revisit something in ways that are productive.

---

[8] If you do form a peer data analysis group, make sure you have ethical clearance to share your data in this way.

[9] Conference presentations – and the conceptual work we do in thinking through the message(s) we present – can provide a useful foundation for developing written reports.

Allowing time for your analytic insights to fully develop

One of the most important issues for quality is time. This means a very practical strategy for ensuring quality is allowing *enough* time to develop an analysis that moves beyond the superficial and obvious meanings in the data, beyond simple **data description** or reduction (Morse, 2020). If there is one *rule* for reflexive TA, it's that it always takes longer than you anticipate. Furthermore, it's crucial to think of time not just in terms of hours of time spent analysing the data, but also a broader expanse of time to think, to reflect, to let ideas percolate; time for moments of clarity, sudden insight or inspiration, time to put things down and walk away for a while. A paper exploring the use of hermeneutic phenomenology in TA, by Hong Kong nursing researchers Ken Ho, Vico Chiang, and Doris Leung (2017), and drawing on a study on foreign domestic helpers in Hong Kong, provides a really nice example of how depth of engagement in reflexive TA is facilitated by time. The paper effectively documents how the first author 'dwelled with' the data, reflecting, asking questions, seeking out theories that might spark insights into particular aspects of the data, interrogating his own assumptions and eventually developing an account of the implicit meanings in the data. This is what we mean by the slow wheel of interpretation (Braun & Clarke, 2021d).

Our first practical tip around time is to try to factor in *double* the time you think you'll need for your analysis. As part of this, don't put off starting your analysis. You don't need to feel completely and utterly ready, having read *everything* on the topic or about the method. Deeper insight often comes from reading literature concurrently with analysis. You might, for instance, notice something interesting in your data, perhaps something you can't fully make sense of, and that prompts a search for unanticipated literature – 'what has been written about X?'. Don't be afraid to get stuck in to the analytic development early on!

PRACTICE POINT We realise planning and being spontaneous aren't entirely compatible, but do try to build in time in your research schedule for taking breaks as needed – including chunks of time away from analysis to allow your analytic ideas to percolate.

If you feel stuck with your analysis or writing, or like you are losing your sense of perspective or judgement, it's useful to move away for a while (physically and intellectually). Things we find helpful include going for a walk or a ride, spending half an hour or so lying on the sofa, or meditating. Find your own thing! Time to ponder – or just to let your mind wander – is an important part of the process. As is simply staring out of a window! Qualitative analysis is not a production line. Analysis is a creative process, and it can be impossible to be creative on demand. We find moments where we take time out often lead to clarity or inspiration.[10] But it's important that such things are not done for the purpose *of* forcing inspiration. Simply take a break and go for a walk/roll/scoot/ride, or lie on the sofa, and let your mind wander. If *all* that happens is that you feel refreshed and reinvigorated for further data analysis, then great! Note that we're *not* suggesting that you give into every whim of distraction – this strategy is one to utilise when you're feeling blocked or stuck. Try to be honest

---

[10]Taking a break can also be useful for dealing with anxiety around analysis, as noted by Elicia Boulton in Box 4.3 in Chapter Four.

with yourself. Is the time you're spending going for long walks, lying on the sofa or reading lots of journal articles and books about your topic *genuinely* helpful? Or is it an anxiety-led displacement activity, a way of avoiding data analysis or writing? It's important to find a balance.

As we noted in Section One, how much time you need to spend on reflexive TA is a thorny question. There is little guidance on how much or what proportion of time researchers should spend analysing their data – there are too many 'it depends' in the equation. Some authors have provided suggestions. Writing as someone engaged in prolonged 'field' data collection, US education researcher Valerie Janesick (2010) recommended that researchers should spend as much time analysing their data as collecting it. In the context of IPA, Jonathan Smith et al. (2009) suggested spending the equivalent of a dedicated week *per interview* engaged in data analysis. It's hard to compartmentalise time in reflexive TA, because, as just noted, you typically interweave things like literature engagement throughout analysis. That acknowledged, in our experience, allocating a third of the *total* time available for your project to *just* analysis would be the *minimum* you'd need to produce quality reflexive TA, especially if you are new to TA. Your planning needs to account for both concentrated time to work on data analysis, and also time to breathe, reflect, and take a break. Good planning around time for analysis means spreading analysis over a longer timeframe – starting early, as we noted – and doing other aspects (e.g. literature engagement, methodology write-up) concurrently, where you can.

> **PRACTICE POINT** It can be helpful to work out how much actual time you have to give to your research practice (e.g. 250 hours), and then plan accordingly.
>
> But: don't expect to write just one research timetable – this is an adventure; the unexpected can occur. Expect to rework your timetable more than once.

Working with an experienced supervisor, mentor or co-researcher

Working with a more *experienced* qualitative researcher as a supervisor, mentor or co-researcher can help you avoid problems like premature closure of the analysis and to manage and contain anxieties about getting analysis 'right' (see Gina Broom's comments in Box 4.4 in Chapter Four). We encourage those new to TA to review and reflect with their supervisor, mentor or co-researcher at all stages of the research process. This might include:

- Reviewing data for quality (such as early interviews or focus groups to ensure depth and richness);
- Sharing initial analytic observations and insights;
- Reviewing initial coding, thematic maps and theme definitions;
- Reviewing a first attempt at a theme write-up;
- And of course the first full draft of your analysis, if the person is your supervisor.

From a quality point of view, the aim of such review and reflection is not to determine whether you have got it 'right' or your mentor or supervisor 'agrees' with your analysis. Rather, it's an opportunity to: explain and clarify your thinking; be questioned; explore alternative ways of making sense of and interpreting the

> **PRACTICE POINT** Supervision/mentoring isn't about seeking your supervisor's approval or agreement, but using them to test out your analytic ideas, to assess whether they stand up to critical questioning and scrutiny, and consider new possibilities.

dataset, coding and patternings that you haven't considered; and reflect on whether your particular standpoints or experiences are (problematically) limiting and constraining how you engage with the data. It's a place where you can develop material for your reflexive journaling; a place where your assumptions can be 'revealed' and interrogated.

Making sure themes are themes, and naming them carefully

Besides the (we hope) *obvious* point that for quality reflexive TA, themes need to be based on shared patterns of meaning, cohering around a central organising concept, theme names matter. Names should convey the 'essence' and 'intent' of a theme. As we discussed in Chapter Four, theme names are like mini-mini 'abstracts' for themes. Individually each provides the reader with the headline to the story of that theme; together they headline the overall story of the analysis. Writing about an interview project with informants/participants who are nurses, Connelly and Peltzer noted:

> **PRACTICE POINT** Good theme names succinctly convey crucial information to the reader about the 'essence' of each theme.

when a researcher designates a 1-word theme, such as 'collaboration,' what does that mean in relationship to the experiences of the informants as interpreted by the researcher? Using only 1 word as a theme, there is no way of knowing, for example, if the experiences with collaboration were positive or negative, or whether collaboration is important to the nurses. One-word themes do not convey what the researcher found out about collaboration. (2016, p. 55)

Poorly named themes are, unfortunately, something we often encounter in both student and published research. In scanning an abstract, we're often struck by what might seem like underdeveloped or topic summary themes – but sometimes this is simply because the themes have not been appropriately named (Braun & Clarke, 2021c). The researcher's job is to do the interpretative work of drawing out what is *meaningful* in the data and telling the reader about it, not leaving the reader to do the interpretative work themselves. Names are part of this.

Drawing inspiration from excellent examples of published research

> **PRACTICE POINT** When you find an example of published TA you really like, try to figure out why it is exactly that you like it – what does it do well? Use that to reflect on your own analytic and writing practice.

It can be hard to know what good practice looks like, in the abstract. Beyond the worked examples we provided in Chapters Four and Five, we recommend identifying examples of published research[11] that exemplify *best practice*

---

[11]We try to ensure that the papers we include on our TA website – www.thematicanalysis.net – do offer examples of good practice. However, rarely does a paper encompass all elements of best practice we've outlined throughout this chapter and book – even our own! We encourage critical interrogation of all the TA (and indeed research) you read, including the papers *we* publish.

for your specific approach to reflexive TA (e.g. inductive or deductive, experiential or critical) – ascertaining whether they *are* indeed best practice using the tools in this chapter (see also Braun & Clarke, 2021c). If the topic is relevant to your topic or field, that can be particularly useful, but it is not essential. Such papers can provide something to model your report on (Connelly & Peltzer, 2016), with the important caveat that local context and guidelines also matter.

Demonstrating quality through an electronic or paper trail

With regard to *demonstrating* quality in a dissertation or thesis, maintaining a detailed electronic or paper 'audit' trail of the analysis is useful (see Connelly & Peltzer, 2016; Nowell et al., 2017), and in some contexts might be required. How much you are expected to include in your final report depends to some extent on local context (so check this). Regardless, there is important value in keeping this material for yourself, to

> **PRACTICE POINT** Maintaining a paper/electronic trail can be challenging for those of us who are a bit more chaotic (ahem Victoria!), so it's really useful to decide at the start of your research how you plan to do this (e.g. box, folders), and keep it updated as you go along.

refer back to, as analysis is not a linear process (as we emphasised in Section One). So what might it be good to keep a record of? The kind of material to keep in a paper/electronic trail includes: examples of coded data items; lists of codes; tables of codes and collated data; all of the (significant) thematic maps; theme definitions; and the final thematic map or theme table. These items are the sorts of things you share with a co-researcher, mentor or supervisor for the purpose of review and reflection, as noted earlier. Your research journal entries are another part of your 'audit trail' – albeit one that might not be shared (some examples of these were generously shared by Rachel Graham in Box 1.3 in Chapter One). When paper/electronic trail items are presented as appendices in a dissertation or thesis, they demonstrate to dissertation markers or thesis examiners that the analytic process has been systematic and rigorous. However, the inclusion of such items should not be used to stand in for a thorough description of your analytic decisions and process (see 'Describing what you actually did during analysis' in Chapter Five).

MANAGING QUALITY *DURING* THE PUBLICATION PROCESS

We briefly mention publishing in this chapter, as the peer review and editing process is – in our experience – a risk to quality (reflexive) TA. We recognise that's a provocative statement, but we feel it is justified (for any editors or reviewers who disagree, see Braun & Clarke, 2021c). As we noted in Chapters One and Six, there is still much *confusion* about TA. Authors are often asked to adhere to standards that are inconsistent

> **ALERT** The peer review process isn't perfect – many journals lack (qualitative) methodological expertise in their reviewer pools, which seems to be a reason why poor-quality TA often gets published.

with their approach to TA (Braun & Clarke, 2021c), or Big Q qualitative research more generally. In a paper outlining new American Psychological Association standards for reporting qualitative research, Levitt et al. noted that authors:

> have suffered from conflicting manuscript expectations in the style or content of reporting [...] they may be asked to adhere to standards and rhetorical styles that are inappropriate for their methods. Authors may also be asked to educate reviewers about basic qualitative methods' assumptions or to defend qualitative methods as a field in articles focused otherwise. (2018, p. 28)

Memorably, a reviewer of one of our TA manuscripts commented that "the authors should discuss how they attempted to avoid bias in their analytic process". We hope we don't need to unpack what's wrong with that here (see Braun & Clarke, 2021c). We chuckled at one reviewer who suggested that we and our co-authors consult Braun and Clarke (2006) for guidance on conducting TA!

Less amusingly, we have been asked by editors and reviewers to change our papers to do the very things we are critical of as practices both for TA (Braun & Clarke, 2021c) and for qualitive research more broadly (Braun & Clarke, 2013). There are some instances when we've had to resign ourselves to complying with such requests, because they are a 'deal breaker' for the editor, such as when a journal editor asked us to include frequency counts in the reporting of themes (see 'Should I use numbers to report theme 'frequency'?' in Chapter Five) and we did so (eventually, reluctantly). In that case, we asked to include an explanatory note in the paper that detailed our reservations about such things (see also Braun & Clarke, 2013):

> **ALERT** Remember: this is an adventure not a recipe, and understanding the principles helps you decide which guidance and criteria you can bend, or break, and when.

> These numbers should be interpreted with a degree of caution. Because of the semi structured and (to some extent) participant-led nature of the interviews, the participants were not asked exactly the same questions, although all of the main topics were discussed with each participant. Therefore, it should not be assumed, for example, when we report that "six women thought that appearance was not as integral to same sex relationships as it was to heterosexual relationships" (see below), that the remaining women thought the opposite. It may be that only some women discussed a particular issue or raised a particular point in their interviews. (Huxley, Clarke, & Halliwell, 2011, p. 419)

The editing and review process can undermine quality if editors do not acknowledge the quality standards for Big Q qualitative research, which are sometimes very *different* from those for postpositivist research. And, indeed, if they do not acknowledge the *divergent* standards associated with particular qualitative methods and paradigms (see next section). If you're new to publishing TA and aren't necessarily certain about things, what should you do when you come up against editorial or reviewer[12] requests you feel are inappropriate? Should

---

[12]This is especially for inappropriate reviewer requests from the ever-notorious 'Reviewer 2' – check out #Reviewer2 on Twitter.

you comply? Or should you argue back and, as Levitt et al. (2018) suggested, educate reviewers and editors about the assumptions underpinning your approach to TA? We support 'arguing back' over compliance, and encourage you to *defend* and *explain* your choices, using the resources we have provided in this book, to

> **PRACTICE POINT** If your research has been subject to inappropriate-for-reflexive-TA quality criteria – by an editor or reviewers – do try arguing back and defending your methodological practice.

support *best* practice in published TA (see also Braun & Clarke, 2021c). We know from experience you are not always going to be successful. If you're not, but publication in a particular journal is important, we encourage you to add cautionary notes, like the one Huxley et al. (2011) added about frequency. However, the onus should *not* be on us as authors to instigate change in the expectations and standards for reporting of qualitative research. We believe this responsibility lies firmly with editors and reviewers.

ARE *GENERIC* QUALITATIVE QUALITY CRITERIA AND STRATEGIES USEFUL IN TA RESEARCH?

We end this chapter by briefly considering how applicable for reflexive TA research *general* or supposedly *universal* qualitative quality criteria and techniques are (e.g. Cassell, n.d.; Elliott et al., 1999; Levitt et al., 2018; Lincoln, 1995; Morrow, 2005; Sparkes & Smith, 2009; Symon & Cassell, 2012; Tong, Sainsbury, & Craig, 2007; Tracy, 2010; Yardley, 2015). Some criteria and techniques for quality have come to occupy the position of common-sense *best practice*. But it's always worthwhile asking: what foundations (conceptual and otherwise) is this criterion based on? Are those foundations consistent with the assumptions and best practice guidelines for reflexive TA? Selecting and applying appropriate 'universal' quality strategies has to be underpinned by theoretical knowingness and reflexivity (Chamberlain, 2004).

> **ALERT** Beware quality criteria presented as universally applicable to all forms of qualitative research! They rarely are.

> **ALERT** Integral to the selection and use of appropriate quality practices and criteria is theoretical knowingness and reflexivity.

Take 'member checking' or 'participant validation', a widely discussed and recommended quality strategy (B. Smith & McGannon, 2018; Varpio et al., 2017), as an example. Participants are asked to read and comment on the analysis and confirm – or not – its accuracy or authenticity as an account of their experiences, views or practices (Lincoln & Guba, 1985). For instance, Elliott et al. (1999) included member checking as a type of 'credibility check' in their widely cited 'publishability guidelines' for qualitative research. Is this evaluative tool useful for reflexive TA? We think it is only meaningful as a quality check when you have produced an interpretation of the data that might be recognisable to participants as an account of their experience. When analysis combines both semantic and latent coding, based in hermeneutics of both empathy and suspicion (Willig, 2013), or uses only *latent* coding and a hermeneutics of *suspicion*, the analysis does not seek to capture participant *perspectives* as such. Such 'critical' analysis might not only be unrecognisable to participants;

it might even upset, offend, or anger them, if it does not resonate with their experience (see Price, 1996; Weatherall et al., 2002). That does not necessarily make it a *poor-quality* analysis of the data – although in evaluating it, we would also need to consider the politics of representation (which we discussed in 'Minimising harm in interpretation: ethics, politics, and representation' in Chapter Seven).

For reflexive TA, 'participant validation' can be an appropriate quality technique "when one of the goals of research is to identify and apply themes that are recognized or used by the people whom one studies" (Ryan & Bernard, 2003, p. 104).[13] It may also be possible to rework the concept of participant validation into something more congruent with the assumptions of reflexive or critical approaches to qualitative research. King and Brooks, for instance, proposed the notion of 'participant feedback', which they conceptualised as "an additional source of information which enriches the analysis but is itself subject to critical reflection as much as the original data" (2018, p. 223). This is similar to Tracy's (2010) notion of 'member reflections' – a wider concept than member checks. Such elements are not essential for TA quality, but if you wish to build something like this into your process, it needs to be done in a way that the process has validity and is ethically appropriate (see B. Smith & McGannon, 2018). This means at the very least, allowing space and *time* to include such reflections or feedback into the analytic process in a *meaningful* way. This means participant feedback needs to be considered early, at the planning and design stages of research, to build in seeking and acting on such feedback.

> **PRACTICE POINT** Quality concepts and practices are not necessarily cast in stone – you may be able to rework them to better suit your research.

Some methodological scholars may present techniques, such as participant validation or **triangulation**,[14] as *universally* applicable quality strategies and criteria for qualitative research (B. Smith & McGannon, 2018). But to do so is to elide the range and diversity of qualitative research, and the various (and sometimes antithetical) theoretical assumptions embedded in the field, *and in* such quality practices. Theoretical/paradigmatic assumptions limit the applicability and usefulness of many quality standards (Braun & Clarke, 2013;

---

[13]Some researchers may nonetheless feel it is important to ask participants to respond to their interpretation of the data for ethical or political reasons. Because they are an 'outsider' researcher or 'representing the Other' (see Box 7.3 in Chapter Seven), for example, or because they are engaged in collaborative or participatory research practice. Some researchers feel it is ethically important to 'return research' to participants, to give participants access to the research they have contributed to. This could mean giving participants access to the full report or a brief summary of the results. 'Returning research' to participants in this way should not be confused with participant validation, but it sometimes is.

[14]Triangulation involves using multiple data sources, participant groups or researchers to gain a richer or multi-faceted account of the phenomena under study. Tracy (2010) suggested the metaphor of 'crystallisation' as a *qualitative* alternative to triangulation. Instead of the realist overtones and suggestion of a singular reality and truth that triangulation embeds, crystallisation – Tracy argued – evokes a goal of capturing a more complex, multi-faceted, but still thoroughly partial, understanding of a phenomenon. We realise only now how well this fits well with our conceptualisation of themes as multi-faceted gems!

Morse, 2020). That acknowledged, there are some more generic principles and criteria that we find useful as starting points for considering quality – because of their (varying levels of) theoretical flexibility and (more or less) wide applicability across a range of research designs and methodological approaches. These include: the 'open-ended, flexible quality principles' outlined by the British health psychologist Lucy Yardley (2000, 2008, 2015); US organisational researcher Sarah Tracy's (2010) eight 'big-tent' (i.e. transtheoretical) quality criteria; and the 'journal reporting standards' developed by US psychologists Levitt et al. (2018).[15] In considering evaluative criteria, hold in mind the concept of methodological integrity (Levitt et al., 2017), and the need to have 'integrity' in the criteria that we apply, within the theoretical frameworks of our research (Morse, 2020).

CHAPTER SUMMARY

How can you have the best TA adventure possible? How can your TA be the best it can be? In this chapter, we engaged with the question of quality in (reflexive) TA by first discussing common problems we encounter in TA research. We introduced our reflexive TA bingo as a fun way you can identify problems in TA research. We outlined a number of strategies for ensuring and demonstrating quality in TA. We discussed the publication process as a particularly risky point for quality – if editors and reviewers lack awareness and knowledge, as can be the case – and suggested strategies to navigate this. We finished up with a discussion of the usefulness of generic quality criteria in thinking about and judging what counts as best practice for TA – and emphasised, once again, the need to be a knowing and reflexively aware researcher.

WANT TO LEARN MORE ABOUT...?

For an in-depth discussion of ***problems in and quality measures for TA***, see: Braun, V., & Clarke, V. (2020). One size fits all? What counts as quality practice in (reflexive) thematic analysis? *Qualitative Research in Psychology*. Advance online publication https://doi.org/10.1 080/14780887.2020.1769238

For a great discussion of problems with ***underdeveloped themes in qualitative research*** (written for a nursing audience, but widely applicable), see: Connelly, L. M., & Peltzer, J. N. (2016). Underdeveloped themes in qualitative research: Relationships with interviews and analysis. *Clinical Nurse Specialist, 30*(1), 52–57.

For an accessible discussion of a wide range of issues related to ***qualitative quality***, and an overview of the concept of ***methodological integrity***, see: Levitt, H. M., Motulsky, S.

---

[15]The Levitt et al. (2018) journal reporting standards do *occasionally* suggest theoretically embedded quality standards and practices as more generally applicable.

L., Wertz, F. J., Morrow, S. L., & Ponterotto, J. G. (2017). Recommendations for designing and reviewing qualitative research in psychology: Promoting methodological integrity. *Qualitative Psychology, 4*(1), 2–22.

For **a critique of common 'universal' standards for quality** in qualitative research, see: Smith, B., & McGannon, K. R. (2018). Developing rigor in qualitative research: Problems and opportunities within sport and exercise psychology. *International Review of Sport and Exercise Psychology, 11*(1), 101–121.

For a discussion of **enhancing the usefulness of qualitative results** (in health research, but again widely applicable), see: Sandelowski, M., & Leeman, J. (2012). Writing usable qualitative health research results. *Qualitative Health Research, 22*(10), 1404–1413.

ACTIVITIES FOR STUDENT READERS

PRACTICE POINT In Google Scholar you can 'search within the citations' of an article – such as Braun and Clarke, 2006 – for a specific topic or key word.

Critically evaluate a published reflexive TA study: Find a recent example of TA claiming to use reflexive TA, or specifically Braun and Clarke (2006), from your field of study (or use one of the two we offer below – available on the companion website):

Marcu, A., Gaspar, R., Rutsaert, P., Seibt, B., Fletcher, D., Verbeke, W., & Barnett, J. (2015). Analogies, metaphors, and wondering about the future: Lay sense-making around synthetic meat. *Public Understanding of Science, 24*(5), 547–562.

Toft, A., Franklin, A., & Langley, E. (2020). "You're not sure that you are gay yet": The perpetuation of the "phase" in the lives of young disabled LGBT+ people. *Sexualities, 23*(4), 516–529.

Using Tables 9.1 and 9.2 to guide you, critically evaluate the paper to identify: (a) any problems; and (b) instances of good practice. Considering the balance between any problems and good practice, how would you rate the paper as an example of reflexive TA? In thinking about evaluating the balance between 'problems' and 'good practice', what was most important in determining your decision, and why? Table 1: Some common problems in published TA research in the additional chapter on the companion website, 'Teaching, supervising, and examining for quality TA', will also be useful for this activity.

If you are part of a group, you could do this individually and then compare your assessments in a group discussion session.

If you're teaching content related to this chapter...
Don't forget to check the companion website for a range of teaching resources:
https://study.sagepub.com/thematicanalysis

FARE-WELL!

Becoming a bold adventurer in the world of reflexive TA

Thank you for allowing us to support and guide your preparations for, and early practice in, doing reflexive TA. With this book, we have aimed to provide you with a rich set of tools and resources to use in your adventuring, to help reduce some of the uncertainty and anxiety that might make the task of 'doing reflexive TA' seem daunting. Coming back to the analogy of an adventure, we hope this book has given you the tools and understandings needed to (more) confidently venture forth, to grapple, to explore, to reflect, and to create as you journey through the world of reflexive TA.

Through framing qualitative analysis – and reflexive TA specifically – as an adventure, rather than a recipe to follow, our aim has been to empower and liberate you. An adventure is not only about reaching a destination; an adventure is also about the journey. Reflexive TA as a process is not a race to the finish line, following the most direct route. It's a meandering path that you help forge. A path that twists in unexpected ways, sometimes even turning back on itself, as you encounter the unanticipated and experience a wide range of emotions. You now understand that doing reflexive TA, and doing reflexive TA *well*, is not about following steps, or applying a formula. Rather, what is required is understanding the conceptual foundations of reflexive TA, and the purpose of reflexive TA. Such knowledge liberates you for practice – practice based on the flexible and situated application of defensible, foundational knowledge.

So, fare *well* in the adventures you have. Our final words of advice are to remember to:

- Be bold
- Be creative
- Be questioning and critical
- And always, always *be reflexive, be be reflexive!*[1]

---

[1] Our phrasing – "be reflexive, be be reflexive!" – riffs off the cheer in the 2000 cheerleading film *Bring it On*: "be aggressive, be be aggressive." It seems apt to end the book with a pop cultural reference, and one that evokes a film we saw together when PhD students at Loughborough University.

GLOSSARY

Actionable outcomes analytic outcomes that have clear implications for practice; that can be readily translated to the real world of social, health and clinical practice.

Analysis the practice of exploring and explaining the meaning and significance of data. In TA research, also the preferred name for the section of a report in which themes are reported.

Analytic foreclosure ceasing data analysis too early, before the researcher has deeply engaged with the complexity of their data and sought to richly interpret and explain their meaning and significance.

Analytic input a tool that guides and shapes, and delimits, the analytic process.

Analytic output the product or products *of* the analytic process (e.g. codes and themes in **reflexive TA**).

Analytic sensibility an orientation to data, which involves taking an inquiring and interpretative stance, exploring meaning beyond the obvious or surface-level content, and examining wider connections or concepts.

Analytic treatment of data a way of working with and reporting data extracts where you comment on and make sense of the specific features of a particular data extract, in order to advance your analytic narrative. Contrasted with an **illustrative use of data**.

Anti-foundationalist theoretical perspectives (such as constructionism) underpinned by an assumption that the truth value or meaningfulness of knowledge cannot be judged with reference to any external foundations (e.g. an objective reality).

A priori themes themes developed *prior* to data analysis, often from existing theory or research.

Big Q qualitative research that involves the use of qualitative tools and techniques within a qualitative paradigm (qualitative values, norms and assumptions). Sometimes referred to as 'fully qualitative' research to capture the emphasis on both qualitative techniques and philosophy.

Big Theory the **philosophical/meta-theories – ontologies** and **epistemologies –** underlying all research; used to acknowledge and distinguish between different 'levels' of theory – lower levels include **explanatory theories.**

Bricolage   the practice of a qualitative researcher flexibility and pragmatically drawing on and combining a range of tools and techniques to address a particular research question or achieve a particular research aim.

Bucket theme   a **topic summary**; the researcher groups data (places them in a metaphorical bucket) related to a topic or data collection question, often with a focus only on semantic or obvious meanings, without considering whether there is shared meaning and a **central organising concept** that unifies the data.

Candidate theme   an initial clustering of codes and a potential theme – one that requires further exploration before it can be considered a more settled theme.

CAQDAS/QDAS   acronym for Computer Assisted/Qualitative Data Analysis Software packages such as NVivo and MAXQDA, which can be used as tools to manage qualitative data coding.

Category   refers to an area, **topic** or **domain** of the data.

Central organising concept   the (sometimes implicit) idea that unifies meaning in a theme; the concept or idea that all the analytic observations that constitute a theme relate to.

Coarse coding   coding that captures meaning at a macro rather than micro level; coding that is too coarse fails to capture different facets of meaning relevant to the developing analysis. See **fine-grained coding**.

Co-construction   the way participants and researchers jointly produce knowledge (e.g. the interviewer's questions inevitably shape the responses from the participant); acknowledges the active role of the researcher in knowledge production.

Code   an analytic tool and output; captures an analytic insight from the researcher's systematic engagement with their data. Codes are the building blocks for themes in reflexive TA.

Code label   a brief phrase that succinctly summarises the analytic ideas and data meanings captured by a code; used to tag every relevant segment of data.

Codebook/coding frame   a structured set of codes or code labels that are developed before data analysis or following (some) data **familiarisation** and then applied to the data (typically by multiple coders working independently, or by a team of researchers). Coding is usually conceptualised as a process of allocating data to pre-determined themes, rather than a precursor to theme development. A codebook can also be used for charting, mapping and displaying the coded data.

Codebook TA   involves a structured and (more or less) fixed approach to coding; a set of codes are developed before data analysis or following (some) data familiarisation, and then applied to the data. Themes are usually conceptualised as **analytic inputs** and coding is a process of allocating data to the pre-determined themes. Reported themes often reflect a **topic summary** conceptualisation. Variations include: **framework analysis**; **template analysis**; **matrix analysis**; **network analysis**.

Coding   the process of using codes and code labels to capture (potentially) relevant meanings in data, in relation to a research question.

Coding accuracy   the notion that it is possible to code data correctly (or incorrectly); underpinned by an assumption that the meaning of data is fixed and not open to interpretation.

Coding reliability (TA)   a type of TA that is broadly (post)positivist in orientation and assumes that coding can be 'accurate' and 'reliable'; the use of a fixed codebook and multiple independent coders are techniques for ensuring and demonstrating reliable coding.

Collaborative coding   a Big Q alternative to **consensus coding**; two or more researchers work together to code data and develop codes through discussing and reflecting on their ideas and assumptions; thus, reflexivity is an essential component of collaborative coding.

Community research   research approaches that centre collaboration with local communities, sometimes involving community members as co-researchers who participate in research design, participant recruitment, data collection and analysis.

Conceptual code   a code that captures implicit meaning underlying the data surface informed by the researcher's conceptual 'take' on the data. See also **latent code** and **researcher-directed code**.

Conceptual coherence   an important principle for research design in TA; the requirement that the different elements of a research design (philosophical and theoretical assumptions, research questions, methods and so on) are in conceptual alignment. See also **'fit'** and **methodological integrity**.

Concrete data   data that are often perfunctory and capture factual information or straightforward descriptions, rather than interpretations and explanations around meaning and experience.

Consensus coding   where two or more coders develop a final set of codes through discussing and agreeing which codes offer a best 'fit' with, or more accurate interpretation of, the data. Codes developed through consensus are assumed to be more reliable, but consensus coding often results in fairly superficial analyses.

Constructionism/social constructionism   a theoretical tradition in qualitative research concerned with the social production of meaning. Meaning and knowledge are conceptualised as socially produced and without external foundation. Often confused with the idea that the social context influences human experiences, constructionism goes further than this and interrogates the categories and ideas that constitute reality.

Content analysis a way of analysing patterns in texts, patterns can be analysed statistically or qualitatively; qualitative versions are typically labelled thematic or **qualitative content analysis.**

Contextualism a theoretical tradition, often classified as an epistemology, concerned with the situated or contextual nature of meaning and the 'person-in-context'; some overlap with **phenomenology.**

Critical qualitative a broad orientation to qualitative research that encapsulates approaches (including critical or constructionist TA) that seek to interrogate patterns of meaning and their effects and implications, and that foreground an understanding of language as performative and active.

Critical realism a **philosophical/meta-theoretical** tradition that assumes that a material reality exists independent of our ideas about it, but that our experiences and representations of reality are mediated by language and culture. Classified by some as an **epistemology,** others as an **onto-epistemology;** we classify it as an **ontology.** See also **realism.**

Critical thematic analysis the use of TA within a critical qualitative orientation, with some similarities to discourse analytic approaches that report broader patterns of meaning (e.g. discourses).

Data description/summary an orientation to data that seeks to merely describe and summarise the data content, often with a concern to accurately represent participants' experiences and perspectives. From the standpoint of **Big Q,** such straightforward representation is not possible as the researcher cannot sweep aside the values and frameworks through which they make meaning of data, which inevitably shape and inflect their meaning-making.

Data item an individual piece of data that forms part of the wider **dataset** (e.g. an interview transcript, newspaper article or survey response).

Dataset the entirety of your data; constituted by all of the individual **data items.**

Deductive TA **coding** and **theme** development informed by pre-existing theory.

Descriptive code a code that captures explicit meanings in data, that aims to stay close to the meanings overtly expressed by participants. See also **semantic code, participant-directed code** and **manifest code/meaning.**

Design thinking an orientation to thinking about research that deliberately considers and selects all the different elements required for a successful project.

Discourse analysis approaches to qualitative research and data analysis strongly associated with **critical qualitative** research, which view meaning as socially produced and negotiated. Analysis is focused on explicating the meaning and function of features of language – ranging from broader patterns of meaning (or discourses) to the fine-grained detail of social interaction (e.g. the function of laughter, pauses and particular word choices).

Discourses broadly defined as patterns of socially located meaning that serve to construct reality and social objects in particular ways.

Domain an area or **category** of the dataset, often easily captured in one word (e.g. gender, shame), and frequently confused with **themes**. See also **topic**.

Emerge (themes) the problematic notion that themes passively 'arise' from data; overlooks the active role of the researcher in creating and generating themes.

Emergent themes the term for lower-level inductive themes in **interpretative phenomenological analysis (IPA)**, and sometimes used to capture themes that are developed inductively from data. Not recommended within reflexive TA. Risks implying that themes passively arise from data without the active input of the researcher, and indeed that themes reside in the data fully formed and are simply 'found' by the researcher.

Epistemic or epistemological violence concept to evoke the harm done to Indigenous, minoritised and/or Othered populations through knowledge and research practices, including representation and 'speaking on behalf' by a privileged, White researcher.

Epistemology a theory of knowledge that captures what it is possible to know and meaningful ways of generating knowledge; one strand of the **philosophical/meta-theories/Big Theories** underpinning all forms of research, sometimes referred to as the 'ologies or 'O&E' stuff.

Essentialist theoretical orientations that assume things and people have an 'essence' that determines their nature and being; there are significant overlaps between essentialism and **realism**.

Experiential qualitative a broad 'camp' (or paradigm) of **Big Q** qualitative research focused on exploring participants' lived experiences and sense-making, their views and perspectives, practices or behaviours. Underpinned by a view of language as more or less transparently communicating meaning.

Explanatory theory a theory that seeks to explain the workings of phenomena.

Familiarisation first phase in **reflexive TA** and many other qualitative analytic approaches; about working closely with the dataset to develop a rich and nuanced understanding of data content. Combines processes of 'immersion' and distancing/'critical reflection'.

Fine-grained coding coding that focuses on detail and meaning at a micro level to parse as much different meaning as possible from data. See also **coarse coding**.

'Fit' (also 'good fit')   describes a research design that is conceptually coherent; also used to describe **codes** that convincingly evoke the data being analysed.

Framework analysis   a **codebook** approach to TA developed by social policy researchers in the UK and designed to enable an efficient and focused analytic process, particularly for researchers working in teams with a pre-determined and clearly defined analytic purpose. The framework is used both for coding and charting data.

Fully qualitative   research that involves both the use of qualitative tools and techniques and qualitative values, norms and assumptions (**Big Q**).

Generalisability   broadly, the notion that research has relevance or meaning beyond the specific setting or 'sample' studied, often equated with *statistical generalisability*, but there are a variety of different conceptualisations of generalisability. See also **transferability**.

'Give voice'   a concern to provide a platform to and amplify the voices and experiences of typically unheard marginalised social groups, often associated with feminist and other politically and social justice orientated research.

Grounded theory   a qualitative methodology that aims to generate theory from the analysis of data; the theory is grounded in the data, hence *grounded* theory. Developed by sociologists in the 1960s in opposition to 'grand theorising' that lacked an empirical base.

Hermeneutics of empathy   an interpretative orientation that seeks to stay close to participants' meanings and capture these in ways that might be recognisable to them.

Hermeneutics of suspicion   an interpretative orientation that interrogates and asks critical questions of the meanings in data and draws more heavily on the researcher's theoretical resources.

Heuristic device   a conceptual tool, designed to aid (systematic, in-depth) understanding of the phenomenon of interest. In reflexive TA, **codes** act as heuristic devices to aid rich, nuanced understanding of the topic of interest in the analysis.

Illustrative use of data   a way of reporting data and analysis in TA, where your data extracts provide illustrative *examples* of analytic points. Contrasted with an **analytic treatment of data**.

...in data   the notion that meaning exists fixed within data and the researcher's task is simply to locate and retrieve it. Due to language limitations, we occasionally use this expression in the book, but it should not be understood to imply fixed and easily-extractable meaning.

Indigenous knowledge frameworks   refers collectively to diverse and expanding theoretical and methodological approaches to knowledge developed by Indigenous researchers and people, based in their worldviews, in contrast to the globally dominant westernised colonial knowledge systems. See also **epistemological violence**.

Inductive TA coding and theme development that strives to be grounded in the data, rather than shaped by pre-existing **explanatory** or **political theories**; remains inescapably shaped by the researcher's positionings and meta-theoretical assumptions.

Information power A model developed by Malterud et al. (2016) for determining the size of dataset ('sample') for a qualitative project. To assess whether a smaller or larger dataset is needed, a range of interconnecting aspects need to be considered in context: research aims; specificity of the 'sample'; theoretical approach taken; quality of the data; and analytic approach.

Insider researcher a researcher who is in some or many ways a member of the group they are studying.

Inter-coder agreement the notion that two coders 'agree' on how to apply a coding frame or codebook to data, an inherently **realist** and **(post)positivist** coding practice, which is premised on the assumption that it is possible to interpret qualitative data 'accurately' and that the meaning of data is fixed. See also **inter-rater/coder reliability**.

Interpretation the analytic practice of making meaning of data, often through the researcher situating data in a wider context and exploring how and why the meanings developed from their engagement with the dataset matter.

Interpretative an orientation to data that seeks to explore and 'unpack' meanings and why those meanings matter; often contrasted with a more **descriptive**-summative orientation.

Interpretative paradigm a term used to describe **Big Q** qualitative research and distinguish it from **positivism**. The term is to some extent a 'historical artefact' and less widely used in the contemporary context, where qualitative approaches are more accepted and established, than in the 'early days' of qualitative research (in the 1960s onwards). Also used to refer to a particular *orientation* to qualitative research that centres on the exploration of participants' meanings and understandings, which we demarcate as **experiential qualitative**.

Interpretative phenomenological analysis (IPA) a popular psychological approach to qualitative data analysis, centred on the exploration of subjective meaning-making and lived experience, and incorporating both **thematic** and idiographic data orientations (idiographic = an orientation to the particular, such as the unique experiences of individual participants).

Inter-rater/coder reliability the level of 'agreement' between coders, measured using statistical tests; high levels of agreement are assumed to indicate a very good level of coding agreement and supposedly reliable and 'accurate' coding. Problematic from a **reflexive TA/Big Q** perspective. See also **inter-coder agreement**.

Intersectionality a hugely influential concept in feminist and social justice research that originated in Black feminist thought. Captures the ways in which different forms of social privilege and marginalisation intersect in human lives, and the ways in which different social systems intersect and shape each other (e.g. dominant constructs of femininity are inherently racialised).

Language practice a fine-grained focus on the things we do with language and the implications and effects of particular linguistic organisations and structures; underpinned by a view of language as active and performative, constructing truths and realities; associated with **critical qualitative** methodologies, including **discourse analysis**.

Latent code a code that captures *implicit* meaning in data or the underlying concepts that allow the overt and obvious meanings to literally 'make sense'. Sometimes assumed (often by psychologists) to refer to unconscious meaning, but this is not generally the intent behind this term. See also **conceptual code** and **researcher-directed code**.

Lived experience personal knowledge derived from direct, first-hand experience of living in the world, often used to refer to the personal knowledge and experience of people from socially marginalised/minoritised and oppressed groups.

Manifest code/meaning meanings overtly expressed in data and the **codes** that captures these. See also **semantic code**, **descriptive code** and **participant-directed code**.

Mash-ups can involve the 'confused' and seemingly unaware mixing of different (conceptually clashing) elements within TA; also the deliberate combining of two or more methods to produce a distinct, hybrid-method (e.g. **thematic narrative analysis**).

Matrix analysis a **codebook** approach to TA in which the codebook, or matrix, is used to guide data coding and collate, chart and display the coded data.

Member checking also referred to as **participant validation**; the process of asking participants to comment on an analysis and whether it resonates with, or is an accurate depiction of, their experience. Widely assumed to offer validity or credibility, certain theoretical assumptions limit its relevance to many forms of qualitative research, including reflexive TA.

Method a tool or technique, usually for collecting or analysing data.

Methodolatry a critical term used to capture a preoccupation with methodological procedures and following them precisely for success, like following baking recipes without any understanding of the purpose and processes of baking. See also **proceduralism**, **techniqueism**.

Methodological bandwidth the extent of an individual's knowledge of the range and diversity of qualitative research (narrow to wide).

Methodological integrity captures when research design, procedures, research questions and theoretical assumptions cohere in a research project to produce a trustworthy and useful outcome.

Methodology a theoretically informed, and delimited, framework for research.

Mind-dependent truth a truth that depends on, and arises from, human perception; associated with **ontologies, epistemologies** and **methodologies** that view truth and meaning as partial and contextual (e.g. **contextualism, phenomenology**).

Mind-independent truth the notion that truth exists *independently* of human practices and our ability to research and understand the world; strongly associated with (**naïve**) **realism** and **positivism**.

Naïve realism a form of **realism** that assumes that the world is as it appears to be, and that it is possible to access reality directly unmediated by language and culture. See also **simple realism, pure realism**.

Narrative analysis a cluster of analytic approaches concerned with narrative or storytelling and the content and structure of the stories people tell and write.

Neo-positivist **positivist** assumptions and values revived and imported into qualitative research, not always knowingly. See also **positivism creep**.

Neo-realist **realist** assumptions and values revived and imported into qualitative research, not always knowingly.

Network analysis a **codebook** approach to TA. The thematic network maps the relationship between the **themes** in a similar way to a **thematic map** in reflexive TA.

Onto-epistemology associated with US feminist philosopher Karen Barad, this philosophical position meshes together being (**ontology**) and knowing (**epistemology**). Later expanded with the incorporation of ethics, into ethico-onto-epistemology.

Ontology philosophies/meta-theories/Big Theories of the nature of reality and being. With **epistemology** (theories of knowledge), sometimes referred to as the 'ologies or 'O&E stuff'.

Outsider researcher a researcher who is not a member of the group they are studying.

Overarching theme in reflexive TA, represents the highest level of theme abstraction; often used as an organising structure for several **themes** (and **subthemes**), rather than being discussed in detail in its own right.

Owning your perspectives the practice of a researcher striving to acknowledge their personal and theoretical assumptions, articulate these, and reflect on how they shape and constrain their research practices, including data collection and analysis.

Paradigm a belief and value system that encompasses meta-theoretical or **ontological, epistemological** and **methodological** assumptions.

Participant-directed code   a code that captures meanings overtly expressed by participants and aims to stay close to these. See also **semantic code, descriptive code** and **manifest code/meaning**.

Participant validation   asking participants to 'validate' the analysis by confirming its authenticity/accuracy or helping the researcher to rework it to become an authentic/accurate account of their experiences and perspectives. Associated with the **experiential** tradition and more **realist** orientations. See also **member checking**.

Participatory research   methods and approaches that seek to overturn the traditional participant–researcher relationship (researchers gather data *from* participants), and involve participants in research as co-researchers or collaborators (potentially from conception to dissemination of the research). Usually has social change goals in the lives of the participants and/or their wider communities alongside, or even ahead of, knowledge generation.

Phenomenology   a research and theoretical tradition centred on the study of first-person lived experience; treats subjective experiences as a valid and meaningful focus of inquiry.

Philosophical assumptions   the 'big' theoretical ideas and values (**paradigms, ontologies** and **epistemologies**) that underlie all research.

Philosophical/meta-theories   the **Big Theories** that underlie all research, including theories of reality (**ontology**) and theories of knowledge (**epistemology**); these capture the assumptions and values that underpin a researcher's practices.

Political theories   in this context refers to theories that provide ideas and assumptions about how (an aspect of) society works, with a particular concern for the operation of lines of power in society. Examples include feminist theory, queer theory and Crip theory, as well as variants of these (e.g. Black feminist theory).

Politics of representation   the ethical and political implications of how we present and interpret participants' experiences, sense-making and so on in our research; also captures broader questions of entitlements to tell stories about and represent particular groups in a historical context in which researchers from socially dominant and privileged groups have researched and represented the Other in harmful ways. See also **representing the Other**.

Positivism   a philosophical tradition, often classified as an **epistemology** or a **paradigm**, associated with the scientific method; values seeking and generating objective knowledge about reality. See **postpositivism, (post)positivism**.

Positivism creep   the unacknowledged and unreflexive adherence to **(post)positivist** assumptions, values and norms in qualitative research; treating (post)positivist assumptions and values as reflecting universal good practice for all research in an unknowing way. See also **neo-positivism**.

Postpositivism retains **positivism**'s belief in the existence of an objective reality; objective knowledge remains an ideal, but possible knowledge of the world is understood to be delimited and imperfect. We use '**(post)positivism**' to capture the blurring of these positions or contexts where it's unclear which is claimed.

Poststructuralism a set of non-realist/**relativist** theoretical traditions, associated with French philosophers Michel Foucault and Jacques Derrida among others, that situate meaning as multiple, socially-constructed, and connected to wider systems (e.g. of knowledge, and power). Unlike the use of *post* in **postpositivist**, here *post* signals a rejection of structuralism; poststructuralism rejects objectivity, linearity and **positivism**.

Practices a term with many meanings. Broadly, refers to socially embedded actions. Can refer to the things participants 'do in the world' (what some psychologists would call 'behaviours'); also refers to the researcher's actions in conducting their research.

Proceduralism a preoccupation with methodological procedures or techniques at the expense of theory, researcher subjectivity and reflexivity; see also **methodolatry**, **techniqueism**.

Pure realism used to distinguish **realism** from **critical realism**; an ontological position that assumes an objective, singular and knowable reality. See also **naïve realism** and **simple realism**.

QDAS acronym for Qualitative Data Analysis Software packages such as NVivo and MAXQDA, which can be used as tools to manage qualitative data coding. See also **CAQDAS**.

Qualitative content analysis a range of approaches to **content analysis**, which focus on text-based meaning and pattern identification; lots of overlap with TA, especially **coding reliability** and **codebook** varieties.

Qualitative paradigm the norms, assumptions, values and beliefs underlying (**Big Q**) qualitative research. There is disagreement about whether there is one qualitative paradigm or several because Big Q qualitative encompasses such a wide range and diversity of theoretical frameworks and research approaches.

Qualitative sensibility an overall research ethos or orientation ('headspace') that is underpinned by (**Big Q**) qualitative norms and values, such as viewing **subjectivity** as a resource, rather than a problem to be managed, and meaning as contextual and situated.

Realism an **ontological** position that assumes the existence of objective reality; since the development of **critical realism**, it is increasingly used as an umbrella term to encompass all forms of realism. See also **critical realism**, **naïve realism**, **pure realism** and **simple realism**.

Reflexive journal a key **reflexivity** tool for researchers. A space to reflect on and interrogate expectations, assumptions, and research **practices**, and how these, alongside design choices, shape their research. Also an important tool for recording analytic insights and reflecting on the emotions evoked by the research, and any challenges and dilemmas encountered.

Reflexive TA   our approach to TA, located within a **qualitative paradigm**. Foregrounds the *active* role of the researcher in **coding** and theme development, the inevitable **subjectivity** of these processes, and the importance of the researcher reflecting on their assumptions and practices, and how these might shape and delimit their data analysis.

Reflexivity   the process and practice of a researcher critically reflecting on how their disciplinary, theoretical and personal assumptions and their design choices shape and delimit the knowledge they produce.

Relativism   an **ontological** position that rejects the idea of an objective, singular reality and instead views *realities* – plural – as the product of human actions and sense-making.

Representation   the practice of telling **stories** about or creating images of social groups or objects in particular contexts. Can relate to representation 'in data' or representation through research.

Representational ethics   relates to the potential for our **representational** practices in research to harm our participants or the communities they belong to. See also **politics of representation**.

Representing the Other   the practice of providing accounts of the lives and experiences of members of socially marginalised groups, particularly by researchers who are not members of those groups – or **outsiders**. The notion of 'the Other' captures social processes that position some socially privileged groups (e.g. White people) as normative, and related socially marginalised or minoritised groups (e.g. people of colour) as 'Other' (to that norm).

Research aims   the intended purpose of the research, which provide direction and focus; in reflexive TA these are not fixed and can evolve. Usually more specific than **research goals**. See also **research questions**.

Research design   the planning of a research study. Encompasses the *informed* choices a researcher makes in relation to theory and concepts, tools and techniques, ethics, their relationship with participants (if relevant), and practical and pragmatic concerns.

Research goals   the purpose of the research, the broad outcomes the researcher expects to achieve. See also **research aims, research questions**.

Research questions   the questions that guide and focus the research, connected to **research goals** and **research aims**. In reflexive TA, questions can evolve throughout the research, often becoming more focused following some analysis, but can also become broader or shift course.

Researcher bias   a **positivist** conceptualisation of the researcher's values and assumptions, to be controlled and eliminated. The language of bias – compared to **subjectivity** – implies that subjective knowledge is a distortion of objective reality.

Researcher-directed code a code that reflects the researcher's interpretative 'take' on the data, likely drawing on their theoretical, substantive and disciplinary knowledge. See also **conceptual code** and **latent code**.

Saturation a common explanation for when data collection was stopped, it is often unclear how the typical meaning of saturation as 'no new information' has been judged or determined. Implicitly **realist** assumptions render its use with **reflexive TA** problematic.

Semantic code a code that captures the surface or obvious meanings in the data. See also **descriptive code, participant-directed code** and **manifest code/meaning**.

Simple realism an **ontological** position that assumes the existence of an objective and directly observable reality; used to distinguish this form of realism from **critical realism**. See also **naïve realism** and **pure realism**.

Small q qualitative research involving the use of qualitative techniques within a **positivist** or **postpositivist** paradigm, occasionally dubbed 'qualitative positivism'. Distinct from **Big Q** qualitative.

Story within **reflexive TA**, we characterise reporting **analysis** as telling a situated *story*. This framing captures the idea that you're not aiming to produce a factual description of data content, but convey vividly and compellingly the important features and meanings of the dataset, as you made sense of it.

Subjectivity the situatedness of the researcher, reflecting their identities, values, experiences and skills. In contrast to the **(post)positivist** concern with **researcher bias**, researcher subjectivity is viewed as resource, and an essential enriching part of analysis, in **Big Q** qualitative.

Subtheme the smallest part of the (final) analytic structure in any **reflexive TA**; used, if needed, to capture and highlight an important facet (or facets) of the **central organising concept** of one **theme**.

Systematic review an alternative to a traditional 'narrative' literature review; requires a systematic approach to collecting, appraising and synthesising relevant literature, often with a focus on quantitative research. See also **thematic synthesis**.

Techniqueism a preoccupation with methodological procedures or techniques at the expense of theory, researcher subjectivity and reflexivity. See also **methodolatry, proceduralism**.

Template analysis a **codebook** approach to TA that centres on the use of a codebook (or template) as a tool for data analysis.

Thematic coding the use of **grounded theory** coding techniques to generate themes from a dataset. Particularly common before the development of widely used procedures for TA; still advocated by some as a distinct type of TA.

Thematic map(ping) a visual representation of **reflexive TA** analysis, which maps themes, and the relationship between themes, and sometimes also themes and codes. Mapping can be used as an analytic technique to aid the researcher at various phases, in developing and refining themes, and the relationship between themes.

Thematic narrative analysis narrative approaches centred on the development of **themes** within and across narratives, and/or hybrid approaches that combine **narrative analysis** and TA to explore both the thematic content of data and narrative structure.

Thematic synthesis an approach to qualitative evidence synthesis associated with the **systematic review** tradition; focused on identifying 'higher level' patterns of meaning across several qualitative studies.

Theme a shared, multi-faceted meaning, patterned across at least some of a qualitative dataset; encapsulates several related analytic insights, unified by a **central organising concept** or idea; developed initially in **reflexive TA** by clustering together **codes**.

Theme definition a concise description of a **theme**, including its central concept, its different facets, what it includes (and maybe excludes), and how it relates to other themes; essentially, an abstract for a theme.

Themes emerged a common but problematic phrase that appears in many TA papers (e.g. five themes emerged...). It suggests the researcher did not play an active role in the creation of themes; that themes exist fully formed in data and are 'harvested' by the researcher during data analysis. *Can* be used to denote inductive theme development, but rarely used in a way that signals the active role of the researcher. Not to be confused with **emergent themes** in IPA.

Theoretical flexibility one of the hallmarks of TA is its lack of inbuilt theoretical assumptions that delimit its use in various ways (although paradigmatic assumptions do provide limits). **Reflexive TA** is 'theoretically flexible' as it can be used with a range of theories – for example, from **(critical) realist** to **constructionist**.

Theoretical knowingness having an understanding of the philosophical and theoretical assumptions that might be embedded in particular approaches or techniques, and striving to use such approaches and techniques with an awareness of those assumptions.

Thick description providing a rich and detailed account of the phenomena of interest.

Topic an area, **domain** or **category** of the dataset, often easily captured in one word (e.g. gender, shame), and frequently confused with **themes**.

Topic summary   an overview of what participants discussed/the data 'showed' in relation to a specific topic, or data collection question; sometimes referred to as a domain summary. Often contains diverse and contradictory perspectives, not connected by a unifying idea or concept. Often used instead of shared-meaning-based **themes** – *not* good practice for reflexive TA.

Transferability   the notion that a qualitative data analysis potentially has relevance beyond the contexts and settings of a particular study and can be 'transferred' to other settings and contexts. See also **generalisability**.

Triangulation   using multiple data sources or researchers to increase the precision or richness of the understanding of the object of study; often assumed to have wide applicability, but can be infused with realist assumptions about improving accuracy.

REFERENCES

Adams, G., & Estrada-Villalta, S. (2017). Theory from the South: A decolonial approach to the psychology of global inequality. *Current Opinion in Psychology, 18*, 37–42.

Adams, N., Pearce, R., Veale, J., Radix, A., Castro, D., Sarkar, A., & Thom, K. C. (2017). Guidance and ethical considerations for undertaking transgender health research and institutional review boards adjudicating this research. *Transgender Health, 2*(1), 165–175.

Aguinaldo, J. P. (2012). Qualitative analysis in gay men's health research: Comparing thematic, critical discourse, and conversation analysis. *Journal of Homosexuality, 59*(6), 765–787.

Ahmed, S. (2000). Who knows? Knowing strangers and strangerness. *Australian Feminist Studies, 15*(31), 49–68.

Ajzen, I. (1991). The theory of planned behavior. *Organizational Behavior and Human Decision Processes, 50*(2), 179–211.

Akala. (2018). *Natives: Race and class in the ruins of empire.* London: Hodder & Stoughton.

Alexander-Floyd, N. G. (2012). Disappearing acts: Reclaiming intersectionality in the social sciences in a post-Black feminist era. *Feminist Formations, 23*(1), 1–25.

Allen, K. R., & Baber, K. M. (1992). Ethical and epistemological tensions in applying a postmodern perspective to feminist research. *Psychology of Women Quarterly, 16*(1), 1–15.

Allen-Collinson, J. (2016). Breathing in life: Phenomenological perspectives on sport and exercise. In B. Smith & A. C. Sparkes (Eds.), *Routledge handbook of qualitative research in sport and exercise* (pp. 33–45). London: Routledge.

Alvesson, M., & Sköldberg, K. (2009). *Reflexive methodology: New vistas for qualitative research* (2nd ed.). London: SAGE.

American Psychological Association. (2020). *Publication manual of the American Psychological Association* (7th ed.). Washington, DC: American Psychological Association.

Anderson, S., & Clarke, V. (2019). Disgust, shame and the psychological impact of skin picking: Evidence from an online support forum. *Journal of Health Psychology, 24*(13), 1773–1784.

Aronson, J. (1995). A pragmatic view of thematic analysis. *The Qualitative Report, 2*(1), https://nsuworks.nova.edu/tqr/vol2/iss1/3/

Attride-Stirling, J. (2001). Thematic networks: An analytic tool for qualitative research. *Qualitative Research, 1*(3), 385–405.

Augoustinos, M., & Every, D. (2007). The language of "race" and prejudice: A discourse of denial, reason and liberal-practical politics. *Journal of Language and Social Psychology, 26*(2), 123–141.

Ayres, L. (2008). Thematic coding and analysis. In L. M. Given (Ed.), *The SAGE encyclopedia of qualitative research methods* (pp. 876–868). Thousand Oaks, CA: SAGE.

Bacsu, J. R., Jeffery, B., Johnson, S., Martz, D., Novik, N., & Abonyi, S. (2012). Healthy aging in place: Supporting rural seniors' health needs. *Online Journal of Rural Nursing and Health Care, 12*(2), 77–87.

Banks, M., & Zeitlyn, D. (2015). *Visual methods in social research*. Los Angeles, CA: SAGE.

Barnes, C. (1992). Qualitative research: Valuable or irrelevant? *Disability, Handicap & Society, 7*(2), 115–124.

Barnes, C. (2003). What a difference a decade makes: Reflections on doing 'emancipatory' disability research. *Disability & Society, 18*(1), 3–17.

Barnett, R. C. (2004). Women and multiple roles: Myths and reality. *Harvard Review of Psychiatry, 12*(3), 158–164.

Basil, P. (2019, October 29). Make yourselves at home: The meaning of hospitality in a divided world, *The Guardian*. Retrieved from www.theguardian.com/food/2019/oct/29/make-yourselves-at-home-the-meaning-of-hospitality-in-a-divided-world

Beauboeuf-Lafontant, T. (2007). You have to show strength: An exploration of gender, race, and depression. *Gender & Society, 21*(1), 28–51.

Bell, G. C., Hopson, M. C., Craig, R., & Robinson, N. W. (2014). Exploring Black and White accounts of 21st-century racial profiling: Riding and driving while Black. *Qualitative Research Reports in Communication, 15*(1), 33–42.

Beres, M. A., & Farvid, P. (2010). Sexual ethics and young women's accounts of heterosexual casual sex. *Sexualities, 13*(3), 377–393.

Berger, P. L., & Luckmann, T. (1967). *The social construction of reality: A treatise in the sociology of knowledge*. London: Allen Lane.

Berger, R. (2015). Now I see it, now I don't: Researcher's position and reflexivity in qualitative research. *Qualitative Research, 15*(2), 219–234.

Bergin, M., Wells, J. S., & Owen, S. (2008). Critical realism: A philosophical framework for the study of gender and mental health. *Nursing Philosophy, 9*(3), 169–179.

Bhaskar, R. (1975). *A realist theory of science*. London: Routledge.

Bhaskar, R. (1979). *The possibility of naturalism: A philosophical critique of the contemporary human sciences*. Atlantic Highlands, NJ: Humanities Press.

Billig, M. (1978). *Fascists: A social psychological view of the National Front*. London: Academic Press.

Billig, M. (2013). *Learn to write badly: How to succeed in the social sciences*. Cambridge: Cambridge University Press.

Bimha, P. Z. J., & Chadwick, R. (2016). Making the childfree choice: Perspectives of women living in South Africa. *Journal of Psychology in Africa, 26*(5), 449–456.

Birks, M., & Mills, J. (2015). *Grounded theory: A practical guide* (2nd ed.). London: SAGE.

Black, N., & Jenkinson, C. (2009). Measuring patients' experiences and outcomes. *British Medical Journal, 339*, b2495.

Blaikie, N. (2010). *Designing social research: The logic of anticipation* (2nd ed.). Cambridge: Polity.

Blee, K. M. (1998). White-knuckle research: Emotional dynamics in fieldwork with racist activists. *Qualitative Sociology, 21*(4), 381–399.

Blockmans, I. G. E. (2015). "Not wishing to be the white rhino in the crowd": Disability-disclosure at university. *Journal of Language and Social Psychology, 34*(2), 158–180.

Boghossian, P. (2007). *Fear of knowledge: Against relativism and constructivism*. Oxford: Clarendon Press.

Boland, A., Cherry, G., & Dickson, R. (2017). *Doing a systematic review: A student's guide.* London: SAGE.

Bond, L. A., Holmes, T. R., Byrne, C., Babchuck, L., & Kirton-Robbins, S. (2008). Movers and shakers: How and why women become and remain engaged in community leadership. *Psychology of Women Quarterly, 32*(1), 48–64.

Borell, B. (2005). Living in the city ain't so bad: Cultural identity for young Māori in South Auckland. In J. H. Liu, T. McCreanor, T. McIntosh & T. Teaiwa (Eds.), *New Zealand identities: Departures and destinations* (pp. 191–206). Wellington: Victoria University Press.

Bowleg, L. (2008). When Black + lesbian + woman ≠ Black lesbian woman: The methodological challenges of qualitative and quantitative intersectionality research. *Sex Roles, 59*(5), 312–325.

Bowleg, L. (2017). Intersectionality: An underutilized but essential theoretical framework for social psychology. In B. Gough (Ed.), *The Palgrave handbook of critical social psychology* (pp. 507–529). London: Palgrave Macmillan.

Boyatzis, R. E. (1998). *Transforming qualitative information: Thematic analysis and code development.* Thousand Oaks, CA: SAGE.

Boynton, P. M. (2016). *The research companion: A practical guide for those in the social sciences, health and development* (2nd ed.). London: Routledge.

Bradbury-Jones, C., Breckenridge, J., Clark, M. T., Herber, O. R., Wagstaff, C., & Taylor, J. (2017). The state of qualitative research in health and social science literature: A focused mapping review and synthesis. *International Journal of Social Research Methodology, 20*(6), 627–645.

Brah, A., & Phoenix, A. (2004). Ain't I a woman? Revisiting intersectionality. *Journal of International Women's Studies, 5*(3), 75–86.

Braun, V. (2008). "She'll be right"? National identity explanations for poor sexual health statistics in Aotearoa/New Zealand. *Social Science & Medicine, 67*(11), 1817–1825.

Braun, V. (2009). "The women are doing it for themselves": The rhetoric of choice and agency around female genital "cosmetic surgery". *Australian Feminist Studies, 24*(60), 233–249.

Braun, V. (2013). "Proper sex without annoying things": Anti-condom discourse and the "nature" of (hetero)sex. *Sexualities, 16*(3–4), 361–382.

Braun, V., & Clarke, V. (2006). Using thematic analysis in psychology. *Qualitative Research in Psychology, 3*(2), 77–101.

Braun, V., & Clarke, V. (2012). Thematic analysis. In H. Cooper, P. M. Camic, D. L. Long, A. T. Panter, D. Rindskopf, & K. J. Sher (Eds.), *APA handbook of research methods in psychology*, Vol. 2. Research designs: Quantitative, qualitative, neuropsychological, and biological (pp. 57–71). Washington, DC: American Psychological Association.

Braun, V., & Clarke, V. (2013). *Successful qualitative research: A practical guide for beginners.* London: SAGE.

Braun, V., & Clarke, V. (2016). (Mis)conceptualising themes, thematic analysis, and other problems with Fugard and Potts' (2015) sample-size tool for thematic analysis. *International Journal of Social Research Methodology, 19*(6), 739–743.

Braun, V., & Clarke, V. (2017). *Yashasvi gunatmak sanshodhan: Navshikya vidyarthyansathi vyavharik margdarshan.* New Delhi: SAGE Publishing India.

Braun, V., & Clarke, V. (2018). *Safal gunaatmak anusandhaan: Naye shodhkartaon ke liye vyaavharik margdarshan.* New Delhi: SAGE Publishing India.

Braun, V., & Clarke, V. (2019a). Reflecting on reflexive thematic analysis. *Qualitative Research in Sport, Exercise and Health, 11*(4), 589–597.

Braun, V., & Clarke, V. (2019b). To saturate or not to saturate? Questioning data saturation as a useful concept for thematic analysis and sample-size rationales. *Qualitative Research in Sport, Exercise and Health, 13*(2), 1–16.

Braun, V., & Clarke, V. (2021a). Can I use TA? Should I use TA? Should I not use TA? Comparing reflexive TA and other pattern-based qualitative analytic approaches. *Counselling and Psychotherapy Research, 21*(2), 37–47.

Braun, V., & Clarke, V. (2021b). Conceptual and design thinking for thematic analysis. *Qualitative Psychology.* Advance online publication https://doi.org/10.1037/qup0000196

Braun, V., & Clarke, V. (2021c). One size fits all? What counts as quality practice in (reflexive) thematic analysis? *Qualitative Research in Psychology, 18*(3), 328–352.

Braun, V., & Clarke, V. (2021d). The ebbs and flows of qualitative research: Time, change and the slow wheel of interpretation. In B. C. Clift, J. Gore, S. Gustafsson, S. Bekker, I. C. Batlle & J. Hatchard (Eds.), *Temporality in qualitative inquiry: Theories, methods and practices* (pp. 22–38). London: Routledge.

Braun, V., & Clarke, V. (2021e). Thematic analysis. In E. Lyons & A. Coyle (Eds.), *Analysing qualitative data in psychology* (3rd ed., pp. 128–147). London: SAGE.

Braun, V., Clarke, V., Boulton, E., Davey, L., & McEvoy, C. (2020). The online survey as a qualitative research tool. *International Journal of Social Research Methodology.* Advance online publication https://doi.org/10.1080/13645579.2020.1805550.

Braun, V., Clarke, V., & Gray, D. (Eds.). (2017a). *Coleta de dados qualitativos: Um guia prático para técnicas textuais, midiáticas e virtuais.* Petrópolis, Brazil: Editora Vozes.

Braun, V., Clarke, V., & Gray, D. (Eds.). (2017b). *Collecting qualitative data: A practical guide to textual, media and virtual techniques.* Cambridge: Cambridge University Press.

Braun, V., Clarke, V., & Hayfield, N. (2019). "A starting point for your journey, not a map": Nikki Hayfield in conversation with Virginia Braun and Victoria Clarke about thematic analysis. *Qualitative Research in Psychology.* Advance online publication https://doi.org/10.1080/14780887.2019.1670765

Braun, V., Clarke, V., Hayfield, N., Moller, N., & Tischner, I. (2019). Qualitative story completion: A method with exciting promise. In P. Liamputtong (Ed.), *Handbook of research methods in health social sciences* (pp. 1479–1496). Singapore: Springer Singapore.

Braun, V., Clarke, V., Hayfield, N., & Terry, G. (2019). Thematic analysis. In P. Liamputtong (Ed.), *Handbook of research methods in health social sciences* (pp. 843–860). Singapore: Springer Singapore.

Braun, V., Clarke, V., & Rance, N. (2014). How to use thematic analysis with interview data. In A. Vossler & N. Moller (Eds.), *The counselling and psychotherapy research handbook* (pp. 183–197). London: SAGE.

Braun, V., Clarke, V., & Terry, G. (2014). Thematic analysis. In P. Rohleder & A. Lyons (Eds.), *Qualitative research in clinical and health psychology* (pp. 95–113). Basingstoke: Palgrave Macmillan.

Braun, V., Clarke, V., & Weate, P. (2016). Using thematic analysis in sport and exercise research. In B. Smith & A. C. Sparkes (Eds.), *Routledge handbook of qualitative research in sport and exercise* (pp. 191–205). London: Routledge.

Braun, V., Schmidt, J., Gavey, N., & Fenaughty, J. (2009). Sexual coercion among gay and bisexual men in Aotearoa/New Zealand. *Journal of Homosexuality, 56*(3), 336–360.

Braun, V., Terry, G., Gavey, N., & Fenaughty, J. (2009). "Risk" and sexual coercion among gay and bisexual men in Aotearoa/New Zealand – key informant accounts. *Culture, Health & Sexuality, 11*(2), 111–124.

Braun, V., Tricklebank, G., & Clarke, V. (2013). "It shouldn't stick out from your bikini at the beach": Meaning, gender, and the hairy/hairless body. *Psychology of Women Quarterly, 37*(4), 478–493.

Breakwell, G. M. (1986). *Coping with threatened identities.* London: Methuen.

Breheny, M., & Stephens, C. (2007). Individual responsibility and social constraint: The construction of adolescent motherhood in social scientific research. *Culture, Health & Sexuality, 9*(4), 333–346.

Brewster, M. E., Velez, B. L., Mennicke, A., & Tebbe, E. (2014). Voices from beyond: A thematic content analysis of transgender employees' workplace experiences. *Psychology of Sexual Orientation and Gender Diversity, 1*(2), 159–169.

Brinkmann, S. (2015). Perils and potentials in qualitative psychology. *Integrative Psychological and Behavioral Science, 49*(2), 162–173.

Brinkmann, S. (2017). Humanism after posthumanism: Or qualitative psychology after the "posts". *Qualitative Research in Psychology, 14*(2), 109–130.

Brinkmann, S., & Kvale, S. (2017). Ethics in qualitative psychological research. In C. Willig & W. Stainton Rogers (Eds.), *The SAGE handbook of qualitative research in psychology* (2nd ed., pp. 259–273). London: SAGE.

British Psychological Society. (2009). *Code of ethics and conduct.* Leicester, UK: The British Psychological Society.

British Psychological Society. (2018). *Code of ethics and conduct.* Leicester, UK: The British Psychological Society.

Brooks, J. M., & King, N. (2012, April 18–20). *Qualitative psychology in the real world: The utility of template analysis.* Paper presented at the British Psychological Society Annual Conference, London.

Brooks, J. M., McCluskey, S., Turley, E., & King, N. (2015). The utility of template analysis in qualitative psychology research. *Qualitative Research in Psychology, 12*(2), 202–222.

Buchanan, K., & Sheffield, J. (2017). Why do diets fail? An exploration of dieters' experiences using thematic analysis. *Journal of Health Psychology, 22*(7), 906–915.

Buetow, S. (2010). Thematic analysis and its reconceptualization as "saliency analysis". *Journal of Health Services Research & Policy, 15*(2), 123–125.

Buolamwini, J. (2019, February 7). Artificial intelligence has a problem with gender and racial bias. Here's how to solve it. *Time.* Retrieved from https://time.com/5520558/artificial-intelligence-racial-gender-bias/

Burr, V. (1998). Overview: Realism, relativism, social constructionism and discourse. In I. Parker (Ed.), *Social constructionism, discourse and realism* (pp. 13–25). London: SAGE.

Burr, V. (2008). A constructivist's journey: From PCP to social constructionism and back? [Keynote presentation]. In *Construing PCP: New contexts and perspectives.* 9th EPCA Conference Proceedings, 2008. Norderstedt: Books on Demand.

Burr, V. (2015). *Social constructionism* (3rd ed.). London: Routledge.

Burr, V., & Dick, P. (2017). Social constructionism. In B. Gough (Ed.), *The Palgrave handbook of critical social psychology* (pp. 59–80). London: Palgrave Macmillan.

Butler, J. (1990). *Gender trouble: Feminism and the subversion of identity*. New York: Routledge.

Butler, J. (1993). *Bodies that matter: On the discursive limits of sex*. New York: Routledge.

Butler, J. (1997). *The psychic life of power: Theories in subjection*. Stanford, CA: Stanford University Press.

Calder-Dawe, O., Witten, K., & Carroll, P. (2020). Being the body in question: Young people's accounts of everyday ableism, visibility and disability. *Disability & Society, 35*(1), 132–155.

Calvocoressi, M. (1931). Rimsky-Korsakov's operas reconsidered. *The Musical Times, 72*(1064), 886–888.

Came, H. A. (2013). Doing research in Aotearoa: A Pākehā exemplar of applying Te Ara Tika ethical framework. *Kōtuitui: New Zealand Journal of Social Sciences Online, 8*(1–2), 64–73.

Carbado, D. W., Crenshaw, K. W., Mays, V. M., & Tomlinson, B. (2014). Intersectionality: Mapping the movements of a theory. *Du Bois Review: Social Science Research on Race, 10*(2), 303–312.

Cargle, R. E. (2018, August 16). When feminism is white supremacy in heels. *Harpers Bazaar*. Retrieved from www.harpersbazaar.com/culture/politics/a22717725/what-is-toxic-white-feminism/

Carless, D. (2012). Negotiating sexuality and masculinity in school sport: An autoethnography. *Sport, Education and Society, 17*(5), 607–625.

Carlston, D. E. (Ed.) (2013). *The Oxford handbook of social cognition*. Oxford: Oxford University Press.

Carminati, L. (2018). Generalizability in qualitative research: A tale of two traditions. *Qualitative Health Research, 28*(13), 2094–2101.

Carmody, M. (2008). *Sex and ethics: Young people and ethical sex*. Sydney, Australia: Palgrave Macmillan.

Carpenter, J. (2008). Metaphors in qualitative research: Shedding light or casting shadows? *Research in Nursing & Health, 31*(3), 274–282.

Carpenter, V. M., & McMurchy-Pilkington, C. (2008). Cross-cultural researching: Māori and Pākehā in Te Whakapakari. *Qualitative Research, 8*(2), 179–196.

Carter, S. M., & Little, M. (2007). Justifying knowledge, justifying method, taking action: Epistemologies, methodologies, and methods in qualitative research. *Qualitative Health Research, 17*(10), 1316–1328.

Cassell, C. (n.d.). Criteria for evaluating papers using qualitative research methods. Retrieved from https://onlinelibrary.wiley.com/page/journal/20448325/homepage/qualitative_guidelines.htm

Cassell, C., & Nadin, S. (2004). Using data matrices. In C. Cassell & G. Symon (Eds.), *Essential guide to qualitative methods in organizational research* (pp. 271–287). London: SAGE.

Cedervall, Y., & Åberg, A. C. (2010). Physical activity and implications on well-being in mild Alzheimer's disease: A qualitative case study on two men with dementia and their spouses. *Physiotherapy Theory and Practice, 26*(4), 226–239.

Chamberlain, K. (2000). Methodolatry and qualitative health research. *Journal of Health Psychology, 5*(3), 285–296.

Chamberlain, K. (2004). Qualitative research, reflexivity and context. In M. Murray (Ed.), *Critical health psychology* (pp. 121–136). London: Macmillan.

Chamberlain, K. (2011). Troubling methodology. *Health Psychology Review, 5*(1), 48–54.

Chamberlain, K. (2012). Do you really need a methodology. *QMiP Bulletin, 13*(59), e63.

Chamberlain, K., Cain, T., Sheridan, J., & Dupuis, A. (2011). Pluralisms in qualitative research: From multiple methods to integrated methods. *Qualitative Research in Psychology, 8*(2), 151–169.

Chandler, D. (2017). *Semiotics: The basics.* London: Routledge.

Charlton, J. (2000). *Nothing about us without us: Disability oppression and empowerment.* Oakland, CA: University of California Press.

Charmaz, K. (2014). *Constructing grounded theory* (2nd ed.). Los Angeles, CA: SAGE.

Chen, E. (2013). Neoliberalism and popular women's culture: Rethinking choice, freedom and agency. *European Journal of Cultural Studies, 16*(4), 440–452.

Chenail, R. J. (2010). Getting specific about qualitative research generalizability. *Journal of Ethnographic & Qualitative Research, 5*(1), 1–11.

Chiari, G., & Nuzzo, M. L. (1996). Psychological constructivisms: A metatheoretical differentiation. *Journal of Constructivist Psychology, 9*(3), 163–184.

Choate, P. W., & Engstrom, S. (2014). The "good enough" parent: Implications for child protection. *Child Care in Practice, 20*(4), 368–382.

Christensen, A.-D., & Jensen, S. Q. (2012). Doing intersectional analysis: Methodological implications for qualitative research. *NORA – Nordic Journal of Feminist and Gender Research, 20*(2), 109–125.

Clark, A. M. (2008). Critical realism. In L. M. Given (Ed.), *The SAGE encyclopedia of qualitative research methods* (pp. 168–170). Thousand Oaks, CA: SAGE.

Clarke, V. (2001). What about the children? Arguments against lesbian and gay parenting. *Women's Studies International Forum, 24,* 555–570.

Clarke, V. (2002). Resistance and normalisation in the construction of lesbian and gay families: A discursive analysis. In A. Coyle & C. Kitzinger (Eds.), *Lesbian and gay psychology: New perspectives* (pp. 98–118). Oxford: BPS Blackwell.

Clarke, V. (2005). "We're all very liberal in our views": Students' talk about lesbian and gay parenting. *Lesbian & Gay Psychology Review, 6*(1), 2–15.

Clarke, V. (@DrVicClarke). (2019, January 21). *Hey Twitter - I need your questions about #thematicanalysis!* ... [Tweet]. Twitter. https://twitter.com/drvicclarke/status/1087313296615706624

Clarke, V., & Braun, V. (2018). Using thematic analysis in counselling and psychotherapy research: A critical reflection. *Counselling and Psychotherapy Research, 18*(2), 107–110.

Clarke, V., & Braun, V. (2019a). Feminist qualitative methods and methodologies in psychology: A review and reflection. *Psychology of Women and Equalities Section Review, 2*(1), 13–28.

Clarke, V., & Braun, V. (2019b). How can a heterosexual man remove his body hair and retain his masculinity? Mapping stories of male body hair depilation. *Qualitative Research in Psychology, 16*(1), 96–114.

Clarke, V., Braun, V., Frith, H., & Moller, N. (2019). Editorial introduction to the special issue: Using story completion methods in qualitative research. *Qualitative Research in Psychology, 16*(1), 1–20.

Clarke, V., Braun, V., & Hayfield, N. (2015). Thematic analysis. In J. A. Smith (Ed.), *Qualitative psychology: A practical guide to research methods* (3rd ed., pp. 222–248). London: SAGE.

Clarke, V., Burgoyne, C., & Burns, M. (2013). Unscripted and improvised: Public and private celebrations of same-sex relationships. *Journal of GLBT Family Studies, 9*(4), 393–418.

Clarke, V., Burns, M., & Burgoyne, C. (2008). "Who would take whose name?" Accounts of naming practices in same-sex relationships. *Journal of Community & Applied Social Psychology, 18*, 420–439.

Clarke, V., Ellis, S. J., Peel, E., & Riggs, D. W. (2010). *Lesbian, gay, bisexual, trans & queer psychology: An introduction.* Cambridge: Cambridge University Press.

Clarke, V., Hayfield, N., Ellis, S. J., & Terry, G. (2018). Lived experiences of childfree lesbians in the United Kingdom: A qualitative exploration. *Journal of Family Issues, 39*(18), 4133–4155.

Clarke, V., Hayfield, N., Moller, N., Tischner, I., & The Story Completion Research Group. (2017). Once upon a time…: Qualitative story completion methods. In D. Gray, V. Clarke & V. Braun (Eds.), *Collecting qualitative data: A practical guide to textual, media and virtual techniques* (pp. 45–69). Cambridge: Cambridge University Press.

Clarke, V., Kitzinger, C., & Potter, J. (2004). "Kids are just cruel anyway": Lesbian and gay parents' talk about homophobic bullying. *British Journal of Social Psychology, 43*(4), 531–550.

Clarke, V., Moller, N., Hayfield, N., & Braun, V. (2021). A critical review of the interdisciplinary literature on voluntary childlessness. In H. A. Cummins, J. A. Rodgers & J. D. Wouk (Eds.), *The truth about (m)otherhood: Choosing to be childfree* (pp. 29–54). Bradford, Ontario: Demeter Press.

Clarkson, P. (2003). *The therapeutic relationship.* London: Whurr Publishers.

Cohen, A. K. (1946). An evaluation of "themes" and kindred concepts. *American Journal of Sociology, 52*(1), 41–42.

Colaizzi, P. F. (1978). Psychological research as the phenomenologist views it. In R. S. Valle & M. King (Eds.), *Existential-phenomenological alternatives for psychology* (pp. 48–71). Dubuque, IA: Kendall/Hunt.

Cole, E. R. (2009). Intersectionality and research in psychology. *American Psychologist, 64*(3), 170–180.

Cole, E. R. (2020). Demarginalizing women of color in intersectionality scholarship in psychology: A Black feminist critique. *Journal of Social Issues, 76*(4), 1036–1044.

Collins, P. H. (2019). *Intersectionality as critical social theory.* Durham, NC: Duke University Press.

Collins, P. H., & Bilge, S. (2016). *Intersectionality.* Malden, MA: Polity.

Combahee River Collective. (1995). Combahee River Collective statement. In B. Guy-Sheftall (Ed.), *Words of fire: An anthology of African-American feminist thought* (pp. 232–240). New York: The New Press.

Connelly, L. M., & Peltzer, J. N. (2016). Underdeveloped themes in qualitative research: Relationship with interviews and analysis. *Clinical Nurse Specialist, 30*(1), 52–57.

Cooke, L. P. (2014). Gendered parenthood penalties and premiums across the earnings distribution in Australia, the United Kingdom, and the United States. *European Sociological Review, 30*(3), 360–372.

Crabtree, B. F., & Miller, W. L. (1999). Using codes and code manuals: A template organizing style of interpretation. In B. F. Crabtree & W. L. Miller (Eds.), *Doing qualitative research* (2nd ed., pp. 163–178). Thousand Oaks, CA: SAGE.

Cram, F., McCreanor, T., Smith, L., Nairn, R., & Johnstone, W. (2006). Kaupapa Māori research and Pākehā social science: Epistemological tensions in a study of Māori health. *Hulili, 3*(1), 41–68.

Crenshaw, K. (1991). Mapping the margins: Intersectionality, identity politics, and violence against women of color. *Stanford Law Review, 43*(6), 1241–1299.

Creswell, J. W., & Poth, C. N. (2016). *Qualitative inquiry and research design: Choosing among five approaches.* London: SAGE.

Crotty, M. (1998). *The foundations of social research: Meaning and perspective in the research process.* London: SAGE.

Crowe, M., Inder, M., & Porter, R. (2015). Conducting qualitative research in mental health: Thematic and content analyses. *Australian & New Zealand Journal of Psychiatry, 49*(7), 616–623.

Cruzes, D. S., & Dybå, T. (2011). *Recommended steps for thematic synthesis in software engineering.* Paper presented at the 2011 International Symposium on Empirical Software Engineering and Measurement.

Cunliffe, A. L. (2004). On becoming a reflexive researcher. *Journal of Management Education, 28*(4), 407–426.

Cunliffe, A. L. (2016). "On becoming a critically reflexive practitioner" redux: What does it mean to be reflexive? *Journal of Management Education, 40*(6), 740–746.

Dahl, C., & Boss, P. (2005). The use of phenomenology for family therapy research: The search for meaning. In D. H. Sprenkle & F. P. Piercy (Eds.), *Research methods in family therapy* (pp. 63–84). New York: Guilford Press.

Danermark, B., Ekström, M., Jakobsen, L., & Karlsson, J. C. (2002). *Explaining society: Critical realism in the social sciences.* London: Routledge.

Dapkus, M. A. (1985). A thematic analysis of the experience of time. *Journal of Personality and Social Psychology, 49*(2), 408–419.

Darnell, S. C., & Hayhurst, L. M. C. (2013). De-colonising the politics and practice of sport-for-development: Critical insights from post-colonial feminist theory and methods. In N. Schulenkorf & D. Adair (Eds.), *Global sport-for-development: Critical perspectives* (pp. 33–61). London: Palgrave Macmillan.

Davey, L., Clarke, V., & Jenkinson, E. (2019). Living with alopecia areata: An online qualitative survey study. *British Journal of Dermatology, 180*(6), 1377–1389.

Davies, B., & Harré, R. (1990). Positioning: The discursive production of selves. *Journal for the Theory of Social Behaviour, 20*, 43–63.

De Finney, S. (2010). "We just don't know each other": Racialised girls negotiate mediated multiculturalism in a less diverse Canadian city. *Journal of Intercultural Studies, 31*(5), 471–487.

de Schipper, T., Lieberman, L. J., & Moody, B. (2017). "Kids like me, we go lightly on the head": Experiences of children with a visual impairment on the physical self-concept. *British Journal of Visual Impairment, 35*(1), 55–68.

de Souza, K. L. (2019). Pesquisa com análise qualitativa de dados: conhecendo a análise temática. *Arquivos Brasileiros de Psicologia, 71*(2), 51–67.

Denzin, N. K. (2013). "The death of data?" *Cultural Studies ↔ Critical Methodologies, 13*(4), 353–356.

Denzin, N. K., & Lincoln, Y. S. (2005). Introduction: The discipline and practice of qualitative research. In N. K. Denzin & Y. S. Lincoln (Eds.), *The SAGE handbook of qualitative research* (2nd ed., pp. 1–32). Thousand Oaks, CA: SAGE.

Denzin, N. K., Lincoln, Y. S., & Smith, L. T. (Eds.). (2008). *Handbook of critical and Indigenous methodologies.* Los Angeles, CA: SAGE.

DePalma, R., & Atkinson, E. (2010). The nature of institutional heteronormativity in primary schools and practice-based responses. *Teaching and Teacher Education, 26*(8), 1669–1676.

DeSantis, L., & Ugarriza, D. N. (2000). The concept of theme as used in qualitative nursing research. *Western Journal of Nursing Research, 22*(3), 351–372.

DiAngelo, R. (2018). *White fragility: Why it's so hard for white people to talk about racism.* Boston, MA: Beacon Press.

DiLapi, E. M. (1989). Lesbian mothers and the motherhood hierarchy. *Journal of Homosexuality, 18*(1–2), 101–121.

Dixon-Woods, M., Agarwal, S., Jones, D., Young, B., & Sutton, A. (2005). Synthesising qualitative and quantitative evidence: A review of possible methods. *Journal of Health Services Research & Policy, 10*(1), 45–53.

Dixon-Woods, M., Bonas, S., Booth, A., Jones, D. R., Miller, T., Sutton, A. J., ... Young, B. (2006). How can systematic reviews incorporate qualitative research? A critical perspective. *Qualitative Research, 6*(1), 27–44.

Downe-Wamboldt, B. (1992). Content analysis: Method, applications, and issues. *Health Care for Women International, 13*(3), 313–321.

Duberley, J., Johnson, P., & Cassell, C. (2012). Philosophies underpinning qualitative research. In G. Symon & C. Cassell (Eds.), *Qualitative organizational research: Core methods and current challenges* (pp. 15–34). London: SAGE.

Duncan, S., Edwards, R., & Song, M. (2002). Social threat or social problem: Media representations of lone mothers and policy implications. In B. Franklin (Ed.), *Social policy, the media and misrepresentation* (pp. 238–252). London: Routledge.

Ebright, P. R., Urden, L., Patterson, E., & Chalko, B. (2004). Themes surrounding novice nurse near-miss and adverse-event situations. *JONA: The Journal of Nursing Administration, 34*(11), 531–538.

Eddo-Lodge, R. (2018). *Why I'm no longer talking to white people about race.* London: Bloomsbury.

Edwards, D., Ashmore, M., & Potter, J. (1995). Death and furniture: The rhetoric, politics and theology of bottom line arguments against relativism. *History of the Human Sciences, 8*, 25–49.

Efran, J. S., McNamee, S., Warren, B., & Raskin, J. D. (2014). Personal construct psychology, radical constructivism, and social constructionism: A dialogue. *Journal of Constructivist Psychology*, *27*(1), 1–13.

Elliott, R., Fischer, C. T., & Rennie, D. L. (1999). Evolving guidelines for publication of qualitative research studies in psychology and related fields. *British Journal of Clinical Psychology*, *38*(3), 215–229.

Ellis, S. J. (2001). Doing being liberal: Implicit prejudice in focus group talk about lesbian and gay human rights issues. *Lesbian & Gay Psychology Review*, *2*(2), 43–49.

Ely, M., Vinz, R., Downing, M., & Anzul, M. (1997). *On writing qualitative research: Living by words*. London: Routledge.

Enriquez, V. (1976). Sikolohiyang Pilipino: Perspektibo at Direksiyon. In L. F. Antonio, E. S. Reyes , R.E. Pe & N.R. Almonte (Eds.), *Ulat ng Unang Pambansang Kumperensya sa Sikolohiyang Pilipino: Ginanap sa Unibersidad ng Pilipinas sa Diliman* (pp. 221–243). Quezon City, Philippines: Pambansang Samahan sa Sikolohiyang Pilipino.

Enriquez, V. (2013). *From colonial to liberation psychology: The Philippine experience*. Manila: DLSU Press.

Evans, G. (2018, March 2). The unwelcome revival of "race science". *The Guardian*. Retrieved from www.theguardian.com/news/2018/mar/02/the-unwelcome-revival-of-race-science

Evers, J. C. (2018). Current issues in Qualitative Data Analysis Software (QDAS): A user and developer perspective. *The Qualitative Report*, *23*(13), 61–73.

Fahs, B. (2012). Breaking body hair boundaries: Classroom exercises for challenging social constructions of the body and sexuality. *Feminism & Psychology*, *22*(4), 482–506.

Fahs, B. (2013). Shaving it all off: Examining social norms of body hair among college men in a women's studies course. *Women's Studies*, *42*(5), 559–577.

Fairchild, S. R. (2002). Women with disabilities. *Journal of Human Behavior in the Social Environment*, *6*(2), 13–28.

Fenaughty, J., Braun, V., Gavey, N., Aspin, C., Reynolds, P., & Schmidt, J. (2006). *Sexual coercion among gay men, bisexual men and takatāpui tāne in Aotearoa/New Zealand*. Auckland: The University of Auckland.

Fine, M. (1992). *Disruptive voices: The possibilities of feminist research*. Ann Arbor, MI: University of Michigan Press

Fine, M., & Torre, M. E. (2004). Re-membering exclusions: Participatory action research in public institutions. *Qualitative Research in Psychology*, *1*(1), 15–37.

Fine, M., & Torre, M. E. (2006). Intimate details: Participatory action research in prison. *Action Research*, *4*(3), 253–269.

Fine, M., Tuck, E., & Zeller-Berkman, S. (2008). Do you believe in Geneva? Methods and ethics at the global–local nexus. In N. K. Denzin, Y. S. Lincoln & L. T. Smith (Eds.), *Handbook of critical and Indigenous methodologies* (pp. 157–179). Los Angeles, CA: SAGE.

Finlay, L. (2002a). Negotiating the swamp: The opportunity and challenge of reflexivity in research practice. *Qualitative Research*, *2*(2), 209–230.

Finlay, L. (2002b). "Outing" the researcher: The provenance, process, and practice of reflexivity. *Qualitative Health Research*, *12*(4), 531–545.

Finlay, L., & Gough, B. (Eds.). (2003). *Reflexivity: A practical guide for researchers in health and social sciences.* Oxford: Blackwell Science.

Flick, U. (2014a). *An introduction to qualitative research* (5th ed.). London: SAGE.

Flick, U. (2014b). Mapping the field. In U. Flick (Ed.), *The SAGE handbook of qualitative data analysis* (pp. 1–18). London: SAGE.

Flick, U. (2018). *An introduction to qualitative research* (6th ed.). London: SAGE.

Flick, U. (2019). The concepts of qualitative data: Challenges in neoliberal times for qualitative inquiry. *Qualitative Inquiry, 25*(8), 713–720.

Floersch, J., Longhofer, J. L., Kranke, D., & Townsend, L. (2010). Integrating thematic, grounded theory and narrative analysis: A case study of adolescent psychotropic treatment. *Qualitative Social Work, 9*(3), 407–425.

Flood, M. (2008). Men, sex, and homosociality: How bonds between men shape their sexual relations with women. *Men and Masculinities, 10*(3), 339–359.

Flowers, P., & Langdridge, D. (2007). Offending the other: Deconstructing narratives of deviance and pathology. *British Journal of Social Psychology, 46*, 679–690.

Ford, A., Moodie, C., Purves, R., & MacKintosh, A. M. (2016). Adolescent girls and young adult women's perceptions of superslims cigarette packaging: A qualitative study. *British Medical Journal Open, 6*(1), e010102.

Fornells-Ambrojo, M., Johns, L., Onwumere, J., Garety, P., Milosh, C., Iredale, C., ... Jolley, S. (2017). Experiences of outcome monitoring in service users with psychosis: Findings from an Improving Access to Psychological Therapies for people with Severe Mental Illness (IAPT-SMI) demonstration site. *British Journal of Clinical Psychology, 56*(3), 253–272.

Foucault, M. (1977). *Discipline and punish: The birth of the prison* (A. Sheridan, Trans.). London: Allen Lane.

Foucault, M. (1978). *The history of sexuality (Volume 1: An introduction)* (R. Hurley, Trans.). London: Penguin.

Fox, K. R., & Corbin, C. B. (1989). The physical self-perception profile: Development and preliminary validation. *Journal of Sport and Exercise Psychology, 11*(4), 408–430.

Frank, E. (2014). Groomers and consumers: The meanings of male body depilation to a modern masculinity body project. *Men and Masculinities, 17*(3), 278–298.

Frost, N., & Nolas, S.-M. (2011). Exploring and expanding on pluralism in qualitative research in psychology. *Qualitative Research in Psychology, 8*(2), 115–119.

Fugard, A., & Potts, H. W. W. (2020). Thematic analysis. In P. Atkinson, S. Delamont, A. Cernat, J. W. Sakshaug & R. A. Williams (Eds.), *SAGE research methods foundations.* London: SAGE.

Gabriel, D. (n.d.). Racial categorisation and terminology. *BlackBritishAcademics.* Retrieved from https://blackbritishacademics.co.uk/about/racial-categorisation-and-terminology/

Gadberry, A. L. (2014). Cross-cultural perspective: A thematic analysis of a music therapist's experience providing treatment in a foreign country. *Australian Journal of Music Therapy, 25*, 66–80.

Gale, N. K., Heath, G., Cameron, E., Rashid, S., & Redwood, S. (2013). Using the framework method for the analysis of qualitative data in multi-disciplinary health research. *BMC Medical Research Methodology, 13*(1), 117.

Garcia, J., Bricker, L., Henderson, J., Martin, M. A., Mugford, M., Nielson, J., & Roberts, T. (2002). Women's views of pregnancy ultrasound: A systematic review. *Birth, 29*(4), 225–250.

Gavey, N. (1989). Feminist poststructuralism and discourse analysis: Contributions to feminist psychology. *Psychology of Women Quarterly, 13*(4), 459–475.

Gavey, N. (2018). *Just sex? The cultural scaffolding of rape* (2nd ed.). London: Routledge.

Gavey, N., Schmidt, J., Braun, V., Fenaughty, J., & Eremin, M. (2009). Unsafe, unwanted: Sexual coercion as a barrier to safer sex among men who have sex with men. *Journal of Health Psychology, 14*(7), 1021–1026.

Gergen, K. J. (1973). Social psychology as history. *Journal of Personality and Social Psychology, 26*(2), 309.

Gergen, K. J. (1999). *An invitation to social construction.* London: SAGE.

Gergen, K. J. (2015). *An invitation to social construction* (3rd ed.). Los Angeles, CA: SAGE.

Gergen, M. M. (1988). Toward a feminist metatheory and methodology in the social sciences. In M. M. Gergen (Ed.), *Feminist thought and the structure of knowledge* (pp. 87–104). New York: New York University Press.

Gergen, M. M. (2017). Qualitative methods in feminist psychology. In C. Willig & W. Stainton Rogers (Eds.), *The SAGE handbook of qualitative research in psychology* (pp. 289–304). London: SAGE.

Gerstl-Pepin, C., & Patrizio, K. (2009). Learning from Dumbledore's Pensieve: Metaphor as an aid in teaching reflexivity in qualitative research. *Qualitative Research, 9*(3), 299–308.

Gibbs, G. R. (2007). *Analysing qualitative data.* London: SAGE.

Giles, D. (2017). Online discussion forums. In V. Braun, V. Clarke & D. Gray (Eds.), *Collecting qualitative data: A practical guide to textual, media and virtual techniques* (pp. 166–188). Cambridge: Cambridge University Press.

Giles, D., Shaw, R. L., & Morgan, W. (2009). Representations of voluntary childlessness in the UK press, 1990–2008. *Journal of Health Psychology, 14*(8), 1218–1228.

Gill, R. (2008). Culture and subjectivity in neoliberal and postfeminist times. *Subjectivity, 25*(1), 432–445.

Gill, R., & Orgad, S. (2018). The amazing bounce-backable woman: Resilience and the psychological turn in neoliberalism. *Sociological Research Online, 23*(2), 477–495.

Gill, R., Henwood, K., & Mclean, C. (2005). Body projects and the regulation of normative masculinity. *Body & Society, 11*(1), 37–62.

Glaser, B. G. (1978). *Theoretical sensitivity: Advances in the methodology of grounded theory.* Mill Valley, CA: Sociology Press.

Glaser, B. G. (1992). *Basics of grounded theory analysis: Emergence vs. forcing.* Mill Valley, CA: Sociology Press.

Glaser, B. G., & Strauss, A. L. (1967). *The discovery of grounded theory.* Chicago, IL: Aldine.

Glaw, X., Inder, K., Kable, A., & Hazelton, M. (2017). Visual methodologies in qualitative research: Autophotography and photo elicitation applied to mental health research. *International Journal of Qualitative Methods, 16*(1).https://journals.sagepub.com/doi/full/10.1177/1609406917748215

Gleeson, K. (2011). Polytextual thematic analysis for visual data: Pinning down the analytic. In P. Reavey (Ed.), *Visual methods in psychology: Using and interpreting images in qualitative research* (pp. 314–329). London: Routledge.

Gleeson, K. (2021). Polytextual thematic analysis for visual data: Analysing visual images. In P. Reavey (Ed.), *A handbook of visual methods in psychology: Using and interpreting images in qualitative research* (pp. 536–554). London: Routledge.

Goodman, S. (2008). The generalizability of discursive research. *Qualitative Research in Psychology, 5*(4), 265–275.

Gough, B. (2002). "I've always tolerated it but...": Heterosexual masculinity and the discursive reproduction of homophobia. In A. Coyle & C. Kitzinger (Eds.), *Lesbian and gay psychology: New perspectives* (pp. 219–239). Oxford: Blackwell.

Gough, B. (2007). Coming out in the heterosexist world of sport: A qualitative analysis of web postings by gay athletes. *Journal of Gay and Lesbian Psychotherapy, 11*(1–2), 153–174.

Gough, B. (2017). Reflexivity in qualitative psychological research. *The Journal of Positive Psychology, 12*(3), 311–312.

Gough, B., & Lyons, A. (2016). The future of qualitative research in psychology: Accentuating the positive. *Integrative Psychological and Behavioral Science, 50*(2), 234–243.

Gough, B., & Madill, A. (2012). Subjectivity in psychological science: From problem to prospect. *Psychological Methods, 17*(3), 374–384.

Graham, M., & Rich, S. (2014). Representations of childless women in the Australian print media. *Feminist Media Studies, 14*(3), 500–518.

Grant, B. M., & Giddings, L. S. (2002). Making sense of methodologies: A paradigm framework for the novice researcher. *Contemporary Nurse, 13*(1), 10–28.

Green, J., & Thorogood, N. (2009). *Qualitative methods for health research* (2nd ed.). Los Angeles, CA: SAGE.

Green, L., & Guinery, C. (2004). Harry Potter and the fan fiction phenomenon. *M/C Journal, 7*(5). https://doi.org/10.5204/mcj.2442

Guba, E. G., & Lincoln, Y. S. (1982). Epistemological and methodological bases of naturalistic inquiry. *Educational Communication and Technology, 30*(4), 233–252.

Guba, E. G., & Lincoln, Y. S. (1994). Competing paradigms in qualitative research. In N. K. Denzin & Y. S. Lincoln (Eds.), *The SAGE handbook of qualitative research* (2nd ed., pp. 105–117). London: SAGE.

Guest, G., MacQueen, K. M., & Namey, E. E. (2012). *Applied thematic analysis.* Los Angeles, CA: SAGE.

Hall, G., Shearer, D., Thomson, R., Roderique-Davies, G., Mayer, P., & Hall, R. (2012). Conceptualising commitment: A thematic analysis of fans of Welsh rugby. *Qualitative Research in Sport, Exercise and Health, 4*(1), 138–153.

Hall, M., & Gough, B. (2011). Magazine and reader constructions of 'metrosexuality' and masculinity: A membership categorisation analysis. *Journal of Gender Studies, 20*(1), 67–86.

Hall, S. (1997). The work of representation. In S. Hall (Ed.), *Representation: Cultural representations and signifying practices* (pp. 13–74). London: SAGE.

Hamilton-Chadwick, A. (2017, August 15). How much does it cost to raise a child in New Zealand? *Juno Investing.* Retrieved from www.junoinvesting.co.nz/personal-finance/2017/8/15/how-much-does-it-cost-to-raise-a-child

Hammersley, M. (1992). *What's wrong with ethnography? Methodological explorations.* London: Routledge.

Haraway, D. (1988). Situated knowledges: The science question in feminism and the privilege of partial perspective. *Feminist Studies, 14*(3), 575–599.

Harding, S. G. (Ed.) (2004). *The feminist standpoint theory reader: Intellectual and political controversies.* New York: Routledge.

Harper, D. A. (2012). *Visual sociology*. London: Routledge.

Harrison, R. (1943). The Thematic Apperception and Rorschach methods of personality investigation in clinical practice. *The Journal of Psychology, 15*(1), 49–74.

Hayes, N. (1997). Theory-led thematic analysis: Social identification in small companies. In N. Hayes (Ed.), *Doing qualitative analysis in psychology* (pp. 93–114). Hove, UK: Psychology Press.

Hayes, N. (2000). *Doing psychological research: Gathering and analyzing data*. Phildelphia, PA: Open University Press.

Hayfield, N., Clarke, V., & Halliwell, E. (2014). Bisexual women's understandings of social marginalisation: "The heterosexuals don't understand us but nor do the lesbians". *Feminism & Psychology, 24*(3), 352–372.

Hayfield, N., & Huxley, C. (2015). Insider and outsider perspectives: Reflections on researcher identities in research with lesbian and bisexual women. *Qualitative Research in Psychology, 12*(2), 91–106.

Hayfield, N., Terry, G., Clarke, V., & Ellis, S. (2019). "Never say never?" Heterosexual, bisexual, and lesbian women's accounts of being childfree. *Psychology of Women Quarterly, 43*(4), 526–538.

Hayhurst, L. M. C., Giles, A. R., Radforth, W. M., & The Vancouver Aboriginal Friendship Centre Society. (2015). "I want to come here to prove them wrong": Using a post-colonial feminist participatory action research (PFPAR) approach to studying sport, gender and development programmes for urban Indigenous young women. *Sport in Society, 18*(8), 952–967.

Heath, N. M., Lynch, S. M., Fritch, A. M., McArthur, L. N., & Smith, S. L. (2011). Silent survivors: Rape myth acceptance in incarcerated women's narratives of disclosure and reporting of rape. *Psychology of Women Quarterly, 35*(4), 596–610.

Hellawell, D. (2006). Inside-out: Analysis of the insider–outsider concept as a heuristic device to develop reflexivity in students doing qualitative research. *Teaching in Higher Education, 11*(4), 483–494.

Hellström, T. (2008). Transferability and naturalistic generalization: New generalizability concepts for social science or old wine in new bottles? *Quality & Quantity, 42*(3), 321–337.

Henriksson, C., & Friesen, N. (2012). Introduction. In N. Friesen, C. Henriksson & T. Saevi (Eds.), *Hermeneutic phenomenology in education: Method and practice* (pp. 1–17). Rotterdam: Sense Publishers.

Henwood, K., & Pidgeon, N. (1994). Beyond the qualitative paradigm: A framework for introducing diversity within qualitative psychology. *Journal of Community & Applied Social Psychology, 4*(4), 225–238.

Hereford Cathedral. (n.d.). *Mappa mundi*. Retrieved from www.themappamundi.co.uk/

Higgins, J. P. T., & Green, S. (Eds.). (2011). *Cochrane handbook for systematic reviews of interventions* (version 5.1.0). Chichester, UK: John Wiley & Sons.

Ho, K. H., Chiang, V. C., & Leung, D. (2017). Hermeneutic phenomenological analysis: The "possibility" beyond "actuality" in thematic analysis. *Journal of Advanced Nursing, 73*(7), 1757–1766.

Holstein, J. A., & Gubrium, J. F. (2011). The constructionist analytics of interpretive practice. In N. K. Denzin & Y. S. Lincoln (Eds.), *The SAGE handbook of qualitative research* (4th ed., pp. 341–358). Thousand Oaks, CA: SAGE.

Holton, G. J. (1973). *Thematic origins of scientific thought: Kepler to Einstein*. Cambridge, MA: Harvard University Press.

Howard, A. (2020, June 4). Dear White people: Get your own house in order. *Daily Beast*. Retrieved from www.thedailybeast.com/dear-white-people-get-your-own-house-in-order

Hruschka, D. J., Schwartz, D., St. John, D. C., Picone-Decaro, E., Jenkins, R. A., & Carey, J. W. (2004). Reliability in coding open-ended data: Lessons learned from HIV behavioral research. *Field Methods, 16*(3), 307–331.

Huxley, C., Clarke, V., & Halliwell, E. (2011). "It's a comparison thing isn't it?": Lesbian and bisexual women's accounts of how partner relationships shape their feelings about their body and appearance. *Psychology of Women Quarterly, 35*(3), 415–427.

Immergut, M. (2002). Manscaping: The tangle of nature, culture, and male body hair. In L. J. Moore & M. Kosut (Eds.), *The body reader: Essential social and cultural readings* (pp. 287–299). New York: NYU Press.

Jackson, K., Paulus, T., & Woolf, N. H. (2018). *The Walking Dead* genealogy: Unsubstantiated criticisms of Qualitative Data Analysis Software (QDAS) and the failure to put them to rest. *The Qualitative Report, 23*(13), 74–91.

Jagose, A. (1996). *Queer theory: An introduction*. Melbourne: Melbourne Univiversity Press.

Janesick, V. J. (2010). *"Stretching" exercises for qualitative researchers* (4 ed.). Los Angeles, CA: SAGE.

Jankowski, G., Braun, V., & Clarke, V. (2017). Reflecting on qualitative research, feminist methodologies and feminist psychology: In conversation with Virginia Braun and Victoria Clarke. *Psychology of Women Section Review, 19*(1), 43–55.

Jaschik, S. (2017, February 27). Professors and politics: What the research says. *Inside Higher Ed*. Retrieved from www.insidehighered.com/news/2017/02/27/research-confirms-professors-lean-left-questions-assumptions-about-what-means

Jaspal, R., & Breakwell, G. M. (2014). *Identity process theory: Identity, social action and social change*. Cambridge: Cambridge University Press.

Jaspal, R., & Cinnirella, M. (2012). Identity processes, threat, and interpersonal relations: Accounts from British Muslim gay men. *Journal of Homosexuality, 59*(2), 215–240.

Jennings, E., Braun, V., & Clarke, V. (2019). Breaking gendered boundaries? Exploring constructions of counter-normative body hair practices in Aotearoa/New Zealand using story completion. *Qualitative Research in Psychology, 16*(1), 74–95.

Joffe, H. (2012). Thematic analysis. In D. Harper & A. R. Thompson (Eds.), *Qualitative research methods in mental health and psychotherapy: A guide for students and practitioners* (pp. 109–223). Chichester: Wiley.

Joffe, H., & Yardley, L. (2004). Content and thematic analysis. In D. Marks & L. Yardley (Eds.), *Research methods for clinical and health psychology* (pp. 56–68). London: SAGE.

Jowett, A. (2014). "But if you legalise same-sex marriage...": Arguments against marriage equality in the British press. *Feminism & Psychology, 24*(1), 37–55.

Kahn, M. (1997). *Between therapist and client: The new relationship*. London: Macmillan.

Kara, H. (2015). *Creative research methods in the social sciences: A practical guide*. Bristol: Policy Press.

Kelly, A., & Ciclitira, K. (2011). Eating and drinking habits of young London-based Irish men: A qualitative study. *Journal of Gender Studies, 20*(3), 223–235.

Kelly, G. (1955). *The psychology of personal constructs*. New York: Norton.

Kelly, M., & Humphrey, C. (2013). Implementation of the care programme approach across health and social services for dual diagnosis clients. *Journal of Intellectual Disabilities, 17*(4), 314–328.

Kennedy, B. L. (2018). Deduction, induction, and abduction. In U. Flick (Ed.), *The SAGE handbook of qualitative data collection* (pp. 49–64). London: SAGE.

Kidder, L. H., & Fine, M. (1987). Qualitative and quantitative methods: When stories converge. In M. M. Mark & L. Shotland (Eds.), *New directions for program evaluation* (pp. 57–75). San Francisco, CA: Jossey-Bass.

Kincheloe, J. L. (2001). Describing the bricolage: Conceptualizing a new rigor in qualitative research. *Qualitative Inquiry, 7*(6), 679–692.

King, N. (1998). Template analysis. In G. Symon & C. Cassell (Eds.), *Qualitative methods and analysis in organizational research: A practical guide* (pp. 118–134). Thousand Oaks, CA: SAGE.

King, N. (2004). Using templates in the thematic analysis of text. In C. Cassell & G. Symon (Eds.), *Essential guide to qualitative methods in organizational research* (pp. 256–270). London: SAGE.

King, N. (2012). Doing template analysis. In G. Symon & C. Cassell (Eds.), *Qualitative organizational research: Core methods and current challenges* (pp. 426–450). London: SAGE.

King, N. (2016). Template analysis. Retrieved from www.hud.ac.uk/hhs/research/template-analysis/

King, N., & Brooks, J. M. (2016). *Template analysis for business and management students.* London: SAGE.

King, N., & Brooks, J. M. (2018). Thematic analysis in organisational research. In C. Cassell, A. L. Cunliffe & G. Grandy (Eds.), *The SAGE handbook of qualitative business management research methods: Methods and challenges* (pp. 219–236). London: SAGE.

King, P., Hodgetts, D., Rua, M., & Whetu, T. T. (2015). Older men gardening on the Marae: Everyday practices for being Māori. *AlterNative: An International Journal of Indigenous Peoples, 11*(1), 14–28.

Kinsky, G., & Strunk, W. O. (1933). Was Mendelssohn indebted to Weber? An attempted solution of an old controversy. *The Musical Quarterly, 19*(2), 178–186.

Kitzinger, C. (1995). Social constructionism: Implications for lesbian and gay psychology. In A. R. D'Augelli & C. J. Patterson (Eds.), *Lesbian, gay, and bisexual identities over the lifespan: Psychological perspectives* (pp. 136–161). New York: Oxford University Press.

Kitzinger, C., & Wilkinson, S. (1996). Theorizing representing the other. In S. Wilkinson & C. Kitzinger (Eds.), *Representing the other: A feminism & psychology reader* (pp. 1–32). London: SAGE.

Kjaran, J. I., & Jóhannesson, I. Á. (2013). Manifestations of heterosexism in Icelandic upper secondary schools and the responses of LGBT students. *Journal of LGBT Youth, 10*(4), 351–372.

Kramer, S. P. (2014, April 26). Sweden pushed gender equality to boost birth rates. *Women's eNews.* Retrieved from https://womensenews.org/2014/04/sweden-pushed-gender-equality-boost-birth-rates/

Kugel, S. (2013, September 6). The gender gap in travel: Myths and revelations. *New York Times.* Retrieved from https://frugaltraveler.blogs.nytimes.com/2011/09/06/the-gender-gap-in-travel-myths-and-revelations/

Lainson, K., Braun, V., & Clarke, V. (2019). Being both narrative practitioner and academic researcher: A reflection on what thematic analysis has to offer narratively informed research. *International Journal of Narrative Therapy & Community Work*, (4), 86–91.

Lampman, C., & Dowling-Guyer, S. (1995). Attitudes toward voluntary and involuntary childlessness. *Basic and Applied Social Psychology*, *17*(1–2), 213–222.

Langdridge, D. (2004). *Introduction to research methods and data analysis in psychology*. London: Pearson Education.

Langdridge, D. (2017). Phenomenology. In B. Gough (Ed.), *The Palgrave handbook of critical social psychology* (pp. 165–183). London: Palgrave Macmillan.

Larsson, E., Lloyd, S., Westwood, H., & Tchanturia, K. (2018). Patients' perspective of a group intervention for perfectionism in anorexia nervosa: A qualitative study. *Journal of Health Psychology*, *23*(12), 1521–1532.

Lather, P. (1991). *Getting smart: Feminist research and pedagogy with/in the postmodern*. New York: Routledge.

Lather, P. (2016). Top ten+ list: (Re)thinking ontology in (post)qualitative research. *Cultural Studies ↔ Critical Methodologies*, *16*(2), 125–131.

Lather, P., & St. Pierre, E. A. (2013). Post-qualitative research. *International Journal of Qualitative Studies in Education*, *26*(6), 629–633.

Lazarsfeld, P. F., & Merton, R. K. (1944). *The psychological analysis of propaganda*. Paper presented at the Writers' Congress. The Proceedings of the Conference held in October 1943 under the sponsorhip of the Hollywood Writers' Mobilization and the University of California.

Le Grice, J. S. (2014). *Māori and reproduction, sexuality education, maternity, and abortion* (PhD thesis). The University of Auckland, Auckland.

Le Grice, J. S., & Braun, V. (2016). Mātauranga Māori and reproduction: Inscribing connections between the natural environment, kin and the body. *AlterNative: An International Journal of Indigenous Peoples*, *12*(2), 151–164.

Le Grice, J. S., & Braun, V. (2017). Indigenous (Māori) perspectives on abortion in New Zealand. *Feminism & Psychology*, *27*(2), 144–162.

Le Grice, J. S., Braun, V., & Wetherell, M. (2017). "What I reckon is, is that like the love you give to your kids they'll give to someone else and so on and so on": Whanaungatanga and mātauranga Māori in practice. *New Zealand Journal of Psychology*, *46*(3), 88–97.

Leal, I., Engebretson, J., Cohen, L., Rodriguez, A., Wangyal, T., Lopez, G., & Chaoul, A. (2015). Experiences of paradox: A qualitative analysis of living with cancer using a framework approach. *Psycho-Oncology*, *24*(2), 138–146.

Lee, J. (2009). Decolonising Māori narratives: Pūrākau as method. *Mai Review*, *91*(2), Article 9. http://www.review.mai.ac.nz/mrindex/MR/article/view/242/268.html

Lenskyj, H. J. (2013). Reflections on communication and sport: On heteronormativity and gender identities. *Communication & Sport*, *1*(1–2), 138–150.

Levitt, H. M., Bamberg, M., Creswell, J. W., Frost, D. M., Josselson, R., & Suárez-Orozco, C. (2018). Journal article reporting standards for qualitative primary, qualitative meta-analytic, and mixed methods research in psychology: The APA Publications and Communications Board task force report. *American Psychologist*, *73*(1), 26–46.

Levitt, H. M., Motulsky, S. L., Wertz, F. J., Morrow, S. L., & Ponterotto, J. G. (2017). Recommendations for designing and reviewing qualitative research in psychology: Promoting methodological integrity. *Qualitative Psychology, 4*(1), 2–22.

Lewis, J., Ritchie, J., Ormston, R., & Morrell, G. (2014). Generalising from qualitative research. In J. Ritchie, J. Lewis, C. McNaughton Nicholls & R. Ormston (Eds.), *Qualitative research practice: A guide for social science students and researchers* (2nd ed., pp. 347–366). London: SAGE.

Li, A. Y., & Braun, V. (2017). Pubic hair and its removal: A practice beyond the personal. *Feminism & Psychology, 27*(3), 336–356.

Lincoln, Y. S. (1995). Emerging criteria for quality in qualitative and interpretive research. *Qualitative Inquiry, 1*(3), 275–289.

Lincoln, Y. S., & Guba, E. G. (1985). *Naturalistic inquiry*. Newbury Park, CA: SAGE.

Lincoln, Y. S., & Guba, E. G. (2000). Paradigmatic controversies, contradictions, and emerging confluences. In N. K. Denzin & Y. S. Lincoln (Eds.), *The SAGE handbook of qualitative research* (2nd ed., pp. 163–188). Thousand Oaks, CA: SAGE.

Lincoln, Y. S., Lynham, S. A., & Guba, E. G. (2011). Paradigmatic controversies, contradictions, and emerging confluences, revisited. In N. K. Denzin & Y. S. Lincoln (Eds.), *The SAGE handbook of qualitative research* (4 ed., pp. 97–128). Thousand Oaks, CA: SAGE.

Lorch, R., Hocking, J., Guy, R., Vaisey, A., Wood, A., Lewis, D., & Temple-Smith, M. (2015). Practice nurse chlamydia testing in Australian general practice: A qualitative study of benefits, barriers and facilitators. *BMC Family Practice, 16*(1), 36.

Luborsky, M. (1994). The identification and analysis of themes and patterns. In J. F. Gubrium & A. Sankar (Eds.), *Qualitative methods in aging research* (pp. 189–210). Thousand Oaks, CA: SAGE.

Lupton, D. (2019). Toward a more-than-human analysis of digital health: Inspirations from feminist new materialism. *Qualitative Health Research, 29*(14), 1998–2009.

Luttrell, W. (2019). Reflexive qualitative research. In G. W. Noblit (Ed.), *The Oxford encyclopedia of qualitative research methods in education*. Oxford: Oxford University Press.

MacKenzie, D., Huntington, A., & Gilmour, J. A. (2009). The experiences of people with an intersex condition: A journey from silence to voice. *Journal of Clinical Nursing, 18*(12), 1775–1783.

Macleod, C. I., Marx, J., Mnyaka, P., & Treharne, G. J. (Eds.). (2018). *The Palgrave handbook of ethics in critical research*. London: Palgrave Macmillan.

MacQueen, K. M., McLellan, E., Kay, K., & Milstein, B. (1998). Codebook development for team-based qualitative analysis. *CAM Journal, 10*(2), 31–36.

Madill, A. (2015). Qualitative research is not a paradigm. *Qualitative Psychology, 2*(2), 214–220.

Madill, A., & Gough, B. (2008). Qualitative research and its place in psychological science. *Psychological Methods, 13*(3), 254–271.

Madill, A., Jordan, A., & Shirley, C. (2000). Objectivity and reliability in qualitative analysis: Realist, contextualist and radical constructionist epistemologies. *British Journal of Psychology, 91*(1), 1–20.

Magnusson, E., & Marecek, J. (2015). *Doing interview-based qualitative research: A learner's guide*: Cambridge: Cambridge University Press.

Malterud, K. (2012). Systematic text condensation: A strategy for qualitative analysis. *Scandinavian Journal of Public Health, 40*(8), 795–805.

Malterud, K. (2016). Theory and interpretation in qualitative studies from general practice: Why and how? *Scandinavian Journal of Public Health, 44*(2), 120–129.

Malterud, K., Siersma, V. D., & Guassora, A. D. (2016). Sample size in qualitative interview studies: Guided by information power. *Qualitative Health Research, 26*(13), 1753–1760.

Manago, A. M. (2013). Negotiating a sexy masculinity on social networking sites. *Feminism & Psychology, 23*(4), 478–497.

Mannay, D. (2015). Achieving respectable motherhood? Exploring the impossibility of feminist and egalitarian ideologies against the everyday realities of lived Welsh working-class femininities. *Women's Studies International Forum, 53*, 159–166.

Mannay, D. (2016). *Visual, narrative and creative research methods: Application, reflection and ethics*. London: Routledge.

Marcu, A., Gaspar, R., Rutsaert, P., Seibt, B., Fletcher, D., Verbeke, W., & Barnett, J. (2015). Analogies, metaphors, and wondering about the future: Lay sense-making around synthetic meat. *Public Understanding of Science, 24*(5), 547–562.

Marfelt, M. M. (2016). Grounded intersectionality: Key tensions, a methodological framework, and implications for diversity research. *Equality, Diversity and Inclusion: An International Journal, 35*(1), 31–47.

Marshall, C., & Rossman, G. B. (2015). *Designing qualitative research*. Los Angeles, CA: SAGE.

Matthews, E. J., & Desjardins, M. (2017). Remaking our identities: Couples' experiences of voluntary childlessness. *The Family Journal, 25*(1), 31–39.

Matthews, S. (2014, May 20). Enough is enough: Poor women are not having babies for money. *Rewire News*. Retrieved from https://rewire.news/article/2014/05/20/enough-enough-poor-women-babies-money/

Maturana, H. R. (1988). Reality: The search for objectivity or the quest for a compelling argument. *The Irish Journal of Psychology, 9*(1), 25–82.

Maxwell, J. A. (2012a). *Qualitative research design* (3rd ed.). Thousand Oaks, CA: SAGE.

Maxwell, J. A. (2012b). *A realist approach for qualitative research*. Thousand Oaks, CA: SAGE.

Maxwell, J. A., & Chmiel, M. (2014). Generalization in and from qualitative analysis. In U. Flick (Ed.), *The SAGE handbook of qualitative data analysis* (pp. 540–553). London: SAGE.

Mayeda, D. T., Keil, M., Dutton, H. D., & Ofamo'Oni, I.-F.-H. (2014). "You've gotta set a precedent": Māori and Pacific voices on student success in higher education. *AlterNative: An International Journal of Indigenous Peoples, 10*(2), 165–179.

McCann, C., & Kim, S.-K. (Eds.). (2013). *Feminist theory reader: Local and global perspectives*. New York: Routledge.

McDermott, M. (2018). The contest of queerbaiting: Negotiating authenticity in fan–creator interactions. *The Journal of Fandom Studies, 6*(2), 133–144.

McDougall, S. D., & McGeorge, C. R. (2014). Utilizing women's feminist identities in family therapy: A phenomenological exploration of the meaning women assign to their feminist identities. *Journal of Feminist Family Therapy, 26*(2), 73–98.

McDowall, A., & Saunders, M. N. K. (2010). UK managers' conceptions of employee training and development. *Journal of European Industrial Training, 34*(7), 609–630.

McGinn, K. L., Ruiz Castro, M., & Lingo, E. L. (2019). Learning from mum: Cross-national evidence linking maternal employment and adult children's outcomes. *Work, Employment and Society, 33*(3), 374–400.

McIntosh, P. (1992). White privilege and male privilege: A personal account of coming to see correspondences through work in women's studies. In M. L. Andersen & P. Hill Collins (Eds.), *Race, class & gender: An anthology* (pp. 70–81). Belmont, CA: Wadsworth.

McLeod, J. (2011). *Qualitative research in counselling and psychotherapy* (2nd ed.). London: SAGE.

McNamee, S. (2004). Relational bridges between constructionism and constructivism. In J. D. Raskin & S. K. Bridges (Eds.), *Studies in Meaning 2: Bridging the personal and social in constructivist psychology* (pp. 37–50). New York: Pace University Press.

McRuer, R. (2006). *Crip theory: Cultural signs of queerness and disability.* New York: New York University Press.

Meth, P. (2017). "Coughing everything out". In D. Gray, V. Clarke & V. Braun (Eds.), *Collecting qualitative data: A practical guide to textual, media and virtual techniques* (pp. 71–93). Cambridge: Cambridge University Press.

Miles, M. B., & Huberman, M. A. (1994). *Qualitative data analysis: An expanded sourcebook* (2nd ed.). Newbury Park, CA: SAGE.

Miller, T., Birch, M., Mauthner, M., & Jessop, J. (Eds.). (2012). *Ethics in qualitative research* (2nd ed.). London: SAGE.

Miller, W. L., & Crabtree, B. F. (1999). Clinical research: A multi-method typology and qualitative roadmap. In B. F. Crabtree & W. L. Miller (Eds.), *Doing qualitative research* (2nd ed., pp. 3–30). Thousand Oaks, CA: SAGE.

Mirza, H. S. (1997). *Black British feminism: A reader.* London: Taylor & Francis.

Mkono, M. (2018). "Troll alert!": Provocation and harassment in tourism and hospitality social media. *Current Issues in Tourism, 21*(7), 791–804.

Moewaka Barnes, H., Gunn, T. R., Barnes, A. M., Muriwai, E., Wetherell, M., & McCreanor, T. (2017). Feeling and spirit: Developing an Indigenous wairua approach to research. *Qualitative Research, 17*(3), 313–325.

Moore, J. (2014). Reconsidering childfreedom: A feminist exploration of discursive identity construction in childfree LiveJournal communities. *Women's Studies in Communication, 37*(2), 159–180.

Moreno-Gabriel, E., & Johnson, K. (2020). Affect and the reparative turn: Repairing qualitative analysis? *Qualitative Research in Psychology, 17*(1), 98–120.

Morison, T., Macleod, C., Lynch, I., Mijas, M., & Shivakumar, S. T. (2016). Stigma resistance in online childfree communities: The limitations of choice rhetoric. *Psychology of Women Quarterly, 40*(2), 184–198.

Morrow, S. L. (2005). Quality and trustworthiness in qualitative research in counseling psychology. *Journal of Counseling Psychology, 52*(2), 250–260.

Morrow, S. L. (2007). Qualitative research in counseling psychology: Conceptual foundations. *The Counseling Psychologist, 35*(2), 209–235.

Morse, J. M. (1991). Qualitative nursing research: A free-for-all? In J. M. Morse (Ed.), *Qualitative nursing research: A contemporary dialogue* (pp. 14–22). Newbury Park, CA: SAGE.

Morse, J. (1997). "Perfectly healthy, but dead": The myth of inter-rater reliability. *Qualitative Health Research, 7*(4), 445–447.

Morse, J. (2010). "Cherry picking": Writing from thin data. *Qualitative Health Research*, *20*(1), 3.

Morse, J. (2020). The changing face of qualitative inquiry. *International Journal of Qualitative Methods*, Advance online publication https://doi.org/10.1177/1609406920909938

Muhammad, S., Milford, D. V., Carson, A., Young, H., & Martin, C. R. (2016). Coping in young people with chronic kidney disease (CKD). *Journal of Renal Care*, *42*(1), 34–42.

Mullings, L. (2000). African-American women making themselves: Notes on the role of black feminist research. *Souls*, *2*(4), 18–29.

Nadar, S. (2014). "Stories are data with Soul" – lessons from black feminist epistemology. *Agenda*, *28*(1), 18–28.

Nadin, S., & Cassell, C. (2006). The use of a research diary as a tool for reflexive practice: Some reflections from management research. *Qualitative Research in Accounting & Management*, *3*(3), 208–217.

Naples, N. A., & Gurr, B. (2014). Feminist empiricism and standpoint theory. In S. N. Hesse-Biber (Ed.), *Feminist research practice: A primer* (pp. 14–41). Thousand Oaks, CA: SAGE.

Norman, L. (2012). Gendered homophobia in sport and coaching: Understanding the everyday experiences of lesbian coaches. *International Review for the Sociology of Sport*, *47*(6), 705–723.

Norris, M. (2015). The complexities of "otherness": Reflections on embodiment of a young White British woman engaged in cross-generation research involving older people in Indonesia. *Ageing & Society*, *35*(5), 986–1010.

Nowell, L. S., Norris, J. M., White, D. E., & Moules, N. J. (2017). Thematic analysis: Striving to meet the trustworthiness criteria. *International Journal of Qualitative Methods*, *16*(1), 1–13.

O'Connor, C., & Joffe, H. (2020). Intercoder reliability in qualitative research: Debates and practical guidelines. *International Journal of Qualitative Methods*. Advance online publication https://doi.org/10.1177/1609406919899220

Obasi, C. (2014). Negotiating the insider/outsider continua: A Black female hearing perspective on research with Deaf women and Black women. *Qualitative Research*, *14*(1), 61–78.

Office for National Statistics. (2016). *Childbearing for women born in different years, England and Wales: 2015*. UK: Retrieved from www.ons.gov.uk/peoplepopulationandcommunity/birthsdeathsandmarriages/conceptionandfertilityrates/bulletins/childbearingforwomenbornindifferentyearsenglandandwales/2015

Ong, M. G. (2015). *"Happy in my own skin": Filipina migrants' embodiment of ageing in New Zealand* (PhD thesis). The University of Auckland, Auckland.

Ong, M. G., & Braun, V. (2016). Erasing/embracing the marks of aging: Alternative discourses around beauty among Filipina migrants. *Social Science Diliman*, *12*(2). https://journals.upd.edu.ph/index.php/socialsciencediliman/article/view/5529

Opler, M. E. (1945). Themes as dynamic forces in culture. *American Journal of Sociology*, *51*(3), 198–206.

Opperman, E., Braun, V., Clarke, V., & Rogers, C. (2014). "It feels so good it almost hurts": Young adults' experiences of orgasm and sexual pleasure. *Journal of Sex Research*, *51*(5), 503–515.

Orteza, G. O. (1997). *Pakikipagkuwentuhan: Isang pamamaraan ng sama-samang pananaliksik, pagpapatotoo at pagtulong sa Sikolohiyang Pilipino (Pakikipagkuwentuhan: A method for participatory research, establishing validity, and contributing to Filipino Psychology)*. Quezon City, Philippines: Philippine Psychology Research and Training House.

Overstreet, N. M., Rosenthal, L., & Case, K. A. (2020). Intersectionality as a radical framework for transforming our disciplines, social issues, and the world. *Journal of Social Issues, 76*(4), 779–795.

Paechter, C. (1998). *Educating the other: Gender, power and schooling*. London: Falmer.

Paechter, C. (2013). Researching sensitive issues online: Implications of a hybrid insider/outsider position in a retrospective ethnographic study. *Qualitative Research, 13*(1), 71–86.

Palomäki, J., Laakasuo, M., & Salmela, M. (2013). "This is just so unfair!": A qualitative analysis of loss-induced emotions and tilting in on-line poker. *International Gambling Studies, 13*(2), 255–270.

Parasuraman, A., Zeithaml, V. A., & Berry, L. L. (1985). A conceptual model of service quality and its implications for future research. *Journal of Marketing, 49*(4), 41–50.

Paredes-Canilao, N., & Babaran-Diaz, M. A. (2013). Sikolohiyang Pilipino: 50 years of critical-emancipatory social science in the Philippines. *Annual Review of Critical Psychology, 10*, 765–783.

Parker, I. (Ed.). (1998). *Social constructionism, discourse and realism*. London: SAGE.

Parkinson, S., Eatough, V., Holmes, J., Stapley, E., & Midgley, N. (2016). Framework analysis: A worked example of a study exploring young people's experiences of depression. *Qualitative Research in Psychology, 13*(2), 109–129.

Paterson, B. L. (2012). "It looks great but how do I know if it fits?": An introduction to meta-synthesis research. In K. Hannes & C. Lockwood (Eds.), *Synthesizing qualitative research: Choosing the right approach* (pp. 1–20). Chichester: Wiley-Blackwell.

Patomäki, H., & Wight, C. (2000). After postpositivism? The promises of critical realism. *International Studies Quarterly, 44*(2), 213–237.

Patton, M. Q. (1999). Enhancing the quality and credibility of qualitative analysis. *Health Services Research, 34*(5), 1189–1208.

Patton, M. Q. (2002). *Qualitative research and evaluation methods* (3rd ed.). Thousand Oaks, CA: SAGE.

Patton, M. Q. (2015). *Qualitative research & evaluation methods: Integrating theory and practice* (4th ed.). Los Angeles, CA: SAGE.

Pepper, S. C. (1942). *World hypotheses: A study in evidence*. Berkeley, CA: University of California Press.

Peterson, B. L. (2017). Thematic analysis/interpretive thematic analysis. In J. Matthes, C. S. Davis & R. F. Potter (Eds.), *The international encyclopedia of communication research methods* (pp. 1–9). London: Wiley-Blackwell.

Peterson, H. (2014). Absent non-fathers: Gendered representations of voluntary childlessness in Swedish newspapers. *Feminist Media Studies, 14*(1), 22–37.

Pettigrew, A. M. (1985). Contextualist research and the study of organizational change processes. In R. H. E. Mumford, G. Fitzgerald & T. Wood-Harper (Eds.), *Research methods in information systems* (Vol. *1*, pp. 53–75). Amsterdam: Elsevier Science.

Pharr, S. (2000). Homophobia: A weapon of sexism. In M. P. L. Umanski (Ed.), *Making sense of women's lives: An introduction to women's studies* (pp. 424–438). Oxford: Rowman and Littlefield.

Phoenix, A. (2006). Interrogating intersectionality: Productive ways of theorising multiple positioning. *Kvinder, Køn & Forskning, 2–3,* 21–30.

Pilgrim, D. (2014). Some implications of critical realism for mental health research. *Social Theory & Health, 12*(1), 1–21.

Pistrang, N., & Barker, C. (2010). Scientific, practical and personal decisions in selecting qualitative methods. In M. Barkham, G. E. Hardy & J. Mellor-Clark (Eds.), *Developing and delivering practice-based evidence* (pp. 65–90). Chichester: Wiley.

Pitama, D., Ririnui, G., & Mikaere, A. (2002). *Guardianship, custody and access: Māori perspectives and experiences.* Wellington, New Zealand: Ministry of Justice.

Polit, D. F., & Beck, C. T. (2010). Generalization in quantitative and qualitative research: Myths and strategies. *International Journal of Nursing Studies, 47*(11), 1451–1458.

Ponterotto, J. G. (2006). Brief note on the origins, evolution, and meaning of the qualitative research concept thick description. *The Qualitative Report, 11*(3), 538–549.

Pope, C., Ziebland, S., & Mays, N. (2006). Analysing qualitative data. In C. Pope & N. Mays (Eds.), *Qualitative research in health care* (3rd ed., pp. 63–81). Oxford: Blackwell.

Potter, J., & Edwards, D. (1999). Social representations and discursive psychology: From cognition to action. *Culture & Psychology, 5*(4), 447–458.

Price, J. (1996). Snakes in the swamp: Ethical issues in qualitative research. In R. Josselson (Ed.), *Ethics and process in the narrative study of lives* (pp. 207–215). Thousand Oaks, CA: SAGE.

Prosser, J. (1998). *Image-based research: A sourcebook for qualitative researchers.* London: Routledge.

Pyett, P. M. (2003). Validation of qualitative research in the "real world". *Qualitative Health Research, 13*(8), 1170–1179.

Ramazanoğlu, C., & Holland, J. (2002). *Feminist methodology: Challenges and choices.* London: SAGE.

Raskin, J. D. (2002). Constructivism in psychology: Personal construct psychology, radical constructivism, and social constructionism. *American Communication Journal, 5*(3), 1–25.

Reavey, P. (Ed.). (2012). *Visual methods in psychology: Using and interpreting images in qualitative research.* London: Routledge.

Reicher, S. (2000). Against methodolatry: Some comments on Elliott, Fischer, and Rennie. *British Journal of Clinical Psychology, 39*(1), 1–6.

Reid, C., & Frisby, W. (2008). Continuing the journey: Articulating dimensions of feminist participatory action research. In P. Reason & H. Bradbury (Eds.), *The SAGE handbook of action research: Participative inquiry and practice* (2nd ed., pp. 93–105). Thousand Oaks, CA: SAGE.

Rice, C. (2009). Imagining the Other? Ethical challenges of researching and writing women's embodied lives. *Feminism & Psychology, 19*(2), 245–266.

Rich, S., Taket, A., Graham, M., & Shelley, J. (2011). "Unnatural", "unwomanly", "uncreditable" and "undervalued": The significance of being a childless woman in Australian society. *Gender Issues, 28*(4), 226–247.

Ricoeur, P. (1970). *Freud and philosophy: An essay on interpretation.* (D. Savage, Trans.). New Haven, CT: Yale University Press.

Ritchie, J., & Lewis, J. (2003). *Qualitative research practice: A guide for social science students and researchers.* London: SAGE.

Ritchie, J., & Spencer, L. (1994). Qualitative data analysis for applied policy research. In A. Bryman & R. G. Burgess (Eds.), *Analyzing qualitative data* (pp. 173–194). London: Routledge.

Ritchie, J., Spencer, L., & O'Connor, W. (2003). Carrying out qualitative analysis. In J. Ritchie & J. Lewis (Eds.), *Qualitative research practice: A guide for social science students and researchers* (pp. 219–262). London: SAGE.

Rivas, C. (2018). Finding themes in qualitative data. In C. Seale (Ed.), *Researching society and culture* (4th ed., pp. 429–453). London: SAGE.

Robinson, O. C. (2021). Conducting thematic analysis on brief texts: The structured tabular approach. *Qualitative Psychology.* Advance online publication https://doi.org/10.1037/qup0000189.

Roditis, M. L., & Halpern-Felsher, B. (2015). Adolescents' perceptions of risks and benefits of conventional cigarettes, e-cigarettes, and marijuana: A qualitative analysis. *Journal of Adolescent Health, 57*(2), 179–185.

Ronkainen, N. J., Watkins, I., & Ryba, T. V. (2016). What can gender tell us about the pre-retirement experiences of elite distance runners in Finland? A thematic narrative analysis. *Psychology of Sport and Exercise, 22,* 37–45.

Rose, G. (2014). On the relation between "visual research methods" and contemporary visual culture. *The Sociological Review, 62*(1), 24–46.

Rubin, H. J., & Rubin, I. S. (2012). *Qualitative interviewing: The art of hearing data* (3rd ed.). Thousand Oaks, CA: SAGE.

Russell-Mundine, G. (2012). Reflexivity in Indigenous research: Reframing and decolonising research? *Journal of Hospitality and Tourism Management, 19,* e7.

Ryan, G. W., & Bernard, H. R. (2003). Techniques to identify themes. *Field Methods, 15*(1), 85–109.

Saad, L. F. (2020). Me and White Supremacy: Combat racism, change the world, and become a good ancestor. Naperville, IL: Sourcebooks, Inc.

Şad, N. S., Özer, N., & Atli, A. (2019). Psikolojide Tematik Analizin Kullanımı. *Eğitimde Nitel Araştırmalar Dergisi, 7*(2), 873–898.

Said, E. W. (1994). *Culture and imperialism.* New York: Vintage.

Saini, A. (2019). *Superior: The return of race science.* London: Fourth Estate.

Saldaña, J. (2013). *The coding manual for qualitative researchers* (2nd ed.). London: SAGE.

Saldaña, J. (2016). *The coding manual for qualitative researchers* (3rd ed.). London: SAGE.

Sandelowski, M. (2001). Real qualitative researchers do not count: The use of numbers in qualitative research. *Research in Nursing & Health, 24*(3), 230–240.

Sandelowski, M. (2004). Using qualitative research. *Qualitative Health Research, 14*(10), 1366–1386.

Sandelowski, M. (2011). When a cigar is not just a cigar: Alternative takes on data and data analysis. *Research in Nursing & Health, 34*(4), 342–352.

Sandelowski, M., & Leeman, J. (2012). Writing usable qualitative health research findings. *Qualitative Health Research, 22*(10), 1404–1413.

Scharff, C. (2016). The psychic life of neoliberalism: Mapping the contours of entrepreneurial subjectivity. *Theory, Culture & Society, 33*(6), 107–122.

Scully, D. (1994). *Understanding sexual violence: A study of convicted rapists.* New York: Routledge.

Shadish, W. R. (1995). Philosophy of science and the quantitative-qualitative debates: Thirteen common errors. *Evaluation and Program Planning, 18*(1), 63–75.

Shavelson, R. J., Hubner, J. J., & Stanton, G. C. (1976). Self-concept: Validation of construct interpretations. *Review of Educational Research, 46*(3), 407–441.

Shaw, R., & Frost, N. (2015). Breaking out of the silo mentality. *The Psychologist, 28*(8), 638–641.

Silver, C., & Bulloch, S. L. (2017). CAQDAS at a crossroads: Affordances of technology in an online environment In N. G. Fielding, R. M. Lee & G. Blank (Eds.), *The SAGE handbook of online research methods* (2nd ed., pp. 470–485). London: SAGE.

Silverman, D. (2017). How was it for you? The Interview Society and the irresistible rise of the (poorly analyzed) interview. *Qualitative Research, 17*(2), 144–158.

Simons, H. (2014). Case study research: In-depth understanding in context. In P. Leavy (Ed.), *The Oxford handbook of qualitative research* (pp. 455–470). Oxford: Oxford University Press.

Sims-Schouten, W., Riley, S. C., & Willig, C. (2007). Critical realism in discourse analysis: A presentation of a systematic method of analysis using women's talk of motherhood, childcare and female employment as an example. *Theory & Psychology, 17*(1), 101–124.

Sinclair, C. (2010). *Grammar: A friendly approach* (2nd ed.). Maidenhead: Open University Press.

Smith, B. (2018). Generalizability in qualitative research: Misunderstandings, opportunities and recommendations for the sport and exercise sciences. *Qualitative Research in Sport, Exercise and Health, 10*(1), 137–149.

Smith, B., & McGannon, K. R. (2018). Developing rigor in qualitative research: Problems and opportunities within sport and exercise psychology. *International Review of Sport and Exercise Psychology, 11*(1), 101–121.

Smith, H., Moller, N. P., & Vossler, A. (2017). Family therapy "lite"? How family counsellors conceptualise their primary care family work. *British Journal of Guidance & Counselling, 45*(5), 562–572.

Smith, J., & Firth, J. (2011). Qualitative data analysis: The framework approach. *Nurse researcher, 18*(2), 52–62.

Smith, J. A. (2019). Participants and researchers searching for meaning: Conceptual developments for interpretative phenomenological analysis. *Qualitative Research in Psychology, 16*(2), 166–181.

Smith, J. A., Flowers, P., & Larkin, M. (2009). *Interpretative phenomenological analysis: Theory, method and research.* London: SAGE.

Smith, L. T. (1992). Kura kaupapa Māori and the implications for curriculum. In G. McCulloch (Ed.), *The school curriculum in New Zealand: History, theory, policy and practice* (pp. 219–231). Palmerston North: Dunmore Press.

Smith, L. T. (1999). *Decolonizing methodologies: Research and Indigenous peoples.* Dunedin, NZ: University of Otago Press.

Smith, L. T. (2013). *Decolonizing methodologies: Research and Indigenous peoples* (2nd ed.). Dunedin, NZ: University of Otago Press.

Smith, L. T., Pihama, L., Cameron, N., Mataki, T., Morgan, H., & Te Nana, R. (2019). Thought space Wānanga – A Kaupapa Māori decolonizing approach to research translation. *Genealogy, 3*(4), 74. https://www.mdpi.com/2313-5778/3/4/74

Smith, L. T., & Reid, P. (2000). Māori research development. *Kaupapa Māori principles and practices: A literature review*. Wellington: Te Puni Kokiri.

Smith, S. E. (2014, April 8). "The people are so beautiful!" That's enough of the colonial tourism. *The Guardian*. Retrieved from www.theguardian.com/commentisfree/2014/apr/08/people-beautiful-colonial-tourism-travel

Sparkes, A. C., & Smith, B. (2009). Judging the quality of qualitative inquiry: Criteriology and relativism in action. *Psychology of Sport and Exercise, 10*, 491–497.

Spiers, J., & Riley, R. (2019). Analysing one dataset with two qualitative methods: The distress of general practitioners, a thematic and interpretative phenomenological analysis. *Qualitative Research in Psychology, 16*(2), 276–290.

Spivak, G. C. (1988). Can the subaltern speak? In C. Nelson & L. Grossberg (Eds.), *Marxism and the interpretation of culture* (pp. 271–313). Basingstoke: Macmillan.

Srivastava, A., & Thomson, S. B. (2009). Framework analysis: A qualitative methodology for applied policy research. *4 Journal of Administration and Governance 72*. Available from https://ssrn.com/abstract=2760705.

St. Pierre, E. A. (2021). Post qualitative inquiry, the refusal of method, and the risk of the new. *Qualitative Inquiry, 27*(1), 3–9.

Stahl, J. V., Taylor, N. E., & Hill, C. E. (2012). Philosophical and historical background of consensual qualitative research. In C. E. Hill (Ed.), *Consensual qualitative research: A practical resource for investigating social science phenomena* (pp. 21–32). Washington, DC: American Psychological Association.

Stake, R. E. (1995). *The art of case study research*. Thousand Oaks, CA: SAGE.

Stephens, M. (1982). A question of generalizability. *Theory & Research in Social Education, 9*(4), 75–89.

Stewart, D. W., & Shamdasani, P. N. (2015). *Focus groups: Theory and practice* (3rd ed.). London: SAGE.

Strawbridge, S., & Woolfe, R. (2003). Counselling psychology in context. In R. Woolfe, W. Dryden & S. Strawbridge (Eds.), *Handbook of counselling psychology* (2nd ed., pp. 3–22). London: SAGE.

Sullivan, N. (2013). *A critical introduction to queer theory*. Edinburgh: Edinburgh University Press.

Swadener, B. B., & Mutua, K. (2008). Decolonizing performances: Deconstructing the global postcolonial. In N. K. Denzin, Y. S. Lincoln & L. T. Smith (Eds.), *Handbook of critical and indigenous methodologies* (pp. 31–44). Thousand Oaks, CA: SAGE.

Swain, J. (2018). A hybrid approach to thematic analysis in qualitative research: Using a practical example. *SAGE Research Methods Cases*. https://dx.doi.org/10.4135/9781526435477

Swallow, V., Newton, J., & Van Lottum, C. (2003). How to manage and display qualitative data using "Framework" and Microsoft® Excel. *Journal of Clinical Nursing, 12*(4), 610–612.

Swauger, M. (2011). Afterword: The ethics of risk, power, and representation. *Qualitative Sociology, 34*(3), 497–502.

Sword, H. (2016). *The writer's diet: A guide to fit prose.* Chicago, IL: University of Chicago Press.

Symon, G., & Cassell, C. (2012). Assessing qualitative research. In G. Symon & C. Cassell (Eds.), *Qualitative organizational research: Core methods and current challenges* (pp. 204–223). London: SAGE.

Tait, A. (2016, September 13). Why do people comment on articles without reading them first? *New Statesman.* Retrieved from www.newstatesman.com/2016/09/why-do-people-comment-articles-without-reading-them-first

Taylor, G. W., & Ussher, J. M. (2001). Making sense of S&M: A discourse analytic account. *Sexualities, 4*(3), 293–314.

Tebes, J. K. (2005). Community science, philosophy of science, and the practice of research. *American Journal of Community Psychology, 35*(3–4), 213–230.

Teo, T. (2010). What is epistemological violence in the empirical social sciences? *Social and Personality Psychology Compass, 4*(5), 295–303.

Teo, T. (2011). Empirical race psychology and the hermeneutics of epistemological violence. *Human Studies, 34*(3), 237–255.

Terry, G. (2010). *Men, masculinity and vasectomy in New Zealand* (PhD thesis). The University of Auckland, Auckland, New Zealand.

Terry, G. (2016). Doing thematic analysis. In E. Lyons & A. Coyle (Eds.), *Analysing qualitative data in psychology* (2nd ed., pp. 104–118). London: SAGE.

Terry, G. (2021). Doing thematic analysis. In E. Lyons & A. Coyle (Eds.), *Analysing qualitative data in psychology* (3rd ed., pp. 148–161). London: SAGE.

Terry, G., & Braun, V. (2009). "When I was a bastard": Constructions of maturity in men's accounts of masculinity. *Journal of Gender Studies, 18*(2), 165–178.

Terry, G., & Braun, V. (2011a). "I'm committed to her and the family": Positive accounts of vasectomy among New Zealand men. *Journal of Reproductive and Infant Psychology, 29*(3), 276–291.

Terry, G., & Braun, V. (2011b). "It's kind of me taking responsibility for these things": Men, vasectomy and "contraceptive economies". *Feminism & Psychology, 21*(4), 477–495.

Terry, G., & Braun, V. (2012). Sticking my finger up at evolution: Unconventionality, selfishness, and choice in the talk of men who have had "preemptive" vasectomies. *Men and Masculinities, 15*(3), 207–229.

Terry, G., & Braun, V. (2013a). To let hair be, or to not let hair be? Gender and body hair removal practices in Aotearoa/New Zealand. *Body Image, 10*(4), 599–606.

Terry, G., & Braun, V. (2013b). "We have friends, for example, and he will not get a vasectomy": Imagining the self in relation to others when talking about sterilization. *Health Psychology, 32*(1), 100–109.

Terry, G., & Braun, V. (2016). "I think gorilla-like back effusions of hair are rather a turn-off": "Excessive hair" and male body hair (removal) discourse. *Body Image, 17,* 14–24.

Terry, G., & Braun, V. (2017). Short but often sweet: The surprising potential of qualitative survey methods. In D. Gray, V. Clarke & V. Braun (Eds.), *Collecting qualitative data: A practical guide to textual, media and virtual techniques* (pp. 15–44). Cambridge: Cambridge University Press.

Terry, G., Braun, V., Jayamaha, S., & Madden, H. (2018). Negotiating the hairless ideal in Aotearoa/New Zealand: Choice, awareness, complicity, and resistance in younger women's accounts of body hair removal. *Feminism & Psychology, 28*(2), 272–291.

Terry, G., Braun, V., Jayamaha, S., & Madden, H. (2021). Choice, awareness, complicity and resistance in younger women's accounts of body hair removal: A reflective account of a thematic analysis study. In E. Lyons & A. Coyle (Eds.), *Analysing qualitative data in psychology* (3rd ed., pp. 365–379). London: SAGE.

Terry, G., Hayfield, N., Clarke, V., & Braun, V. (2017). Thematic analysis. In C. Willig & W. Stainton Rogers (Eds.), *The SAGE handbook of qualitative research in psychology* (2nd ed., pp. 17–36). London: SAGE.

Thomas, C. (1997). The baby and the bath water: Disabled women and motherhood in social context. *Sociology of Health & Illness, 19*(5), 622–643.

Thomas, J., & Harden, A. (2008). Methods for the thematic synthesis of qualitative research in systematic reviews. *BMC Medical Research Methodology, 8*(24). https://doi.org/10.1186/1471-2288-8-45

Throsby, K., & Evans, B. (2013). "Must I seize every opportunity?" Complicity, confrontation and the problem of researching (anti-) fatness. *Critical Public Health, 23*(3), 331–344.

Thwaites, T., Davis, L., & Mules, W. (2002). *Introducing cultural and media studies: A semiotic approach* (2nd ed.). Basingstoke: Palgrave.

Tischner, I., & Malson, H. (2012). Deconstructing health and the un/healthy fat woman. *Journal of Community & Applied Social Psychology, 22*(1), 50–62.

Toft, A., Franklin, A., & Langley, E. (2020). "You're not sure that you are gay yet": The perpetuation of the "phase" in the lives of young disabled LGBT+ people. *Sexualities, 23*(4), 516–529.

Tolich, M., & Tumilty, E. (2020). Practicing ethics and ethics praxis. *The Qualitative Report, 25*(13), 16–30.

Tong, A., Sainsbury, P., & Craig, J. (2007). Consolidated criteria for reporting qualitative research (COREQ): A 32-item checklist for interviews and focus groups. *International Journal for Quality in Health Care, 19*(6), 349–357.

Torrance, H. (2018). Data as entanglement: New definitions and uses of data in qualitative research, policy, and neoliberal governance. *Qualitative Inquiry, 25*(8), 734–742.

Tracy, S. J. (2010). Qualitative quality: Eight "big-tent" criteria for excellent qualitative research. *Qualitative Inquiry, 16*(10), 837–851.

Trainor, L. R., & Bundon, A. (2020). Developing the craft: Reflexive accounts of doing reflexive thematic analysis. *Qualitative Research in Sport, Exercise and Health*. Advance online publication https://doi.org/10.1080/2159676X.2020.1840423 .

Tremeer, E. (2019, January 8). Is it cultural appropriation to use drag slang and AAVE? *Babbel*. Retrieved from www.babbel.com/en/magazine/cultural-appropriation-drag-slang-aave

Truth, S. (1851). Ain't I a Woman?. Speech delivered December 1851 at Women's Convention, Akron, Ohio. *Modern history sourcebook*. https://sourcebooks.fordham.edu/mod/sojtruth-woman.asp

Tuffin, K. (2008). Racist discourse in New Zealand and Australia: Reviewing the last 20 years. *Social and Personality Psychology Compass, 2*(2), 591–607.

Ulmer, J. B. (2017). Posthumanism as research methodology: Inquiry in the Anthropocene. *International Journal of Qualitative Studies in Education, 30*(9), 832–848.

Ushioda, E. (2009). A person-in-context relational view of emergent motivation, self and identity. In Z. Dörnyei & E. Ushioda (Eds.), *Motivation, language identity and the L2 self* (pp. 215–228). Bristol: Multilingual Matters.

Vaismoradi, M., Jones, J., Turunen, H., & Snelgrove, S. (2016). Theme development in qualitative content analysis and thematic analysis. *Journal of Nursing Education and Practice, 6*(5), 100–110.

Vaismoradi, M., Turunen, H., & Bondas, T. (2013). Content analysis and thematic analysis: Implications for conducting a qualitative descriptive study. *Nursing & Health Sciences, 15*(3), 398–405.

Van Brunt, B., Zedginidze, A. A., & Light, P. A. (2016). The unfit parent: Six myths concerning dangerousness and mental illness. *Family Court Review, 54*(1), 18–28.

Varpio, L., Ajjawi, R., Monrouxe, L. V., O'Brien, B. C., & Rees, C. E. (2017). Shedding the cobra effect: Problematising thematic emergence, triangulation, saturation and member checking. *Medical Education, 51*(1), 40–50.

Varpio, L., O'Brien, B., Rees, C. E., Monrouxe, L., Ajjawi, R., & Paradis, e. (2021). The applicability of generalisability and bias to health professions education's research. *Medical Education, 55*(2), 167–173.

Vincent, B. W. (2018). Studying trans: Recommendations for ethical recruitment and collaboration with transgender participants in academic research. *Psychology & Sexuality, 9*(2), 102–116.

Wainwright, E. (@Dr_wainright). (2020, March 27). *I know #themesdonotemerge but is it OK to feel that analysis has been like wrestling with a sea-monster? ...* [Tweet]. Twitter. https://twitter.com/dr_wainright/status/1243618377467342854

Ward, D. J., Furber, C., Tierney, S., & Swallow, V. (2013). Using framework analysis in nursing research: A worked example. *Journal of Advanced Nursing, 69*(11), 2423–2431.

Ware, F., Breheny, M., & Forster, M. (2017). The politics of government "support" in Aotearoa/New Zealand: Reinforcing and reproducing the poor citizenship of young Māori parents. *Critical Social Policy, 37*(4), 499–519.

Watson, N. (@Watson_N_E). (2018, June 21). *Every time I think my MSc dissertation is sorted* [Tweet]. Twitter. https://twitter.com/Watson_N_E/status/1009822742793871364

Weatherall, A., Gavey, N., & Potts, A. (2002). So whose words are they anyway? *Feminism & Psychology, 12*(4), 531–539.

Wetherell, M. (1998). Positioning and interpretative repertoires: Conversation analysis and post-structuralism in dialogue. *Discourse & Society, 9*, 387–412.

Wetherell, M. (2015). Trends in the turn to affect: A social psychological critique. *Body & Society, 21*(2), 139–166.

Wetherell, M., Taylor, S., & Yates, S. (2001). *Discourse theory and practice: A reader*. London: SAGE.

White, K. M., Jimmieson, N. L., Obst, P. L., Graves, N., Barnett, A., Cockshaw, W., Gee, P., Haneman, L., Page, K., & Campbell, M. (2015). Using a theory of planned behaviour framework to explore hand hygiene beliefs at the "5 critical moments" among Australian hospital-based nurses. *BMC Health Services Research, 15*(59). https://doi.org/10.1186/s12913-015-0718-2.

Wiggins, S. (2017). *Discursive psychology: Theory, method and applications.* London: SAGE.

Wilkinson, S. (1988). The role of reflexivity in feminist psychology. *Women's Studies International Forum, 11*(5), 493–502.

Wilkinson, S. (2001). Theoretical perspectives on women and gender. In R. K. Unger (Ed.), *Handbook of the psychology of women and gender* (pp. 17–28). Hoboken, NJ: Wiley.

Wilkinson, S., & Kitzinger, C. (Eds.). (1996). *Representing the other: A feminism & psychology reader.* London: SAGE.

Wilkinson, S., & Kitzinger, C. (2013). Representing our own experience: Issues in "insider" research. *Psychology of Women Quarterly, 37*(2), 251–255.

Willig, C. (1999). Beyond appearances: A critical realist approach to social constructionist work. In D. J. Nightingale & J. Cromby (Eds.), *Social constructionist psychology: A critical analysis of theory and practice* (pp. 37–52). Buckingham, UK: Open University Press.

Willig, C. (2001). *Introducing qualitative research in psychology: Adventures in theory and method.* Buckingham: Open University Press.

Willig, C. (2013). *Introducing qualitative research in psychology* (3rd ed.). Maidenhead, UK: Open University Press.

Willig, C. (2017). Interpretation in qualitative research. In C. Willig & W. Stainton Rogers (Eds.), *The SAGE handbook of qualitative research in psychology* (2nd ed.). London: SAGE.

Willig, C., & Stainton Rogers, W. (2008). Introduction. In C. Willig & W. Stainton Rogers (Eds.), *The SAGE handbook of qualitative research in psychology* (pp. 1–12). Los Angeles, CA: SAGE.

Willig, C., & Wirth, L. (2018). A meta-synthesis of studies of patients' experience of living with terminal cancer. *Health Psychology, 37*(3), 228–237.

Willis, T. (2015). Kicking down barriers: Gay footballers, challenging stereotypes and changing attitudes in amateur league play. *Soccer & Society, 16*(2–3), 377–392.

Winder, A. E., & Hersko, M. (1958). A thematic analysis of an outpatient psychotherapy group. *International Journal of Group Psychotherapy, 8*(3), 293–300.

Wittgenstein, L. (1953). *Philosophical investigations.* Oxford: Basil Blackwell.

Wood, M. (2016). Onward gay Christian soldiers? Exploring the positioning of lesbian, gay and bisexual Christians in the "battle" against religious homophobia. *Psychology of Sexualities Review, 7*(1), 98–106.

Woods, P. (1999). *Successful writing for qualitative researchers.* London: Routledge.

Wright, J., & Clarke, G. (1999). Sport, the media and the construction of compulsory heterosexuality: A case study of women's rugby union. *International Review for the Sociology of Sport, 34*(3), 227–243.

Xu, W., & Zammit, K. (2020). Applying thematic analysis to education: A hybrid approach to interpreting data in practitioner research. *International Journal of Qualitative Methods.* Advance online publication https://doi.org/10.1177/1609406920918810

Yardley, L. (2000). Dilemmas in qualitative health research. *Psychology & Health, 15,* 215–228.

Yardley, L. (2008). Demonstrating validity in qualitative psychology. In J. A. Smith (Ed.), *Qualitative psychology: A practical guide to research methods* (2nd ed., pp. 235–251). London: SAGE.

Yardley, L. (2015). Demonstrating validity in qualitative psychology. In J. A. Smith (Ed.), *Qualitative psychology: A practical guide to research methods* (2nd ed., pp. 257–272). London: SAGE.

Ymous, A., Spiel, K., Keyes, O., Williams, R. M., Good, J., Hornecker, E., & Bennett, C. L. (2020). *"I am just terrified of my future": Epistemic violence in disability related technology research.* In Extended Abstracts of the 2020 CHI Conference on Human Factors in Computing Systems, Honolulu, HI.

Zhao, P., Li, P., Ross, K., & Dennis, B. (2016). Methodological tool or methodology? Beyond instrumentality and efficiency with qualitative data analysis software. *Forum Qualitative Sozialforschung/Forum: Qualitative Social Research, 17*(2). http://www.qualitative-research.net/index.php/fqs/article/view/2597

INDEX

Page numbers in *italic* indicate figures and in **bold** indicate tables, glossary items are indicated by a letter g following the page number, footnotes are indicated by a letter n following the page number.

actionable outcomes, 247, 283g
activities (for readers)
  analytic writing, 151–2
  coding, 60, 73
  critical evaluation of published studies, 257, 280
  design thinking, 29–30
  familiarisation, 45, 50
  interpretation, 221–2
  reflexivity, 16–18, 50
  themes, 116
  theoretical assumptions, 193
ADHD, 95–6
African Caribbean women, 20–2, 161, 200
alopecia areata research, 126–7, 204
American Psychological Association, 219, 276
analysis, defined, 283g
analytic foreclosure, 12, 54, **263–4**, 266–7, 283g
analytic inputs, 237, 242, 244, 283g
analytic outputs, 8, 230, 237, 283g
analytic reports, 36, 117–52
  activities, 151–2
  analysis section, 128–46
  analytic process write-up, 124–8, 129
  analytic treatment of data, 137, 138, 283g
  common problems, 138–9, **264–5**
  conclusions section, 145–8
  contextualising data extracts, 140
  critical reflective evaluation, 148–9
  data extract selection, 133–5
  editing, 149
  generalisability, 142–6, **144**, 288g
  good practice, **264–5**, **269**, 272–3
  illustrative use of data, 135, 136, 288g
  literature review/introduction section, 119–21
  method/methodology section, 121–8
  ordering themes, 140–1
  peer review process, 112, 275–7
  rationale for use of TA, 122–4, **123**, **124**, 125
  separate results and discussion sections, 131–3

  theme frequency counts, 141–2, 276
  theme summary tables, 130, **130**
  thick description, 140, 296g
analytic sensibility, 44, 283g
analytic treatment of data, 137, 138, 283g
analytical generalisability, **144**
anti-foundationalism, 174, 183, 283g
anxiety management, 92, 93–6
a priori codes/themes, **236**, 243, 244, 283g
Aronson, Jodi, 227
audit trails, 245, 275

Bacsu, Juanita R., **231**
Basil, Priya, 118
Beres, Melanie, 210, 267
Berger, Peter, 180
Berger, Roni, 13
Bernard, H. Russell, 241, 278
Bhaskar, Roy, 170
bias
  implicit, 189
  researcher, 8, 294g
  see also subjectivity
Big Q qualitative research, 5, 7, *159*, 228, 232, 235, 283g
Big Theory, **6**, 156, 283g
  see also theory
body hair norms research, 121, **124**, 143–5, 200–1, **231**
Bond, Lynne A., 239–40
Boulton, Elicia, 93–4
Boyatzis, Richard, 227, 229, **236**, 238, 239, 241, **248**
Bradbury-Jones, Caroline, 254
bricolage, 254, 284g
Brooks, Joanna M., 234, 239, 249, 278
Broom, Gina, 95–6
bucket themes, 230n, 284g
Bundon, Andrea, 61, 70, 118, 128, 224, 268
Burgoyne, Carol, 101
Burns, Maree, 101
Butler, Judith, 180

candidate themes, 284g
developing and reviewing, 35, 97–108, *103*, *104*
generating, 35, 78–92, *80*, **82–4**, *86*
CAQDAS/QDAS (Computer Assisted/ Qualitative Data Analysis Software), 65–9, 239, 284g
case-to-case generalisability, **144**
categories, defined, 284g
central organising concepts, 35, 77–8, 88, 89, 284g
Charmaz, Kathy, 5n
cherry-picking, 54, 101
Chiang, Vico, 272
childfree dataset example, 37–41, **40**
analytic writing, 129, 133, 134, 136–7, 146–7
coding, 59–65, **63**, 69
contradiction in themes, 107–8, 109–10
familiarisation, 45, 47, 48
interpretation, 198n, 203–4, 208, 212–13, 215
naming themes, 112, 113–14
reflexivity exercise, 50
research question, 41–2
thematic mapping, 85–6, *86*, 102–3, *103*, *104*
theme definitions, 111
theme generation, 81, **82–4**, 85–6, *86*
topic summaries, 77, 104–7
Ciclitira, Karen, 120
Cinnirella, Marco, **189**
coarse coding, 240, 284g
co-construction, **176**, 183n, 284g
code labels
defined, 52, 53, 284g
guidelines for, 58–9, **60**
codebook TA, 235, **236**, 242–7, **248**, 284g
framework analysis, 227, 242, 244–6, 288g
matrix analysis, 242, 290g
network analysis, 242, 291g
template analysis, 227, **236**, 242–4, 295g
codebooks/coding frames, 237–8, 239, 242, 243, 245, 284g
codes
a priori, 243, 244, 283g
defined, 52, 53, 284g
guidelines for, 58–9
coding, 4, 6, 35, 51–73
activities, 60, 73
coarse, 240, 284g
in codebook TA, **236**, 242, 243, 244, 245
in coding reliability TA, **236**, 237–8, 239–40
collaborative, 8, 285g
consensus, 188, 232, 238, 285g
deductive orientation, 55–6, 57, 64
definitions, 52, 53, 285g

good practice, **269**
guidelines for codes and code labels, 58–9, **60**
inductive orientation, 55–6, 64
initial coding process, 59–65, **63**
insight and rigour, 54
latent codes/coding, 35, 52, 57–8, **58**, 59, 62–5, 277–8, 290g
multiple rounds of, 70–1
as an organic and evolving process, 54–5
overly-fine-grained, 69, 80–1
refining, 69–71
semantic codes/coding, 35, 52, 57–8, **58**, 59, 62–5, 295g
stopping, 71–2
as a subjective process, 55
as a systematic process, 53–4
technologies, 65–9
variation across TA approaches, 229, **236**
coding accuracy, 232, 285g
coding reliability TA, 167n, 168, 235, **236**, 237–42, **248**, 285g
Colaizzi, Paul F., 226
collaborative coding, 8, 285g
community research, **261**, 285g
conceptual codes, 52, 285g
see also latent codes/coding
conceptual coherence, 26, 167, **263**, 267–8, 279, 285g
concrete data, 230, 246, 266, 285g
Connelly, Lynne M., 266, 274
consensus coding, 188, 232, 238, 285g
constructionism, 9, **10**, 179–80, 182–4, 185–6, 243, 285g
theories of language, 164, 165, 179–80
constructivism, 183–4, **190**
content analysis, 226, 286g
contextualism, 178–9, 185, 286g
contradictory meanings, 107–8, 109–10
co-researchers, 273–4
correspondence theory of truth, 169
Cowie, Lucy, 172–3
Crabtree, Benjamin F., 242
Crenshaw, Kimberlé, 218
critical engagement, 43–4
critical qualitative approaches, 9, **10**, *159*, 160, 187–8, 286g
analytic treatment of data, 137, 138, 283g
generalisability, **144**, 145
hermeneutics of suspicion, 160, 277–8, 288g
interpretation, 204–7
language, 142, 164
research examples, **124**, 162
critical realism, 167, 169–73, 286g
critical thematic analysis, **124**, 255, 286g
culture, influence on reality, 169–70

Dapkus, Marilyn A., 226
data
  analytic treatment of, 137, 138, 283g
  concrete, 230, 246, 266, 285g
  illustrative use of, 135, 136, 288g
  '...in data' concept, 288g
  quality, 28
  saturation, 28, 295g
data coding *see* coding
data description/summary, 272, 286g
data items, 286g
datasets, 4, 286g
  basing analyses on part of, 101
  design, 27–8
  men and healthy eating, 50, 73, 116,
    151, 221–2
  see also childfree dataset example
Davey, Louise, 126–7, 204
de Saussure, Ferdinand, 180
de Schipper, Tessa, **190**
deconstructionism, 180
deductive orientation, 9, **10**, 228, 286g
  codebook TA, 242, 243, 245
  coding, 55–6, 57, 64
  coding reliability TA, 237–8
  interpretation, 208–11
  qualitative evidence synthesis, 250
Denzin, Norman, 13
Derrida, Jacques, 180
DeSantis, Lydia, 229–30, 255
descriptive codes, 52, 243, 286g
  see also semantic codes/coding
design, research, 26–32, 294g
design coherence, 26, 29–30, 167, 167n
design thinking, 4, 29–30, 286g
disciplinary reflexivity, 13, 17–18
discourse analysis, 48, 254, 255, 286g
discourse-located analysis, 213
discourses, defined, 287g
domains, defined, 287g

electronic/paper trails, 275
Elliott, Robert, 13, 15, 277
Ely, Margot, 233
emergent themes, 287g
'emerging themes' concept, 227, 232–3,
    234, 287g
empathy, hermeneutics of, 160, 288g
epistemic violence, 217, 287g
epistemological violence, 217, 287g
epistemology, **6**, 163, 166–7, 175–86, 287g
  constructionism, 179–80, 182–4,
    185–6, 285g
  contextualism, 178–9, 185, 286g
  positivism/postpositivism, 177–8,
    185, 292g
  relativism, 171

essentialism, 9, **10**, 287g
ethical considerations, 28, 197, 214–20,
    278, 294g
ethnicity-specific equity (ESE) programmes,
    172–3
experiential qualitative approaches, 9, **10**,
    159–60, *159*, 287g
  generalisability, **144**
  hermeneutics of empathy, 160, 288g
  illustrative use of data, 135, 136, 288g
  interpretation, 204–7
  language, 163–4
  research examples, **124**, 161
explanatory theories, 157, 189, **189–90**,
    209, 287g

familiarisation, 6, 35, 42–9, 70, 287g
  activities, 45, 50
  critical engagement, 43–4
  immersion, 43, 44
  interpretation during, 197
  note-making, 36, 46–8, *46*, *47*
Farvid, Panteá, 210, 267
feminism, 12n, 13–14, 17, **124**, 127, 161, 180,
    189, **189**, **190**, 199, 202n, 209, 217, 218
Filipina migrants, 181–2
Fine, Michelle, 7, **144**, 145
fine-grained coding, 69, 80–1, 287g
fit, 26, 167, **263**, 267–8, 279, 288g
flexible generalisability, **144**
Flick, Uwe, 224, 249
Foucault, Michel, 180
framework analysis, 227, 242, 244–6, 288g
Fugard, Andrew, 227
fully qualitative research, 7, 228, 235, 288g
functional reflexivity, 13, 17–18

gender
  body hair norms research, 121, **124**, 143–5,
    200–1, **231**
  clothing and, 180
  feminist identities, **189**
  intersectionality, 218–19, 289g
  men and healthy eating research, 50, 73,
    116, 120, 151, 221–2
  'strong Black woman' construct, 20–2, 161
  see also childfree dataset example; LGBT
    (lesbian, gay, bisexual and trans)
    research
generalisability, 142–6, **144**, 288g
Gergen, Ken, 180
Gerstl-Peplin, Cynthia, 19
Gibbs, Graham R., 248, 249
Gibson, Alexandra, 68–9
'give voice', 14, 56, 160, 217, 217n, 288g
Gleeson, Kate, 250, 251
good practice *see* quality

Gough, Brendan, 158, 168, 268
Graham, Rachel, 19–22, 161, 200
grounded theory, 5n, 66, 224, 249, 250, 288g
Guba, Egon, 166–7, 171, 177
Guest, Greg, 167n, 227, 237, 238, 240

hair loss research, 126–7, 204
Hall, Stuart, 164
Hayes, Nicky, 251
Hayfield, Nikki, **124**, 130
Hayhurst, Lyndsay M. C., **190**
health
    healthy ageing research, **231**
    men and healthy eating research, 50, 73,
        116, 120, 151, 221–2
    sexual health research, 91, 165, 204
Heath, Nicole M., 239
hermeneutic phenomenology, **190**, 272
hermeneutics of empathy, 160, 288g
hermeneutics of suspicion, 160, 277–8, 288g
heterosexism research, 57, **124**, **190**, 206–7
heuristic devices, 59, 288g
historically-located analysis, 212–13
Ho, Ken, 272
Holton, Gerald, 226
Huxley, Caroline, 276

identity process theory (IPT), **189**
ideologically-located analysis, 211–12
idiographic generalisability, **144**
illustrative use of data, 135, 136, 288g
immersion, 43, 44
implicit bias, 189
'...in data' concept, 288g
Indigenous knowledge frameworks, 172,
    180–2, **190**, 288g
inductive orientation, 9, **10**, 228, 289g
    codebook TA, 242, 243, 245
    coding, 55–6, 64
    coding reliability TA, 237, 238
    qualitative evidence synthesis, 250
    see also experiential qualitative approaches
inferential generalisability, **144**
information power, 28
insider researchers, 18, 216–17, 289g
intentional theories of language, 164, 165
inter-coder agreement, 232, 238, 240,
    241, 289g
interpretation, 55, 195–222
    activities, 221–2
    analytic foreclosure, 12, 54, **263–4**,
        266–7, 283g
    common problems, **264–5**, 266
    critical approaches, 204–7
    deductive orientation, 208–11
    defensible, 200–3
    defined, 199–201, 289g

descriptive analysis and, 203–4
ethical considerations, 214–20
experiential approaches, 204–7
familiarisation and, 197
good practice, **264–5**, **269**, 272–3
interpretative analysis and, 203–4
locating within wider context, 211–14
reporting, 131, 138, 139, 140, **264–5**
research questions and, 198
theme development and, 197–8
theory and, 208–11
interpretative orientation, 9, 289g
interpretative paradigm, 289g
    see also Big Q qualitative research
interpretative phenomenological analysis
    (IPA), 196n, 226n, 273, 289g
inter-rater/coder reliability, 188, 240,
    241, 289g
intersectional generalisability, **144**
intersectionality, 218–19, 289g

Janesick, Valerie, 273
Jaspal, Rusi, **189**
Joffe, Hélène, 226, 227, 240
Jóhannesson, Ingólfur Á., 57, **124**, **190**
journaling, reflexive, 19–22, 23–4, 36, 232,
    270, 293g
Jowett, Adam, 130

Kaupapa Māori research, 172–3, 181
Kelly, Aiden, 120
Kelly, George, 184
Kidder, Louise, 7
King, Nigel, 227, **236**, 239, 242, 243, **248**,
    249, 278
Kitzinger, Celia, 217
Kjaran, Jón I., 57, **124**, **190**

language
    critical approaches, 142, 164
    ethical considerations, 219–20
    experiential approaches, 163–4
    influence on reality, 169–70
    theories of, 163–6, 179–80
language practice, **261**, 289g
latent approaches, 9, **10**
latent codes/coding, 35, 52, 57–8, **58**, 59,
    62–5, 277–8, 290g
Le Grice, Jade, 181–2, 216, 216n
Leeman, Jennifer, 247
Leung, Doris, 272
Levitt, Heidi M., 267, 276, 277, 279
LGBT (lesbian, gay, bisexual and trans)
    research
    bisexual women and marginalisation,
        124, 130
    heterosexism in schools, 57, **124**, **190**

lesbian and gay parenting, 39
LGB Christians, 162
Muslim gay men, **189**
religious homophobia, 162
same-sex marriage, 101, 130
women's team sports, 206–7
Lincoln, Yvonna, 13, 166–7, 171, 177, 196n
literature review, 119–21
lived experience, defined, 290g
Luckmann, Thomas, 180
Luttrell, Wendy, 15
Lyons, Antonia, 168, 268

McDougall, Sarah D., **189**
McGeorge, Christi R., **189**
McNamee, Sheila, 183
MacQueen, Kathleen, 167n, 227
Madill, Anna, 158, 159, 169, 179
manifest codes, 52, 290g
   see also semantic codes/coding
Māori, 172–3, 181, 213
mapping, thematic, 85–7, 86, 102–4, 103,
   104, 296g
mash-ups, 228, 254–5, 290g
materially-located analysis, 212–13
matrix analysis, 242, 290g
Maxwell, Joseph, 170, 171
member checking, 188, 277–8, 290g
men and healthy eating research, 50, 73,
   116, 120, 151, 221–2
mentors, 273–4
method, defined, 4, 290g
method/methodology section of report,
   121–8
methodolatry, 128, 249, 290g
methodological bandwidth, 290g
methodological integrity, 26, 167, **263**,
   267–8, 279, 290g
methodological pluralism, 254n
methodology, defined, 4, 290g
Microsoft Word, 65, 68
Miller, William L., 242
mind-dependent truths, 164, 290g
mind-independent truths, 164, 168, 291g
Morse, Janice, 196n, 240

naïve realism, 168–9, **176**, 291g
Namey, Emily, 167n, 227
narrative analysis, 254, 291g
naturalistic generalisability, **144**
neoliberalism, 147, 207, 211–12
neo-positivism, 244, 291g
neo-realism, 291g
network analysis, 242, 291g
note-making, 46–8, 46, 47
Nowell, Lorelli, 270
NVivo, 66, 67–9, 239

obsessive-compulsive disorder (OCD), 93–4
O'Connor, Cliodhna, 240
Ong, Michelle, 181–2
onto-epistemologies, 167n, 291g
ontology, **6**, 163, 166–75, 291g
   critical realism, 167, 169–73, 286g
   realism, 167, 168–9, **176**, 293g
   relativism, 167, 173–5, **176**, 294g
Otherness, 216–18
outsider researchers, 18, 216–17, 278n, 291g
overarching themes, 87–8, 291g
owning your perspectives, 13, 15, 291g

paper/electronic trails, 275
paradigms, 5, 166–7, 291g
   see also qualitative paradigms
paraphrasing, 138, 139
Parkinson, S., 245, 246
participant validation, 188, 277–8, 292g
participant-directed codes, 291g
   see also semantic codes/coding
participatory action research, **190**
participatory research, 217n, 278n, 292g
Patrizio, Kami, 19
Patton, Michael Quinn, 156, 186, 197
peer data analysis groups, 271
peer review process, 112, 275–7
Peltzer, Jill N., 266, 274
pensieve, 19
Pepper, Stephen, 178
personal construct psychology, 184
personal reflexivity, 13, 14–15, 16–17
phenomenology, 177n, **189**, **190**, 226, 226n,
   272, 292g
philosophical assumptions, 292g
   see also epistemology; ontology; paradigms
philosophical/meta-theories, 156, 166, 292g
   see also theory
physical self-concept (PSC) model, **190**
policy-located analysis, 213
political theories, 189, **189–90**, 209, 292g
   feminism, 12n, 13–14, 17, **124**, 127, 161,
      180, 189, **189**, **190**, 199, 202n, 209,
      217, 218
   postcolonial theory, **190**, 209, 217
   queer theory, 17, **124**, 189, **190**, 209
politically-located analysis, 212
politics, personal, 14, 17
politics of representation, 197, 214–20,
   278, 292g
polytextual TA, 251
Ponterotto, Joseph G., 140
positivism creep, 7, 188, 270, 292g
positivism/postpositivism, 7, 158, 177–8, 185,
   228, 237, 239, 243, 244, 292g
postcolonial theory, **190**, 209, 217
postmodernism, 180, **189**

post-qualitative enquiry, 187
poststructuralism, 158, 180, 181, 182, 255, 293g
Potts, Henry W. W., 227
practices, defined, 293g
premature closure of analysis *see* analytic
  foreclosure
presentations, 261, 271
proceduralism, 128, 249, 293g
Psychology of Women Quarterly, 148
*Publication manual of the American
  Psychological Association*, 219
publishing, 112, 275–7
pure realism, 168–9, **176**, 293g

QDAS (Qualitative Data Analysis Software),
  65–9, 239, 293g
qualitative content analysis, 226, 293g
qualitative evidence synthesis, 250–1
qualitative paradigm(s), 5, **6**, 7, 158–9, 166–7,
  187, 228, 232, 293g
qualitative sensibility, 7–8, 270, 293g
quality, 259–80
  audit trails, 275
  common problems, 260–7, *262*, **263–5**
  data, 28
  design coherence, 26, 29–30, 167, 167n
  generic quality criteria, 277–9
  methodological integrity, 26, 167, **263**,
    267–8, 279, 290g
  publication process, 275–7
  reflexive journaling, 19–22, 23–4, 36, 232,
    270, 293g
  strategies for ensuring, 268–75, **269**
quantitative paradigm(s), **6**, 7
queer theory, 17, **124**, 189, **190**, 209

realism, **10**, 167, 168–9, **176**, **189**, **190**, 293g
  see also critical realism
reflective theories of language, 164
reflexive journaling, 19–22, 23–4, 36, 232,
  270, 293g
reflexive TA
  comparison with other TA approaches, 235,
    236, **248**
  core assumptions, 8
  defined, 5, 293g
  guidelines, not rules, 10–11
  overview of process, 6, 34–7
  strengths and limitations of, **261**
  variations, 9, **10**, 159–63, *159*
Reflexive TA Bingo card, 261, *262*
reflexivity, 5, 7–8, 13–19, 294g
  activities, 16–18, 50
  disciplinary, 13, 17–18
  functional, 13, 17–18
  personal, 13, 14–15, 16–17
  topic-based, 18, 50

Reicher, Stephen, 235
relativism, **10**, 167, 173–5, **176**, 294g
reports *see* analytic reports
representation, 27, 294g
representational ethics, 28, 197, 214–20,
  278, 294g
representational generalisability, **144**
representing the Other, 217–18, 278n, 294g
research aims, 9, 294g
research design, 26–32, 294g
research goals, 294g
research questions, 7, 27, 41–2, 294g
  coding and, 53, 59
  interpretation and, 198
  theme development and, 85, 89, 90, 91,
    97, 99, 102
research reports *see* analytic reports
research timetable, 29–30, 272–3
researcher bias, 8, 294g
researcher-directed codes, 294g
  see also latent codes/coding
Ricoeur, Paul, 160n
Ritchie, Jane, 227
Rivas, Carol, 249
Ryan, Gery W., 241, 278

Saldaña, Johnny, 230
saliency analysis, 250
same-sex marriage research, 101, 130
Sandelowski, Margarete, 101n, 247
saturation, 28, 295g
semantic approaches, 9, **10**
semantic codes/coding, 35, 52, 57–8, **58**, 59,
  62–5, 295g
semiotics, 180, 252
sensibility
  analytic, 44, 283g
  qualitative, 7–8, 270, 293g
Seven Sharp see childfree dataset example
sexual ethics research, 210
sexual health research, 91, 165, 204
Sikolohiyang Pilipino (Indigenous Filipino
  psychology), 181–2
Sillars, Matt, 250, 252–4, *252*, *253*
Sills, Sophie, 200, 205, 206–7
simple realism, 168–9, **176**, 295g
small q qualitative research, 7, 228, 232,
  235, 295g
small q TA *see* coding reliability TA
Smith, Harriet, 122
Smith, Jonathan, 196n, 273
social constructionism *see* constructionism
Spencer, Liz, 227
Stainton Rogers, Wendy, 201
stories, 295g
  see also analytic reports

'strong Black woman' construct, 20–2, 161
subjectivity, **6**, 7–8, 12–13, 55, 295g
  in codebook TA, **236**
  in coding reliability TA, **236**, 238,
    239–40, 241
  realism and, 168
  variation across TA approaches,
    232, **236**
subthemes, 85, 86–7, 88, 295g
supervisors, 273–4
SurveyMonkey, 65
suspicion, hermeneutics of, 160, 277–8, 288g
systematic review, 250, 295g
systematic text condensation, 250

techniqueism, 128, 295g
technologies, coding, 65–9
template analysis, 227, **236**, 242–4, 295g
Terry, Gareth, 67–8, **124**, 142, 143–5, **231**
thematic analysis (TA), 4–5, 224
  coding reliability TA, 167n, 168, 235, **236**,
    237–42, **248**, 285g
  history of, 224–7
  mash-ups, 228, 254–5, 290g
  misunderstandings and myths, 224, **225**
  polytextual TA, 251
  for qualitative evidence synthesis, 250–1
  variation of core concepts across
    approaches, 228–33, **231**, **236**
  for visual data analysis, 250, 251, 252–4,
    252, *253*
  see also codebook TA; reflexive TA
thematic coding, 224, 248–50, 295g
thematic mapping, 85–7, *86*, 102–4, *103*,
  104, 296g
thematic narrative analysis, 296g
thematic synthesis, 250–1, 296g
themes, 4, 6, 75–116, 296g
  activities, 116
  a priori, **236**, 243, 244, 283g
  central organising concepts, 35, 77–8, 88,
    89, 284g
  in codebook TA, **236**, 242, 243, 244, 245
  in coding reliability TA, **236**, 237–8,
    239, 240
  common problems, **263–4**, 266
  contradiction in, 107–8, 109–10
  developing and reviewing, 35, 97–108,
    103, *104*
  frequency counts, 141–2, 276
  generating initial, 35, 78–92, *80*, **82–4**, *86*
  good practice, **263–4**, **269**, 274
  interpretation and, 197–8
  levels of, 87–8
  naming, 36, 111–14, 274
  number of, 89–90, 91
  overarching themes, 87–8, 291g

  as shared-meaning patterns, 35, 77–8,
    104–7, 229–30, **231**
  subthemes, 85, 86–7, 88, 295g
  theme definitions, 36, 108, 111, 296g
  theme summary tables, 130, **130**
  'themes emerging' concept, 227, 232–3,
    234, 296g
  vs. topic summaries, 77, 104–7, 230–1,
    231, 266
  variation across TA approaches, 229–31,
    231, 232–3, **236**
  visual mapping, 85–7, *86*, 102–4, *103*,
    104, 296g
theory, **6**, 155–93
  activities, 193
  analytic foreclosure and, 267
  constructionism, 9, **10**, 179–80, 182–4,
    185–6, 243, 285g
  constructivism, 183–4, **190**
  contextualism, 178–9, 185, 286g
  critical realism, 167, 169–73, 286g
  explanatory, 157, 189, **189–90**, 209, 287g
  Indigenous knowledge frameworks, 172,
    180–2, **190**, 288g
  interpretation and, 208–11
  positivism/postpositivism, 7, 158, 177–8,
    185, 228, 237, 239, 243, 244, 292g
  poststructuralism, 158, 180, 181, 182,
    255, 293g
  realism, **10**, 167, 168–9, **176**, **189**,
    190, 293g
  relativism, **10**, 167, 173–5, **176**, 294g
  research examples, 188–9, **189–90**
  theoretical awareness, 188, 189
  theoretical flexibility, 162–3, 296g
  theoretical knowingness, 268, 277, 296g
  theories of knowledge, 175–86
  theories of language, 163–6, 179–80
  theories of reality, 167–75, **176**
  using, 186–8
  see also political theories
theory of planned behaviour (TPB), **190**
thick description, 140, 296g
time-management, 95–6
timetable, research, 29–30, 272–3
topic summaries, 77, 104–7, 230–1, **231**,
  266, 296g
topics, defined, 296g
Tracy, Sarah, 278, 278n, 279
Trainor, Lisa, 61, 70, 80, *80*, 118, 128, 224, 268
transcription, 27, **269**
transferability, 143, **144**, 211, 297g
triangulation, 278, 278n, 297g
Truth, Sojourner, 218

Ugarriza, Doris, 229–30, 255
uncertainty, 11–12

values, personal, 14, 17
vertical generalisability, **144**
visual data analysis, 250, 251, 252–4, *252*, *253*
visual mapping of themes, 85–7, *86*, 102–4, *103*, *104*, 296g

White, Katherine M., **190**
Wilkinson, Sue, 13, 217
Willig, Carla, 177n, 196n, 201, 214

Wittgenstein, Ludwig, 180
Wood, Matthew, 46, *46*, *47*, 162
writing
    familiarisation notes, 36, 46–8, *46*, *47*
    reflexive journaling, 19–22, 23–4, 36, 232, 270, 293g
    see also analytic reports

Yardley, Lucy, 227, 279